# MOUNTAIN BIKE!
# Oregon

## A GUIDE TO THE CLASSIC TRAILS

## CHRIS AND LAURIE LEMAN

Menasha
Ridge
Press

Library of Congress Cataloging-in-Publication Data:
Leman, Chris.
Mountain bike! Oregon: a guide to the classic trails/
Chris and Laurie Leman. — 1st ed.
p.    cm. — (America by mountain bike series)
Includes index.
ISBN 0-89732-281-9 (pbk.)
1. All terrain cycling — Oregon — Guidebooks.
2. Bicycle trails — Oregon — Guidebooks
3. Oregon — Guidebooks.
I. Leman, Laurie. II. Title.
GV1045.5.07L44 1998
796.6'3'09795 — dc21 98-30987
CIP

Photos by the authors unless otherwise credited
Maps by Bryan Steven Jones and Jeff Goodwin
Cover and text design by Suzanne Holt
Cover photo by Dennis Coello

Menasha Ridge Press
700 South 28th Street
Suite 206
Birmingham, Alabama 35233-3417

All the trails described in this book are legal for mountain bikes. But rules can change — especially for off-road bicycles, the new kid on the outdoor recreation block. Land access issues and conflicts between bicyclists, hikers, equestrians, and other users can cause the rewriting of recreation regulations on public lands, sometimes resulting in a ban of mountain bike use on specific trails. That's why it's the responsibility of each rider to check and make sure that he or she rides only on trails where mountain biking is permitted.

CAUTION

Outdoor recreational activities are by their very nature potentially hazardous. All participants in such activities must assume the responsibility for their own actions and safety. The information contained in this guidebook cannot replace sound judgment and good decision-making skills, which help reduce risk exposure, nor does the scope of this book allow for disclosure of all the potential hazards and risks involved in such activities.

Learn as much as possible about the outdoor recreational activities in which you participate, prepare for the unexpected, and be cautious. The reward will be a safer and more enjoyable experience.

To our parents, Chuck and Dot and Bob and Marg

# CONTENTS

# AMERICA BY MOUNTAIN BIKE MAP LEGEND

Ride trailhead

Steep grade

Optional trailhead

Primary bike trail

Direction of travel

(arrows point downhill)

Optional bike trail

Restricted area

Hiking trail

Interstate highways (with exit no.)

US routes

Oregon state routes

Covell Blvd.

Other paved roads

Unpaved, gravel, or dirt roads (may be 4WD only)

US Forest Service roads

Portland ◉ Cities

Prospect ◉ Towns or settlements

Dam Lake

River, stream, or canal

0    ½    1
MILES
Approximate scale in miles

**N** True north

TOPANGA ST. PK.
Public Lands*

International border

State border

✈ Airport

✖ Ski Area

🌳 Orchard

▲ Campground (CG)

≡ Cattle guard

◼ Spring

⬆ Park

Cliff, escarpment, or outcropping

Drinking water

Power Plant

Fire tower or lookout

🅸🅾 Food

Gate

House, shelter, or cabin

Lodging

Mountain or butte

Mountain pass

Mountain summit
3312 (elevation in feet)

Rest room

✕ Mine

Museum

Observatory

Park office or ranger station

Ħ Picnic area

Sno-Park

Power line or pipeline

Ranch or stable

Swimming Area

Transmission towers

Tunnel or bridge

*Remember, private property exists in and around our National Forests.

# OREGON • Ride Locations

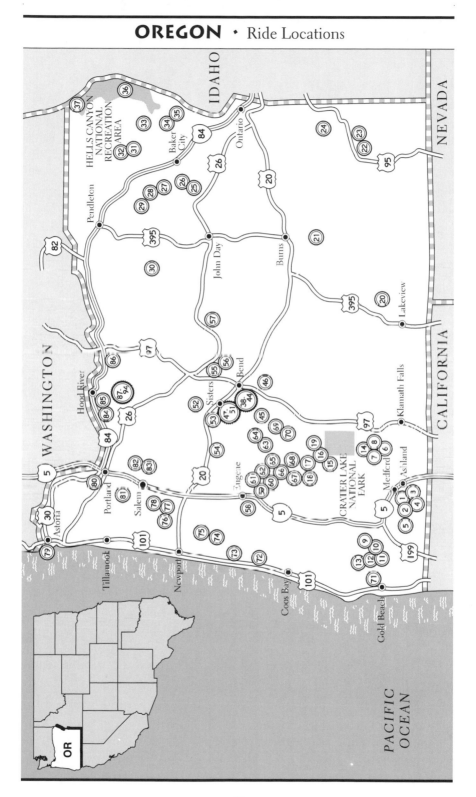

# LIST OF MAPS

# FOREWORD

Welcome to *America by Mountain Bike*, a series designed to provide all-terrain bikers with the information they need to find and ride the very best trails around. Whether you're new to the sport and don't know where to pedal, or an experienced mountain biker who wants to learn the classic trails in another region, this series is for you. Drop a few bucks for the book, spend an hour with the detailed maps and route descriptions, and you're prepared for the finest in off-road cycling.

My role as editor of this series was simple: First, find a mountain biker who knows the area and loves to ride. Second, ask that person to spend a year researching the most popular and very best rides around. And third, have that rider describe each trail in terms of difficulty, scenery, condition, elevation change, and all other categories of information that are important to trail riders. "Pretend you've just completed a ride and met up with fellow mountain bikers at the trail-head," I told each author. "Imagine their questions, be clear in your answers."

As I said, the *editorial* process—that of sending out riders and reading the submitted chapters—is a snap. But the work involved in finding, riding, and writing about each trail is enormous. In some instances our authors' tasks are made easier by the information contributed by local bike shops or cycling clubs, or even by the writers of local "where-to" guides. Credit for these contributions is provided, when appropriate, in each chapter, and our sincere thanks goes to all who have helped.

All of the rides in this guide have been pedaled by our authors themselves, then compared with dozens of other routes to determine if they qualify as "classic"—that area's best in scenery and cycling fun. If you've ever had the experience of pioneering a route from outdated topographic maps, or entering a bike shop to request information from local riders who would much prefer to keep their favorite trails secret, or know how it is to double- and triple-check data to be positive your trail info is correct, then you have an idea of how each of our

Single-track excitement.

authors has labored to bring about these books. You and I, and all the mountain bikers of America, are the richer for their efforts.

You'll get more out of this book if you take a moment to read the Introduction explaining how to read the trail listings. The "Topographic Maps" section will help you understand how useful topos will be on a ride, and will also tell you where to get them. And though this is a "where-to," not a "how-to" guide, those of you who have not traveled the backcountry might find "Hitting the Trail" of particular value.

In addition to the material above, newcomers to mountain biking might want to spend a minute with the Glossary, page 388, so that terms like *hardpack*, *single-track*, and *waterbars* won't throw you when you come across them in the text.

All the best.

*Dennis Coello*
*St. Louis*

# PREFACE

Oregon encompasses a huge variety of spectacular landscapes. The Oregon coast offers hundreds of miles of beaches, rolling sand dunes, and sublime scenery. Moving inland, coastal mountains and agricultural valleys quickly give way to the Cascades. The volcanoes that are part of this mountain range create a remarkable backdrop for central Oregon. Majestic snowy peaks rise from verdant forests, filling the horizon with their great presence. Sparkling snow fields and glaciers are created as moist ocean air is wrung dry by the mountains. Vast deserts have formed on the leeward sides of these giants. Heading northeast, sage and juniper give way to alpine terrain and the beginning of the Rockies. The extreme northeastern corner of the state is home to Hells Canyon, another world altogether.

This state is rich with public lands and opportunities for active recreation and adventure. The mountain biking in Oregon is exceptional, offering an inviting array of trails. Gravel roads crisscross forests, climb mountains to stunning views, and reach across deserts. Single-tracks follow rivers, traverse rocky canyons, and wind through rainforests. Easy and demanding, long and short, road and single-track—the cycling opportunities in Oregon are limitless. Some places in the state are home to networks of bike routes, making them attractive vacation destinations. Other areas offer trips through remote backcountry, longer trails over ridge tops, or easy pedals down forest roads. This guidebook will direct you to routes suited to all skill levels and tastes.

It has been our goal to present timely and accurate information in this book—after all, a guidebook should be useful for guiding. This book also contains information about access issues and the responsibilities involved in the use of shared trails. We hope that you find this book helpful in locating great trails and that it provides insights into the places you visit.

We spent months looking for (and pedaling) outstanding mountain bike rides in Oregon. Weeks of planning, letter writing, and phone calls preceded our trips into the field. As always, we visited ranger stations and bike shops, scoured guidebooks and brochures, and consulted maps. People we met recommended favorite outings, described concerns they had about certain trails, and helped us understand the ins and outs of particular regions and rides. The riding was

Queen of Hearts
Trail, Ashland.

incredible; our interactions were fruitful and fun. Our thanks to all of the forest rangers, land managers, bike shop folks, and cyclists who helped us shape this book. We also wish to thank the individuals and groups who perform volunteer maintenance on trails, and those who are involved in mountain bicycle advocacy and trail access issues. You are doing great work!

We have made every attempt to portray accurately the difficulty of each ride. Keep in mind that "difficulty" is a subjective matter. Some cyclists will find our descriptions understated, while others will find them overly cautious. We suggest that you start with an easier ride, especially if your fitness level is low or if your bike-handling skills could use some work. This will give you a gauge for our rating scale and provide you with a more appropriate setting in which to strengthen your riding abilities.

Mountain biking can be arduous. After logging many miles researching guidebooks, we half-expected to tire of the sport. On the contrary, increased strength and bike-handling ability make mountain biking more fun for us. Now, we find ourselves looking for longer rides and more technical terrain, and our explorations have become more fulfilling. Here's hoping that your adventures are gratifying, too.

## SAFETY, COURTESY, AND RESPONSIBILITY

*Be completely self-sufficient.* Be prepared to find your own way if you get lost. Use all available maps and carry a compass. Information is often inaccurate on maps—check their data and make comparisons. Take note of landmarks and keep track of where you are and where you came from. Stop often and look behind you; it may be necessary to turn around and retrace your path. Tell someone where you plan to go, your route of travel, your anticipated time of return, and what to do if you do not return by that time. Ride with others who may be able to provide help in an emergency, especially in remote areas. Always call ahead to check on trail and road conditions, closures, or special circumstances that could affect your ride. Learn first aid and how to deal with hypothermia, dehydration, heat stroke, snake and tick bites, and other ailments and injuries that could befall backcountry travelers. Carry good first-aid and repair kits. Keep your bicycle in good working order and know how to make roadside repairs (like how to fix a flat). Develop a checklist of what to take with you when you go riding. Wear a helmet, cycling gloves, and protective eyewear. Oregon state law requires children under the age of 16 to wear a helmet while riding on a bicycle.

*Ride within your limitations.* Turn around if the weather becomes threatening or if you find the ride more difficult than you had expected. Keep your speed under control at all times. Descend at a rate that will allow you to stop well in advance of meeting others on the trails. Play it safe on narrow roads, trails, and when approaching blind corners; someone may be coming from the other direction. Stay to the right and ride defensively and predictably. If the route involves highway or city riding, avoid rush-hour traffic. Wait until the off-season to visit areas that are popular with tourists. Steer clear of ongoing logging operations, and avoid backcountry rides during hunting season.

*As relative newcomers, mountain bikers should make an extra effort to be courteous and ride safely.* Get in the habit of yielding to others. On trails, bikes should always stop and yield to hikers, runners, and equestrians. A "thank you" is in order if someone moves aside to wave you through. Do your best to avoid startling people; announce your presence well in advance of overtaking or approaching others. Be mindful of the special needs of equestrians. Horses have poor eyesight, are naturally skittish, and can cause serious injury when startled. Horses instinctively flee in the face of danger, and they are notoriously poor judges of what constitutes a threat. The slightest change in their surroundings may trigger a flight response. If you meet horses on the trail, dismount and move well away from the trail to the downhill side (horses may feel an attack is imminent if you are above them). Never hide in an attempt to allow equestrians an unburdened passing. When the horses do detect your presence (which is nearly a certainty), they will likely bolt. When approaching from behind, stop well in back of the riders and announce your presence. Always talk to horseback riders; ask them if their horses are easily spooked and ask for instructions on how they would prefer you to facilitate passing. Your voice will be helpful to the horse in recognizing you as a human. Be patient, the equestrians may require some time to calm their mounts and find a place where a pass can be negotiated.

*Be prepared for extreme riding conditions.* Weather conditions can change rapidly—especially at higher elevations. Carry rain gear, warm gloves, and other protective clothing to change into. Dress in layers so you can adjust your clothing to meet any number of riding conditions. Ultraviolet radiation from the sun becomes more intense as you climb higher; wear protective sunglasses and apply sunscreen rated SPF 15 or higher. Reapply sunscreen frequently. Lower air humidity and loss of water through increased respiration can cause rapid dehydration at higher elevations. Carry water from a safe source and bring more than you expect to need. Force yourself to drink even if you are not thirsty, especially on hot days. Once you become dehydrated, you will not be able to rehydrate and continue cycling. Carry high-energy foods and eat often; drink water with your snacks and meals.

*Respect the environment you are riding through.* Bicycles are not permitted in designated wilderness areas or on the Pacific Crest Trail. Some public lands restrict bicycle use to designated trails and roads only. Obey all signs indicating road or trail closings. Never trespass on private property or block access with your parked vehicle. Always stay on trails and roads; cross-country riding is inappropriate and often illegal. Never travel on worn trails where cycling will cause further damage. Carry your bike over degraded sections of the trail, or turn around and return the way you came. If you encounter isolated wet conditions and you feel it is appropriate to continue on, carry your bike while remaining on the trail. Carrying around wet areas widens the area of impact and causes "braided" trail conditions. Do not shortcut switchbacks or ride around waterbars placed in the trail; help control erosion instead of creating further degradation. It is never appropriate to skid your tires on trails. If you cannot control your speed without skidding, dismount and walk your bike down the hill to gentler terrain. Skidding through switchbacks is extremely hard on trails. If switchbacks are too tight to roll through, walk your bike down them. Resource damage can result from riding on wet trails. Wait until the spring thaw is over and trails are dry before riding. Pack out your own trash and, when possible, remove other people's litter as well. Leave gates as you find them; close them behind you if they were closed.

*Call or visit the ranger station (or other land management office) that is responsible for the lands you will be traveling on.* At the time of our last visit, a pass was required for parking at many National Forest trailhead facilities in Oregon. Parking passes were available for purchase at district ranger stations. (A season parking pass cost $25 and was good in eight National Forests in Oregon and Washington.) For trail and road information, ask to speak with a trail coordinator or a recreation specialist. Find out when the trail was last maintained, what condition it is in, and if there are any special circumstances that could affect your ride. It is also a good idea to inquire about ranger station office hours, for they vary widely from district to district. Forest Service maps are great sources of information. Obtain both the general map of the forest and the district map (district maps are sometimes referred to as "fire maps"). The general map will provide you with an overview of the region and helpful information about the area. The district map (topographic) is more detailed and is helpful as a directional aid. Ranger districts produce handouts that describe recreation opportunities in the forest. Most ranger districts distribute recreation opportunity guides that are specific to mountain biking. Feedback about trail conditions and your impressions of the ride are helpful to the rangers.

*Become an informed participant and get involved in managing the lands you use for recreation.* Many groups are active in trail building and maintenance efforts. Motorized off-road-vehicle users and equestrians have a record of involvement that speaks well of their concern for public lands. Mountain bike clubs throughout Oregon are actively involved in trail access issues, public education programs, and ongoing trail maintenance and construction projects. The efforts of these clubs have been instrumental in keeping trails open to bikes and in broadening the influence that trail bicyclists have on land management decisions. Get in touch with a local cycling club or bike shop that works to keep trails open to mountain bikes and promotes responsible riding. Attend meetings where management and recreation plans are discussed. Ask to be placed on a mailing list for volunteer work building or repairing trails.

Conflicts and closures are still problematic, but mountain biking has grown out of its infancy to become an accepted form of recreation. We seem to be getting along better with other trail users. Land managers across Oregon welcome mountain bikers; they only ask that cyclists ride responsibly.

*Chris and Laurie Leman*

## Family

7  Fish Lake Trail
8  High Lakes Trail
9  Burnt Timber Trail 1148
25  Phillips Reservoir Loop
40  Deschutes River Trail
47  Sisters Mountain Bike Trail/Eagle Rock Loop
51  Suttle Tie Trail/Suttle Lake Loop Trail
67  Middle Fork Willamette Trail
78  McDonald Research Forest/Vineyard Mountain Loop
79  Fort Stevens Bicycle Trails
80  Forest Park/Leif Erikson Drive
81  Champoeg State Park
82  Molalla River Corridor
83  Silver Falls State Park Bike Path
86  Deschutes River State Recreation Area Bike Path

## Novice and Beginner

7  Fish Lake Trail
8  High Lakes Trail
9  Burnt Timber Trail 1148
15  Minnehaha Loop
17  Umpqua Hot Springs
18  North Umpqua Trail/Tioga Section (first couple of miles)
21  Diamond Craters
25  Phillips Reservoir Loop
26  Indian Rock
40  Deschutes River Trail
41  Tumalo Falls
47  Sisters Mountain Bike Trail/Eagle Rock Loop
48  Sisters Mountain Bike Trail/Peterson Ridge Loop
51  Suttle Tie Trail/Suttle Lake Loop Trail
54  McKenzie River National Recreation Trail (lower reaches of the trail)
58  South Hills Ridgeline Trail (first couple of miles)
59  Row River Trail
66  Larison Creek Trail (first couple of miles)
67  Middle Fork Willamette Trail
70  Summit Lake Trail/Meek Lake Trail
72  Siltcoos Lake Trail
78  McDonald Research Forest/Vineyard Mountain Loop
79  Fort Stevens Bicycle Trails
80  Forest Park/Leif Erikson Drive
81  Champoeg State Park
82  Molalla River Corridor
83  Silver Falls State Park Bike Path
86  Deschutes River State Recreation Area Bike Path
87  East Fork Trail
91  Eightmile Loop Trail

## Intermediate and Advanced—Short Rides

3  White Rabbit Trail
11  Onion Way/Briggs Creek Loop
14  Rustler Peak Lookout
28  Anthony Lakes/Elkhorn Crest Trail
33  Tenderfoot Wagon Trail
34  Sugarloaf/Deadman Trails
37  Imnaha River Trail
39  Shevlin Park
49  Upper Three Creek Lake Sno-Park/Short Loop
56  Gray Butte Loop
58  South Hills Ridgeline Trail
60  Brice Creek Trail
61  Goodman Trail
62  Hardesty Trail
63  Flat Creek Trail/Dead Mountain
64  Blair Lake Loop
65  Larison Rock Trail
66  Larison Creek Trail
70  Summit Lake Trail/Meek Lake Trail
74  Burnt Timber Mountain
77  McDonald Research Forest/Dan's Trail—Horse Trail
82  Molalla River Corridor
84  Post Canyon/Seven Streams
85  Post Canyon/Mitchell Ridge

## Intermediate and Advanced—Short Rides (continued)

87  East Fork Trail
90  Knebal Springs Loop

91  Eightmile Loop Trail
93  Gunsight Trail

## Intermediate and Advanced—Long Rides

1  Watershed Loop
2  Horn Gap
4  Siskiyou Crest
5  Applegate Lake Loop
6  Brown Mountain Trail
10  Taylor Creek Trail
12  Chrome Ridge Loop
13  Illinois River Road
16  Sherwood Butte
18  North Umpqua Trail/Tioga Section
19  North Crater Trail/Crater Trail Loop
20  Hart Mountain/Guano Creek Loop
22  Owyhee Spring Loop
23  Owyhee Rim
24  Leslie Gulch
27  Twin Lakes Loop
29  Lehman Hot Springs
30  Copple Butte Trail
31  Mt. Fanny
32  Point Prominence
35  Horse Lake/Buck's Crossing
36  Windy Ridge
38  Phil's, Jim's, and Kent's Trails
42  Skyliners Loop
43  Tangent/Quarry Site 1041 Loop

44  Ridge Trail Loop
45  Cultus Lake Loop
46  Peter Skene Ogden Trail
50  Upper Three Creek Lake Sno-park/Long Loop
52  Green Ridge Lookout Loop
53  Cache Mountain Loop
54  McKenzie River National Recreation Trail
55  Burma Road/Smith Rock State Park
57  Round Mountain
66  Larison Creek Trail
68  Moon Point/Youngs Rock Trail
69  Waldo Lake
71  Lower Rogue River Trail
75  Marys Peak
76  McDonald Research Forest/McCulloch Peak
82  Molalla River Corridor
88  Surveyor's Ridge Trail
89  High Prairie Loop
92  Fifteenmile Creek Trail/Cedar Creek Trail
93  Gunsight Trail
94  Frog Lake Buttes

## Loops

1  Watershed Loop
2  White Rabbit Trail
5  Applegate Lake Loop
6  Brown Mountain Trail
9  Burnt Timber Trail 1148
11  Onion Way/Briggs Creek Loop
12  Chrome Ridge Loop
13  Illinois River Road
15  Minnehaha Loop
16  Sherwood Butte
18  North Umpqua Trail/Tioga Section
19  North Crater Trail/Crater Trail Loop
20  Hart Mountain/Guano Creek Loop
25  Phillips Reservoir Loop
27  Twin Lakes Loop
29  Lehman Hot Springs
33  Tenderfoot Wagon Trail
34  Sugarloaf/Deadman Trails

35  Horse Lake/Buck's Crossing
39  Shevlin Park
42  Skyliners Loop
44  Ridge Trail Loop
45  Cultus Lake Loop
46  Peter Skene Ogden Trail
50  Upper Three Creek Lake Sno-park/Long Loop
53  Cache Mountain Loop
57  Round Mountain
60  Brice Creek Trail
61  Goodman Trail
64  Blair Lake Loop
65  Larison Rock Trail
66  Larison Creek Trail
67  Middle Fork Willamette Trail
68  Moon Point/Youngs Rock Trail
69  Waldo Lake

## Single-track (continued)

7  Fish Lake Trail
8  Burnt Timber Trail 1148
10  Taylor Creek Trail
11  Onion Way/Briggs Creek Loop
12  Chrome Ridge Loop
15  Minnehaha Loop
17  Umpqua Hot Springs
18  North Umpqua Trail/Tioga Section
19  North Crater Trail/Crater Trail Loop
25  Phillips Reservoir Loop
26  Indian Rock
27  Twin Lakes Loop
28  Anthony Lakes/Elkhorn Crest Trail
29  Lehman Hot Springs
30  Copple Butte Trail
31  Mt. Fanny
34  Sugarloaf/Deadman Trails
36  Windy Ridge
37  Imnaha River Trail
38  Phil's, Jim's, and Kent's Trails
39  Shevlin Park
40  Deschutes River Trail
41  Tumalo Falls
42  Skyliners Loop
45  Cultus Lake Loop
46  Peter Skene Ogden Trail
47  Sisters Mountain Bike Trail/Eagle Rock Loop
48  Sisters Mountain Bike Trail/Peterson Ridge Loop
49  Upper Three Creek Lake Sno-Park/Short Loop
50  Upper Three Creek Lake Sno-Park/Long Loop
51  Suttle Tie Trail/Suttle Lake Loop

53  Cache Mountain Loop
54  McKenzie River National Recreation Trail
55  Burma Road/Smith Rock State Park
56  Gray Butte Loop
57  Round Mountain
58  South Hills Ridgeline Trail
60  Brice Creek Trail
61  Goodman Trail
62  Hardesty Trail
63  Flat Creek Trail/Dead Mountain
64  Blair Lake Loop
65  Larison Rock Trail
66  Larison Creek Trail
67  Middle Fork Willamette Trail
68  Moon Point/Youngs Rock Trail
69  Waldo Lake
70  Summit Lake Trail/Meek Lake Trail
71  Lower Rogue River Trail
72  Siltcoos Lake Trail
75  Marys Peak
77  McDonald Research Forest/Dan's Trail—Horse Trail
82  Molalla River Corridor
84  Post Canyon/Seven Streams
85  Post Canyon/Mitchell Ridge
87  East Fork Trail
88  Surveyor's Ridge Trail
89  High Prairie Loop
90  Knebal Springs Loop
91  Eightmile Loop Trail
92  Fifteenmile Creek Trail/Cedar Creek Trail
93  Gunsight Trail

## Great Scenery

4  Siskiyou Crest
5  Applegate Lake Loop
7  Fish Lake Trail
27  Twin Lakes Loop
28  Anthony Lakes/Elkhorn Crest Trail
32  Point Prominence
34  Sugarloaf/Deadman Trails
36  Windy Ridge
37  Imnaha River Trail
40  Deschutes River Trail
46  Peter Skene Ogden Trail
52  Green Ridge Lookout Loop

53  Cache Mountain Loop
54  McKenzie River National Recreation Trail
55  Burma Road/Smith Rock State Park
56  Gray Butte
64  Blair Lake Loop
65  Larison Rock Trail
69  Waldo Lake
70  Summit Lake Trail/Meek Lake Trail
75  Marys Peak
88  Surveyor's Ridge Trail
89  High Prairie Loop

90  Knebal Springs Loop
91  Eightmile Loop Trail

93  Gunsight Trail

## Wildlife Viewing

4  Siskiyou Crest
18  North Umpqua Trail/Tioga Section
20  Hart Mountain/Guano Creek Loop
22  Owyhee Spring Loop
23  Owyhee Rim
24  Leslie Gulch
27  Twin Lakes Loop
83  Silver Falls State Park Bike Path
86  Deschute River State Recreation

Area Bike Path
88  Surveyor's Ridge
90  Knebal Springs Loop
91  Eightmile Loop Trail
92  Fifteenmile Creek Trail/Cedar
    Creek Trail
93  Gunsight Trail
94  Frog Lake Buttes

## High-Speed Cruising

1  Watershed Loop
2  Horn Gap
4  Siskiyou Crest
12  Chrome Ridge Loop
16  Sherwood Butte
31  Mt. Fanny
32  Point Prominence
44  Ridge Trail Loop

46  Peter Skene Ogden Trail
52  Green Ridge Lookout Loop
74  Burnt Timber Mountain
76  McDonald Research
    Forest/McCulloch Peak
93  Gunsight Trail
94  Frog Lake Buttes

## Technical Heaven

3  White Rabbit Trail
18  North Umpqua Trail/Tioga Section
28  Anthony Lakes/Elkhorn Crest Trail
34  Sugarloaf/Deadman Trails
46  Peter Skene Ogden Trail
50  Upper Three Creek Lake Sno-
    park/Long Loop
54  McKenzie River National
    Recreation Trail
60  Brice Creek Trail

62  Hardesty Trail
63  Flat Creek Trail/Dead Mountain
68  Moon Point/Youngs Rock Trail
69  Waldo Lake
71  Lower Rogue River Trail
75  Marys Peak
89  High Prairie Loop
92  Fifteenmile Creek Trail/Cedar
    Creek Trail
93  Gunsight Trail

## Tough Climb

1  Watershed Loop
3  White Rabbit Trail
12  Chrome Ridge Loop
13  Illinois River Road
16  Sherwood Butte
27  Twin Lakes Loop
31  Mt. Fanny
42  Skyliners Loop
46  Peter Skene Ogden Trail
52  Green Ridge Lookout Loop

53  Cache Mountain Loop
56  Burma Road/Smith Rock State Park
57  Round Mountain
65  Larison Rock Trail
68  Moon Point/Youngs Rock Trail
73  North Fork Siuslaw River Loop
75  Marys Peak
92  Fifteenmile Creek Trail/Cedar
    Creek Trail
93  Gunsight Trail

# INTRODUCTION

TRAIL DESCRIPTION OUTLINE

Each trail in this book begins with key information that includes length, configuration, aerobic and technical difficulty, trail conditions, scenery, and special comments. Additional description is contained in 11 individual categories. The following will help you to understand all of the information provided.

**Trail name:** Trail names are as designated on United States Geological Survey (USGS) or Forest Service or other maps, and/or by local custom.

### At a Glance Information

**Length/configuration:** The overall length of a trail is described in miles, unless stated otherwise. The configuration is a description of the shape of each trail—whether the trail is a loop, out-and-back (that is, along the same route), figure eight, trapezoid, isosceles triangle, decahedron . . . (just kidding), or if it connects with another trail described in the book. See the Glossary for definitions of *point-to-point, combination,* and *out-and-back,* or see "Ride Configurations" on page 4.

**Aerobic difficulty:** This provides a description of the degree of physical exertion required to complete the ride.

**Technical difficulty:** This provides a description of the technical skill required to pedal a ride. Trails are often described here in terms of being paved, unpaved, sandy, hard-packed, washboarded, two- or four-wheel-drive, single-track or double-track. All terms that might be unfamiliar to the first-time mountain biker are defined in the Glossary.

*Note:* For both the aerobic and technical difficulty categories, authors were asked to keep in mind the fact that all riders are not equal, and thus to gauge the trail in terms of how the middle-of-the-road rider—someone between the newcomer and Ned Overend—could handle the route. Comments about the trail's length, condition, and elevation change will also assist you in determining the difficulty of any trail relative to your own abilities.

**Scenery:** Here you will find a general description of the natural surroundings during the seasons most riders pedal the trail, and a suggestion of what is to be found at special times (like great fall foliage or cactus in bloom).

**Special comments:** Unique elements of the ride are mentioned.


### Category Information

**General location:** This category describes where the trail is located in reference to a nearby town or other landmark.

**Elevation change:** Unless stated otherwise, the figure provided is the total gain and loss of elevation along the trail. In regions where the elevation variation is not extreme, the route is simply described as flat, rolling, or possessing short steep climbs or descents.

**Season:** This is the best time of year to pedal the route, taking into account trail conditions (for example, when it will not be muddy), riding comfort (when the weather is too hot, cold, or wet), and local hunting seasons.

   *Note:* Because the exact opening and closing dates of deer, elk, moose, and antelope seasons often change from year to year, riders should check with the local fish and game department or call a sporting goods store (or any place that sells hunting licenses) in a nearby town before heading out. Wear bright clothes in fall, and don't wear suede jackets while in the saddle. Hunter's-orange tape on your helmet is also a good idea.

**Services:** This category is of primary importance in guides for paved-road tourers, but is far less crucial to most mountain bike trail descriptions because there are usually no services whatsoever to be found. Authors have noted when water is available on desert or long mountain routes and have listed the availability of food, lodging, campgrounds, and bike shops. If all these services are present, you will find only the words "All services available in . . ."

**Hazards:** Special hazards like steep cliffs, great amounts of deadfall, or barbed-wire fences very close to the trail are noted here.

**Rescue index:** Determining how far one is from help on any particular trail can be difficult due to the backcountry nature of most mountain bike rides. Authors therefore state the proximity of homes or Forest Service outposts, nearby roads where one might hitch a ride, or the likelihood of other bikers being encountered on the trail. Phone numbers of local sheriff departments or hospitals are hardly ever provided because phones are usually not available. If you are able to reach a phone, the local operator will connect you with emergency services.

**Land status:** This category provides information regarding whether the trail crosses land operated by the Forest Service, Bureau of Land Management, or a city, state, or national park; whether it crosses private land whose owner (at the time the author did the research) has allowed mountain bikers right of passage; and so on.

Note: Authors have been extremely careful to offer only those routes that are open to bikers and are legal to ride. However, because land ownership changes over time, and because the land-use controversy created by mountain bikes still has not completely subsided, it is the duty of each cyclist to look for and to heed signs warning against trail use. Don't expect this book to get you off the hook when you're facing some small-town judge for pedaling past a Biking Prohibited sign erected the day before you arrived. Look for these signs, read them, and heed the advice. And remember there's always another trail.

**Maps:** The maps in this book have been produced with great care and, in conjunction with the trail-following suggestions, will help you stay on course. But as every experienced mountain biker knows, things can get tricky in the backcountry. It is therefore strongly suggested that you avail yourself of the detailed information found in the 7.5 minute series USGS topographic maps. In some cases, authors have found that specific Forest Service or other maps may be more useful than the USGS quads and tell how to obtain them.

**Finding the trail:** Detailed information on how to reach the trailhead and where to park your car is provided here.

**Sources of additional information:** Here you will find the address and/or phone number of a bike shop, governmental agency, or other source from which trail information can be obtained.

**Notes on the trail:** This is where you are guided carefully through any portions of the trail that are particularly difficult to follow. The author also may add information about the route that does not fit easily in the other categories. This category will not be present for those rides where the route is easy to follow.

ABBREVIATIONS

The following road-designation abbreviations are used in *Mountain Bike! Oregon:*

| | | | |
|---|---|---|---|
| CR | County Road | I- | Interstate |
| FS | Forest Service Road | US | United States highway |

State highways are designated with the appropriate two-letter state abbreviation, followed by the road number. Example: OR 35 = Oregon State Highway 35.

## SPECIAL TERMS

The following terms, used throughout this book, deserve special attention:

| | |
|---|---|
| *BLM* | Bureau of Land Management, an agency of the federal government |
| *Carsonite sign* | a small, thin, and flexible fiberglass signpost used extensively by the Forest Service and BLM to mark roads and trails (often dark brown in color) |
| *decomposed granite* | an excellent, fine- to medium-grain, trail and road surface material; typically used in native surface road and trail applications (not trucked in); results from the weathering of granite |
| *pummy* | soil with high pumice content produced by volcanic activity in the Pacific Northwest and elsewhere; light in consistency and easily pedaled; trails with such soil often become thick with dust |
| *recreation opportunity guides (R.O.G.)* | handouts which identify and describe resources available to the public on national forest lands (camping facilities, trails, wildlife viewing opportunities, etc.); often available for the asking at Forest Service ranger stations throughout the Pacific Northwest |
| *skid road* | the path created when loggers drag trees through the forest with heavy equipment |

## RIDE CONFIGURATIONS

**Combination:** This type of route may combine two or more configurations. For example, a point-to-point route may integrate a scenic loop or an out-and-back spur midway through the ride. Likewise, an out-and-back may have a loop at its farthest point (this configuration looks like a cherry with a stem attached; the stem is the out-and-back, the fruit is the terminus loop). Or a loop route may have multiple out-and-back spurs and/or loops to the side. Mileage for a combination route is for the total distance to complete the ride.

**Loop:** This route configuration is characterized by riding from the designated trailhead to a distant point, then returning to the trailhead via a different route (or simply continuing on the same in a circle route) without doubling back. You always move forward across new terrain, but return to the starting point when finished. Mileage is for the entire loop from the trailhead back to trailhead.

**Out-and-back:** A ride where you will return on the same trail you pedaled out. While this might sound far more boring than a loop route, many trails look very different when pedaled in the opposite direction.

**Point-to-point:** A vehicle shuttle (or similar assistance) is required for this type of route, which is ridden from the designated trailhead to a distant location, or endpoint, where the route ends. Total mileage is for the one-way trip from the trailhead to endpoint.

**Spur:** A road or trail that intersects the main trail you're following.

TOPOGRAPHIC MAPS

The maps in this book, when used in conjunction with the route directions present in each chapter, will in most instances be sufficient to get you to the trail and keep you on it. However, you will find superior detail and valuable information in the 7.5 minute series USGS topographic maps. Recognizing how indispensable these are to bikers and hikers alike, many bike shops and sporting goods stores now carry topos of the local area.

But if you're brand new to mountain biking you might be wondering "What's a topographic map?" In short, these differ from standard "flat" maps in that they indicate not only linear distance, but elevation as well. One glance at a topo will show you the difference, for "contour lines" are spread across the map like dozens of intricate spider webs. Each contour line represents a particular elevation, and at the base of each topo a particular "contour interval" designation is given. Yes, it sounds confusing if you're new to the lingo, but it truly is a simple and wonderfully helpful system. Keep reading.

Let's assume that the 7.5 minute series topo before us says "Contour Interval 40 feet," that the short trail we'll be pedaling is two inches in length on the map, and that it crosses five contour lines from its beginning to end. What do we know? Well, because the linear scale of this series is 2,000 feet to the inch (roughly 2 3/4 inches representing 1 mile), we know our trail is approximately 4/5 of a mile long (2 inches × 2,000 feet). But we also know we'll be climbing or descending 200 vertical feet (5 contour lines × 40 feet each) over that distance. And the elevation designations written on occasional contour lines will tell us if we're heading up or down.

The authors of this series warn their readers of upcoming terrain, but only a detailed topo gives you the information you need to pinpoint your position exactly on a map, steer yourself toward optional trails and roads nearby, plus let you know at a glance if you'll be pedaling hard to take them. It's a lot of information for a very low cost. In fact, the only drawback with topos is their size — several feet square. I've tried rolling them into tubes, folding them carefully, even cutting them into blocks and photocopying the pieces. Any of these systems is a pain, but no matter how you pack the maps you'll be happy they're along. And you'll be even happier if you pack a compass as well.

In addition to local bike shops and sporting goods stores, you'll find topos at major universities and some public libraries where you might try photocopying the ones you need to avoid the cost of buying them. But if you want your own and can't find them locally, contact:

USGS Map Sales
Box 25286
Denver, CO 80225
(800) HELP MAP (435-7627)

VISA and MasterCard are accepted. Ask for an index while you're at it, plus a price list and a copy of the booklet *Topographic Maps*. In minutes you'll be reading them like a pro.

A second excellent series of maps available to mountain bikers is that produced by the United States Forest Service. If your trail runs through an area designated as a national forest, look in the phone book (white pages) under the United States Government listings, find the Department of Agriculture heading, and then run your finger down that section until you find the Forest Service. Give them a call and they'll provide the address of the regional Forest Service office, from which you can obtain the appropriate map.

## TRAIL ETIQUETTE

Pick up almost any mountain bike magazine these days and you'll find articles and letters to the editor about trail conflict. For example, you'll find hikers' tales of being blindsided by speeding mountain bikers, complaints from mountain bikers about being blamed for trail damage that was really caused by horse or cattle traffic, and cries from bikers about those "kamikaze" riders who through their antics threaten to close even more trails to all of us.

The authors of this series have been very careful to guide you to only those trails that are open to mountain biking (or at least were open at the time of their research), and without exception have warned of the damage done to our sport through injudicious riding. All of us can benefit from glancing over the following International Mountain Bicycling Association (IMBA) Rules of the Trail before saddling up.

1. *Ride on open trails only.* Respect trail and road closures (ask if not sure), avoid possible trespass on private land, obtain permits and authorization as may be required. Federal and state wilderness areas are closed to cycling.

2. *Leave no trace.* Be sensitive to the dirt beneath you. Even on open trails, you should not ride under conditions where you will leave evidence of your passing, such as on certain soils shortly after rain. Observe the different types of soils and trail construction; practice low-impact cycling. This also means staying on the trail and not creating any new ones. Be sure to pack out at least as much as you pack in.

3. *Control your bicycle!* Inattention for even a second can cause disaster. Excessive speed can maim and threaten people; there is no excuse for it!

4. *Always yield the trail.* Make known your approach well in advance. A friendly greeting (or a bell) is considerate and works well; startling someone may cause loss of trail access. Show your respect when passing others by slowing to a walk or even stopping. Anticipate that other trail users may be around corners or in blind spots.

5. *Never spook animals.* All animals are startled by an unannounced approach, a sudden movement, or a loud noise. This can be dangerous for you, for others, and for the animals. Give animals extra room and time to adjust to you. In passing, use special care and follow the directions of horseback riders (ask if uncertain). Running cattle and disturbing wild animals is a serious offense. Leave gates as you found them, or as marked.

6. *Plan ahead.* Know your equipment, your ability, and the area in which you are riding—and prepare accordingly. Be self-sufficient at all times. Wear a helmet, keep your machine in good condition, and carry necessary supplies for changes in weather or other conditions. A well-executed trip is a satisfaction to you and not a burden or offense to others.

For more information, contact IMBA, P.O. Box 7578, Boulder, CO 80306; (303) 545-9011.

## HITTING THE TRAIL

Once again, because this is a "where-to," not a "how-to" guide, the following will be brief. If you're a veteran trail rider these suggestions might serve to remind you of something you've forgotten to pack. If you're a newcomer, they might convince you to think twice before hitting the backcountry unprepared.

**Water:** I've heard the questions dozens of times. "How much is enough? One bottle? Two? Three?! But think of all that extra weight!" Well, one simple physiological fact should convince you to err on the side of excess when it comes to deciding how much water to pack: a human working hard in 90-degree temperature needs approximately ten quarts of fluids every day. Ten quarts. That's two and a half gallons—12 large water bottles, or 16 small ones. And, with water weighing in at approximately 8 pounds per gallon, a one-day supply comes to a whopping 20 pounds.

In other words, pack along two or three bottles even for short rides. And make sure you can purify the water found along the trail on longer routes. When writing of those routes where this could be of critical importance, each author has provided information on where water can be found near the trail—if it can be found at all. But drink it untreated and you run the risk of disease. (See *Giardia* in the Glossary.)

One sure way to kill the protozoans, bacteria, and viruses in water is to boil it. Right. That's just how you want to spend your time on a bike ride. Besides, who wants to carry a stove, or denude the countryside stoking bonfires to boil water?

Luckily, there is a better way. Many riders pack along the inexpensive and only slightly distasteful tetraglycine hydroperiodide tablets (sold under the names Potable Aqua, Globaline, and Coughlan's, among others). Some invest in portable, lightweight purifiers that filter out the crud. Unfortunately, both iodine *and* filtering are now required to be absolutely sure you've killed all the nasties you can't see. Tablets or iodine drops by themselves will knock off the well-known *Giardia*, once called "beaver fever" for its transmission to the water through the feces of infected beavers. One to four weeks after ingestion, *Giardia* will have you bloated, vomiting, shivering with chills, and living in the bathroom. (Though you won't care while you're suffering, beavers are getting a bum rap, for other animals are carriers also.)

But now there's another parasite we must worry about—*Cryptosporidium*. "Crypto" brings on symptoms very similar to *Giardia*, but unlike that fellow protozoan it's equipped with a shell sufficiently strong to protect it against the chemical killers that stop *Giardia* cold. This means we're either back to boiling or on to using a water filter to screen out both *Giardia* and crypto, plus the iodine to knock off viruses. All of which sounds like a time-consuming pain, but really isn't. Some water filters come equipped with an iodine chamber, to guarantee full protection. Or you can simply add a pill or drops to the water you've just filtered (if you aren't allergic to iodine, of course). The pleasures of backcountry biking—and the displeasure of getting sick—make this relatively minor effort worth the few minutes involved.

**Tools:** Ever since my first cross-country tour in 1965 I've been kidded about the number of tools I pack on the trail. And so I will exit entirely from this discussion by providing a list compiled by two mechanic (and mountain biker) friends of mine. After all, since they make their livings fixing bikes and get their kicks by riding them, who could be a better source?

These two suggest the following as an absolute minimum:

tire levers
spare tube and patch kit
air pump
Allen wrenches (3, 4, 5, and 6 mm)
six-inch crescent (adjustable-end) wrench
small flat-blade screwdriver
chain rivet tool
spoke wrench

But, while they're on the trail, their personal tool pouches contain these additional items:

channel locks (small)
air gauge
tire valve cap (the metal kind, with a valve-stem remover)
baling wire (ten or so inches, for temporary repairs)
duct tape (small roll for temporary repairs or tire boot)
boot material (small piece of old tire or a large tube patch)
spare chain link
rear derailleur pulley
spare nuts and bolts
paper towel and tube of waterless hand cleaner

**First-aid kit:** My personal kit contains the following, sealed inside double Ziploc bags:

sunscreen
aspirin
butterfly-closure bandages
Band-Aids
gauze compress pads (a half dozen 4" × 4")
gauze (one roll)
ace bandages or Spenco joint wraps
Benadryl (an antihistamine, in case of allergic reactions)
water purification tablets / water filter (on long rides)
moleskin / Spenco "Second Skin"
hydrogen peroxide, iodine, or Mercurochrome (some kind of antiseptic)
snakebite kit

**Final considerations:** The authors of this series have done a good job in suggesting that specific items be packed for certain trails—rain gear in particular seasons, a hat and gloves for mountain passes, or shades for desert jaunts. Heed their warnings, and think ahead. Good luck.

*Dennis Coello*

AND NOW, A WORD ABOUT CELLULAR PHONES . . .

Thinking of bringing the Flip-Fone along on your next off-road ride? Before you do, ask yourself the following questions:

- Do I know where I'm going? Do I have an adequate map? Can I use a compass effectively? Do I know the shortest way to civilization if I need to bail out early and find some help?

- If I'm on the trail for longer than planned, am I ready for it? Do I have adequate water? Have I packed something to eat? Will I be warm enough if I'm still out there after dark?

- Am I prepared for possible injuries? Do I have a first-aid kit? Do I know what to do in case of a cut, fracture, snakebite, or heat exhaustion?

- Is my tool kit adequate for likely mechanical problems? Can I fix a flat? Can I untangle a chain? Am I prepared to walk out if the bike is unridable?

If you answered "yes" to *every* question above, you may pack the phone, but consider a good whistle instead. It's lighter, cheaper, and nearly as effective.

If you answered "no" to *any* of these questions, be aware that your cellular phone does little to reduce your risks in the wilderness. Sure, being able to dial 911 in the farthest corner of the Cascade Mountains sounds like a great idea, but this ain't downtown, friend. If disaster strikes, and your call is routed to some emergency operator in Portland or Hillsboro, and it takes awhile to figure out which ranger, sheriff, or search-and-rescue crew to connect you with, and you can't tell the authorities where you are because you're really not sure, and the closest they can come to pinpointing your location is a cellular tower that serves 62 square miles of dense woods, and they start searching for you but dusk is only two hours away, and you have no signaling device and your throat is too dry to shout, and meanwhile you can't get the bleeding stopped, you are out of luck. I mean *really* out of luck.

And when the battery goes dead, you're on your own again. Enough said.

*Jeff Faust*
*Author of* Mountain Bike! New Hampshire

# SOUTHWEST OREGON

Mountain ranges and huge tracts of timber dominate southwest Oregon. This area is defined by the Siskiyou Mountains to the south, the Klamath Mountains and Coastal Range to the west, and the Cascades to the east. The northern limit of this region (for the purposes of this book) is the North Umpqua River.

The weather in the valleys of western Oregon is generally moderate. Extreme temperatures are rare. Rain is common in the winter and spring. Summers are often dry, with daytime temperatures seldom climbing higher than the 80s. Evenings are pleasantly cool. The higher elevations see snow in the winter and a wider range of temperatures year-round.

We begin this book with rides near the cities of Ashland and Medford. Today, the area is a center of art, culture, and commerce. This broad, flat valley was once the home of Native Americans who fiercely defended their homeland. Early French-Canadian trappers called them *les Coquins*, the Rogues. In the late 1880s, the valley was chosen as the route for the Oregon-California Railroad. A train depot was built at Medford, and the rails were pushed south over Siskiyou Pass. This route provided a link to a newly completed national network of railways and had a huge impact on the future of southwestern Oregon.

Heading west, we explore rides near Grants Pass in the Siskiyou National Forest. The Galice and Illinois Valley Ranger Districts are becoming popular destinations for mountain bikers. The rangers in these regions are working hard to develop trails that meet the needs of this growing population.

To the north are riding opportunities in the Rogue and Umpqua National Forests. Crater Lake National Park is bounded by these forests and is an outstanding feature of the area. Mountain biking is almost nonexistent in this park, but the breathtaking beauty of the lake should not be missed. Not far from the park is Diamond Lake, which can provide some good cycling. Farther to the north is the North Umpqua River Trail. It follows the North Umpqua River for 80 miles and offers a variety of outstanding recreation experiences. The Tioga section of the trail is explored in this guidebook; the remaining 65 miles are left to intrepid cyclist-adventurers.

## **RIDE 1** · Watershed Loop

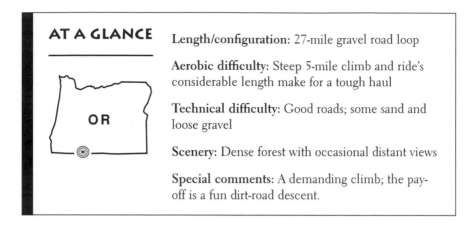

**AT A GLANCE**

**OR**

**Length/configuration:** 27-mile gravel road loop

**Aerobic difficulty:** Steep 5-mile climb and ride's considerable length make for a tough haul

**Technical difficulty:** Good roads; some sand and loose gravel

**Scenery:** Dense forest with occasional distant views

**Special comments:** A demanding climb; the payoff is a fun dirt-road descent.

Ashland is a bustling tourist center known for its Shakespearean theater, splendid Victorian homes, and flower-filled landscapes. Two-wheel enthusiasts are drawn here by the area's outstanding mountain biking. A popular local's ride is the 27-mile Watershed Loop. The trip begins and ends in the center of Ashland in Lithia Park.

We rate this ride as difficult. The circuit's length and a steep, five-mile climb make it strenuous. The 3,000-foot ascent is followed by 15 miles of level pedaling and easy hills. The loop ends with a six-mile descent back into town. Most of the riding is on good gravel roads. (There are also 1.5 miles of pavement.)

**General location:** Ashland is 15 miles north of the California border on Interstate 5.

**Elevation change:** The parking area in Lithia Park lies at 2,080'. The route climbs to 4,400' at an intersection of roads known as Four Corners. From Four Corners, you continue to ascend, but the climbing is hardly noticeable compared with the monster you just completed. You will encounter some rolling terrain before you reach a high point of 5,000'. These ups and downs add about 200' of climbing to the trip. Total elevation gain: 3,120'.

**Season:** Snow may linger at higher elevations along the route in the spring. Most of the loop is within the Ashland Watershed. Entry into the watershed may be restricted during periods of high fire danger.

**Services:** Water is available at the trailhead in Lithia Park. All services can be obtained in Ashland.

**Hazards:** Be mindful that you may encounter motor vehicles and descending cyclists on your climb up Forest Service Road 2060. The watershed is popular with hikers, runners, and dog walkers. Slow down and give others advance warning of your approach—share, don't scare. The ride ends with a long descent that contains many blind curves. Control your speed and anticipate others approaching from around the next bend.

# RIDE 1 · Watershed Loop

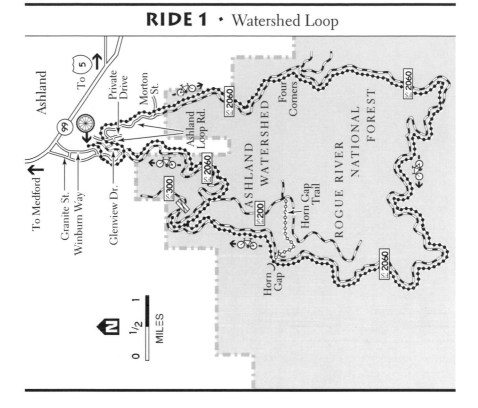

**Rescue index:** Help can be found in Ashland.

**Land status:** The Rogue River National Forest and the City of Ashland.

**Maps:** The district map of the Ashland Ranger District is a good guide to this ride. USGS 7.5 minute quads: Ashland, Mt. Ashland, Siskiyou Peak, and Talent.

**Finding the trail:** From I-5 in Ashland, take Exit 14 and travel west on OR 66/Ashland St. After 1.3 miles, turn right onto OR 99 North/Siskiyou Boulevard. In another mile, the road's name changes to Lithia Way, and it becomes a one-way street. Follow Lithia Way for 0.4 mile (get in the left-hand lane before you cross the bridge over Lithia Creek). Turn left immediately after crossing the bridge to follow a sign reading "City Center, Lithia Park, Southbound." Turn left onto North Main, then immediately turn right onto Granite Street. Go up Granite Street for 0.3 mile to a stop sign. Turn left onto Nutley Street, then right onto Winburn Way. Follow Winburn Way up through the park for 0.4 mile to parking at the Upper Duck Pond on the left.

Forest Service
Road 2060.

**Sources of additional information:**

Ashland Ranger District
645 Washington Street
Ashland, OR 97520
(541) 482-3333

Ashland Chamber of Commerce
P.O. Box 1360
Ashland, OR 97520
(541) 482-3486

**Notes on the trail:** From the parking lot, turn left onto Granite Street. The road changes to dirt after about 0.5 mile, and then you reach the intersection of

Rogue River
National Forest.

Granite Street and Glenview Drive. Turn left onto Glenview Drive; follow it for 0.5 mile, then turn right onto Ashland Loop Road. Climb steeply to a **T** intersection and pavement. Turn left, then stay to the right and continue gently uphill on Ashland Loop Road. At the intersection with Morton Street, go right and uphill, remaining on Ashland Loop Road. Shortly, the pavement ends, the road enters the national forest, and its designation changes to FS 2060. At Four Corners, turn right and proceed on FS 2060 toward Horn Gap. Remain on FS 2060 to return to Lithia Park.

## RIDE 2 · Horn Gap

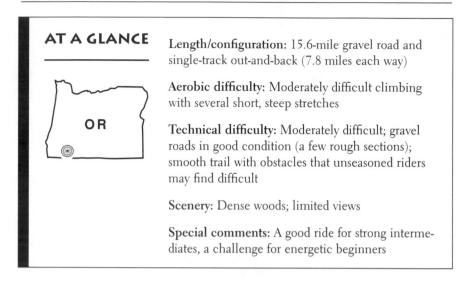

**AT A GLANCE**

**Length/configuration:** 15.6-mile gravel road and single-track out-and-back (7.8 miles each way)

**Aerobic difficulty:** Moderately difficult climbing with several short, steep stretches

**Technical difficulty:** Moderately difficult; gravel roads in good condition (a few rough sections); smooth trail with obstacles that unseasoned riders may find difficult

**Scenery:** Dense woods; limited views

**Special comments:** A good ride for strong intermediates, a challenge for energetic beginners

Horn Gap Trail was built as a mountain bike "tie trail." It provides a link from Ashland Loop Road (Forest Service Road 2060) to a less traveled side road, FS 200. This connection has opened up some new opportunities for mountain biking in the Ashland Watershed. We describe a 15.6-mile out-and-back trip (7.8 miles each way) that begins and ends in Lithia Park.

Most of the climbing on the roads is moderately difficult, but there are a number of short, steep sections. These make the climb more demanding, but they quickly give way to less taxing segments. Horn Gap Trail is only 1.3 miles long, but it makes for a fun little climb and an exciting, twisting descent. Novices may have difficulty with the trail's tight turns and short, moderately steep grades.

Horn Gap Trail is in fine shape, thanks in large part to the Southern Oregon Cycling Association. This group has volunteered to maintain this trail as a part of the U.S. Forest Service Adopt-A-Trail Program. Budget cuts for recreation and increased trail use have left forest service crews scrambling to get their work accomplished. Increasingly, trails are in need of maintenance. By adopting trails, individuals, businesses, and groups throughout Oregon are helping with this important work.

The roads on this trip are very good. They are categorized as "native surface"—built with material that was readily available when the road was cut. Happily for us, that material is decomposed granite, undoubtedly the best stuff for rolling tires over. You will find some ruts, minor washboarding, and short sections of coarse gravel.

Views on this ride are limited by the dense forest that lines the roads and trail. You can catch a glimpse of Mt. Ashland from Horn Gap Trail, or take an optional

View from Forest Service Road 250.

side trip on an old spur road to an open area. Here you get a view of grassy foothills to the north and east of Ashland, forested ridges to the southeast, and Mt. Ashland to the south.

**General location:** Ashland is 15 miles north of the California border on Interstate 5.

**Elevation change:** The ride starts in Lithia Park at an elevation of 2,080'. A high point of 4,680' is reached at the top of Horn Gap Trail. Total elevation gain: 2,600'.

**Season:** Horn Gap Trail is often dry and able to support traffic from the late spring through the fall. The trail is quite high and it is well shaded by trees; it can remain snow-covered for some time. Please stay off the trail when it is wet. The gravel and native surface roads in the area are generally suitable for travel well before the region's single-track. Call ahead to check on trail conditions and seasonal closures. The entire watershed may be closed to all during times of high fire danger.

**Services:** You will find toilets and drinking fountains in Lithia Park. All services are available in Ashland.

**Hazards:** Some (not all) of the roads in the Ashland Watershed are closed to private motor vehicles. Administrative traffic is common. The roads and trails contain blind corners and are popular with all manner of huffing, puffing people. Slow down as you descend, and watch out for people who may be hidden from view. As you are climbing, consider that you may meet cyclists who are descending without the forethought that you are being asked to consider.

# RIDE 2 · Horn Gap

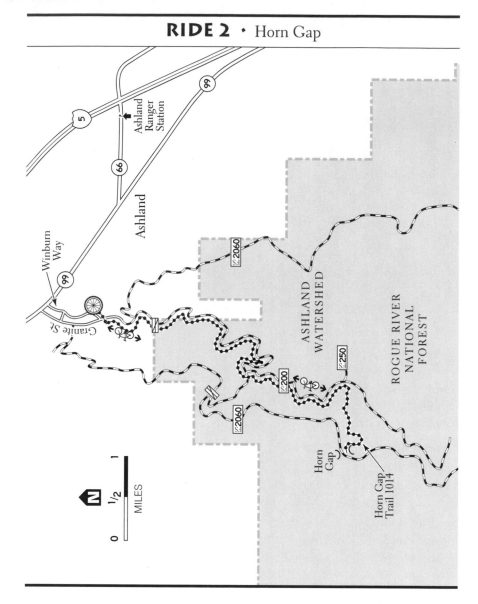

**Rescue index:** Help can be found in Ashland.

**Land status:** The Rogue River National Forest and the City of Ashland.

**Maps:** We recommend that you carry the district map of the Ashland Ranger District. However, this map does not show Horn Gap Trail. You will find the trail delineated on an Ashland Ranger District recreation opportunity guide titled "Horn Gap Mountain Bike Trail, #1014." You can pick one up at the ranger station when you purchase your district map. USGS 7.5 minute quad: Ashland.

**Finding the trail:** From I-5 in Ashland, take Exit 14 and travel west on OR 66/Ashland St. In 1.3 miles, turn right onto OR 99 North/Siskiyou Boulevard. In another mile the road's name changes to Lithia Way and it becomes a one-way street. Follow Lithia Way for 0.4 mile (get in the left-hand lane before you cross the bridge over Lithia Creek). Turn left immediately after crossing the bridge to follow the sign: "City Center, Lithia Park, Southbound." Turn left onto North Main, then immediately turn right onto Granite Street. Go up Granite Street for 0.3 mile to a stop sign. Turn left onto Nutley Street, then right onto Winburn Way. Follow Winburn Way up through the park for 0.4 mile to parking on the left at the Upper Duck Pond.

## Sources of additional information:

Ashland Ranger District
645 Washington Street
Ashland, OR 97520
(541) 482-3333

Ashland Chamber of Commerce
P.O. Box 1360
Ashland, OR 97520
(541) 482-3486

Southern Oregon Cycling Association
P.O. Box 903
Ashland, OR 75520
(541) 488-2453

**Notes on the trail:** From the parking lot, turn left onto Granite Street. The road changes to dirt after about 0.5 mile, and then you reach the intersection of Granite Street and Glenview Drive. Continue straight on Granite Street. Stay on the main road, climbing to a metal barrier. Pass your bikes over the barrier and continue with the climb. In another 3.5 miles you will reach FS 200 on the left at a sign for Horn Gap Trail 1014. Turn left and ride up FS 200 for 1.8 miles to FS 250 on the left (FS 250 is marked with a brown Carsonite sign). Option — ride up FS 250 for 0.2 mile to a viewpoint, then turn around and return to the intersection of FS 200 and FS 250. After riding to the viewpoint and back (or foregoing that option), continue on FS 200 for another 50' to single-track Horn Gap Trail on the right. Ride up the trail. It is 1.3 miles to the top of the trail at Horn Gap and FS 2060. Return the way you came.

You can add a couple of miles to this ride by following FS 200 to its southern terminus (see map).

**RIDE 3** · White Rabbit Trail

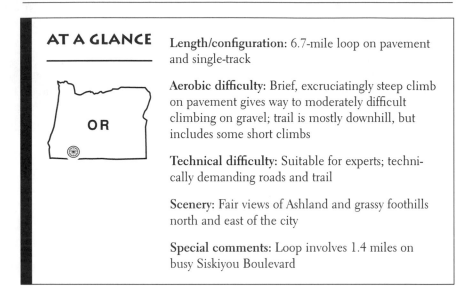

**AT A GLANCE**

**Length/configuration:** 6.7-mile loop on pavement and single-track

**Aerobic difficulty:** Brief, excruciatingly steep climb on pavement gives way to moderately difficult climbing on gravel; trail is mostly downhill, but includes some short climbs

**Technical difficulty:** Suitable for experts; technically demanding roads and trail

**Scenery:** Fair views of Ashland and grassy foothills north and east of the city

**Special comments:** Loop involves 1.4 miles on busy Siskiyou Boulevard

With a length of 2.3 miles, White Rabbit Trail is short, but it's no bunny hill. We describe a 6.7-mile loop that takes you to the top of the trail on roads. Climbing on roads facilitates a descent on the trail—well, it's mostly downhill. White Rabbit Trail can be ridden as an out-and-back, but climbing up on the trail would be extremely demanding. Getting to the top of this trail by taking roads is also difficult. The loop begins on a busy city thoroughfare, Siskiyou Boulevard. Next comes incredibly steep Morton Street. It is so steep that your bike will slide down the hill if you set it down to remove a layer of clothing! Sound like a fun ride? Well, you have the devil to pay, but White Rabbit Trail is fun, and in Ashland, "near to town" single-track is hard to come by.

The roads are in good condition with some ruts on gravel Ashland Loop Road. The upper portion of White Rabbit Trail is in great shape. This single-track is another Adopt-A-Trail success story—accolades to adoptee Dr. William S. Epstein. The trail is jazzed up with small side loops that add difficulty and excitement to the basic route. The forested upper reaches of the trail involve some climbing, then the path pops out of the woods onto an open ridge with views of Ashland. From here, White Rabbit descends rapidly through switchbacks and sharp, rutted turns. The bottom of the trail follows old, decomposed granite roads that are becoming trail-like as the surrounding vegetation grows in. Some of these "troads" are steep and eroded.

**General location:** Ashland is 15 miles north of the California border on Interstate 5.

**Elevation change:** Starts at 2,160' and reaches a high point of 3,275'. There is about 300' of additional climbing along the route. Total elevation gain: 1,415'.

# RIDE 3 · White Rabbit Trail

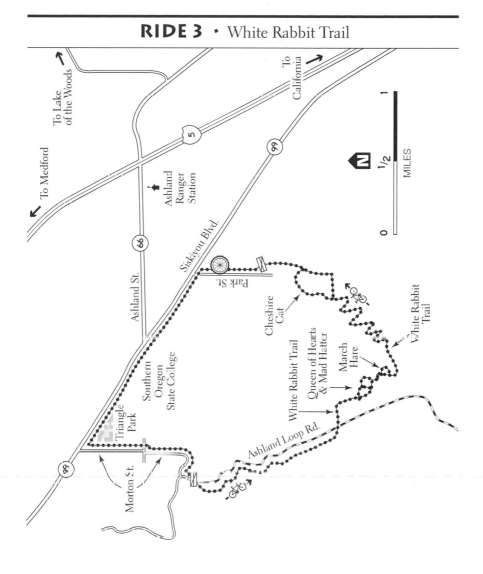

**Season:** You can usually plan on riding here from the spring through the fall. During periods of wet weather, restrict your travels to the vast network of nearby gravel roads. Call or visit the Ashland Ranger Station for road ride ideas and information on trail conditions and seasonal closures.

**Services:** All services are available in Ashland.

**Hazards:** The loop begins with 1.4 miles on busy Siskiyou Boulevard; probably the most dangerous portion of the ride. If riding in city traffic makes you uncomfortable but you are determined to do this ride, consider some alternatives. You could choose to ride up the sidewalk that parallels Siskiyou Boulevard, but this poses other safety concerns. If you decide to ride up the sidewalk, stop at each intersection and make sure that cars aren't turning off of (or onto) the boulevard without seeing you. Another option is to follow side streets and avoid Siskiyou Boulevard all together. Get a city map from the Chamber of Commerce; the street connections are convoluted. Another option is to use two vehicles to create a shuttle ride (lots of driving for a short ride). If you follow our "Notes on the trail," consider pushing your bike up Morton Street. Do not climb this steep hill by weaving from side to side. Riding in a predictable and defensive manner is an important aspect of sharing roads with motor vehicles. Watch for cars on gravel Ashland Loop Road; there are several blind corners. Parts of White Rabbit Trail contain technical sections and dangerous exposures.

**Rescue index:** Help can be found in Ashland.

**Land status:** City of Ashland and the Rogue River National Forest.

**Maps:** We were not able to find White Rabbit Trail 1002 on any maps, but it is delineated on an Ashland Ranger District recreation opportunity guide titled "White Rabbit Trail, #1002." We recommend that you carry the district map of the Ashland Ranger District and the R.O.G.; both are available at the ranger station in Ashland. (The ranger station is on Washington Street; which is just west of I-5 Exit 14.) USGS 7.5 minute quad: Ashland.

**Finding the trail:** From I-5 in Ashland, take Exit 14 and travel west on OR 66/Ashland Street. In 1.3 miles, turn left onto OR 99 South/Siskiyou Boulevard. Turn right in 0.6 mile onto Park Street. Park your vehicle curbside on Park Street.

**Sources of additional information:**

Ashland Ranger District
645 Washington Street
Ashland, OR 97520
(541) 482-3333

Ashland Chamber of Commerce
P.O. Box 1360
Ashland, OR 97520
(541) 482-3486

**Notes on the trail:** Turn left (northwest) onto Siskiyou Boulevard and ride 1.4 miles to Morton Street (1 block past Triangle Park). Turn left onto Morton Street and climb up the hill. Morton Street makes a couple of turns; keep an eye on the street signs. Turn left onto Ashland Loop Road at the terminus of Morton Street. Shortly, the pavement ends at a green metal gate. Climb up the gravel road for a little over a mile to a small parking area on the left. Turn left and follow signed White Rabbit Trail 1002. Several side-loop trails branch off of White Rabbit Trail (see map). Take these well-marked, short detours. They are fun in both directions. (Can you climb up Mad Hatter? We couldn't!) Soon after pass-

White Rabbit Trail.

ing the intersections with March Hare Trail, White Rabbit Trail climbs steeply to an open ridge. Here, a red arrow on a green sign directs you to continue straight on the main trail. Descend through switchbacks and sharp turns. Intersections are well marked; follow the signs for White Rabbit Trail and Park Street. Pass around a green metal gate to reach paved Park Street. Follow Park Street down to your vehicle.

## RIDE 4 · Siskiyou Crest

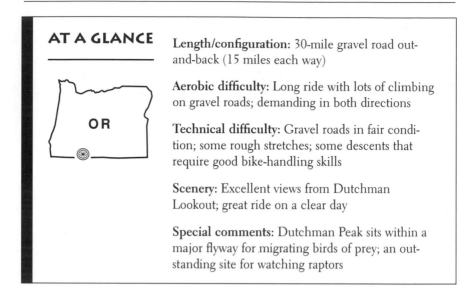

**AT A GLANCE**

**Length/configuration:** 30-mile gravel road out-and-back (15 miles each way)

**Aerobic difficulty:** Long ride with lots of climbing on gravel roads; demanding in both directions

**Technical difficulty:** Gravel roads in fair condition; some rough stretches; some descents that require good bike-handling skills

**Scenery:** Excellent views from Dutchman Lookout; great ride on a clear day

**Special comments:** Dutchman Peak sits within a major flyway for migrating birds of prey; an outstanding site for watching raptors

This is a demanding 30-mile out-and-back ride. It begins at Mt. Ashland Ski Area and follows gravel roads to the lookout on Dutchman Peak. The length of the trip and the amount of elevation gained make this a difficult outing. There is a lot of easy to moderately difficult climbing, and there are about two miles of steep uphills. The trip includes several long descents. The roads are in fair condition, with some washboarding and rocky sections. The return is almost as demanding as the first half of the tour.

Built in 1927, Dutchman Lookout is one of the few remaining cupola-style lookouts in the Pacific Northwest. The structure has two floors—a "fire-finder" room is stacked on top of the living quarters. The view from the lookout is panoramic.

We had the good fortune to meet Lillian Deala (the lookout) and her faithful watchdog Fluffy on our visit to Dutchman Peak. Lillian pointed out the mountains for us; Fluffy let us play with her ball. On a clear day you can look north across nearly half of the state to Diamond Peak (near Waldo Lake). Closer peaks are Mt. Bailey, Mt. Thielsen (near Diamond Lake), and Mt. Scott (on the rim of Crater Lake). Mt. McLoughlin is prominent in the northeast. To the south, the ridge riding offers views of Cottonwood Valley, the Marble and Scott mountain ranges, Mt. Shasta, and Pilot Rock.

The area around Dutchman Peak is a major flyway for migrating birds of prey. Hawkwatch International, a nonprofit research group, uses the peak as a counting station and bird-banding facility. Volunteers compile data that are used by scientists involved in ecosystem and wildlife research. Being at the top of their particular food chain, raptors are good indicators of the overall health of an ecosystem.

# RIDE 4 · Siskiyou Crest

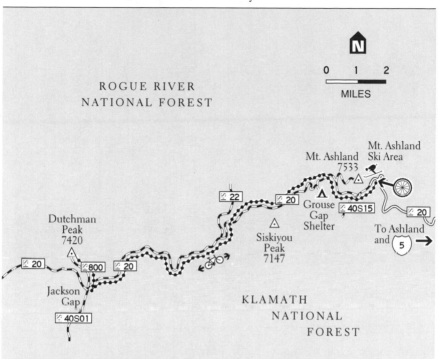

**General location:** Mt. Ashland Ski Area is approximately 18 miles southwest of Ashland.

**Elevation change:** The ride begins at 6,600' and tops out at 7,420' on Dutchman Peak. Undulations along the route add an estimated 2,000' of climbing to the trip. Total elevation gain: 2,820'.

**Season:** Generally, the roads are free of snow and open between July and November. In the summer, the rocky meadows near Dutchman Peak contain many wildflowers. The route follows part of a popular 85-mile auto tour, and the roads can get busy on weekends and during hunting season.

**Services:** There is no water on this ride—bring all you will need with you. All services are available in Ashland.

**Hazards:** Loose rocks, gravel, ruts, and washboarding occur on the steeper sections of the route. The descent from Meridian Overlook to Siskiyou Gap is particularly rough. On bright days, this downhill stretch is made more treacherous by sun and shadow. Trees border the road and create patches of deep shade, which are followed by patches of blinding sunshine. Seeing the obstacles in the road becomes difficult under these conditions, so descend slowly. All of the riding is at high altitude; use sunscreen and drink plenty of water. Watch for traffic.

Dutchman Lookout.

**Rescue index:** Help can be found in Ashland.

**Land status:** Rogue River National Forest.

**Maps:** The route travels through the Ashland and Applegate Ranger Districts. Used together, the district maps from these two agencies make a good guide to this ride. USGS 7.5 minute quads: Mt. Ashland, Siskiyou Peak, and Dutchman Peak.

**Finding the trail:** From Ashland, follow Interstate 5 south for 8.5 miles and take Exit 6 for Mt. Ashland. Follow the signs for Mt. Ashland. (You will be paralleling the highway for 0.6 mile.) Then turn right onto Colestin Road/Forest Service Road 20 and head toward Mt. Ashland Ski Area. Follow the road for 8.9 miles to the ski area parking lot on the right.

The view to the south from FS 20 is excellent, there is a good pullout on the left just before milepost 5.

**Sources of additional information:**

Ashland Ranger District
645 Washington Street
Ashland, OR 97520
(541) 482-3333

Applegate Ranger District
Star Ranger Station
6941 Upper Applegate Road
Jacksonville, OR 97530
(541) 899-1812

**Notes on the trail:** Follow paved FS 20 southwest. The road surface changes to gravel in 0.3 mile (at a gate). At intersections, stay on FS 20 and follow the signs toward Dutchman Peak. You arrive at Jackson Gap and FS 800 after pedaling 13.7 miles. Turn right onto FS 800 and follow the sign for Dutchman Peak. You reach the lookout in another 1.4 miles. Return the way you came. The Pacific Crest Trail parallels FS 20 for most of the route, but it is closed to bicycles.

A brochure titled "The Siskiyou Loop" can be purchased at the Ashland Ranger Station. It is filled with interesting information about the area.

## RIDE 5 · Applegate Lake Loop

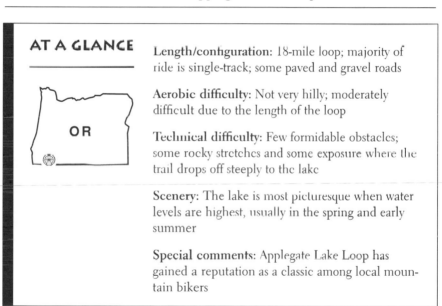

**AT A GLANCE**

**Length/configuration:** 18-mile loop; majority of ride is single-track; some paved and gravel roads

**Aerobic difficulty:** Not very hilly; moderately difficult due to the length of the loop

**Technical difficulty:** Few formidable obstacles; some rocky stretches and some exposure where the trail drops off steeply to the lake

**Scenery:** The lake is most picturesque when water levels are highest, usually in the spring and early summer

**Special comments:** Applegate Lake Loop has gained a reputation as a classic among local mountain bikers

This 18-mile loop uses 12.5 miles of single-track, 3 miles of pavement, and 2.5 miles of gravel roads. The trail follows the fingered shoreline of Applegate Lake and climbs many short, moderately difficult hills. There are two steep climbs on the south side of the reservoir, both about one-quarter mile long. The trail is never too technical, but it is challenging enough to stay exciting. The trail surface is crushed rock, clay loam, and decomposed granite. The trail is generally in good condition. Expect some rocks and windfalls. The roads are in good condition.

The most scenic portion of the ride occurs north of Watkins Campground. Wildflowers do well here, and there is a nice view of Elliott Creek Ridge across the lake. Harr Point is a good place for a lunch break. It is a sunny spot and surrounded by water.

**General location:** The ride starts at French Gulch Trailhead, approximately 25 miles southwest of Medford.

**Elevation change:** The ride begins at 2,000' and reaches a high point of 2,200' at the top of Manzanita Creek Road. Many lesser ups and downs add an estimated 800' of climbing to the trip. Total elevation gain: 1,000'.

**Season:** If the weather has been unseasonably dry, the spring is a nice time for a visit. The lake and its facilities are often busy during the summer. Typically, dry conditions contribute to good fall cycling, and a smattering of deciduous trees along the lakefront provide nice color at that time of year.

**Services:** Water can be obtained seasonally on the north shore at Watkins Campground and Hart-tish Park. Limited groceries are available in Ruch. All services are available in Jacksonville. The nearest hospital is in Medford.

**Hazards:** In places, the single-track drops off steeply to the lake. Portions of the trail are rocky. Expect traffic on the roads. Watch for hikers and other trail users.

**Rescue index:** Help may be found at the Star Ranger Station (on Upper Applegate Road) during regular business hours. There is also a pay phone at the ranger station.

**Land status:** Rogue River National Forest.

**Maps:** The district map for the Applegate Ranger District is a good guide to this route. USGS 7.5 minute quads: Squaw Lakes and Carberry Creek.

**Finding the trail:** From Interstate 5, take Exit 27 for Medford and Jacksonville. After exiting the highway, go west on Barnett Road (follow the signs toward Jacksonville). Get in the right-hand lane and turn right onto OR 99 North/Riverside Avenue. Follow OR 99 for 1 mile, then turn left onto OR 238/East Main Street. Bear right in 0.4 mile, remaining on OR 238. You will enter Jacksonville in 4 miles. About 0.7 mile into the town of Jacksonville, bear right at a **T** intersection, remaining on OR 238. This will take you through the "Old Town" section of Jacksonville. Note your mileage as you exit Jacksonville on OR 238. In 7.3 miles you will drive past Ron's Market on your right. Turn left at the next intersection onto Upper Applegate Road. Follow signs for the Star Ranger Station and Applegate Dam. Follow Upper Applegate Road for 15 miles to Squaw Creek Road on the left. Turn left onto Squaw Creek Road and follow it over Applegate Dam. Proceed on Squaw Creek Road for 1 mile and turn right into the parking area for French Gulch Trailhead.

From Grants Pass, follow OR 238 East for 24 miles to Hamilton Road (on the right). Turn right and drive 2.1 miles to Upper Applegate Road. Turn right and proceed 13 miles to Squaw Creek Road on the left. Turn left onto Squaw Creek Road and follow it over the dam. Stay on Squaw Creek Road for 1 mile and then turn right into the parking area for French Gulch Trailhead.

# RIDE 5 · Applegate Lake Loop

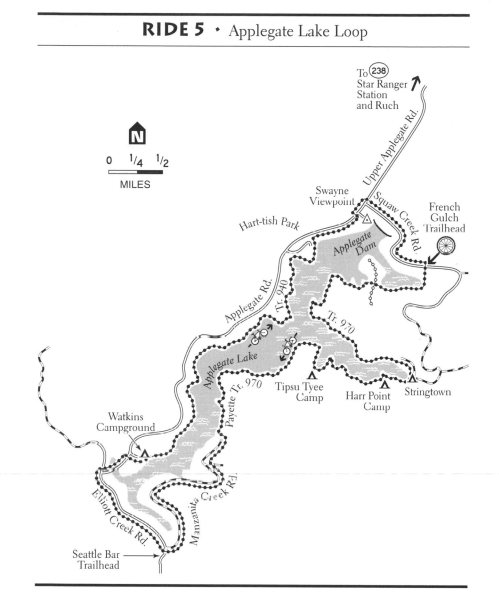

**Source of additional information:**

Applegate Ranger District
Star Ranger Station
6941 Upper Applegate Road
Jacksonville, OR 97530
(541) 899-1812

Da-Ku-Be-Te-De Trail
at Applegate Lake.

**Notes on the trail:** At the French Gulch Trailhead, follow the single-track Payette Trail 970. In approximately 1 mile (at the top of a steep little hill), stay left and descend as a trail goes right to a viewpoint and another trail goes hard left to signed Calsh Trail 971. Follow the signs to Stringtown. The trail becomes an overgrown double-track. At an intersection with a road (4.5 miles into the ride), go downhill and follow the road to a signed day-use area (Stringtown). Turn right and carry your bike over log stringers. The logs are a temporary replacement for an earthen bridge that was washed out by flooding in 1997. Replacement of the bridge is expected in 1999. After a short uphill, turn right to go through a barbed wire fence at a **V**-shaped gate. Follow the trail past Harr Point and Tipsu Tyee Camp. Stay on the single-track as it follows the shoreline and passes innumerable inlets. The trail ends at an abandoned fire road and a sign for Payette Trail/French Gulch 9.2 miles. Go uphill through a narrow fence opening and ride up the steep road. Stay right at the **Y** intersection near the top of the hill, and immediately arrive at a main gravel road (unsigned Manzanita Creek Road). Continue straight (right) and descend on Manzanita Creek Road. Turn right when you reach paved Elliott Creek Road (Seattle Bar Trailhead is directly across from this intersection). Proceed on Elliott Creek Road for about

1 mile and turn right onto Applegate Road. Turn right into Watkins Campground after just 0.3 mile on Applegate Road. Bear left through the campground's small parking area to find Trail 940 heading east and downhill out of the campground. (On our most recent visit the trail was marked with a temporary sign for Watkins Loop Trail.) Follow the trail along the north shore of the reservoir. Trail 940 becomes a paved path after 3.3 miles (nearing Hart-tish Park). Ride up through picnic sites on the paved trail. Stay on the main path, passing a drinking fountain, toilets, and wooden handrails. You will arrive at a parking area and a boat ramp. Ride through the parking area and look for a trail near the boat ramp. The trail is signed: Da-Ku-Be-Te-De Trail 940. Pedal up the trail for 0.5 mile to Swayne Viewpoint. Ride out to Applegate Road and turn right. Turn right on Squaw Creek Road. Ride over the dam and to your car at French Gulch Trailhead.

## RIDE 6 · Brown Mountain Trail

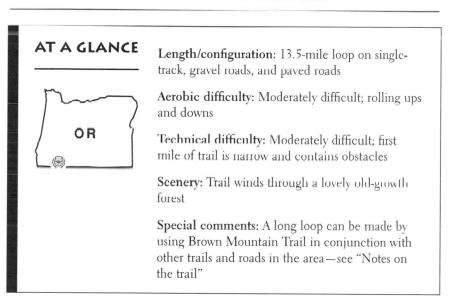

**AT A GLANCE**

OR

**Length/configuration:** 13.5-mile loop on single-track, gravel roads, and paved roads

**Aerobic difficulty:** Moderately difficult; rolling ups and downs

**Technical difficulty:** Moderately difficult; first mile of trail is narrow and contains obstacles

**Scenery:** Trail winds through a lovely old-growth forest

**Special comments:** A long loop can be made by using Brown Mountain Trail in conjunction with other trails and roads in the area—see "Notes on the trail"

This is a moderately difficult 13.5-mile loop (including 5.5 miles of single-track). The climbing on Brown Mountain Trail is mostly easy, but the riding is made more difficult by protruding obstacles like rocks and roots. The condition of the trail improves after the first mile. The route follows gravel roads for 4.7 miles, paved roads for 3.3 miles. The cycling on the roads is divided between easy uphill pedaling on one half and level pedaling and downhill cruising on the other. The ride ends with a moderately difficult (but short) ascent.

Brown Mountain Trail twists and turns its way through a lovely old-growth forest. Morel mushroom hunting in the late spring and huckleberry picking in

Brown Mountain Trail 1005.

the late summer can be productive. Orchids, trilliums, and other shade-loving wildflowers blanket the forest floor in the early summer. Near the end of the trail, you pass by 15,000-year-old lava flows at the base of Brown Mountain.

**General location:** Begins near Lake of the Woods, about 30 miles northeast of Ashland, and approximately 40 miles west of Klamath Falls.

**Elevation change:** The trailhead lies at 4,850'. A high point of 5,730' is attained on FS 700. Undulations add about 200' of climbing to the ride. Total elevation gain: 1,080'.

**Season:** Plan on cycling here from mid-May to October. Striking fall color and wildflower displays in the spring and summer provide seasonal interest.

**Services:** There is no water on this ride. Water can be obtained seasonally at Fish Lake Campground. Food, lodging, and pay phones can be found at Fish Lake Resort and Lake of the Woods Resort. All services are available in Ashland, Medford, and Klamath Falls.

**Hazards:** Brown Mountain Trail is popular with hikers and equestrians. Watch for motorists while traveling on the forest roads.

**Rescue index:** You may be able to obtain assistance in an emergency at one of the many developed recreation facilities in the area. There is a visitor center at Lake of the Woods. Emergency services are located in Ashland.

**Land status:** Rogue River National Forest and Winema National Forest.

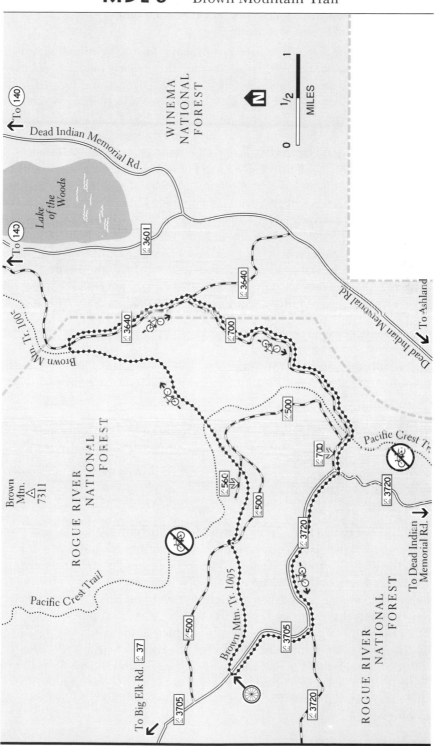

**Maps:** The district map of the Ashland Ranger District of the Rogue River National Forest is a good guide to this ride. USGS 7.5 minute quads: Lake of the Woods South and Brown Mountain.

**Finding the trail:** From Interstate 5 at Ashland, take Exit 14 and go east on Main Street/OR 66 East. Turn left (toward the airport) onto Dead Indian Memorial Road after 0.7 mile on OR 66. Drive 21 miles and turn left onto Forest Service Road 37/Big Elk Road (0.8 miles past a large wood sign on the right for the Rogue River National Forest). Follow FS 37 for 6 miles and turn right onto FS 3705. Stay on FS 3705 for 3.3 miles; there you will see Brown Mountain Trail 1005 on the left. Park on the right, opposite the trailhead.

From I-5 at Medford, take Exit 30 and follow Crater Lake Highway/OR 62 northeast toward Crater Lake. In approximately 5.5 miles, turn right onto Lake of the Woods Highway/OR 140. Turn right onto FS 37/Big Elk Road after about 30 miles on OR 140. Follow FS 37 for 2 miles and turn left onto FS 3705. Stay on FS 3705 for 3.3 miles to the trailhead for Brown Mountain Trail 1005 on the left. There is a parking area across from the trailhead.

From Klamath Falls, drive northwest on OR 140/Lake of the Woods Highway. After approximately 40 miles on OR 140, turn left onto FS 37/Big Elk Road (2 miles beyond Fish Lake Recreation Area). Follow FS 37 for 2 miles, then turn left onto FS 3705. Stay on FS 3705 for 3.3 miles to Brown Mountain Trail 1005 on the left. There is a parking area on the right side of the road.

**Sources of additional information:**

Ashland Ranger District
645 Washington Street
Ashland, OR 97520
(541) 482-3333

Klamath Ranger District
1936 California Avenue
Klamath Falls, OR 97601
(541) 885-3400

**Notes on the trail:** Head east on Brown Mountain Trail 1005. In 1.7 miles you will reach FS 500. Turn right onto the road, then immediately turn left back onto the trail. Continue on Trail 1005 where it crosses FS 560. You will cross the Pacific Crest Trail in another 0.5 mile. (No bikes are allowed on the Pacific Crest Trail.) Continue straight at this intersection to remain on Brown Mountain Trail; follow the sign for Lake of the Woods. At the next intersection (after more than 2 miles), Lake of the Woods is signed to the left. Turn right here and pedal a short distance to FS 3640. Turn right onto FS 3640. After 1.5 miles, turn right onto FS 700. Follow FS 700 for 3.2 miles (past FS 500) to a **T** intersection. Turn right onto paved FS 3720, following the sign for FS 37. In 2 miles turn right onto FS 3705, continuing toward FS 37. Follow FS 3705 to your vehicle.

Those interested in a longer ride can combine Brown Mountain Trail, High Lakes Trail, Fish Lake Trail, and forest roads to create a loop. This makes for an outing of about 22 miles. Follow the above directions to the intersection of trails where Lake of the Woods is signed to the left. Turn left to stay on Brown Mountain Trail. In about 1.5 miles the trail arrives at FS 3640. Turn left onto the road and ride 0.3 mile to the trailhead for High Lakes Trail on the left. Turn left toward Fish Lake. Pick up the Fish Lake Trail at Fish Lake Campground and continue west to FS 37. Go left on FS 37 and travel about 2 miles on the pavement to FS 3705 on the left. Pedal up this paved road for 3.3 miles to complete the loop.

## RIDE 7 · Fish Lake Trail

**AT A GLANCE**

**Length/configuration:** 7-mile single-track out-and-back (3.5 miles each way)

**Aerobic difficulty:** Easy; some short, minor climbs

**Technical difficulty:** Easy; the first 0.5 mile is the most demanding; beginners may need to walk their bikes

**Scenery:** West end—charming Little Butte Creek; middle—old-growth and meadows speckled with wildflowers; east end—views across Fish Lake to Brown Mountain

**Special comments:** Short but sweet; Fish Lake Trail can be used in conjunction with other trails and roads in the area to form longer rides—see "Notes on the trail"

We were smiling after our ride on Fish Lake Trail. The beginning is circuitous, passing between rocks and bouncing you over roots. This half-mile stretch (along Little Butte Creek) is the most technical part of the trail. Casual riders may find this section difficult to negotiate. If you like, you can walk your bike through this part. There are some small hills along the remainder of the route, but beginners should have little difficulty with them. The outing is a seven-mile out-and-back trip on single-track (3.5 miles each way).

The trail moves away from Little Butte Creek after passing Fish Lake Dam (after the first half-mile). The trail enters the woods and winds through pockets of old-growth forest and small meadows. Fish Lake Trail then skirts the north

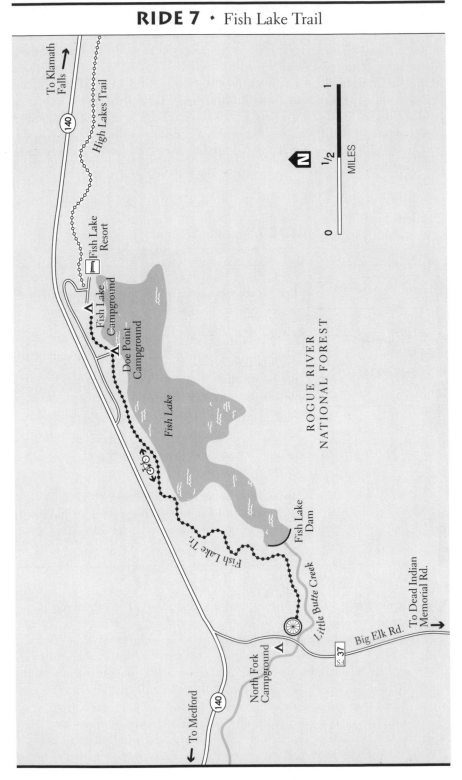

shore of its namesake (keep an eye out for ospreys and bald eagles). Across the water is Brown Mountain, a young shield volcano. Thousands of years ago, a lava flow from Brown Mountain formed a dam that created Fish Lake (originally about one-third its present size). A canal was dug in the early 1900s to bring additional water to the lake from Four Mile Lake. Then the dam was fortified, and Fish Lake grew to its present size.

There are campgrounds at both ends of the trail. North Fork Campground is small and affords good access to trout fishing on Little Butte Creek. Fish Lake Campground and the adjacent Fish Lake Resort offer more developed facilities. The cafe at the resort provides a setting where you can rest and purchase refreshments.

Fish Lake Trail is a small gem; a great ride for intrepid families or scout troops. Skip this trail if your criteria for a good ride includes bragging to your buddies about how gnarly your last outing was.

**General location:** Begins near Fish Lake, about 30 miles northeast of Ashland, and approximately 40 miles west of Klamath Falls.

**Elevation change:** The trailhead at Forest Service Road 37 is at 4,560'. The high point of the ride is 4,635' at Fish Lake. Ups and downs along the route add about 100' of climbing to the trip. Total elevation gain: 175'.

**Season:** The trail is usually free of snow from May through October. Campgrounds, lakes, and other recreation sites in the area are often busy during the summer. Wildflowers and uncrowded conditions make the spring a nice time for a visit, but stay off of the trail if it is wet. Call ahead to ask if the trail is dry and if it has been cleared of windfalls.

**Services:** Water can be obtained seasonally at Fish Lake Campground. There is a cafe, a store, and a pay phone at Fish Lake Resort. All services are available in Ashland, Medford, and Klamath Falls.

**Hazards:** The first 0.5 mile of the trail weaves through large rocks. Although technically easy, the trail does contain small obstacles like protruding roots and rocks.

**Rescue index:** You may be able to obtain assistance in an emergency at one of the many developed recreation facilities in the area. There is a pay phone at Fish Lake Resort. Emergency services are located in Ashland.

**Land status:** Rogue River National Forest.

**Maps:** A recreation opportunity guide titled "Fish Lake Trail 1013," is available from the Ashland Ranger District. It includes a map that is suitable as a guide to this ride. USGS 7.5 minute quad: Mt. McLoughlin.

**Finding the trail:** From Interstate 5 at Ashland, take Exit 14 and go east on Main St./OR 66 East. Turn left (toward the airport) onto Dead Indian Memorial Road after 0.7 mile on OR 66. Drive 21 miles and turn left onto FS 37/Big Elk Road (0.8 mile past a large wood sign on the right for the Rogue River National Forest). Follow FS 37 for 7.5 miles to the trailhead for Fish Lake Trail 1013 on the right.

Meadows of mullein
near Fish Lake.

From I-5 at Medford, take Exit 30 and follow Crater Lake Highway/OR 62 northeast toward Crater Lake. In about 5.5 miles, turn right onto Lake of the Woods Highway/OR 140. Turn right on FS 37/Big Elk Road after approximately 30 miles on OR 140. Follow FS 37 for about 0.5 mile to the trailhead for Fish Lake Trail 1013 on the left.

From Klamath Falls, follow Lake of the Woods Highway/OR 140 west for approximately 43 miles to FS 37/Big Elk Road (2 miles beyond Fish Lake Recreation Area). Turn left onto FS 37 and drive about 0.5 mile to the trailhead for Fish Lake Trail 1013 on the left.

**Source of additional information:**

Ashland Ranger District
645 Washington Street
Ashland, OR 97520
(541) 482-3333

**Notes on the trail:** The trail is well marked at intersections. Follow the signs to Fish Lake Campground. Return the way you came. You can add a little distance to the ride by exploring side trails at Fish Lake Dam, Doe Point Campground, and Fish Lake. For a longer out-and-back trip, combine this ride with High Lakes Trail (Ride 8). A long loop can be formed by linking the above rides with Brown Mountain Trail. See the "Notes on the trail" section of Brown Mountain Trail (Ride 6).

## RIDE 8 · High Lakes Trail

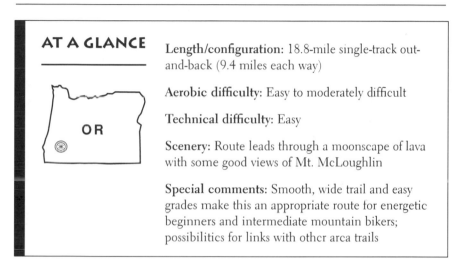

**AT A GLANCE**

**Length/configuration:** 18.8-mile single-track out-and-back (9.4 miles each way)

**Aerobic difficulty:** Easy to moderately difficult

**Technical difficulty:** Easy

**Scenery:** Route leads through a moonscape of lava with some good views of Mt. McLoughlin

**Special comments:** Smooth, wide trail and easy grades make this an appropriate route for energetic beginners and intermediate mountain bikers; possibilities for links with other area trails

High Lakes Trail is a new path that winds through the lava fields between Fish Lake and Lake of the Woods. Riding out and back on this wide, smooth trail makes for an 18.8-mile excursion (9.4 miles each way). The development of High Lakes Trail has provided a link between Brown Mountain Trail and Fish Lake Trail. Tying these three trails together makes a loop of approximately 22 miles.

High Lakes Trail is wheelchair-accessible. It's buffed out—you won't be dealing with many obstacles. There are some hills to climb, but they are short and easy. Overall, the trail gradually gains elevation from west to east. Fit cyclists will negotiate the trail with ease; beginners and out-of-shape riders may find the trip more demanding. If you like, you can follow the "Notes on the trail" for a comfortable distance, then turn around. The return trip will be easier than the first half, especially if you turn around before passing the high point of the trail (3.5 miles into the ride).

Trailheads and intersections are well marked and the trail is dotted with interpretive displays describing the areas geology and natural history. Nearby OR 140 is well hidden along most of the route, but traffic noise is often audible. On clear days the massive peak of Mt. McLoughlin is visible from select points along the trail.

High Lakes Trail.

**General location:** Begins near Lake of the Woods, about 30 miles northeast of Ashland and approximately 40 miles west of Klamath Falls.

**Elevation change:** The western trailhead for High Lakes Trail (at Fish Lake Campground) is at 4,635'. The trail's high point (5,200') is about 3.5 miles east of Fish Lake Campground. Undulations along the trail add about 300' of climbing to this out-and-back trip. Overall elevation gain: 865'.

**Season:** Barring unseasonable weather, you can expect the trail to be snow-free and rideable from mid-May through October. The summer months are busy with people enjoying the lakes and recreation facilities in the area.

**Services:** Limited supplies and accommodations are available seasonally at Fish Lake Resort and Lake of the Woods Resort. Water can be obtained seasonally at Fish Lake and Aspen Point Campgrounds. All services are available in Ashland and Medford.

**Hazards:** High Lakes Trail was designed and built to be approachable and inviting to all manner of forest users. Older visitors, the physically challenged, and less active people can follow this trail and enjoy a moment in the forest. We

# RIDE 8 · High Lakes Trail

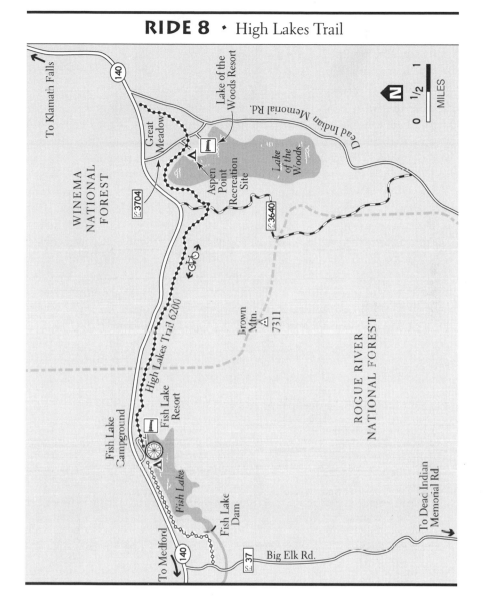

encourage you to travel at a modest pace and to use common sense while riding on this path.

**Rescue index:** You may be able to obtain assistance in an emergency at one of the many developed recreation facilities in the area. There is a Visitor Center at Lake of the Woods. Emergency services are located in Ashland.

**Land status:** Rogue River National Forest and Winema National Forest.

**Maps:** This new trail was not delineated on any maps at the time of our visit.

We recommend that you carry the district map of the Ashland Ranger District, Rogue River National Forest. You may wish to inquire about a recreation opportunity guide/map at the Lake of the Woods Visitor Center; one may be available by the time you visit the area. USGS 7.5 minute quads: Lake of the Woods North and Mt. McLoughlin.

**Finding the trail:** From Interstate 5 at Ashland, take Exit 14 and go east on Main Street/OR 66 east. Turn left (toward the airport) onto Dead Indian Memorial Road after 0.7 mile on OR 66. Drive 21 miles and turn left onto Forest Service 37/Big Elk Road (0.8 mile past a large wood sign on the right for the Rogue River National Forest). Follow FS 37 for 8 miles to Lake of the Woods Highway/OR 140. Turn right onto OR 140 and drive 2 miles to Fish Lake Recreation Area on the right. Turn right and follow the signs for Fish Lake. Park in the day-use parking area.

From I-5 at Medford, take Exit 30 and follow Crater Lake Highway/OR 62 northeast toward Crater Lake. In approximately 5.5 miles, turn right onto Lake of the Woods Highway/OR 140. Turn right into Fish Lake Recreation Area after about 33 miles on OR 140 (0.5 mile beyond Doe Point Campground). Follow the signs for Fish Lake and park in the day-use parking area.

From Klamath Falls, follow Lake of the Woods Highway/OR 140 west for approximately 40 miles to Fish Lake Recreation Area on the left (about 6 miles west of Lake of the Woods). Turn left into Fish Lake Recreation Area and follow the signs for Fish Lake. Park in the day-use parking area.

**Sources of additional information:**

Ashland Ranger District
645 Washington Street
Ashland, OR 97520
(541) 482-3333

Klamath Ranger District
1936 California Avenue
Klamath Falls, OR 97601
(541) 885-3400

**Notes on the trail:** From the day-use parking at Fish Lake Campground, backtrack up the campground access road to the trailhead for High Lakes Trail 6200 on the right. Follow the trail east through the woods. Intersections are well marked—follow the signs for Lake of the Woods. After 6 miles you will arrive at a developed trailhead at FS 3640. Cross the road and continue east on the single-track. (The trail crosses FS 3640 just north of the trailhead.) In another 1.5 miles you will arrive at Aspen Point Recreation Site. Turn left just before the developed trailhead to stay on the trail and pass through the recreation site. The route soon crosses the recreation site entrance road and then arrives at a **Y** intersection. Turn left to remain on High Lakes Trail. From this turn it is 1.6 miles to a large paved parking area for Great Meadow. This is the end of High Lakes Trail. Return the way you came to Fish Lake.

Those interested in a longer ride can combine High Lakes Trail with Fish Lake Trail for a 25.8-mile out-and-back excursion. A good loop can be created by linking these trails with Brown Mountain Trail. See "Notes on the trail" for Brown Mountain Trail (Ride 6) for more information about this loop.

## RIDE 9 · Burnt Timber Trail 1148

**AT A GLANCE**

OR

**Length/configuration:** 1.7-mile single-track loop

**Aerobic difficulty:** Mostly easy with one moderately steep climb

**Technical difficulty:** Easy; good trail with a few minor obstacles

**Scenery:** Passes through meadows and woodlands; interpretive signs highlight aspects of the ecosystem

**Special comments:** A great beginner ride; intrepid families can tackle this loop—may require walking bikes over obstacles, pushing up hills, and lots of water breaks

Burnt Timber Trail forms a pleasant 1.7-mile single-track loop. It is well suited to beginning mountain bikers. There is a moderately steep one-quarter-mile climb near the end of the circuit where novices may have to push their bikes. The trail is well maintained, but it does contain minor technical challenges.

The first portion of this interpretive trail passes through open woodlands and a meadows. Then it descends into a fern-filled old-growth forest. Live oak, madrone, and maples grow as understory trees below stately firs and cedars. After you cross lovely Burnt Timber Creek, your attention is focused on a challenging climb out of the drainage. The loop is short but fun enough to do twice—perhaps in the opposite direction.

**General location:** The trailhead is about 20 miles northwest of Grants Pass.

**Elevation change:** The ride begins at 1,500', drops to a low point of 1,350', then ascends back to the trailhead. Ups and downs add approximately 50' of climbing to the loop. Total elevation gain: 200'.

**Season:** Early spring through fall.

**Services:** There is no water on the ride. Water can be found seasonally at Indian

# RIDE 9 · Burnt Timber Trail 1148

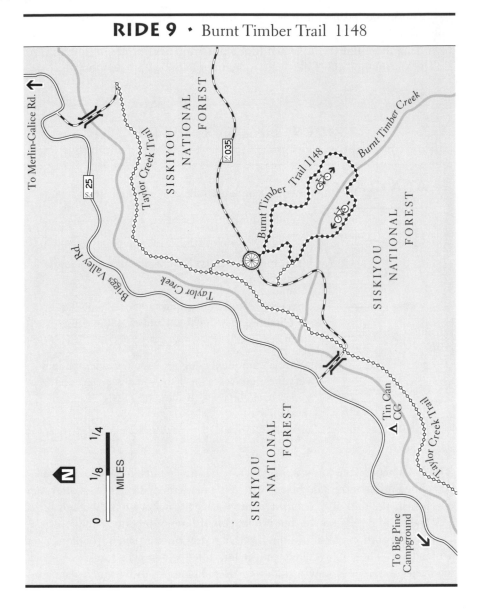

Mary Campground. This campground is on the way to the trailhead on the Merlin-Galice Road. Food, lodging, groceries, and gas can be obtained in Merlin. All services are available in Grants Pass.

**Hazards:** The trail contains some tight turns and crosses some wooden bridges that can be slick when wet. Portions of the path are bordered by poison oak.

**Rescue index:** There is a pay phone at Indian Mary Campground on the Merlin-Galice Road (approximately 1.4 miles east of the intersection with Forest

Burnt Timber
Interpretive Trail.

Service Road 25). Help can be found in Merlin. Emergency services are located in Grants Pass.

**Land status:** Siskiyou National Forest.

**Maps:** Burnt Timber Trail is not delineated on the district map of the Galice Ranger District. Inquire at the Galice Ranger Station (in Grants Pass) about mountain bike recreation opportunity guides for the area. USGS 7.5 minute quads: Onion Mountain and Galice.

**Finding the trail:** Take Interstate 5 to Exit 61 (3 miles north of Grants Pass). Exit the highway and follow Merlin-Galice Road toward Merlin. Continue through Merlin on Merlin-Galice Road. From Merlin, it is 8.5 miles to Morrison's Lodge on the right. After the lodge, Merlin-Galice Road crosses a concrete bridge over Taylor Creek and immediately comes to Briggs Valley Road/FS 25. Turn left onto this paved one-lane road. Follow FS 25 for 4.9 miles to FS 035. Turn left onto FS 035 and travel 0.6 mile to the trailhead (on the right). Park in the pullout on the left.

**Source of additional information:**

Galice Ranger District
200 N.E. Greenfield Road
P.O. Box 440
Grants Pass, OR 97528
(541) 471-6500

**Notes on the trail:** From the trailhead, descend on signed Burnt Timber Trail 1148. After passing an interpretive sign for "Poison Oak," you will immediately arrive at an interpretive sign describing "Forest Habitats." Stay left at the **Y** intersection at the "Forest Habitats" sign. Pass through a meadow and then enjoy a good stretch of downhill. A couple of small bridges span an intermittent creek, then you cross a couple of larger bridges over Burnt Timber Creek. After the second of these more substantial bridges, you arrive at an unsigned intersection of trails. To remain on Burnt Timber Trail, turn hard to the right and climb steeply. Bear left when you arrive back at the "Forest Habitats" sign. Pedal back to the trailhead.

## RIDE 10 · Taylor Creek Trail

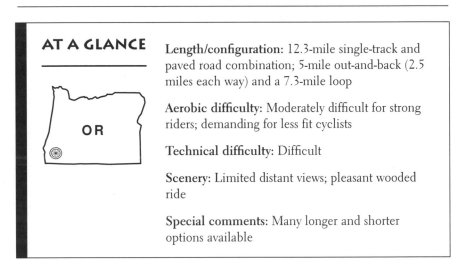

**AT A GLANCE**

**Length/configuration:** 12.3-mile single-track and paved road combination; 5-mile out-and-back (2.5 miles each way) and a 7.3-mile loop

**Aerobic difficulty:** Moderately difficult for strong riders; demanding for less fit cyclists

**Technical difficulty:** Difficult

**Scenery:** Limited distant views; pleasant wooded ride

**Special comments:** Many longer and shorter options available

Do you remember the scene from *Return of the Jedi* where Luke Skywalker is pursued through a forest of giant trees? It's an exciting, fast-paced chase on futuristic rocket bikes. Local riders were reminded of that scene when they came up with a nickname for a portion of Taylor Creek Trail (the segment between Forest Service Road 2509 and FS 121). "Jedi Trail" is the perfect moniker for this piece of downhill single-track. The trail dips, rolls, and swoops around trees. A local mountain bike race follows Taylor Creek Trail, using it as

Hiking Taylor
Creek Trail.

a link between the forest roads that make up the bulk of the race circuit. The race is named "Return on the Jedi." (You've got to love a race promoter with a sense of humor.) May the forest be with you!

The ride we describe is 12.3 miles long; a 5-mile out-and-back spur (2.5 miles each way) and a 7.3-mile loop. Fit racer types will have little difficulty with the moderately difficult climbing and somewhat technical descents found on the single-track sections of the ride. Casual riders can give this route a go and bail out if they find the trail too demanding. (See "Notes on the trail" for bail-out options.) The trail surface includes rocks, roots, sandy sections, and narrow areas where riders are exposed to steep drop-offs.

Taylor Creek Trail can be combined with area forest roads and single-tracks to create longer or shorter options. We have yet to explore the lowest segment of the trail; it runs east (from the trailhead we describe) to English Meadow. You might consider connecting this lower section of Taylor Creek Trail with Burnt Timber Trail. Taylor Creek Trail can also be linked with riding on Chrome Ridge and with the network of single-track trails found in Briggs Valley. Mountain bikers who enjoy long days of exploring will love this region.

# RIDE 10 · Taylor Creek Trail

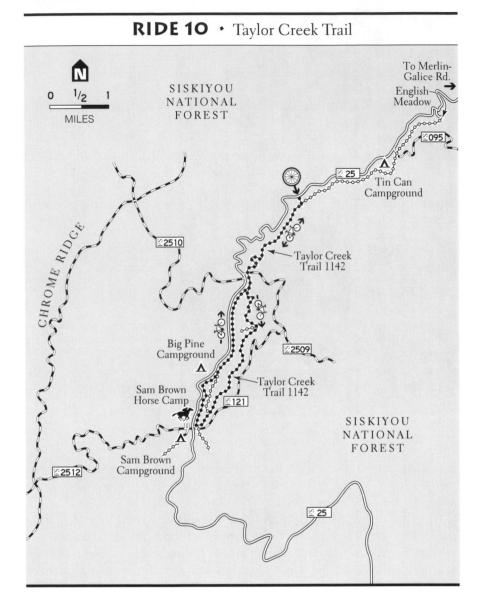

**General location:** The trailhead is about 25 miles northwest of Grants Pass.

**Elevation change:** The ride starts at 1,500' and climbs to a high point on Taylor Creek Trail of 2,800'. The southern terminus of Taylor Creek Trail (at its intersection with FS 121) is at an elevation of 2,080'. Then the route follows FS 25 to 2,640'. The ride ends with a single-track descent back to the trailhead. Ups and downs add about 200' of climbing to the ride. Total elevation gain: 2,060'.

**Season:** Taylor Creek Trail can typically be used from the early spring through the late fall. Stay off the trail when it is wet.

**Services:** Water can be obtained seasonally at Big Pine Campground, Sam Brown Campground, and Sam Brown Horse Camp. Food, lodging, groceries, and gas can be found in Merlin. All services are available in Grants Pass.

**Hazards:** We had the opportunity to chat with a couple of hikers on the trail. They mentioned that there have been some problems between trail user-groups lately. We've also had communications with area rangers about the recent conflicts. It is their hope that everyone will make a strong effort to practice trail etiquette and be courteous. Please approach blind corners slowly, anticipating that there may be someone around the next bend. The trails in the area are very popular with equestrians. When approaching horses, stop and dismount to yield the trail. (When approaching from behind, stop well in back of equestrians and announce your presence; do your utmost to avoid spooking the animals.) Talk to the riders in a normal tone of voice; ask if their horses are easily spooked and for instructions on how the equestrians would prefer you to facilitate passing. Your voice will help the horses recognize you as human.

**Rescue index:** There is a pay phone at Indian Mary Campground on the Merlin-Galice Road (approximately 1.4 miles east of the intersection with FS 25). Help can be found in Merlin. Rescue services are located in Grants Pass.

**Land status:** Siskiyou National Forest.

**Maps:** Taylor Creek Trail is not shown on the district map of the Galice Ranger District. It is delineated on a recreation opportunity guide for Taylor Creek Trail 1142. You can pick one up at the ranger station in Grants Pass. USGS 7.5 minute quads: Chrome Ridge and Mt. Peavine.

**Finding the trail:** Take Interstate 5 to Exit 61 (3 miles north of Grants Pass). Exit the highway and follow Merlin-Galice Road toward Merlin. Continue through Merlin on this road. From Merlin, it is 8.5 miles to Morrison's Lodge (on the right). After the lodge, Merlin-Galice Road crosses a bridge over Taylor Creek and immediately comes to Briggs Valley Road/FS 25. Turn left onto this paved one lane road. Follow FS 25 for 7.4 miles to Taylor Creek Trail on the left at a gravel parking area. (This parking area is 0.4 mile beyond the trailhead for China Creek Trail.)

## Source of additional information:

Galice Ranger District
200 N.E. Greenfield Road
P.O. Box 440
Grants Pass, OR 97528
(541) 471-6500

**Notes on the trail:** The trail begins near the southwest end of the parking area and is signed Taylor Creek Trail West. Follow the trail across two footbridges to a **T** intersection. Turn right and climb up Taylor Creek Trail for 2.5 miles to FS 25 and FS 2509. Cross FS 2509 and bear left to regain Taylor Creek Trail. The trail rolls up and down (mostly up) for 1.8 miles to an intersection. Bear left to remain on Taylor Creek Trail. Bear left at the next intersection (1.7 miles from the last intersection) and continue with a fun descent. Bear right when you reach gravel FS 121 and ride a short distance to paved FS 25. Turn right onto FS 25 and pedal 2.9 miles to FS 2509 and Taylor Creek Trail on the right. Return down Taylor Creek Trail to your parked vehicle.

The easiest way to shorten this ride is to turn around if you find the climbing too demanding on Taylor Creek Trail. Another option is to form a short loop by riding up Taylor Creek Trail to the intersection of FS 25 and FS 2509—turn right and descend back to the trailhead on paved FS 25. Keep your speed under control and watch for approaching traffic. Exploring the trails that go to the right off of Taylor Creek Trail is yet another option. (We are referring to the section of Taylor Creek Trail between FS 2509 and FS 121.) We have not been down these side trails, but we believe they lead out to FS 25.

To lengthen the trip, consider starting the ride at the northern terminus of Taylor Creek Trail—English Meadow. (We have not been on this section of trail.) Burnt Timber Trail, Onion Way Trail, Secret Way Trail, and Briggs Creek Trail can also be tied together with Taylor Creek Trail. You can also link up to good gravel roads on Chrome Ridge. Another forest road alternative is to take FS 121 and FS 2509 as substitutes to the paved portion of the basic ride described above.

## RIDE 11 · Onion Way/Briggs Creek Loop

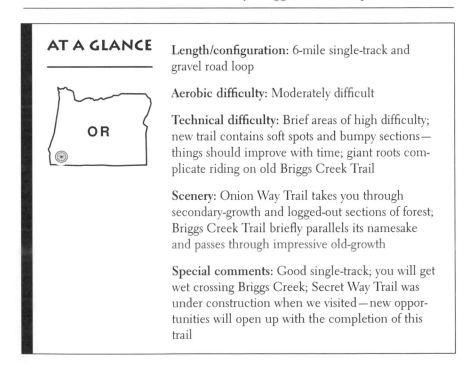

**AT A GLANCE**

OR

**Length/configuration:** 6-mile single-track and gravel road loop

**Aerobic difficulty:** Moderately difficult

**Technical difficulty:** Brief areas of high difficulty; new trail contains soft spots and bumpy sections— things should improve with time; giant roots complicate riding on old Briggs Creek Trail

**Scenery:** Onion Way Trail takes you through secondary-growth and logged-out sections of forest; Briggs Creek Trail briefly parallels its namesake and passes through impressive old-growth

**Special comments:** Good single-track; you will get wet crossing Briggs Creek; Secret Way Trail was under construction when we visited—new opportunities will open up with the completion of this trail

Onion Way Trail and Briggs Creek Trail combine to form a moderately difficult six-mile loop. Onion Way Trail travels through areas that the forest service refers to as "harvest units." We call them "places where the trees have been cut down." Parts of this trail are very pleasant, passing through stands of young fir and madrone. Other sections feel more raw. Briggs Creek Trail is lovely, and the creek is beautiful. Maples hang over the bubbling stream, and everything seems to drip with green moss. Stately old-growth firs line the lower reaches of the trail.

Onion Way Trail was brand-new at the time of our research. Lumps, bumps, and soft sections were predominant. These conditions should give way to an improved riding surface as the trail sees more traffic. Briggs Creek Trail is a time-worn path, long popular with horsemen and hikers. The passing of thousands of hooves has created a tread that is sunken in places. It is a challenge to pass through these trench-like segments without hanging your pedals up on the trail's steep sidewalls. Massive roots of old trees have been exposed here as well. These root mazes will stump all but the most skilled riders. Accessing Briggs Creek Trail from Onion Way Trail involves a short stretch on roads and a fording of Briggs Creek (you will get wet).

**General location:** Begins near Sam Brown Campground, approximately 30 miles west of Grants Pass.

**Elevation change:** Starts at 2,080' and reaches a high point of 2,300' on Onion Way Trail. The low point of the ride is at the crossing of Briggs Creek at 1,870'. Undulations along the course of the ride add a significant amount of climbing to the trip—about 500'. Total elevation gain: 930'.

**Season:** The loop includes the crossing of Briggs Creek at a ford. Crossing in the spring can be dangerous due to high water. The summer and fall are good times of year for riding this route.

**Services:** Water can be obtained seasonally at Big Pine Campground, Sam Brown Campground, and Sam Brown Horse Camp. Food, lodging, groceries, and gas can be obtained in Merlin. All services are available in Grants Pass.

**Hazards:** The trails in the area are multiple-use. Practice trail etiquette and common courtesy. Lines of sight are limited on portions of the trails and roads. When approaching horses, stop and dismount to yield the trail. (When approaching from behind, stop well in back of equestrians and announce your presence; do your utmost to avoid spooking the animals.) Talk to the riders in a normal tone of voice; ask if their horses are easily spooked and for instructions on how the equestrians would prefer you to facilitate passing. Your voice will help the horses recognize you as a human. Do not attempt to ford Briggs Creek during periods of high water.

**Rescue index:** There is a pay phone at Indian Mary Campground on the Merlin-Galice Road (about 1.4 miles east of the intersection with Forest Service Road 25). Help can be found in Merlin. Emergency services are located in Grants Pass.

# RIDE 11 · Onion Way/Briggs Creek Loop

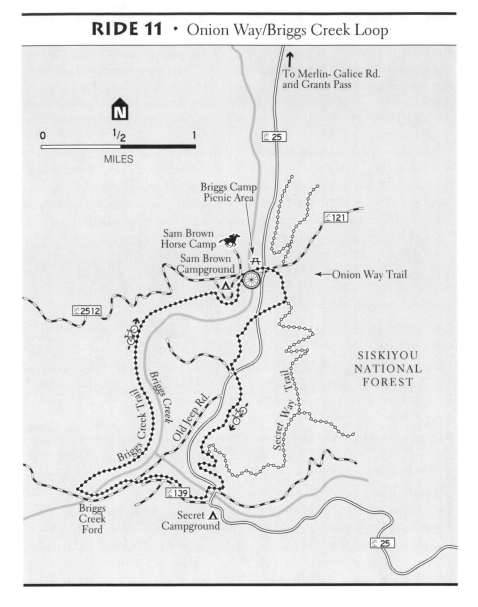

**N**

0        1/2        1
MILES

To Merlin- Galice Rd.
and Grants Pass

25

Briggs Camp
Picnic Area

121

Sam Brown
Horse Camp

Sam Brown
Campground

2512

←Onion Way Trail

SISKIYOU
NATIONAL
FOREST

Briggs Creek Trail

Briggs Creek

Old Jeep Rd.

Secret Way Trail

139

Briggs
Creek
Ford

Secret
Campground

25

**Land status:** Siskiyou National Forest.

**Maps:** Briggs Creek Trail is shown on the district map of the Galice Ranger District. Onion Way Trail was not shown on any maps at the time of our research. Inquire at the ranger station in Grants Pass about recreation opportunity guides for these trails. USGS 7.5 minute quad: Chrome Ridge.

**Finding the trail:** Take Interstate 5 to Exit 61 (3 miles north of Grants Pass). Exit the highway and follow Merlin-Galice Road toward Merlin. Continue through Merlin on this road. From Merlin, it is 8.5 miles to Morrison's Lodge (on the right). After the lodge, Merlin-Galice Road crosses a bridge over Taylor Creek and immediately comes to Briggs Valley Road/FS 25. Turn left onto this paved one-lane road. Follow FS 25 for 13 miles and turn right onto FS 2512 (1 mile beyond Big Pine Campground). Immediately (before the concrete bridge) turn right onto FS 011 and park in Briggs Camp Picnic Area.

## Source of additional information:

Galice Ranger District
200 N.E. Greenfield Road
P.O. Box 440
Grants Pass, OR 97528
(541) 471-6500

**Notes on the trail:**  At the time of our visit, signs had not yet been installed on Onion Creek Trail, and many signs on Briggs Creek Trail had been vandalized. We had to poke around to stay oriented. We have given rather fussy directions in an attempt to keep you from getting lost. You may discover improved signage. If so, you're likely to have an easier time with route finding than the "Notes on the trail" indicate.

Turn left out of Briggs Camp Picnic Area and cross FS 25. Ride up gravel FS 121 for 0.1 mile and turn right onto Onion Way Trail. Bear right after 0.2 mile on the trail to remain on Onion Way Trail (Secret Way Trail goes left here). Onion Way Trail crosses paved FS 25 in another 0.2 mile—jog right on the road to regain the trail. There is another road crossing in 0.6 mile; turn left onto a gravel spur road that takes you out to FS 25. Regain the trail on the opposite side of FS 25. The high point of the ride is reached shortly after this road crossing. The trail takes you downhill from this high point, taking you past Secret Way Trail (it comes in from the left). Then you come out onto a gravel road near Secret Creek Campground. Turn right onto the gravel road, and then turn left immediately onto paved FS 25. In less than 0.1 mile you will come to FS 139 on the right. Turn right onto this gravel road. FS 139 climbs for 0.4 mile to a **Y** intersection. Stay right and descend to the end of the road. An overgrown trail goes steeply downhill from here. Take it down to an old jeep trail that parallels Briggs Creek. Turn left onto the jeep trail and ride past mining claims to Briggs Creek. Ford the creek and push your bike up the rough jeep trail. It is about 40 yards from the creek crossing to Briggs Creek Trail on the right. Turn right onto the single-track. In 1.2 miles, the trail leads out onto a double-track—continue straight. Follow the double-track, crossing a creek in 0.1 mile. Continue straight after crossing the creek. In another 0.1 mile you will arrive at an intersection where a minor road goes right to cross another creek. (There is a "mining claim" sign here; it's high in a tree to the right.) Continue straight (bear left, do not cross the creek) and climb up the main double-track. Look to the right as you climb. You soon arrive at a single-track on the right. Bear right onto the trail. Follow this segment of Briggs Creek Trail for 0.4 mile. It will take you over a couple of creek crossings and out to an intersection with a rough gravel road.

On her way on
Onion Way.

Continue straight across the road to continue on Briggs Creek Trail. In 0.2 mile,
bear left at an intersection of trails. Briggs Creek Trail ends in another 0.2 mile
at a day-use parking area in Sam Brown Campground. Turn right at the toilet to
follow the campground loop road out to FS 2512. Turn right onto FS 2512, cross
the bridge, turn left into Briggs Camp Picnic Area.

## RIDE 12 · Chrome Ridge Loop

**AT A GLANCE**

OR

**Length/configuration:** 20.5-mile gravel road and single-track loop

**Aerobic difficulty:** Demanding; begins with a difficult 5-mile climb; ends on Taylor Creek Trail (not all downhill)

**Technical difficulty:** Moderately difficult to difficult; gravel roads run the gamut from good to rough and eroded; single-track in fair condition with areas that require good bike-handling skills

**Scenery:** Nice views of Briggs Valley and Onion Mountain from Chrome Ridge

**Special comments:** Tough climb, nice views, great gravel road descent, ends with fun single-track; a nice ride

Chrome Ridge Loop is a demanding 20.5-mile ride. Pleasant views from the ridge and an exciting descent highlight the gravel road riding on this outing. The circuit ends on a fun note—four miles on single-track Taylor Creek Trail. The path follows a shady route through a forest of madrone, live oak, and conifers. The trail surface is in pretty good shape with some technical challenges like rocks and sandy sections.

The trip starts with a difficult five-mile gravel road climb to Chrome Ridge. This climb is followed by easier riding on rough and eroded Chrome Ridge Road. The gravel road descent off of Chrome Ridge is fast, fun, and somewhat technical (due to loose gravel). This descent brings you to Taylor Creek Trail. The first 2.5 miles on the single-track are moderately difficult. The last 1.5 miles of the trail are mostly downhill.

**General location:** Begins near Sam Brown Campground, approximately 30 miles west of Grants Pass.

**Elevation change:** The elevation at the trailhead is 2,080'. A high point of 4,240' occurs on Chrome Ridge. Ups and downs on the ridge and trail add about 500' of climbing to the loop. Total elevation gain: 2,660'.

**Season:** The higher elevations along the route are generally free of snow from June through October. Stay off Taylor Creek Trail when it is wet (complete the loop on Forest Service Road 25).

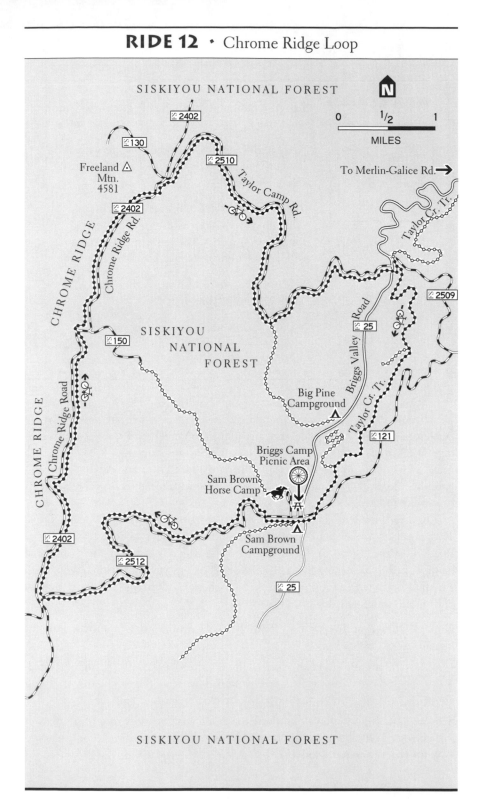

SISKIYOU NATIONAL FOREST

N

0    1/2    1

MILES

2402

130

2510

Freeland △
Mtn.
4581

Taylor Camp Rd.

To Merlin-Galice Rd. →

Taylor Cr. Tr.

2402

CHROME RIDGE

Chrome Ridge Rd.

2509

150

SISKIYOU
NATIONAL
FOREST

Briggs Valley Road

FS 25

CHROME RIDGE

Chrome Ridge Road

Big Pine
Campground

Taylor Cr. Tr.

Briggs Camp
Picnic Area

121

Sam Brown
Horse Camp

2402

Sam Brown
Campground

2512

25

SISKIYOU NATIONAL FOREST

Riding Chrome Ridge.

**Services:** Water can be obtained seasonally at Big Pine Campground, Sam Brown Campground, and Sam Brown Horse Camp. Food, lodging, groceries, and gas can be found in Merlin. All services are available in Grants Pass.

**Hazards:** The ride is long and exposed. Watch for traffic on the roads; especially on the descent off of the ridge. Anticipate other trail users—the area is popular with equestrians. Control your speed and approach blind corners carefully.

**Rescue index:** There is a pay phone at Indian Mary Campground on the Merlin-Galice Road (approximately 1.4 miles east of the intersection with FS 25). Help can be found in Merlin. Emergency services are located in Grants Pass.

**Land status:** Siskiyou National Forest.

**Maps:** Taylor Creek Trail is not shown on the district map of the Galice Ranger District. It is delineated on a recreation opportunity guide for Taylor Creek Trail 1142. You can get this guide at the ranger station in Grants Pass. We recommend carrying the district map and the R.O.G. USGS 7.5 minute quads: Chrome Ridge and Mt. Peavine.

**Finding the trail:** Take Interstate 5 to Exit 61 (3 miles north of Grants Pass). Exit the highway and follow Merlin-Galice Road toward Merlin. Continue through Merlin on this road. From Merlin, it is 8.5 miles to Morrison's Lodge (on the right). After the lodge, Merlin-Galice Road crosses a bridge over Taylor Creek and immediately comes to Briggs Valley Road/FS 25. Turn left onto this paved one-lane road. Follow FS 25 for 13 miles and turn right onto FS 2512 (1 mile beyond Big Pine Campground). Immediately (before the concrete bridge) turn right onto FS 011 and park in Briggs Camp Picnic Area.

**Source of additional information:**

Galice Ranger District
200 N.E. Greenfield Road
P.O. Box 440
Grants Pass, OR 97528
(541) 471-6500

**Notes on the trail:** Turn right onto FS 2512 and begin the grind to Chrome Ridge. Turn right when you reach FS 2402/Chrome Ridge Road. Follow this main road for nearly 6 miles, to a major intersection where FS 130 goes left and FS 2510/Taylor Camp Road goes right. Turn right onto FS 2510 toward Briggs Valley Road. Proceed on the main road to FS 25 (Briggs Valley Road). Turn left onto FS 25; you will immediately arrive at Lone Tree Pass and the junction of FS 2509 (Onion Mountain Road) and Taylor Creek Trail. FS 2509 heads east from the pass. Taylor Creek Trail goes north and south from FS 2509. Turn right (south) onto Taylor Creek Trail. (Do not go north on Taylor Creek Trail toward China Creek Trail or English Meadow.) You will arrive at an intersection in 1.8 miles—bear left to remain on Taylor Creek Trail. Bear left at the next intersection (1.7 miles from the last intersection) and continue with a fun descent. Turn right when you reach gravel FS 121 and ride a short distance to paved FS 25 and your parked vehicle in Briggs Camp Picnic Area.

## **RIDE 13** · Illinois River Road

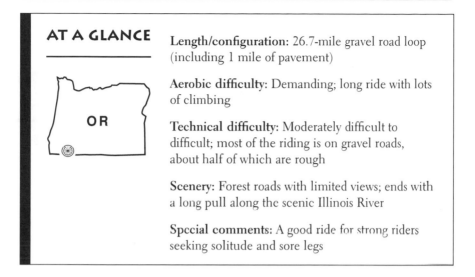

**AT A GLANCE**

**OR**

**Length/configuration:** 26.7-mile gravel road loop (including 1 mile of pavement)

**Aerobic difficulty:** Demanding; long ride with lots of climbing

**Technical difficulty:** Moderately difficult to difficult; most of the riding is on gravel roads, about half of which are rough

**Scenery:** Forest roads with limited views; ends with a long pull along the scenic Illinois River

**Special comments:** A good ride for strong riders seeking solitude and sore legs

This 26.7-mile loop is strenuous, with many ups and downs. The trip begins with 14 miles on gravel Forest Service Road 4105. This stretch contains several long ascents and descents. The climbing on FS 4105 breaks down as follows: two miles of easy, four miles of moderately difficult, and two miles of steep pedaling. This climb is followed by a rugged 1.2-mile descent to the Illinois River. Illinois River Road travels alongside the scenic waterway. The road is rough and the terrain is demanding. After 7.5 miles of unmerciful undulations, Illinois River Road changes to a paved surface. The last mile of the circuit is a grueling grind.

This loop makes a good training ride for powerful cyclists. The sight of your parked car may be a highlight of the trip. Reduced logging operations in the surrounding forest and the rough character of Illinois River Road help keep traffic light. The river is beautiful and is a favorite among kayakers and rafters.

**General location:** Begins 7 miles west of Selma. Selma is 23 miles southwest of Grants Pass.

**Elevation change:** The first part of the ride (on FS 4105) is characterized by long climbs and descents. The terrain over the second half is made up of many shorter ups and downs. The loop starts on FS 4105 at 1,500'. The road climbs to 2,480' after 3.4 miles, and then drops to 2,220' by the 5-mile mark. The trip's high point of 2,800' occurs in another 1.8 miles. This peak is followed by a 1.5-mile descent to 2,240', then a 1-mile climb to 2,420'. Next, the route goes downhill for 3.2 miles to 1,520'. The intersection of FS 152 and FS 4105 is at 1,680'. FS 152 drops and connects up with Illinois River Road. Illinois River Road continues the descent to the ride's low point of 880'. From this low point, Illinois River Road rises and falls for the remainder of the circuit. The pedaling on this

Gazing down on the
Wild and Scenic
Illinois River.

road contributes about 1,700' of climbing to the ride. Lesser hills on FS 4105 add approximately 200' of climbing to the trip. Total elevation gain: 3,800'.

**Season:** This excursion is suitable for year-round use.

**Services:** There is no water on this ride. Water, food, lodging, groceries, and gas can be obtained in Selma and Cave Junction.

**Hazards:** The greatest threat to a safe completion of this tour may be exhaustion. You may be fatigued by the time you reach Illinois River Road. The river road is exceedingly rough with rocks, and the hills seem endless. Control your speed on the descents and watch for loose gravel. FS 152 sees limited maintenance and can be strewn with windfalls.

**Rescue index:** The nearest pay phone is in Selma. Help can be found in Selma and Cave Junction. Emergency services are located in Grants Pass.

**Land status:** Siskiyou National Forest lands and public right-of-way through private property.

**Maps:** The district map of the Illinois Valley Ranger District is suitable as a guide to this ride, but the map's depiction of the intersection of FS 4105 and FS 152 is incorrect. USGS 7.5 minute quads: Eight Dollar Mountain, Pearsoll Peak, Chrome Ridge, and York Butte.

# RIDE 13 · Illinois River Road

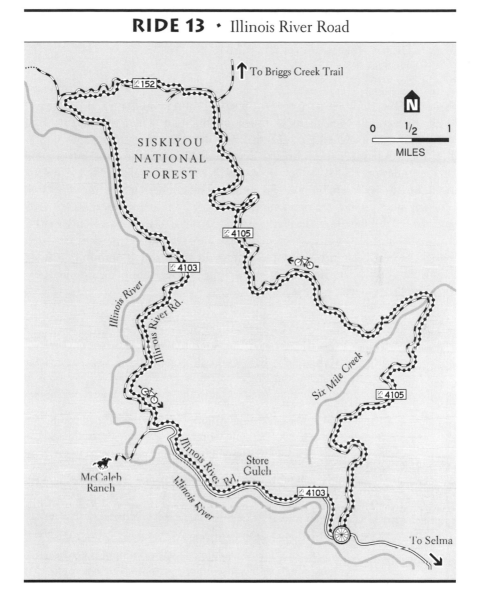

**Finding the trail:** From Grants Pass, Oregon, follow US 199 southwest for 23 miles to Selma. From Crescent City, California, drive northeast on US 199 for 65 miles to Selma. In Selma, turn west onto Illinois River Road/FS 4103 and follow it for 6.8 miles to FS 4105, on the right. Continue on Illinois River Road for about 50 feet and turn left to park in a paved parking area.

**Source of additional information:**

Illinois Valley Ranger District
26568 Redwood Highway
Cave Junction, OR 97523
(541) 592-2166

**Notes on the trail:** Head north up FS 4105. You encounter a short stretch of broken pavement after about 11 miles on this road. Then you find yourself cycling next to unsigned Soldier Creek and through some older stands of timber. You will pass a sign for Briggs Creek Trail 1132 (on the right) after a total of 13.1 miles on FS 4105. From this sign, it is about 1 mile to FS 152 on the right. FS 152 is signed, but the sign and the road are hard to see from FS 4105. The landmark to look for is a sign on the left of FS 4105; it identifies FS 4105 and reads, "Road 4103 — 14 miles, Selma — 21 miles." Here, turn right onto FS 152 and follow it for 1.2 miles to Illinois River Road (signed for McCaleb Ranch, Store Gulch, Six Mile Creek, and Selma). Turn left onto Illinois River Road; the road to the right leads into private property. Stay on Illinois River Road for the remainder of the loop.

## RIDE 14 · Rustler Peak Lookout

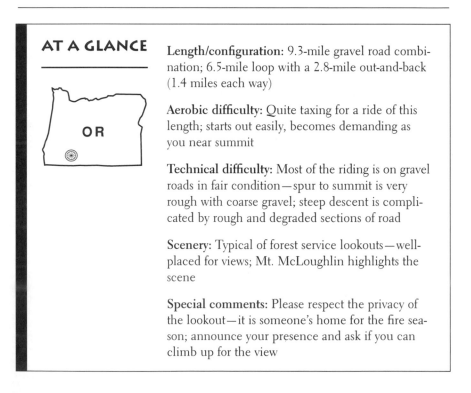

**AT A GLANCE**

**Length/configuration:** 9.3-mile gravel road combination; 6.5-mile loop with a 2.8-mile out-and-back (1.4 miles each way)

**Aerobic difficulty:** Quite taxing for a ride of this length; starts out easily, becomes demanding as you near summit

**Technical difficulty:** Most of the riding is on gravel roads in fair condition — spur to summit is very rough with coarse gravel; steep descent is complicated by rough and degraded sections of road

**Scenery:** Typical of forest service lookouts — well-placed for views; Mt. McLoughlin highlights the scene

**Special comments:** Please respect the privacy of the lookout — it is someone's home for the fire season; announce your presence and ask if you can climb up for the view

# RIDE 14 · Rustler Peak Lookout

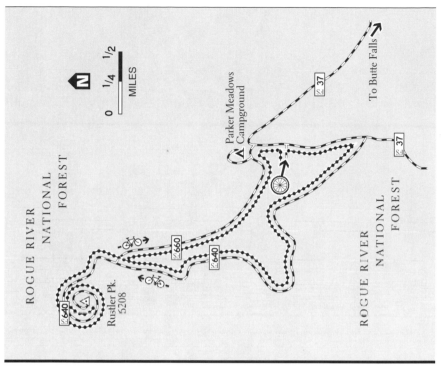

This is a tough 9.3-mile ride. It includes a 6.5-mile loop, and a side trip to the top of Rustler Peak. The spur to the summit is a 2.8-mile out-and-back (1.4 miles each way). The climbing starts out easily and becomes increasingly difficult as you near the summit. The route follows gravel roads in mostly fair condition. The final, steep push to the top is made more challenging by stretches of coarse gravel. The view from the lookout is expansive. The return descent is steep and degraded.

**General location:** Begins near Parker Meadows Campground, approximately 25 miles northeast of Butte Falls. (Butte Falls is a small town about 30 miles northeast of Medford.)

**Elevation change:** The ride begins at 5,100', climbs 40', and then drops quickly to 4,980' at the turn for Forest Service Road 640. From here, FS 640 climbs steadily to 6,208' atop Rustler Peak. Undulations in the topography add about 200' of climbing to the circuit. Total elevation gain: 1,468'.

**Season:** These roads are usually free of snow by late June.

**Services:** Water can be obtained seasonally at Parker Meadows Campground. Food, lodging, gas, and groceries are available in Butte Falls.

**Hazards:** Although traffic is usually light, you may share these roads with motorists. Control your speed while descending; FS 640 is rough with coarse

Riding with John
McBurney.

gravel and washboarding. FS 660 is eroded and contains areas of loose soil, ruts, and rocks.

**Rescue index:** Help can be found during regular business hours at the ranger station in Butte Falls. Emergency services are located in Medford.

**Land status:** Rogue River National Forest.

**Maps:** The district map of the Butte Falls Ranger District is a good guide to this trip. USGS 7.5 minute quad: Rustler Peak.

**Finding the trail:** From the community of Butte Falls, follow Butte Falls Road east for 0.9 mile and turn left onto Butte Falls-Prospect Road. Stay on Butte Falls-Prospect Road for 9 miles to Lodgepole Road/FS 34. Turn right onto FS 34. In 7.7 miles you pass South Fork Campground, and then cross the South Fork of the Rogue River. After the river you will pass FS 3775 (on the left) then arrive at an intersection with Parker Meadows Road/FS 37. Turn right to follow FS 37 south for 7.4 miles. This road brings you to FS 660, on the right, which leads into Parker Meadows Campground. Continue on FS 37 for 0.3 mile to a closed road on the right. There is room to park one vehicle here. Additional parking can be found farther up FS 37 on the left.

This ride can also be approached from the south, from the Fish Lake/Lake of the Woods region of the Rogue River National Forest. We haven't driven the route, but from our maps it looks like you can make the connections (probably involving some gravel roads). Near the west end of Fish Lake, FS 37/Butte Falls—Fish Lake Road heads north from OR 140/Lake of the Woods Highway. Follow FS 37 north for about 25 miles to Parker Meadows Campground. (The forest service map of the Rogue River National Forest and a compass may come in handy on this drive.)

**Source of additional information:**

Butte Falls Ranger District
P.O. Box 227
Butte Falls, OR 97522
(541) 865-2700

**Notes on the trail:** Ride south on FS 37. After a short, gentle climb you will begin a fast descent. From this crest, it is 0.4 mile to FS 640, on the right. (Watch carefully; this road is easy to miss.) Turn right onto FS 640 and stay on this main road to reach Rustler Peak. Return down FS 640 for 1.4 miles to FS 660. Turn left onto FS 660 and drop to Parker Meadows Campground. Stay to the right, on FS 660, through the campground. Turn right onto FS 37 and ride to your vehicle.

## **RIDE 15** · Minnehaha Loop

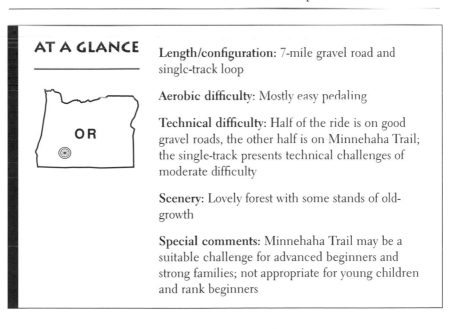

**AT A GLANCE**

**OR**

**Length/configuration:** 7-mile gravel road and single-track loop

**Aerobic difficulty:** Mostly easy pedaling

**Technical difficulty:** Half of the ride is on good gravel roads, the other half is on Minnehaha Trail; the single-track presents technical challenges of moderate difficulty

**Scenery:** Lovely forest with some stands of old-growth

**Special comments:** Minnehaha Trail may be a suitable challenge for advanced beginners and strong families; not appropriate for young children and rank beginners

Minnehaha Trail.

This is an easy seven-mile loop that you can start from your campsite in Hamaker Campground. Half of the ride is on gravel roads in good condition; the other half is on a single-track trail in fair condition, with some tree roots, windfalls, and several soft sections of trail. The circuit passes through lovely meadows and a forest of lodgepole pine, western white pine, and old-growth Douglas fir.

**General location:** The trailhead in Hamaker Campground is about 15 miles northwest of Crater Lake (as the crow flies).

**Elevation change:** The ride begins at 3,980', and a high point of 4,400' is attained at the footbridge at Soda Springs. Total elevation gain: 420'.

**Season:** The trail is fragile and should be avoided when wet. The driest time of year is generally June through September.

**Services:** Water can be obtained seasonally at Hamaker Campground. Food, lodging, gas, and limited groceries are available in Prospect and at Diamond Lake.

**Hazards:** Stay alert for traffic on the roads in the forest. The Minnehaha Trail is eroded in places and contains some exposed tree roots. Some areas along the

# RIDE 15 · Minnehaha Loop

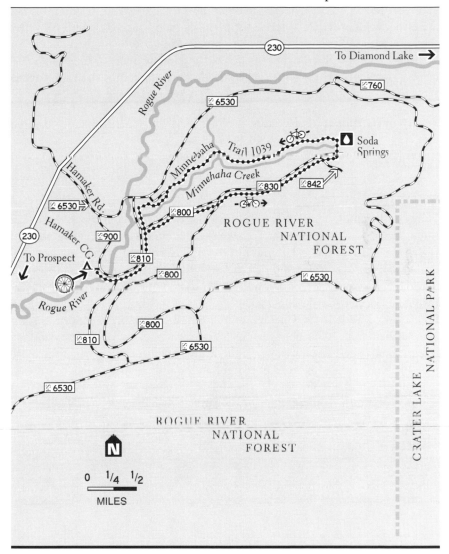

trail are soft with accumulations of pumice dust. The trail is a popular day hike; control your speed and anticipate other trail users.

**Rescue index:** Help is available in Prospect and at Diamond Lake. Emergency services are located in Medford.

**Land status:** Rogue River National Forest.

**Maps:** The district map of the Prospect Ranger District is a good guide to this trip. The Rogue River National Forest map also shows this trail adequately. USGS 7.5 minute quad: Hamaker Butte.

**Finding the trail:** From Prospect, follow OR 62 north for 11 miles, to the junction with OR 230. Stay left to follow OR 230 for approximately 12 miles, to Hamaker Road/Forest Service Road 6530 (on the right). From Diamond Lake, drive southwest on OR 230 for about 11 miles to Hamaker Road/FS 6530 (on the left). Turn onto Hamaker Road and proceed in a southeasterly direction for 0.6 mile to FS 900. Turn right onto FS 900 and follow it for 0.8 mile to FS 930 (on the right). FS 930 leads into Hamaker Campground. Turn right and park in the campground if you intend to camp; otherwise, park along FS 900.

### Source of additional information:

Prospect Ranger District
47201 Highway 62
Prospect, OR 97536
(541) 560-3400

**Notes on the trail:** Cross the bridge over the Rogue River and pass your bike under the gate on the other side. Follow the double-track and turn left at the first intersection (a sign points left toward OR 230). Turn right at the next intersection (a sign points both left and right toward OR 230). You are now on unsigned FS 800. Follow this road for 0.9 mile, then turn left onto FS 830. The road narrows to an overgrown double-track after 1.5 miles. This double-track leads to Soda Springs Trail 1039. Turn left onto the trail. The trail becomes unsigned Minnehaha Trail 1039 after passing Soda Springs. This single-track follows Minnehaha Creek downstream for about 1.5 miles and then becomes more road-like. In 0.3 mile, the road goes right and uphill; continue straight instead, following the trail into the woods. Turn left on reaching unsigned FS 800. Pedal 0.3 mile, and turn right onto unsigned FS 810 to backtrack to your vehicle.

## RIDE 16 · Sherwood Butte Loop

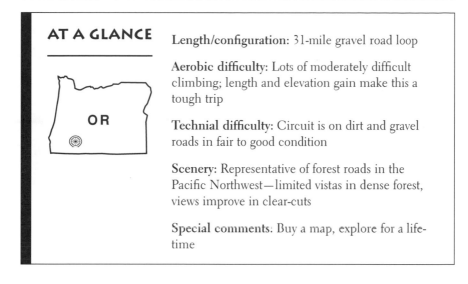

**AT A GLANCE**

**Length/configuration:** 31-mile gravel road loop

**Aerobic difficulty:** Lots of moderately difficult climbing; length and elevation gain make this a tough trip

**Technial difficulty:** Circuit is on dirt and gravel roads in fair to good condition

**Scenery:** Representative of forest roads in the Pacific Northwest—limited vistas in dense forest, views improve in clear-cuts

**Special comments:** Buy a map, explore for a lifetime

Sherwood Butte Loop is 31 miles long and mostly follows moderately difficult terrain. The gravel and dirt roads traveled on this route are in fair to good condition. There is some steep climbing, and the length of the ride makes this a taxing trip.

Typical of forests throughout the Pacific Northwest, the Rogue River and Umpqua National Forests are loaded with logging roads. A spirit of adventure and a good map will make finding mountain bike routes as simple as getting out there and going for it. The Hamaker Campground makes a nice base of operations for exploring the region.

**General location:** Hamaker Campground is about 15 miles northwest of Crater Lake (as the crow flies).

**Elevation change:** The ride starts at 4,000' at Hamaker Campground and ascends to 5,100' at Lake West. Beyond the lake, over rolling terrain, the route gains elevation to 5,420' before reaching OR 230. From the highway, the ride climbs on Forest Service Road 3703 for 4 miles, to 6,100', and then drops for about 1 mile, to 5,880'. The trip reaches 6,080' near Three Lakes and then begins a long descent. This downhill stretch starts out gradually and becomes increasingly steep. The turn onto FS 100 lies at 4,880'. This road leads to FS 37, at 4,480'. The riding is uphill on FS 37 for 2.3 miles, to the Rogue-Umpqua Divide, at 5,040'. A long drop ensues from the divide to OR 230, at 4,140'. Pedaling from the highway to the campground is mostly level and downhill. Rolling topography and shorter hills over the course of the ride add an additional 500' of climbing to the circuit. Total elevation gain: 3,360'.

**Season:** These roads are usually free of snow from June through September.

Road riding in the Rogue River.

**Services:** Water is available seasonally at Hamaker Campground. Food, lodging, gas, and limited groceries are available in Prospect and at Diamond Lake.

**Hazards:** Expect logging trucks and loose gravel on the roads. This route briefly follows OR 230.

**Rescue index:** Help is available in Prospect and at Diamond Lake. Emergency services are located in Medford.

**Land status:** Rogue River National Forest and Umpqua National Forest.

**Maps:** The district map of the Prospect Ranger District of the Rogue River National Forest is an excellent guide to the forest roads of this region. USGS 7.5 minute quads: Pumice Desert West, Hamaker Butte, Diamond Lake, and Garwood Butte.

**Finding the trail:** From Prospect, follow OR 62 north for 11 miles, to the junction with OR 230. Stay left, following OR 230 for approximately 12 miles to Hamaker Road/FS 6530 (on the right). From Diamond Lake, drive southwest on OR 230 for about 11 miles to Hamaker Road/FS 6530 (on the left). Turn onto Hamaker Road and proceed in a southeasterly direction for 0.6 mile to FS 900. Turn right onto FS 900 and follow it for 0.8 mile to FS 930, on the right. FS 930 leads into Hamaker Campground. Turn right and park in the campground if you intend to camp; otherwise, park along FS 900.

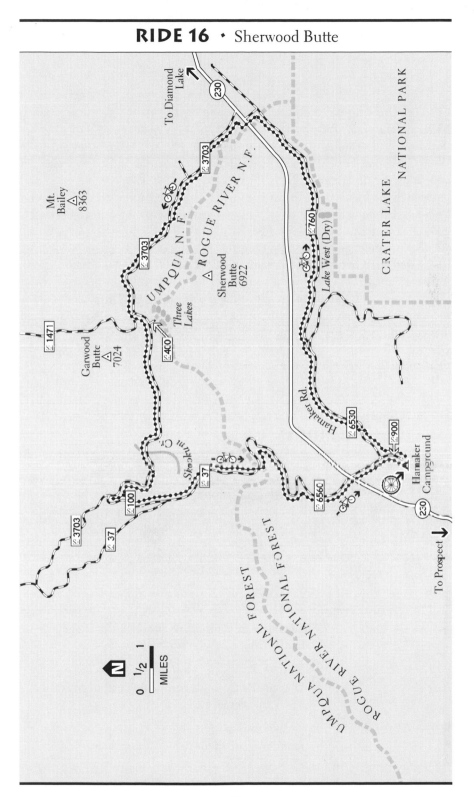

**Source of additional information:**

Prospect Ranger District
47201 Highway 62
Prospect, OR 97536
(541) 560-3400

**Notes on the trail:** Ride back out FS 900 and turn right onto FS 6530 at the stop sign. After 4 miles of riding, turn left onto FS 760, heading toward Lake West. Cycle past Lake West and continue to a sign on the right that points left and reads, "State Highway 230—.25 miles." Turn left at this intersection and proceed to the highway. Turn right onto OR 230. In 0.3 mile, turn left at a sign for South Umpqua Road/FS 3703. You will pass a spur road to Three Lakes (FS 400) after 6 miles of cycling on FS 3703. You will cross over Skookum Creek after 3 more miles and then start losing elevation rapidly. Approximately 2 miles past Skookum Creek, turn left onto Three Lakes Connector Road/FS 100. Arrive at signed Fish Creek Road/FS 37 after 1.7 miles on FS 100. Turn left and uphill onto FS 37. Continue straight at the top of the Rogue-Umpqua Divide as the Fish Creek Road designation changes from FS 37 to FS 6560. The long descent on FS 6560 ends as you cross Muir Creek. It is 0.5 mile from Muir Creek to OR 230. Cross the highway and follow FS 6530 to signed FS 900. Turn right and follow FS 900 to your vehicle.

## RIDE 17 · Umpqua Hot Springs

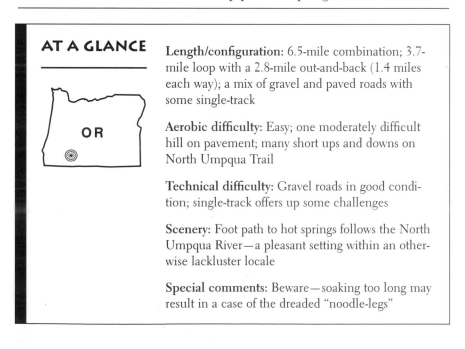

**AT A GLANCE**

**Length/configuration:** 6.5-mile combination; 3.7-mile loop with a 2.8-mile out-and-back (1.4 miles each way); a mix of gravel and paved roads with some single-track

**Aerobic difficulty:** Easy; one moderately difficult hill on pavement; many short ups and downs on North Umpqua Trail

**Technical difficulty:** Gravel roads in good condition; single-track offers up some challenges

**Scenery:** Foot path to hot springs follows the North Umpqua River—a pleasant setting within an otherwise lackluster locale

**Special comments:** Beware—soaking too long may result in a case of the dreaded "noodle-legs"

This easy ride is 6.5 miles long. It includes a 3.7-mile loop and an out-and-back that is 2.8 miles long (1.4 miles each way). There is a moderately difficult half-mile stretch of paved cycling on Forest Sevice Road 34, and there are some moderately difficult rolling hills on the North Umpqua Trail 1414. The hike to the springs is short but steep. The ride begins with about one mile of pavement, then travels over a gravel road in good condition for 3.5 miles. The rest of the trip is on a single-track trail in fair to good condition.

Umpqua Hot Springs is a small "tub" that has been carved out of the travertine that surrounds the springs. This soaking hole is very popular, and nudity is common. The single-track cycling is on the Hot Springs segment of the North Umpqua Trail. Rolling hills along this trail add a touch of excitement to the circuit.

**General location:** The ride starts at Toketee Lake Campground near Clearwater. Clearwater is approximately 60 miles east of Roseburg and about 20 miles northwest of Diamond Lake.

**Elevation change:** From 2,440' at Toketee Lake Campground, the ride ascends to 2,680' at the parking area and trailhead for the springs. The hiking trail to the springs climbs about 150'. The route returns from the hot springs parking area to the North Umpqua Trail, at 2,600'. There are many small hills on this trail. Ups and downs add an estimated 200' of climbing to the trip. Total elevation gain: 440' (hike not included)

**Season:** The hot springs can be enjoyed year-round. In general, the region sees the most precipitation in the winter and the spring. Portions of the North Umpqua Trail are vulnerable to erosion. If the single-track appears to be wet, please return on the roads.

**Services:** There is no water on this ride, nor is there water at Toketee Lake Campground. The nearby community of Clearwater has limited services. All services can be obtained in Roseburg.

**Hazards:** Part of the route is on paved and gravel roads that see fair amounts of traffic. The water in the hot springs can be very hot (typically 108 degrees). The twisting and rolling nature of the North Umpqua Trail creates some blind spots; anticipate others approaching from the opposite direction. Walk your bike over degraded sections of the trail. We recommend carrying a lock on this ride so you can secure your bikes at the trailhead for the hot springs.

**Rescue index:** Help can be found at the Toketee Ranger Station in Clearwater during regular business hours. Emergency services are located in Roseburg.

**Land status:** Umpqua National Forest.

**Maps:** The district map of the Diamond Lake Ranger District is a good guide to this ride. USGS 7.5 minute quads: Potter Mountain and Toketee Falls.

**Finding the trail:** From Roseburg, travel east on OR 138 for approximately 60 miles to FS 34 (on the left). From Diamond Lake, follow OR 138 west for about 20 miles to FS 34 (on the right). Turn north onto FS 34 (the west entrance to

Footbridge over the
North Umpqua River.

Toketee Ranger Station). At the bottom of the hill, turn left and cross two concrete bridges, staying on FS 34 where FS 100 goes right toward the Toketee Ranger Station. Drive another 1.2 miles (along the west shore of Toketee Lake) to Toketee Lake Campground on the right. Turn into the campground and follow the entrance road past the boat ramp to the day-use parking on the right.

**Source of additional information:**

Diamond Lake Ranger District
2020 Toketee Ranger Station Road
Idleyld Park, OR 97447
(541) 498-2531

**Notes on the trail:** Exit Toketee Lake Campground and turn right onto paved FS 34. Continue on FS 34 as it passes Lemolo Power Plant No. 2 and crosses a bridge over the North Umpqua River. After the bridge, the road climbs moderately to FS 3401 (Thorn Prairie Road). Turn right onto FS 3401. Go over the next bridge. Note that the North Umpqua Trail crosses FS 3401 here; you will pick up the North Umpqua Trail at this point on your return from the springs.

# RIDE 17 · Umpqua Hot Springs

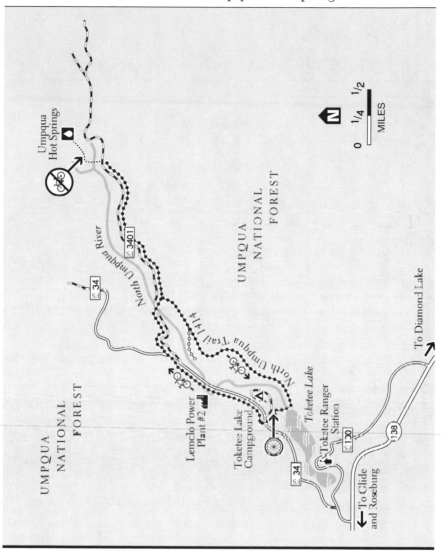

Cycle another 1.4 miles on FS 3401 to an unsigned parking area for the Umpqua Hot Springs on the left. Lock your bike and cross the footbridge. (Bikes are not allowed on the trail to the hot springs.) Turn right after the bridge to follow the trail to the hot springs. After your soak, return the way you came on FS 3401. Turn left onto North Umpqua Trail 1414. In about 1 mile, turn left, following signed North Umpqua Trail. In another mile you will come to an intersection where the dirt single-track meets a gravel path. Turn right onto this gravel path and stay to the right; you will then reach a footbridge over the North

Umpqua River. Cross the bridge into the day-use parking area of Toketee Lake Campground.

## RIDE 18 · North Umpqua Trail/Tioga Section

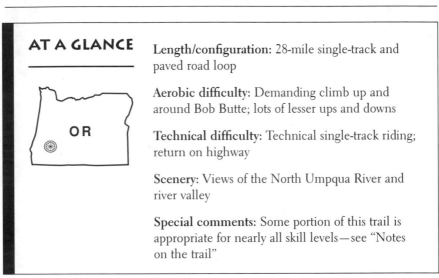

**AT A GLANCE**

OR

**Length/configuration:** 28-mile single-track and paved road loop

**Aerobic difficulty:** Demanding climb up and around Bob Butte; lots of lesser ups and downs

**Technical difficulty:** Technical single-track riding; return on highway

**Scenery:** Views of the North Umpqua River and river valley

**Special comments:** Some portion of this trail is appropriate for nearly all skill levels—see "Notes on the trail"

The North Umpqua Trail parallels the North Umpqua River for approximately 80 miles. Our route covers 15 miles of this single-track trail (the Tioga Section). The return to the trailhead is on OR 138. It is a strenuous 28-mile loop and requires good bike-handling skills. The most challenging climb is a switchbacking ascent around Bob Butte, which you will encounter about three miles into the ride. In general, the route is well maintained. Some of the trail's steeper sections are degraded and rocky. There may also be some windfalls blocking the single-track.

The first few miles of the trail are very scenic. It rolls up and down, passing over several wooden footbridges spanning small waterfalls and creeks. An interpretive display near the start of the ride offers visitors a scenic spot to watch migrating salmon. The North Umpqua is famous for its steelhead fishing.

**General location:** This trip begins at the Swiftwater County Park, 6 miles east of Glide. This trailhead is the western terminus of the North Umpqua Trail.

**Elevation change:** The trip begins at 1,200' and reaches a high point of 2,000' near Bob Butte. The undulating character of the loop adds about 1,500' of climbing to the ride. Total elevation gain: 2,300'.

**Season:** Wet weather and windfalls may preclude traveling on this loop in the winter and spring; phone ahead to check on conditions. Stay off the trail when

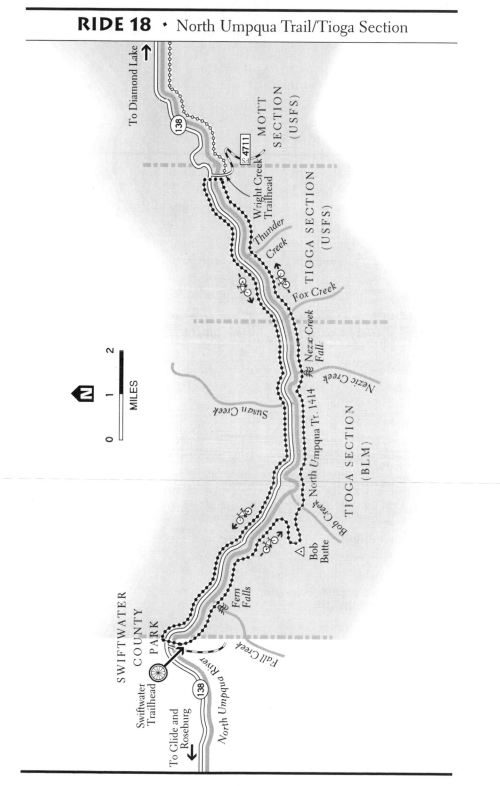

it is wet. The river is popular for both summer and winter steelhead fishing. You can often see chinook salmon spawning in September and October.

**Services:** There is no potable water available on this ride. Water, food, lodging, groceries, and gas can be obtained in Glide.

**Hazards:** This narrow trail sees traffic from pack and saddle stock, hikers, fishermen, and mountain bikers. The descent from Bob Butte involves a series of steep, rocky switchbacks. Some of the cycling is along sections of trail that drop off steeply to the river. Walk your bike where you encounter dangerous conditions. Rattlesnakes may be present in the rocky, drier areas. Poison oak borders the trail in places. The return to the trailhead is via OR 138. This two-lane highway has no shoulder and can see heavy traffic from logging trucks and recreational vehicles.

**Rescue index:** Help can be found in Glide. There are no bail-out points on the 15-mile stretch of single-track. If an emergency presents itself, you will need to consider how best to exit the trail. Once past Bob Butte, backtracking becomes more difficult. Emergency services are located in Roseburg.

**Land status:** Lands administered by the Bureau of Land Management, Umpqua National Forest, and county government.

**Maps:** A pamphlet called "North Umpqua Trail" contains a passable map of the route as well as interesting interpretive information. It is available at the North Umpqua Ranger Station in Glide; you can also get a copy by writing the Bureau of Land Management Office in Roseburg. USGS 7.5 minute quads: Glide, Mace Mountain, and Old Fairview.

**Finding the trail:** From Interstate 5 in Roseburg, drive east on OR 138 for 23 miles (6 miles east of Glide) to the Swiftwater County Park, on the right side of the highway. Turn and proceed over the bridge that spans the North Umpqua River. Immediately after crossing the bridge, turn left into the parking area for the North Umpqua Trail.

**Sources of additional information:**

Bureau of Land Management
Roseburg District
777 N.W. Garden Valley Boulevard
Roseburg, OR 97470
(541) 440-4930

Umpqua National Forest
North Umpqua Ranger District
18782 N. Umpqua Highway
Glide, OR 97443
(541) 496-3532

**Notes on the trail:** Ride upstream on the North Umpqua Trail. You will follow this trail for 15.3 miles to Forest Service Road 4711 at Wright Creek. Turn left onto FS 4711 and cross the bridge over the North Umpqua River. Turn left onto

One of many bridges on
the North Umpqua Trail.

OR 138. Ride west on OR 138 for 12.1 miles to the entrance road for the
Swiftwater County Park on the left.

Advanced beginners and intermediate mountain bikers may wish to turn
around before passing the high point of the ride (at Bob Butte). The first few
miles of the trail roll up and down and are very scenic. Strong cyclists can ride
out-and-back on the Tioga Section of the trail (a 30-mile outing). This option
avoids the highway, but it is a more demanding trip than the described loop.
Further explorations of the 80-mile-long North Umpqua Trail can be under-
taken by adventurous cyclists. Recreation opportunity guides for the North
Umpqua Trail are available at the ranger station in Glide; they provide a brief
outline of the trail's many segments. The R.O.G.s are not comprehensive;
seek out additional information from a district recreation specialist or trail
coordinator.

## RIDE 19 · North Crater Trail/Crater Trail Loop

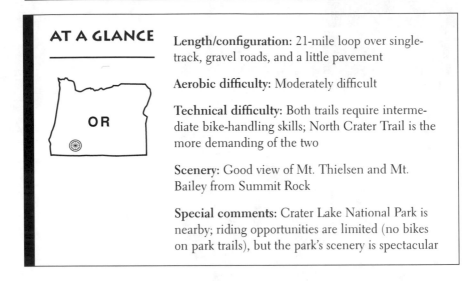

**AT A GLANCE**

OR

**Length/configuration:** 21-mile loop over single-track, gravel roads, and a little pavement

**Aerobic difficulty:** Moderately difficult

**Technical difficulty:** Both trails require intermediate bike-handling skills; North Crater Trail is the more demanding of the two

**Scenery:** Good view of Mt. Thielsen and Mt. Bailey from Summit Rock

**Special comments:** Crater Lake National Park is nearby; riding opportunities are limited (no bikes on park trails), but the park's scenery is spectacular

This is a moderately difficult 21-mile loop near Diamond Lake. The circuit follows trails and roads that are in mostly good condition. North Crater Trail is a single-track that rolls up and down for several miles. Then it commences an easy to moderately difficult six-mile climb to the North Crater Trailhead. Next, the ride follows OR 138 for 1.5 miles. This highway leads to an abandoned fire road known as Crater Trail. Crater Trail includes a pleasant four-mile descent, several miles of easy riding, and some short, moderately difficult climbs.

North Crater Trail is well maintained and just challenging enough to make your ride exciting. The path travels through a forest of fir and lodgepole pine, and passes a few open meadows with good wildflowers in the spring. A spur road leads to a viewpoint at Summit Rock, where you can see Mt. Thielsen and Mt. Bailey in the distance.

**General location:** This ride begins at the Howlock Mountain Trailhead, near Diamond Lake Resort. Diamond Lake lies within the Umpqua National Forest, just north of Crater Lake National Park on OR 138.

**Elevation change:** The ride starts at 5,360' and follows North Crater Trail to 5,860' at the North Crater Trailhead. The high point is 6,060' at Summit Rock. Undulations in the trails and roads add about 500' of climbing to the loop. Total elevation gain: 1,200'.

**Season:** It may be late spring before the snow has melted and the trails are dry around Diamond Lake. Phone the Forest Service for current conditions. Arrive before Memorial Day or after Labor Day to avoid the busy season.

**Services:** Water is available seasonally at the Forest Service campgrounds on Diamond Lake. Food, lodging, gas, limited groceries, and mountain bike rentals can be found at Diamond Lake Resort.

**Hazards:** The trails around Diamond Lake are popular with hikers and equestrians. Watch for loose gravel and sandy areas while descending. There are several highway crossings and 1.5 miles of cycling along the narrow shoulder of OR 138.

**Rescue index:** Help is available at Diamond Lake Resort or at the Forest Service's Information Center on the east shore of Diamond Lake. The Information Center is open seasonally and during regular business hours.

**Land status:** Umpqua National Forest.

**Maps:** The district map of the Diamond Lake Ranger District is a good guide to this ride. USGS 7.5 minute quads: Pumice Desert East, Pumice Desert West, Mount Thielsen, and Diamond Lake.

**Finding the trail:** From US 97 at Diamond Lake Junction, travel west on OR 138. Follow OR 138 for approximately 23 miles to the northern entrance of Diamond Lake Recreation Area, on the left (west) side of the highway. From Interstate 5 in Roseburg, take OR 138 east for about 76 miles to the northern entrance of Diamond Lake Recreation Area, on the right (west) side of the highway. At the northern entrance to the recreation area, turn west onto Forest Sevice Road 4795. Drive 0.3 mile on FS 4795 and turn left into the Howlock Mountain Trailhead. Proceed past the corrals to the farthest parking area.

## Sources of additional information:

Diamond Lake Ranger District
2020 Toketee Ranger Station Road
Idleyld Park, OR 97447
(541) 498-2531

Diamond Lake Resort
HC 30, Box 1
Diamond Lake, OR 97731-9708
(541) 793-3333

**Notes on the trail:** From the Howlock Mountain Trailhead, bear right onto North Crater Trail 1410. Continue in a southerly direction on North Crater Trail as it passes behind the corrals. Follow the signs toward South Shore. Take note of the blue diamond-shaped markers that have been placed at intervals on the trees that border the trail. Follow the blue diamonds to remain on North Crater Trail. The trail crosses OR 230 after about 5 miles of pedaling. It crosses OR 138 in another 0.3 mile. From this highway crossing it is 1.5 miles to a point where the single-track meets an abandoned dirt road. Turn left onto this double-track road. It climbs gently for 0.8 mile and then switchbacks hard to the left. Look to the right at this switchback for an easy-to-miss single-track that is marked with blue diamonds. Turn right to follow this trail. It climbs steeply at first and then deposits you at another abandoned road. Ride across the road to continue on the trail marked by the blue diamonds. The trail rolls up and down and widens to a double-track. This portion of the route is marked by orange and blue diamonds. It is 0.4 mile from the last road crossing to a single-track that breaks

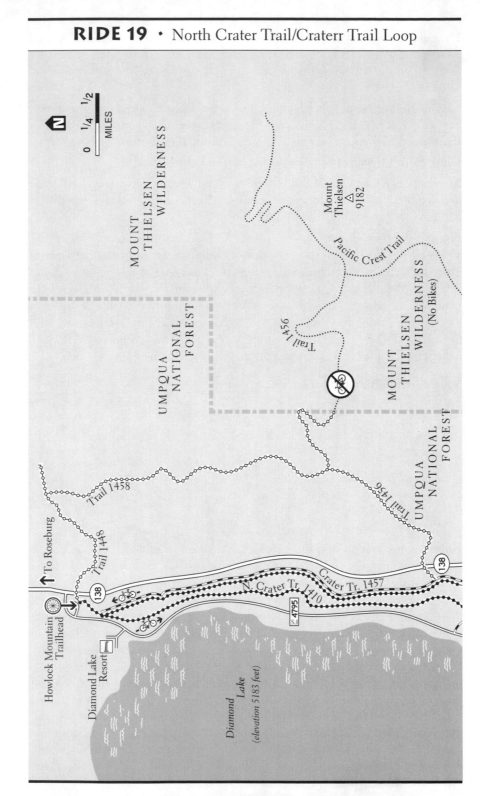

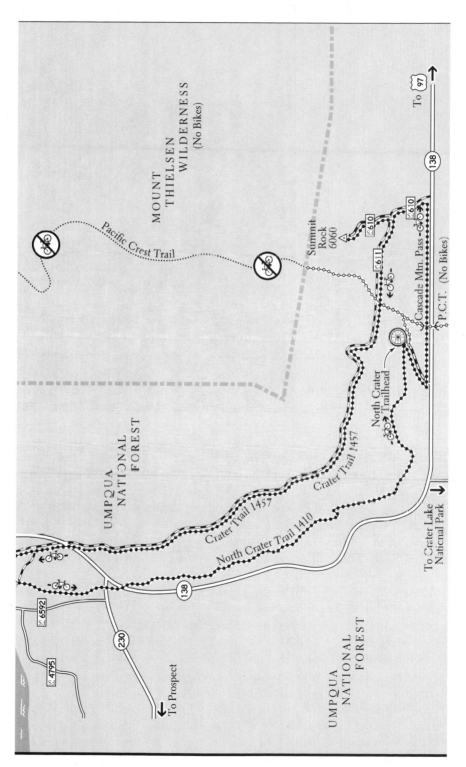

MOUNT THIELSEN WILDERNESS (No Bikes)

Pacific Crest Trail

UMPQUA NATIONAL FOREST

Summit Rock 6060

S. 610

S. 610

S. 611

Cascade Mtn. Pass

P.C.T. (No Bikes)

To 97

138

North Crater Trailhead

Crater Trail 1457

Crater Trail 1457

North Crater Trail 1410

To Crater Lake National Park

138

S. 6592

230

S. 4795

To Prospect

UMPQUA NATIONAL FOREST

View of Mt. Thielsen
from Summit Rock.

off to the right (marked by blue diamonds). Turn right and follow this trail to a
horse camp and a gravel road at the North Crater Trailhead. Follow the gravel
road to OR 138 and turn left. You will reach signed Cascade Mountain Pass after
0.5 mile on OR 138, then you will begin a gentle descent. Turn left onto
unmarked FS 610, 1 mile past the summit and the first road on the left. FS 610
brings you to FS 611. Continue straight on FS 610, following the sign for
Summit Rock. The road enters a clearing and then climbs steeply up to the
viewpoint.

Return the way you came to the intersection of FS 610 and FS 611. Turn
right onto FS 611. Shortly, the road crosses the Pacific Crest Trail (closed to
bicycles) and begins a long descent. At this point the road's designation changes
from FS 611 to Crater Trail 1457. Stay on Crater Trail and follow the signs for
Diamond Lake. You will arrive at OR 138 after descending for approximately 4
miles. Cross the highway and continue on Crater Trail for another 4 miles to
your vehicle at the Howlock Mountain Trailhead.

You may wish to check out The Diamond Lake Bicycle Path while visiting
the area. Linking this trail with FS 4795 creates a pleasant 11-mile loop around
the lake. A handout describing the path's points of interest can be obtained at
the Diamond Lake Visitor Information Center.

# SOUTHEAST OREGON

The Oregon Desert dominates southeastern Oregon. This huge sagebrush plateau, which covers roughly 45,000 square miles, accounts for approximately one-quarter of the state's area. Most of the land is owned by the government and administered by the Bureau of Land Management. Portions of the desert are bordered by National Forests.

The Hart Mountain National Antelope Refuge is in the southwestern corner of the desert, about 70 miles northeast of Lakeview, Oregon. The refuge is a vast haven for pronghorn antelope, California bighorn sheep, mule deer, jackrabbits, golden eagles, and many other species of mammals and birds. Traveling through this remote region has been likened to going on safari. Lovers of starkness and spaciousness will delight in riding over the quiet roads of the refuge.

Farther to the northeast is Diamond Craters Outstanding Natural Area. Geologists marvel at the diverse volcanic features found here. To most visitors, Diamond Craters is acres of sagebrush and some lava flows. We appreciated it for its remoteness, and for the early season ride it afforded us. The mountain biking in Diamond Craters is limited to the site's one cinder road.

If you do visit Diamond Craters, you aren't far from some highly regarded riding opportunities. Nearby, and dominating the landscape, is 9,773-foot Steens Mountain. Jack Remington in *Mountain Bike Guide to Oregon* describes a long, demanding, back-road loop on the western flanks of Steens Mountain. Mr. Remington exclaims that the trip is "one of the greatest mountain bike rides you can ever take!" To our knowledge, his mountain bike guidebook was the first to cover rides throughout the state of Oregon. We believe it is out of print; it was published by Oregon State Parks and Recreation Division. We have seen copies for sale on occasion. If you come across one, you might want to snatch it up, especially if you are a fan of long rides and overnight trips. (You will not find a ride on Steens Mountain in our book. Our research took us longer than we'd planned, so the late season and looming deadline nixed it.)

Vast desert expanses are also found on the eastern side of Steens Mountain. Here, as far as recreation goes, the Owyhee River is the main attraction. In the spring, the river rages, swollen from melting snow. Kayakers and rafters flock to the river's white water rapids and quiet backwater campsites. Typically, mountain biking is an afterthought for visitors to the area. That's understandable; you won't find much in the way of single-track here, and the area's back-road opportunities remain largely undocumented. However, the tablelands bordering the Owyhee are perfect for cyclists with an adventurous bent and a hankering to get away from it all. These plateaus are laced with double-tracks and dirt roads; wildlife sightings and views of the Owyhee Canyon often highlight outings here. If you're planning a river trip to the Owyhee, or just passing through to greener pastures, consider bringing your bike along.

Austere beauty and spaciousness abound in southeastern Oregon. The climate is dry, with an abundance of sunny days throughout the year. Services are a long way apart in this part of the country—you will want to come prepared. Get the car tuned up, fill a lot of water bottles, and set out for the openness and freedom found only in great desert spaces.

## RIDE 20 · Hart Mountain/Guano Creek Loop

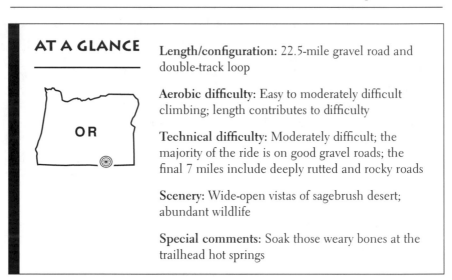

**AT A GLANCE**

**OR**

**Length/configuration:** 22.5-mile gravel road and double-track loop

**Aerobic difficulty:** Easy to moderately difficult climbing; length contributes to difficulty

**Technical difficulty:** Moderately difficult; the majority of the ride is on good gravel roads; the final 7 miles include deeply rutted and rocky roads

**Scenery:** Wide-open vistas of sagebrush desert; abundant wildlife

**Special comments:** Soak those weary bones at the trailhead hot springs

This trip is a 22.5-mile loop through a portion of the Hart Mountain National Antelope Refuge. The ride is long and exposed and lies at a relatively high elevation. There is a lot of climbing, but it is all easy to moderately difficult. The first 15.5 miles are over two-wheel-drive gravel roads that are in mostly good condition. These roads contain some loose gravel and washboarding. The remaining seven miles are on four-wheel-drive roads in fair condition, with some deep ruts and large rocks. The most degraded section of road occurs on the final descent.

Pedaling through this sagebrush desert is a treat for those seeking a more remote riding experience—you may even find yourself humming "Home On The Range." Bands of pronghorn antelope are a common sight, as are mule deer

## RIDE 20 • Hart Mountain/Guano Creek Loop

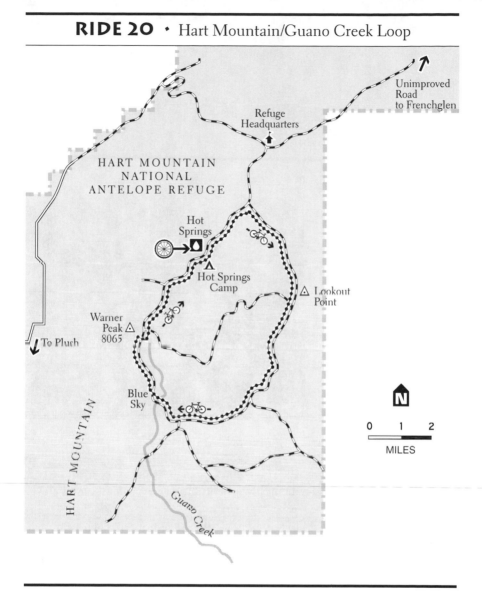

and coyote. Aspen thickets dot the hillsides of Hart Mountain and add a splash of fall color to the landscape along Guano Creek. A soak in the hot springs (at the trailhead) caps off a nice day of cycling.

**General location:** This ride begins near Hot Springs Camp in the Hart Mountain National Antelope Refuge; approximately 70 miles northeast of Lakeview. (Lakeview sits near the Oregon border; close to both California and Nevada.)

**Elevation change:** The loop starts at 5,600' and rolls up and down to reach

Hart Mountain National
Antelope Refuge.

6,185' at Lookout Point. The ride's high point—6,860'—is attained near the end of the trip. Undulations add about 700' of climbing to the circuit. Total elevation gain: 1,960'.

**Season:** The best time to ride here is from the beginning of August through October. The main roads are closed from November to Memorial Day, and the four-wheel-drive roads are closed until August 1. Road conditions and wildlife protection practices may limit access to parts of the area at any time; call ahead to check on closures.

**Services:** Water can be obtained at the refuge headquarters. Gas, limited groceries, and a pay phone can be found in the town of Plush (approximately 28 miles from the campground). All services are available in Lakeview.

**Hazards:** Although traffic is usually light, don't be lulled into a false sense of security; watch for motorists. Some of the descents go over coarse gravel, ruts, and large rocks. Be prepared for changes in the weather and emergencies on this exposed and remote ride.

**Rescue index:** Help can be obtained at the refuge headquarters or in the towns of Plush or Lakeview.

**Land status:** Public lands administered by the Department of the Interior.

**Maps:** A Hart Mountain Refuge brochure, which can be obtained at the refuge headquarters, is an adequate guide to this outing. USGS 7.5 minute quads: Campbell Lake, Flook Lake, Swede Knoll, and Warner Peak.

**Finding the trail:** From Lakeview, follow US 395 north for 4.5 miles to its junction with OR 140. Turn right onto OR 140 and drive 16 miles to the intersection of County Road 313/Plush Cutoff Road (a sign points left toward Plush and Hart Mountain Refuge). Turn left and follow CR 313 for 19 miles. Follow the road through Plush and turn right onto Hart Mountain Road (where a sign for Hart Mountain Refuge points right). This paved road changes to dirt after winding through farmland for 13.6 miles. Continue on the dirt road for another 10 miles, until you reach the refuge headquarters. From the headquarters, drive south for 1.7 miles to a **Y** intersection. Bear right and travel 2.5 miles to the hot springs on the right. Turn right toward the hot springs and park your vehicle.

## Source of additional information:

Sheldon-Hart Mountain Refuges
P.O. Box 111
18 South G Street, #301
Lakeview, OR 97630
(541) 947-3315

**Notes on the trail:** Turn left out of the hot springs parking area and follow the road back toward the refuge headquarters. Turn right at the next intersection. A sign here reads "Road Closed November 1–May 25 due to Hazardous Conditions and to Reduce Wildlife Disturbance." After pedaling 4.2 miles on this road you will come to a sign that directs you left toward Lookout Point. Turn left and ride 0.1 mile to the viewpoint. Return to the main road and turn left to continue on the loop. Several jeep trails branch off from the route; stay on the main road. It is 8.4 miles from the lookout to a culvert where Guano Creek passes under the road. Soon after passing over the creek, you will come to a road that leads left toward Blue Sky (a private hunting camp); stay to the right, on the main road. After this intersection the route begins to climb more steeply and changes from a two-wheel-drive to a four-wheel-drive road. This climb tops out at a gate. Go through the gate and descend. The road rolls up and down and crosses two shallow creeks. This leg is followed by an easy climb that crests at a **Y** intersection. Here, continue straight on the main road as a lesser road goes left and uphill. Descend to your vehicle.

## RIDE 21 · Diamond Craters

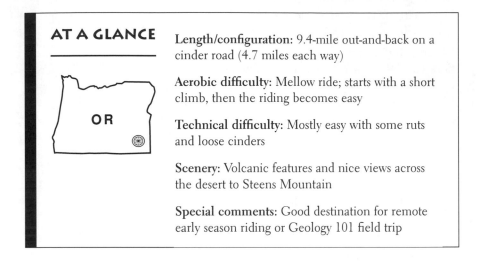

**AT A GLANCE**

OR

**Length/configuration:** 9.4-mile out-and-back on a cinder road (4.7 miles each way)

**Aerobic difficulty:** Mellow ride; starts with a short climb, then the riding becomes easy

**Technical difficulty:** Mostly easy with some ruts and loose cinders

**Scenery:** Volcanic features and nice views across the desert to Steens Mountain

**Special comments:** Good destination for remote early season riding or Geology 101 field trip

This is a tame 9.4-mile out-and-back ride. Diamond Craters is said to have the "best and most diverse basaltic volcanic features in the United States." We enjoyed the area most for its remoteness. The surrounding sage and rock desert is stark, but beautiful. The view to the south is filled by broad-shouldered, mile-high Steens Mountain.

You probably need to be a geologist to fully appreciate the region's volcanic diversity, but a mountain biker can have a good time here, too. When the snow is still deep on the mountain trails, this isolated route will be dry and rideable. The cycling is on a four-wheel-drive, cinder road. The road is rough and impassable to low-clearance vehicles for the first mile. The road improves, but it contains some pockets of loose cinders.

**General location:** This high desert ride is in Diamond Craters Natural Area; about 55 miles southeast of Burns.

**Elevation change:** The ride begins at 4,300' and climbs to a high point of 4,420' in the first mile. The road rolls up and down to reach a low point of 4,220'. Undulations in the terrain add about 50' of climbing to the ride. Total elevation gain: 370'.

**Season:** The best times to ride here are the spring and fall. Temperatures in the summer can soar.

**Services:** No water is available on this ride. Water, food, lodging, groceries, and gas can be obtained in Burns. You will find gas, limited groceries, and lodging in Diamond and French Glen.

**Hazards:** The first mile of road is rutted; be careful on the return descent. Wide tires are recommended for negotiating the sometimes loose roadbed. Be prepared for any emergency; you are a long way from help. Rattlesnakes reside in this natural area.

Lava pit crater.

**Rescue index:** Inquiries seem to indicate that you will find pay phones in French Glen and Diamond. (If there are no pay phones in these small communities, you should be able to make a call for emergency assistance from places of business.) The nearest hospital is in Burns.

**Land status:** Lands administered by the Bureau of Land Management.

**Maps:** The BLM pamphlet "Self-Guided Auto Tour of Diamond Craters" contains a useful map. The brochure gives a detailed description of the area's geology and makes the trip much more interesting. USGS 7.5 minute quads: Diamond and Diamond Swamp.

**Finding the trail:** From Burns, follow OR 78 east for 1.6 miles and turn right onto OR 205. A sign here reads "Frenchglen 59, Fields 111, Denio 132." Drive 40 miles on OR 205 to Diamond Junction. Turn left at Diamond Junction onto Diamond Grain Camp Road/CR 409. Follow this road for 6.7 miles, then turn left onto Lava Beds Road/CR 404. Drive 1.8 miles on Lava Beds Road; you will pass a large sign on the left announcing the Diamond Craters Outstanding Natural Area. Turn left in another 1.4 miles onto a hard-packed cinder pullout. The route heads west from this parking area. Diamond Craters can also be accessed from the east by following OR 78 to New Princeton. In New Princeton, take Lava Beds Road south. In 1.5 miles, follow the road as it curves right and heads west. In another 1.5 miles, turn left (south) to stay on Lava Beds Road. You will arrive at an intersection and the Peter French Round Barn in 10.5 miles. Stay to the right toward Diamond Craters (the road to the left goes toward Happy

# RIDE 21 · Diamond Craters

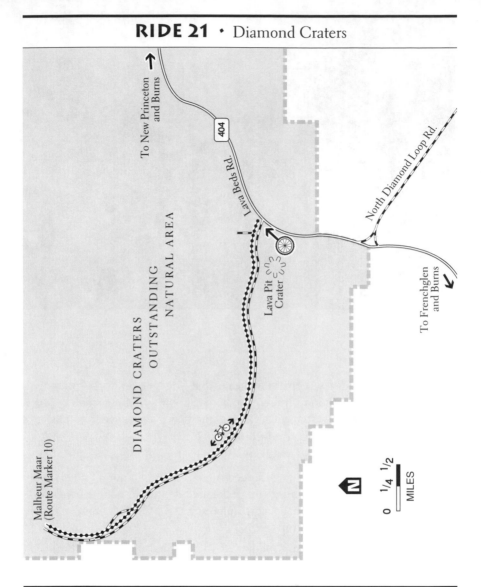

Valley and the small town of Diamond). Turn right in about 7 miles onto a hard-packed cinder pullout. The route heads west from this parking area.

## Source of additional information:

Bureau of Land Management
Burns District Office
HC 74-12533 Highway 20 West
Hines, OR 97738
(541) 573-4400

**Notes on the trail:** From the parking area, follow the rough cinder road uphill. Stay left to remain on the main road. The route is well marked with numbered signs and arrows for the interpretive auto tour. Follow the markers to #10. Turn around and return to your vehicle.

## RIDE 22 · Owyhee Spring Loop

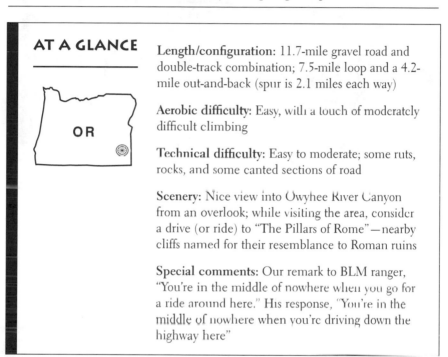

**AT A GLANCE**

**OR**

**Length/configuration:** 11.7-mile gravel road and double-track combination; 7.5-mile loop and a 4.2-mile out-and-back (spur is 2.1 miles each way)

**Aerobic difficulty:** Easy, with a touch of moderately difficult climbing

**Technical difficulty:** Easy to moderate; some ruts, rocks, and some canted sections of road

**Scenery:** Nice view into Owyhee River Canyon from an overlook; while visiting the area, consider a drive (or ride) to "The Pillars of Rome"—nearby cliffs named for their resemblance to Roman ruins

**Special comments:** Our remark to BLM ranger, "You're in the middle of nowhere when you go for a ride around here." His response, "You're in the middle of nowhere when you're driving down the highway here"

In the spring, Rome, Oregon is a popular destination for white-water enthusiasts. A "put-in" spot provides kayakers and rafters access to the Owyhee River. They come to float through steep-walled canyons and run rapids with names like Widow Maker, Raft Flip, and Upset. The mountain bike routes in the area are less exciting than these attractions, but adrenaline junkies can get their fix on the river, then mellow out with a quiet desert ride.

The described ride is 11.7 miles long. It is formed by following a gravel road and old double-tracks. The gravel road is in good condition with minor washboarding and some loose gravel. The double-tracks have seen better days. They contain ruts and rocks, and there is a stretch of roadbed that is canted off to the side. The outing involves a loop of 7.5 miles and a 4.2-mile out-and-back spur (2.1 miles each way). It's an easy ride with a bit of moderately difficult climbing. The gravel road takes you up through a shallow gulch—the double-tracks

Owyhee River Canyon.

wander about through the desert. Highlighting the double-track riding is an overlook that provides a good view of the river.

Owyhee Spring is a reservoir at an old homestead above the river. A short side trip off of the main route leads to this small pond. We set up camp at the pond and poked around in the site's old buildings before dinner. There is little left of the buildings, but the masonry employed in the foundations is impressive. At dusk, a dozen nighthawks gathered to make a feast of flying insects. It was delightful to sit and watch the sun go down as the nighthawks soared and swooped over our heads. Slowly, frogs began to sound off in the pond. All this seemed a fitting end to a fine day. Around bedtime, the pond's big kahunas started in with their megaphone croaks. We couldn't believe the racket those giant bullfrogs put out. Sleep was out of the question. Thankfully, it's a big desert, with lots of frog-free zones. We broke camp and moved a half-mile away for a good night's rest.

**General location:** The loop is just south of Rome, a tiny community on US 95 (the Idaho-Oregon-Nevada Highway). This town is about 13 miles east of the intersection of US 95 and OR 78 at Burns Junction.

**Elevation change:** This high desert ride begins at 3,600'. The high point of the ride is at 3,900'. Ups and downs add about 100' of climbing to the route. Total elevation gain: 400'.

**Season:** The spring and fall are the best times of year for riding in this desert. Summer temperatures can be unbearable. Periods of rain and lingering snow are common in the winter. The roads in the area become impassable when wet.

**Services:** There is no water on this ride. Water can be obtained seasonally at the Rome/Owyhee River Ranger Station. This BLM–managed launch site and campground is 0.4 mile east of Rome (on the south side of the highway). There is a cafe and a gas station in Rome. Gas, food, and lodging are available in Burns Junction (13 miles west of Rome, at the intersection of US 95 and OR 78). Gas, food, lodging, and groceries can be obtained in Jordan Valley (33 miles east of Rome on US 95).

**Hazards:** Watch for motor vehicles. Portions of the route follow double-tracks that are rocky and rutted. A short stretch of double-track hugs a hillside; the road is canted here. Do not travel on any of the region's dirt roads if wet conditions are encountered or are expected. The roads in the area become impassable when wet. Rattlesnakes inhabit the desert.

**Rescue index:** The Rome/Owyhee River Ranger Station is staffed seasonally, typically from March through September. There are pay phones at the Rome cafe and gas station.

**Land status:** Lands administered by the Bureau of Land Management.

**Maps:** The BLM Vale District Recreation Guide/Jordan Resource Area shows most of the roads and double-tracks followed on this route. USGS 7.5 minute quads: Scott Reservoir and Rome.

**Finding the trail:** From Burns, drive southeast on OR 78 for about 92 miles to Burns Junction and US 95. Turn left onto US 95 and proceed east for 13 miles to Rome. From McDermitt, on the Oregon/Nevada border, go north on US 95 for approximately 55 miles to Burns Junction. Bear right to remain on US 95 and travel 13 miles to Rome. From Jordan Valley (near the Oregon/Idaho border), follow US 95 southwest for 33 miles to Rome. Park in the large dirt parking area adjacent to the highway, just west of the cafe and gas station.

**Source of additional information:**

Bureau of Land Management
Vale District Office
100 Oregon Street
Vale, OR 97918
(541) 473-3144

**Notes on the trail:** Ride up the gravel road that heads south from the highway. (This road is just west of the Rome landing strip; it is marked by a small sign at the highway for Owyhee Canyon.) Stay on the main road; please respect private property by heeding the no trespassing signs. You will come to a **Y** intersection after pedaling 2.1 miles. (We understand that since our visit, a sign has been installed at this intersection reading, "Welcome to the Owyhee Desert.") Bear left to continue on the main road. In another 2.9 miles you will cross a cattle guard and come to a fork in the road. Turn left after the cattle guard and climb to the ride's high point. Descend for a little over 1 mile to an opening in a wire

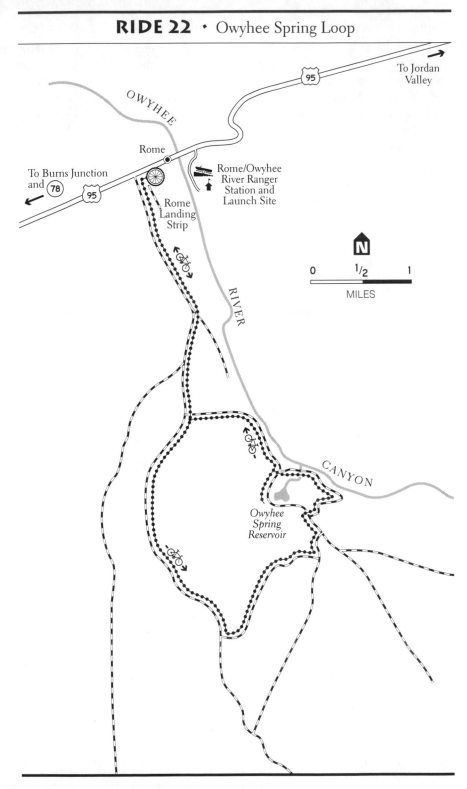

To Jordan
Valley

95

O W Y H E E

Rome

Rome/Owyhee
River Ranger
Station and
Launch Site

To Burns Junction
and 78   95

Rome
Landing
Strip

R I V E R

N

0          1/2          1

MILES

C A N Y O N

Owyhee
Spring
Reservoir

fence. Stay to the left after passing through the fence opening. You will pass a couple of fence posts (made of rock) in another 0.3 mile. (These landmarks are cylinders of wire fencing that are filled with rocks.) After the fence posts, look to the right for a faint double-track. Turn right and descend on the faint double-track to an unmarked overlook. Walk out for a view of the river. Back at your bike, ride west (downhill) on the double-track. You will cross a creek, then arrive at a barbed-wire fence. Pass your bike over the fence and ride up to a well-traveled double-track. Turn left onto the double-track and ride uphill a short distance to Owyhee Spring Reservoir (a small pond). From the pond, return the way you came, riding downhill and passing the double-track you just came off of. Stay on the main double-track as it takes you close to the river and then swings around to the left. Turn right when you reach the main gravel road. Ride out to the highway and your vehicle.

While visiting the area you may wish to ride out to see "The Pillars of Rome." These cliffs can be reached by following back roads that head northwest from Rome. Ride up the main gravel road (across the highway from the cafe/gas station). The road bends sharply right in 1.8 miles, then you will arrive at an intersection in 0.3 mile. Turn left to ride up a short steep hill, the cliffs will come into view at the top. You can continue on back roads to come out on US 95, then return to Rome on the highway (use the recommended map and a compass), or return the way you came to Rome.

## RIDE 23 · Owyhee Rim

**AT A GLANCE**

OR

**Length/configuration:** 22.7-mile gravel road and double-track combination; 15.7-mile loop and a 7-mile out-and-back segment (3.5 miles each way)

**Aerobic difficulty:** Difficult; long ride with many short ups and downs; bone-jarring conditions add to the ride's difficulty

**Technical difficulty:** Very rough double-tracks create handling problems; gravel road and paved highway in good condition

**Scenery:** Nice high desert landscape near beginning of ride; outstanding Owyhee Canyon overlook at midpoint

**Special comments:** Alert visitors may discern ruins of ancient Indian structures at overlook; please do not disturb this site

Our first stop in Rome (not built in one day), Oregon was the BLM ranger station at the Owyhee River Launch Site. We met the ranger, John Shipp, and asked him if he could direct us to any good riding in the area. He told us that he enjoyed a ride that paralleled the rim of the Owyhee Canyon. Following his directions, we set off to explore the route.

The double-track paralleling the canyon rim was extremely rough with tire ruts and bovine hoof prints. Apparently, local road conditions vary from year to year. When the roads get wet they become squishy; anything that travels on them leaves a lasting impression. We found the road along the rim to be very bumpy in the summer of 1997. We stopped often, taking time to enjoy the scenery, and picking up gear that had rattled off our bikes. The view across the canyon was delightful. The desert stretched out before us for miles, and Steens Mountain, to the west, was an impressive sight.

The double-track lead to a gravel road that was in fair condition with some washboarding and sandy sections. We followed the gravel road to another double-track, which headed out to a cliff and a breathtaking view of the river. Archaeologists have determined that this site was once used by native peoples. What at first appear to be random piles of rocks are actually the remnants of old Indian structures. With a little imagination, crumbled walls can be discerned. It doesn't take a huge leap of faith to imagine that Indians would choose to inhabit this beautiful place. Sitting and gazing out over a wide landscape of rock, water, and sky invites speculation. We found ourselves wondering what went on here so many years before.

The ride is 22.7 miles long; a 15.7-mile loop and an out-and-back spur of 7 miles (3.5 miles each way). There are no long, steep hills on the ride, but we rate the outing as difficult. It is a long, exposed ride with many ups and downs over rough roads. Staying oriented is another challenging aspect of this ride. There are few landmarks and getting lost is a distinct possibility, especially for those who are less than adept at route-finding.

**General location:** These roads are just east of Rome, Oregon. Rome is a remote outpost in the southeastern Oregon desert. The town (a cafe and gas station) is on US 95, about 13 miles east of the intersection of US 95 and OR 78.

**Elevation change:** The ride begins at approximately 3,800' and climbs to a high point of about 4,100'. Undulations along the route add about 400' of climbing to the trip. Total elevation gain: 700'.

**Season:** The best seasons for riding here are the spring and fall. Temperatures in the summer can be oppressive, while rain and snow are common in the winter. Area roads become impassable when wet.

**Services:** There is no water on this ride. Water can be obtained seasonally at the Rome/Owyhee River Ranger Station. This BLM–managed launch site and campground is 0.4 mile east of Rome (on the south side of the highway). There is a cafe and gas station in Rome. Gas, food, and lodging are available in Burns Junction (13 miles west of Rome, at the intersection of US 95 and OR 78). Gas, food, lodging, and groceries can be obtained in Jordan Valley (33 miles east of Rome on US 95).

Riding the rim.

**Hazards:** Carry the recommended maps, a compass, and be completely self-sufficient. Bike handling can be a problem on the ride's rough roads—rocks, loose gravel, and sand complicate matters. The route includes a 2 mile stretch on US 95. Be prepared for emergencies and changing weather conditions; the route is exposed and remote. Do not attempt this ride if there is a chance of rain—the roads become an impassable quagmire when wet. Rattlesnakes are indigenous to the desert.

**Rescue index:** The Rome/Owyhee River Ranger Station is staffed seasonally—usually from March through September. There are pay phones at the Rome cafe and gas station.

**Land status:** Lands administered by the Bureau of Land Management.

**Maps:** The BLM Vale District Recreation Guide/Jordan Resource Area shows most of the roads and double-tracks followed on this route. USGS 7.5 minute quad: Scott Reservoir.

**Finding the trail:** See "Finding the trail" for Owyhee Spring Loop (Ride 22) for information on getting to Rome, Oregon. From Rome, drive east on US 95 for 1.7 miles, climbing out of the Owyhee River Canyon to a pullout on the right. Park well off the highway in the pullout.

# RIDE 23 · Owyhee Rim

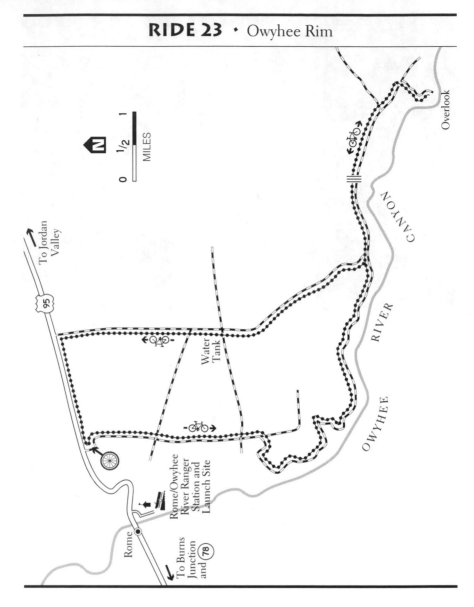

**Source of additional information:**

Bureau of Land Management
Vale District Office
100 Oregon Street
Vale, OR 97918
(541) 473-3144

**Notes on the trail:** This ride passes through fenced grazing allotments. Leave gates as you find them—if they were closed, close them behind you.

From the highway, follow a faint double-track that briefly parallels the highway, then heads south (away from the highway). Soon the double-track passes through a wire gate. Stay on the main double-track where side roads branch off. It is about 1 mile from the first wire gate to another wire gate (1.5 miles into the ride). You pass a couple of intersections after the second wire gate; continue straight at these to arrive at a third wire gate (3 miles from the start of the ride). After the third gate, the double-track bears to the right and descends a little. This brings you beside a small side canyon. The road slowly swings to the left and out to Owyhee Canyon. Again, stay on the main double-track, heading in a southeasterly direction along the canyon rim. Turn right when you arrive at a main gravel road (8.5 miles from the start of the ride). In another mile, pass over a cattle guard. It is 1.4 miles from the cattle guard to a dip in the road and a double-track that goes right. (The main gravel road begins to swing to the left/northeast near this landmark/intersection.) Turn right onto the double-track and pedal 0.4 mile to a wire gate. Pass through the gate and ride 0.2 mile to a **Y** intersection. Take the right fork and travel 0.6 mile to the end of this double-track. Walk out to the canyon overlook and Indian ruins.

Return the way you came, riding back to the main gravel road and turning left to backtrack. At the intersection with the rough double-track you came off of earlier (1 mile past the cattle guard), continue straight to stay on the main gravel road. Remain on the primary gravel road (head north), passing a water tank and more cattle guards to arrive at the highway. Turn left onto US 95 and ride 2 miles to your vehicle.

## RIDE 24 · Leslie Gulch

| **AT A GLANCE** | **Length/configuration:** 12-mile gravel road out-and-back (6 miles each way) |
|---|---|
| | **Aerobic difficulty:** Moderately difficult; first half is a 6-mile climb |
| OR | **Technical difficulty:** Easier road riding; some loose gravel, ruts, and rocks |
| | **Scenery:** Rock formations reminiscent of the desert southwest |
| | **Special comments:** Opportunities for viewing bighorn sheep (if you are lucky) |

W e read about this narrow canyon in our handy "Oregon Atlas and Gazetteer," published by DeLorme Mapping. Leslie Gulch sounded like an interesting place, and we would be passing the area on our way to Rome, Oregon. We drove to Leslie Gulch and found that it stood up nicely to the Gazetteer's description. It really did contain "towering red spires, sheer rock walls, and pinnacles as high as 2,000' rising from the canyon floor." We visited the area on a sun-baked day in July. The searing heat and vertical rock formations reminded us of rides we had done in Utah's canyon country.

The mountain biking in Leslie Gulch is restricted to existing roads. We describe a 12-mile out-and-back route (6 miles each way) that begins at Lake Owyhee and has a turnaround point in Dago Gulch. Strong cyclists will find that the climb up from the lake is pretty easy—they will be able to stay in their middle chain ring. Intermediate bicyclists and beginners may find themselves shifting into their "granny gear." The gravel road through Leslie Gulch is in good condition with some loose gravel. The double-track in Dago Gulch is rougher with some ruts, rocks, and soft tread.

**General location:** Leslie Gulch is a remote canyon in southeastern Oregon. The nearest city is Boise, Idaho, approximately 75 miles away. The small town of Jordan Valley, Oregon, is about 35 miles south of Leslie Gulch.

**Elevation change:** The ride starts near Lake Owyhee at 2,655'. The high point of the ride is 3,900' in Dago Gulch. Total elevation gain: 1,245'.

**Season:** The spring is a good time of year for a ride in Leslie Gulch; wildflower displays can be good. The fall is also a good season for a visit; temperatures are cooler and traffic is usually light. High temperatures are a hindrance to summertime rides.

**Services:** There is no potable water available in Leslie Gulch—bring all you will need with you. There are vault toilets at several locations within the gulch. Gas, food, lodging, and groceries can be obtained in Jordan Valley.

**Hazards:** Control your speed when descending; especially through Dago Gulch (where the road is somewhat degraded). Watch for traffic in Leslie Gulch. Rattlesnakes inhabit the region.

**Rescue index:** Help can be found in Jordan Valley. Emergency services are located in Boise.

**Land status:** Lands administered by the Bureau of Land Management.

**Maps:** The BLM Vale District/Malheur Resource Area Recreation Guide shows the roads followed on this ride. USGS 7.5 minute quads: Bannock Ridge and Rooster Comb.

**Finding the trail:** From Boise, Idaho, follow US 26/20 west to US 95 near Parma. Drive south on US 95 for about 35 miles to McBride Creek Road on the right. Turn onto McBride Creek Road (gravel) and drive 8.5 miles to an intersection of roads in Rockville (an old ranching community—nearly a ghost town). Turn right to follow the signs for Leslie Gulch Turnoff and Succor Creek

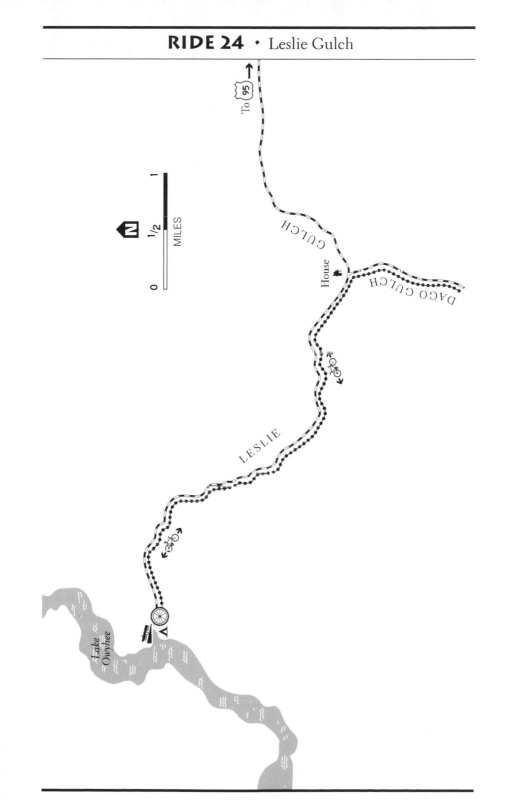

Dago Gulch
double-track.

State Park. You will arrive at another signed intersection in 1.7 miles. Turn left to follow the sign for Leslie Gulch. In another 5.8 miles you enter Leslie Gulch. Drive to the end of the road (8.3 miles down the canyon). Park in the day-use area at the Lake Owyhee boat ramp. From Jordan Valley, follow Highway 95 north 17.7 miles to Succor Creek Road on the left. Turn onto Succor Creek Road (gravel) and drive 8 miles to an intersection of roads at the Rockville site. Bear left to follow the signs for Leslie Gulch and Succor Creek State Park. In 1.7 miles turn left at the sign for Leslie Gulch. Stay on this road for just over 14 miles to arrive at Lake Owyhee. Park in the day-use lot at the boat ramp.

**Source of additional information:**

Bureau of Land Management
Vale District Office
100 Oregon Street
Vale, Oregon 97918
(541) 473-3144

**Notes on the trail:** Ride uphill on the gravel road. After 4.7 miles of riding you will pass an interpretive display about bighorn sheep. Ride another 0.3 mile to a double-track on the right (across from a house). Ride up the double-track through Dago Gulch for 1 mile to a wire fence across the road. Turn around and return the way you came.

If you would prefer a longer, more demanding ride, follow the main gravel road to the top of Leslie Gulch. This adds a total of 7 miles to the trip.

# NORTHEAST OREGON

Most of the recreational lands in northeastern Oregon are in the 2.4-million-acre Wallowa-Whitman National Forest. Although the forest includes four wilderness areas that are off-limits to bikes, you should have little difficulty finding places to ride. There are 9,000 miles of dirt roads and 750 miles of trails open to two-wheeled travel.

Varied terrain is the hallmark of northeastern Oregon. The Blue Mountains parade through the region, with many peaks reaching upwards of 10,000 feet. Some of the individual mountain groups within this range are extremely rugged, especially the Wallowas.

The Blue Mountains contain not only lofty peaks but also Hells Canyon, the deepest canyon in the United States. This 6,000-foot-deep gorge on the Snake River separates the Wallowas from the Seven Devils Mountain Range of northern Idaho. The size and scale of the canyon is awe-inspiring.

The region that includes Enterprise, Joseph, and Imnaha was the land of Chief Joseph and the Nez Perce Indians (the Nee-Me-Poo people). The tribe spent their summers beside Wallowa Lake and wintered near the mouth of Joseph Creek at the Snake River. Hostilities between the Nez Perce and whites reached a fever pitch when gold was discovered in Orofino, Idaho. Suddenly adding to the trespasses of cattlemen and settlers were 10,000 miners searching for gold.

After years of broken treaties, misunderstandings, and conflicts, the U.S. government forced the Nez Perce to leave their homeland and move to a reservation in Idaho. As the displaced Indians neared their new home, a small band of young warriors turned back and raided a white settlement. The cavalry was sent to bring in the Nez Perce.

Like Sitting Bull after defeating Custer, the Nez Perce decided to flee to Canada. The retreat, led by Chief Joseph, was an incredible march; every mile was filled with danger. After several horrible battles, and a flight of 2,000 miles in four months, the Indians were defeated—just 40 miles from the Canadian border.

The Nee-Me-Poo National Recreation Trail in Hells Canyon offers hikers a chance to walk in the footsteps of the Nez Perce. You can obtain an informative brochure about the trail at the Wallowa Mountains Visitor Center in Enterprise.

The center's interpretive displays alone are worth a stop. The place is sure to please history buffs and windshield naturalists. The rangers at the center are very helpful and are armed with maps and handouts.

Towns throughout the region are home to district ranger stations. Take the opportunity to visit these posts; information on mountain biking is often available for the asking. There is great cycling near La Grande, near Baker, and in the mountains between Joseph and Halfway. Explorations in these areas are easy in a four-wheel-drive vehicle, but a high-clearance, two-wheel-drive car will do the trick too.

Winters in northeastern Oregon are generally cold and damp; rain and snow are common. The spring and fall tend to be mild, while summers are hot and dry. Hells Canyon experiences temperate winters and hot summers.

## RIDE 25 · Phillips Reservoir Loop

**AT A GLANCE**

**Length/configuration:** 16-mile road and single-track loop

**Aerobic difficulty:** Easy; mostly mellow ups and downs

**Technical difficulty:** Easy; 11 miles of single-track with some rocky and sandy spots

**Scenery:** Trail winds around the lakeshore with views of Elkhorn Crest

**Special comments:** Families may enjoy all or part of this ride

Phillips Reservoir Loop is a 16-mile ride suitable for strong beginners. Eleven miles of mellow, single-track cycling on Shoreline Trail highlight the trip. The trail runs along the lakeshore contours and offers views of Elkhorn Crest and of boats bobbing on the water.

The riding is easy, but not totally free of obstacles. A couple of rocky and sandy sections help keep the trail interesting. Ups and downs on the route are nicely graded and easy to handle. There are three miles of pedaling on paved and dirt forest roads in good condition. A downside to the loop is a two-mile stretch on OR 7.

**General location:** The trailhead is located approximately 20 miles southwest of Baker City.

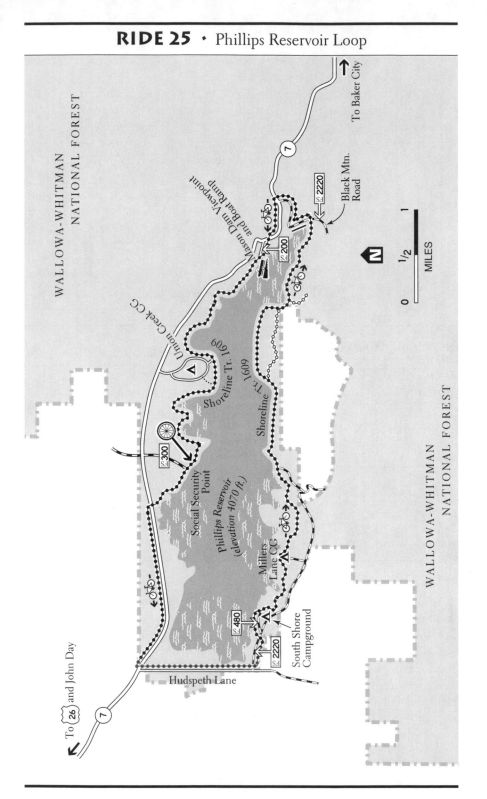

**Elevation change:** The ride begins at 4,100' and varies little over the course of the outing. Ups and downs on the route add up to about 500' of climbing.

**Season:** Pedal around the lake on a fall weekday and you'll have the place to yourself—or nearly so. The reservoir is a popular summer destination, and the trail may be busy with hikers (especially on weekends). The lakeshore trails see occasional use by equestrians. Avoid riding in early spring when the trail may be wet and easily damaged.

**Services:** Water can be found seasonally at Union Creek Campground. There is a pay phone near the entrance to the campground. All services are available in Baker City.

**Hazards:** Ride with care on OR 7; the shoulder width varies from zero to three feet, and traffic moves rapidly. Watch for loose rocks, sandy spots, and other trail users on Shoreline Trail.

**Rescue index:** You may be able to obtain emergency assistance at Union Creek Campground during the summer. Emergency services are located in Baker City.

**Land status:** Wallowa-Whitman National Forest.

**Maps:** The district map for the Baker Ranger District is a good guide to this route. A recreation opportunity guide describing this route is available from the Baker Ranger District. USGS 7.5 minute quads: Phillips Lake and Blue Canyon.

**Finding the trail:** From Interstate 84, take Exit 304 and follow the signs to Baker City. In 1.1 miles turn left onto Main Street/OR 7. Follow OR 7 south for approximately 20 miles to the Union Creek Recreation Area Campground, on the left. Continue west past the campground for 0.9 mile, to Forest Service Road 300. Turn left onto FS 300 toward Social Security Point. Drive down the road 0.4 mile to a parking area on the left.

This is just one of many trailheads on the lake, others include Mason Dam Boat Launch, Union Creek Day-Use Area, Mowich Loop Picnic Area, and South Shore Campground.

**Source of additional information:**

Baker Ranger District
3165 10th Street
Baker City, OR 97814
(541) 523-4476

**Notes on the trail:** From the trailhead across from the parking area, follow signed Shoreline Trail west. After 1 mile you reach Deer Creek (there is a green shed here). Walk up to the highway and turn left onto OR 7. Follow OR 7 for 1.5 miles, then turn left onto Hudspeth Lane. In 1.2 miles, turn left onto gravel FS 2220 toward South Shore Campground. Follow FS 2220 for about 0.5 mile; turn left onto FS 480 to enter the campground. Follow the campground road east to the end of a cul-de-sac and the trail. Turn right onto the single-track. Stay

Shoreline Trail.

on Shoreline Trail where side trails go right. You will pass a ditch as you near the east end of the lake. Then turn left to cross a footbridge, and then left again to regain the trail. When you reach the gravel road at Mason Dam, turn left. Pedal over the dam and out to OR 7. Turn left onto the highway. In 0.5 mile, turn left into the Mason Dam Viewpoint and Boat Ramp (FS 200). Ride down toward the water, and turn right onto the trail near the parking area. Shoreline Trail changes to a paved surface as it passes through Union Creek Campground. Continue straight across the large boat ramp to pick up the trail on the other side. In another 0.4 mile, bear left onto a dirt single-track. The paved path will lead up to day-use parking if you miss the turn onto the dirt trail. Continue around the lakeshore (crossing several bridges and catwalks) to arrive back at your vehicle.

## RIDE 26 · Indian Rock

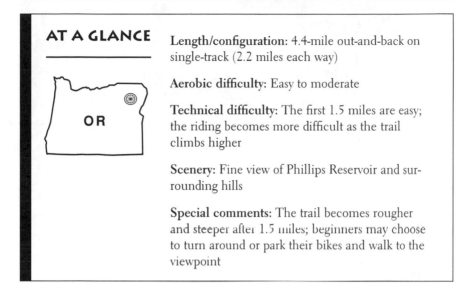

**AT A GLANCE**

**OR**

**Length/configuration:** 4.4-mile out-and-back on single-track (2.2 miles each way)

**Aerobic difficulty:** Easy to moderate

**Technical difficulty:** The first 1.5 miles are easy; the riding becomes more difficult as the trail climbs higher

**Scenery:** Fine view of Phillips Reservoir and surrounding hills

**Special comments:** The trail becomes rougher and steeper after 1.5 miles; beginners may choose to turn around or park their bikes and walk to the viewpoint

Indian Rock Trail is a lonely little single-track; it could use some friends. If it could, it might place an ad in the personals section of the classifieds. Sticks, pinecones, and rocks have piled up and obscured portions of the trail. Passing feet and rolling tires would help move some of that debris aside.

Following this path takes you on a pleasant 2.2-mile ride to Indian Rock (a 4.4-mile out-and-back trip). The trail climbs easily at first. After 1.5 miles, the climbing becomes moderately difficult. It gets steep and technical just before you reach Indian Rock. Park your bike and hike up this last stretch. You get a nice view of Phillips Reservoir from the rock. The lake provides a setting where relaxation and exhilaration mingle sluggish fishing boats contrast with whirling jet skis. The same can be said for Indian Rock Trail. Quiet pedaling brings you to a promontory that invites you to linger over a nice view. The return down the trail is the exciting part of the ride. It is a short but sweet descent.

**General location:** The trailhead is located approximately 20 miles southwest of Baker City.

**Elevation change:** The ride begins at 4,100' and rises to a high point of 4,700' at Indian Rock. Total elevation gain: 600'.

**Season:** Though Phillips Reservoir is a popular summer destination, this trail is not heavily used. The trail is open from the spring through the fall.

**Services:** Water can be found seasonally at the trailhead in Union Creek Campground. There is a pay phone near the entrance to the campground. All services are available in Baker City.

Climbing to Indian Rock.

**Hazards:** Cross OR 7 with care. Forest litter obscures the trail in places. Watch for loose rocks and soft sections of trail.

**Rescue index:** You may be able to obtain emergency assistance at Union Creek Campground during the summer. Emergency services are located in Baker City.

**Land status:** Wallowa-Whitman National Forest.

**Maps:** The district map for the Baker Ranger District shows the roads and trails followed on this ride. USGS 7.5 minute quad: Phillips Lake.

**Finding the trail:** From Interstate 84, take Exit 304 and follow the signs to Baker City. In 1.1 miles turn left onto Main Street/OR 7. Follow OR 7 south for approximately 20 miles and turn left into the Union Creek Recreation Area Campground. Park in the day-use area (near the boat ramp).

**Source of additional information:**

Baker Ranger District
3165 10th Street
Baker City, OR 97814
(541) 523-4476

**Notes on the trail:** From the day-use area, ride back up the pavement to OR 7. Look across the highway and slightly to the right to find the faint trail. (Be careful crossing the highway.) Follow the trail and immediately arrive at a stile that passes over a barbed wire fence. Carry your bike up and over the steps. Continue

# RIDE 26 · Indian Rock

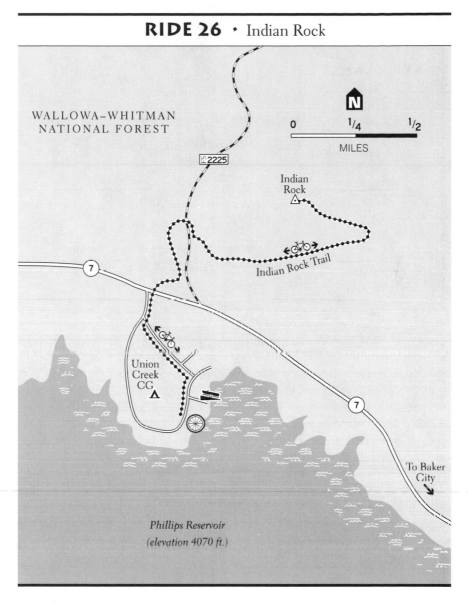

WALLOWA–WHITMAN
NATIONAL FOREST

2225

Indian
Rock

Indian Rock Trail

7

Union
Creek
CG

7

To Baker
City

Phillips Reservoir
*(elevation 4070 ft.)*

0    1/4    1/2

MILES

on the trail, crossing 2 footbridges to meet a gravel road (Forest Service Road 2225). Cross the road to find unsigned Indian Rock Trail 1648 heading uphill to the right. The trail peters out just before reaching Indian Rock. Park your bike and walk to the rocky viewpoint. Return the way you came.

## RIDE 27 · Twin Lakes Loop

---

**AT A GLANCE**

---

**OR**

**Length/configuration:** 17.8-mile loop; single-track, double-track, and forest roads

**Aerobic difficulty:** Extremely demanding

**Technical difficulty:** Tough; in places the trail is steep, rutted, rocky, and narrow

**Scenery:** Big views from Elkhorn Crest of alpine lakes, the Wallowa Mountains, and the Blue Mountains

**Special comments:** Good possibility of spying mountain goats on the crags above Twin Lakes Basin

---

In a recreation opportunity guide for Twin Lakes Loop, the Baker Ranger District warns that this 17.8-mile loop "is not for the faint of heart." We would add that it is not for the wimpy of leg. The climb on forest roads to Marble Pass Trailhead gains over 3,200 feet. A turn onto Forest Service Road 6510 (3.5 miles into the ride) signals the start of an excruciatingly steep half-mile climb through a quarry. If you find that you are already fatigued upon reaching FS 6510, turn around. You will have a real struggle on your hands if you choose to continue on. Once through the quarry, however, the views start to open up and the ascent becomes more moderate (from torturous to merely painful).

The loop is composed of 8 miles of trails and 9.8 miles of forest roads. The forest roads are in fair to good condition. The trails vary greatly in their condition and technical difficulty. This route follows a small segment (3.8 miles) of the 22.6-mile long Elkhorn Crest Trail 1611. The portion of the trail followed on this loop is in fair to good condition with some rocks and loose gravel.

Elkhorn Crest Trail winds through outcroppings as it passes across Elkhorn Crest. You are right on the ridge of the mountain. Each bend in the trail provides another canyon to look down, or a fresh perspective on a wider landscape. At times, you are looking north into Baker Valley with the Wallowa Mountains as a backdrop. Then, as you come around a corner, new views open up over your other shoulder. To the southwest, the Blue Mountains and hundreds of square miles of forest stretch out below you. Riders should take in this scenery with at least one foot on the ground. The trail drops off steeply in places; an ill-timed glance could spell disaster.

The 1.1-mile drop from Elkhorn Crest into Twin Lakes Basin (on Twin Lakes Trail 1633) is tightly switchbacked over loose, rocky terrain. Live to see another

# RIDE 27 · Twin Lakes Loop

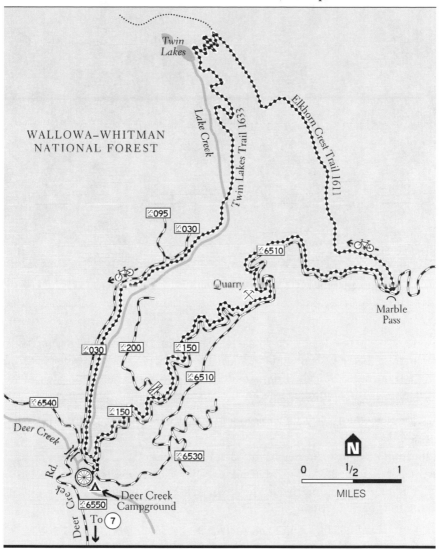

day; walk your bike down these severe switchies. Walking also provides an opportunity to take in another eyeful of incredible scenery. Below you are two beautiful alpine lakes, their glimmering surfaces framed by towering granite walls. The spectacular crags behind Twin Lakes are home to mountain goats. Look for them on the ridge to the west of the lakes.

Continuing downhill from Twin Lakes, Trail 1633 takes a turn for the worse. This three-mile section of single-track sees a good amount of saddle and pack stock traffic, and little maintenance. It is a nasty trail that goes straight down

Twin Lakes from the Elkhorn Crest Trail.

some steep pitches. Rocky, ditch-like conditions are common, and at one point the trail has been washed out by a creek. This creek crossing makes for wet feet and a short, tricky stretch of route finding. The last three miles are a fun flight back to the campground on forest roads.

**General location:** Deer Creek Campground is approximately 28 miles southwest of Baker City.

**Elevation change:** The ride begins at 4,300' at Deer Creek Campground and ascends to 7,542' at Marble Pass Trailhead. The Elkhorn Crest Trail reaches a high point of approximately 8,240'. Ups and downs add about 200' of climbing to the trip. Total elevation gain: 4,140'.

**Season:** Due to its high elevation, Elkhorn Crest Trail may not be free of snow until July. Snow showers are common at these elevations in the late spring and early fall. Summer is a good time of year to travel on Elkhorn Crest Trail.

**Services:** There is no water on this ride. Water can be obtained seasonally at Union Creek Campground (on the north shore of Phillips Reservoir). There are pit toilets at Deer Creek Campground. All services can be found in Baker City.

**Hazards:** This loop presents problems typical of remote, high-altitude trails. You are exposed to extreme conditions and are far from assistance in an emergency. Please take a moment to review the information about safety at the front of the book—especially the paragraphs on self-sufficiency and extreme riding conditions. You will pass dangerous rock ledges on Elkhorn Crest Trail. In places, Twin Lakes Trail is a steep, rocky ditch. Walk your bike if you are uncomfortable with any portions of the trails. Watch for other trail users, especially on Twin Lakes Trail (popular with equestrians). Expect vehicular traffic on the forest roads.

**Rescue index:** There is a phone at Union Creek Campground (on the north shore of Phillips Reservoir). Help can be obtained in Baker City.

**Land status:** Wallowa-Whitman National Forest.

**Maps:** The district map of the Baker Ranger District is a good guide to this route. USGS 7.5 minute quads: Elkhorn Peak and Phillips Lake.

**Finding the trail:** From Interstate 84, take exit 304 and follow the signs to Baker City. In 1.1 miles turn left onto Main Street/OR 7. Follow OR 7 south for approximately 20 miles to Union Creek Recreation Area Campground on the left. Continue west past the campground for 3.7 miles to FS 6550 (Deer Creek Road). Turn right and immediately bear left at the **Y** intersection to stay on FS 6550. Stay on the main road for about 4 miles to a bridge over Deer Creek and a major intersection. Turn right to follow the sign for FS 6530/Deer Creek Campground. Turn right into Deer Creek Campground (FS 100) in 0.3 mile.

**Source of additional information:**

Baker Ranger District
3165 10th Street
Baker City, OR 97814
(541) 523-4476

**Notes on the trail:** Turn left out of Deer Creek Campground and pedal 0.1 mile to FS 150 on the right (across from a sign for Deer Creek Campground). Turn onto FS 150 and climb for 1.6 miles to a sharp turn in the road. Here, the main road switchbacks hard to the left and its designation changes to FS 200. (FS 200 is gated.) Do not follow the switchback (FS 200) to the left. Instead, continue straight to pass through a couple of tank traps and remain on FS 150. FS 150 climbs some more, then drops to meet FS 6510 at a **T** intersection. Turn left onto FS 6510 and begin the tough climb through the quarry. Marble Pass is 3.2 miles up FS 6510. Turn left onto single-track Elkhorn Crest Trail at the summit. (The trail is marked by a sign for Marble Pass Trailhead.) Elkhorn Crest Trail meets signed Twin Lakes Trail in 3.8 miles. Turn left and descend on Twin Lakes Trail. Twin Lakes Basin is reached in about 1 mile. Stay on the main trail through the basin. From the lakes, you will ride about 2 miles to reach a wire fence and a **V**-shaped gate. Pass your bike through the gate and continue down Twin Lakes Trail. In another 0.7 mile the trail deposits you on the banks of Lake Creek. Here, at the time of our visit, the trail was washed out and tangled with debris—the creek and trail were one and the same. Follow the creek a short distance downstream (less than 0.1 mile) to find the trail on the opposite bank. After the creek crossing, the trail becomes more of a double-track, then meets a maintained gravel road. Continue downhill on the gravel road. At the next intersection, turn left to continue descending on FS 030 (FS 095 goes right here). FS 030 brings you to FS 6530 in another 2.4 miles. Turn left onto FS 6530 and ride 0.3 mile to Deer Creek Campground on the right.

## RIDE 28 · Anthony Lakes/Elkhorn Crest Trail

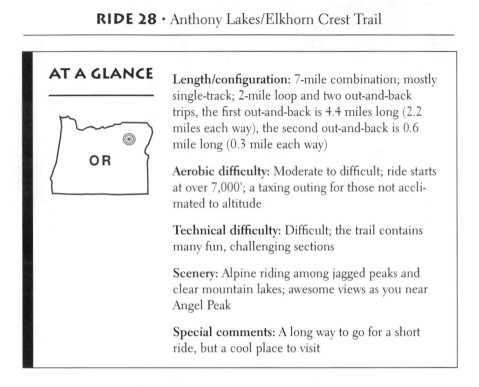

**AT A GLANCE**

**Length/configuration:** 7-mile combination; mostly single-track; 2-mile loop and two out-and-back trips, the first out-and-back is 4.4 miles long (2.2 miles each way), the second out-and-back is 0.6 mile long (0.3 mile each way)

**Aerobic difficulty:** Moderate to difficult; ride starts at over 7,000'; a taxing outing for those not acclimated to altitude

**Technical difficulty:** Difficult; the trail contains many fun, challenging sections

**Scenery:** Alpine riding among jagged peaks and clear mountain lakes; awesome views as you near Angel Peak

**Special comments:** A long way to go for a short ride, but a cool place to visit

Anthony Lakes Recreation Area is located high in the Blue Mountains of eastern Oregon. This beautiful alpine region is enjoyed by outdoorsmen throughout the year. In winter, trails are groomed for Nordic skiing, and a ski lift services alpine runs. The area's trails are popular with hikers and equestrians in the summer.

Anthony Lakes is adjacent to a portion of the North Fork John Day Wilderness. Unfortunately, this proximity to the Wilderness Area limits the number of trails open to cycling.

This ride covers a total of seven miles. About one mile of the trip is on forest roads, the rest is on trails. The route involves a two-mile loop and two out-and-back spurs. The out-and-back portions of the trip are 4.4 miles long (2.2 miles each way) and 0.6 mile long (0.3 mile each way). Included in the outing are 2.7 miles of fine single-track on Elkhorn Crest Trail. Skilled technical riders will love the challenging mix of rocks, big check dams, and roots that this trail throws their way.

Fun single-track near
Anthony Lakes.

The high point of the ride is reached on Elkhorn Crest Trail; near Angel Peak. Up high, the trail becomes very rough (we parked our bikes and walked the last bit). There are great views into the North Fork John Day Wilderness from the turnaround point. The return is a fun descent, but please keep your speed under control and remember to tread lightly.

**General location:** Anthony Lakes is located approximately 35 miles northwest of Baker City.

**Elevation change:** The low point of the ride is 7,130' near Anthony Lakes. The high point, 8,200', occurs on Elkhorn Crest Trail. Ups and downs add about 200' of climbing to the tour. Total elevation gain: 1,270'.

**Season:** The trails in the area may not be dry until July. Anthony Lakes Recreation Area is a popular summer destination. For a quieter experience, plan on visiting in the fall.

**Services:** Water can be found seasonally at the Anthony Lake picnic area, and at the campground. All services are available in Baker City.

**Hazards:** These trails contain many obstacles and present some dangerous

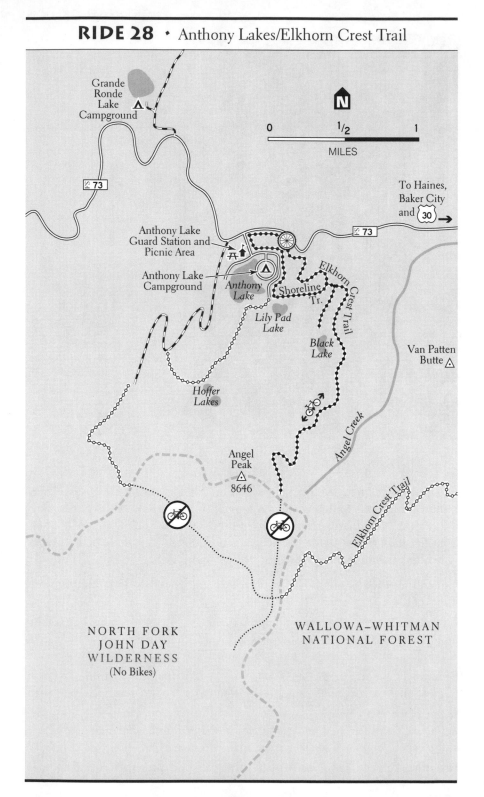

Grande
Ronde
Lake
Campground

N

0            1/2            1

MILES

73

To Haines,
Baker City
and 30

Anthony Lake
Guard Station and
Picnic Area

73

Elkhorn Crest Trail

Anthony Lake
Campground

Anthony
Lake

Shoreline
Tr.

Van Patten
Butte

Lily Pad
Lake

Black
Lake

Hoffer
Lakes

Angel Creek

Angel
Peak
8646

Elkhorn Crest Trail

NORTH FORK
JOHN DAY
WILDERNESS
(No Bikes)

WALLOWA–WHITMAN
NATIONAL FOREST

exposures. The high altitude of the outing could pose problems for cyclists arriving from lower elevations. Watch for others while descending; these trails are extremely popular with hikers and equestrians. Good alpine riding is hard to find—please help protect this unique place and our access to it (don't skid).

**Rescue index:** There is a guard station on the north side of Anthony Lake. You may be able to obtain help in an emergency there. Emergency services are located in Baker City.

**Land status:** Wallowa-Whitman National Forest.

**Maps:** The forest service pamphlet "Anthony Lakes Recreation Area" is a helpful guide to the trails in the area. It is available at the ranger station in Baker City. The route is also indicated on the district map of the Baker Ranger District. USGS 7.5 minute quad: Anthony Lakes.

**Finding the trail:** From Baker City, follow US 30 north for 10 miles to Haines. In Haines, turn left onto County Road 1146. This road twists and turns its way through the countryside. Stay on the main road; follow the signs for the Elkhorn Drive National Scenic Byway. The road's designation changes to Forest Service Road 73 at the forest boundary. The road climbs steeply through the forest for approximately 8 miles to the Elkhorn Crest Trailhead on the left. (You have overshot the trailhead by 0.3 mile if you arrive at the entrance to Anthony Lakes Campground.) Park at the Elkhorn Crest Trailhead.

**Source of additional information:**

Baker Ranger District
3165 10th Street
Baker City, OR 97814
(541) 523-4476

**Notes on the trail:** Ride up signed Elkhorn Crest Trail 1611. Bear left in 0.5 mile to remain on Elkhorn Crest Trail where Shoreline Trail goes right. Immediately arrive at another intersection. Stay left where a trail goes right toward Black Lake. After traveling a total of 2.7 miles you will reach a saddle near the wilderness boundary. (Bicycles are not allowed in designated wilderness areas.) Turn around and return the way you came. On your return trip, ride out and back on the trail to Black Lake. Then follow Shoreline Trail to Lily Pad Lake. Continue on Shoreline Trail to a boat launch at Anthony Lake. Follow the road out to FS 73. Turn right onto FS 73 and pedal back to the Elkhorn Crest Trailhead.

# RIDE 29 · Lehman Hot Springs

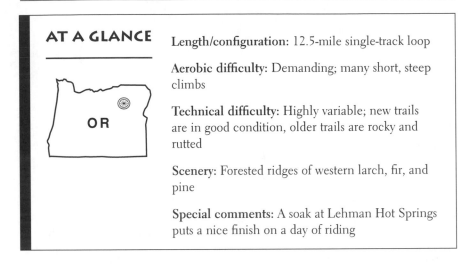

**AT A GLANCE**

**OR**

**Length/configuration:** 12.5-mile single-track loop

**Aerobic difficulty:** Demanding; many short, steep climbs

**Technical difficulty:** Highly variable; new trails are in good condition, older trails are rocky and rutted

**Scenery:** Forested ridges of western larch, fir, and pine

**Special comments:** A soak at Lehman Hot Springs puts a nice finish on a day of riding

Lehman Hot Springs is a good starting point for exploring the Winom-Frazier Off Highway Vehicle (OHV) Complex. The area offers over 100 miles of challenging trails to off-road riders and other trail users. The proprietors of Lehman Hot Springs operate a large hot mineral pool and a snack bar. Cabin rentals and full service RV hook-ups are available. There are several forest ser-

Butcher Knife Trail.

vice campgrounds nearby, and the surrounding area abounds with opportunities for dispersed camping.

Are you hankering to test your mettle against other two-wheeled enthusiasts? If so, consider entering "The Battle in the Blues" mountain bike race. This annual event is held on the trails that radiate out from Lehman Hot Springs. The beginner leg of the 1997 race followed the 12.5-mile loop described in this chapter. Routes for the race change from year to year, but riding this loop will provide you with a sense of what to expect if you enter as a novice.

Longer, more challenging rides are available, but you may wish to start with this outing; it is demanding. Typical of trails designed for motorized use, these paths climb steeply at times. The riding here is a mix of conditions and difficulties. One minute you are struggling with a steep hill, the next is a curvy cruise through the trees. Smooth tread can instantly give way to sandy, rocky, and rutted conditions.

Getting lost is a possibility for those venturing out onto OHV trails. OHV areas are notorious for bootleg trails. These paths are cut by renegades who show little interest in staying on designated routes. Their machines supply them with the power to go where they wish, and new trails are always popping up. Finding your way can be a challenge when you are confronted with a spider web of unmarked and unmapped trails. Motorized riders are at an advantage here; their engines provide them with the means to explore vast areas in short periods of time. Preparedness, patience, and a good attitude are keys to enjoying the sport of mountain bicycling. These attributes are even more important to riders who want to safely enjoy trails in OHV areas.

**General location:** The trailhead at Lehman Hot Springs is about 35 miles west of La Grande and about 12 miles east of Ukiah.

**Elevation change:** The ride begins at about 4,200' and reaches a high point of approximately 5,200'. Ups and downs along the course of the loop add about 800' of climbing to the outing. Total elevation gain: 1,800'.

**Season:** Trails in the area are usually free of snow and rideable from mid-June through October. Expect short-term closures for trail maintenance and during periods of wet weather.

**Services:** Water can be obtained at Lehman Hot Springs. Limited groceries and gas are available in Ukiah. All services are available in La Grande.

**Hazards:** Watch for other trail users. You may encounter unsigned and unmapped trails while following the described route. Take care to stay oriented. The ride includes downhill sections that are sandy. Some of the descents are rough and rocky.

**Rescue index:** You can obtain help in an emergency at Lehman Hot Springs. There are hospitals in Pendleton and La Grande.

**Land status:** Umatilla National Forest.

**Maps:** A trail map and user guide for the Winom-Frazier OHV Complex is available at Lehman Hot Springs or from the Umatilla and Wallowa-Whitman National Forests. It shows some of the trails and intersections encountered on the described route. USGS 7.5 minute quads: Pearson Ridge and Lehman Springs.

**Finding the trail:** Take Interstate 84 to Exit 252. (Exit 252 is about 9 miles west of La Grande, and approximately 43 miles east of Pendleton.) Exit the Interstate and follow OR 244 for approximately 30 miles to the paved entrance road to Lehman Hot Springs. (The road that leads into the hot springs is 1 mile west of Forest Service Road 5226/Frazier Campground.) Turn left and drive 1.3 miles to the parking area at Lehman Hot Springs.

## Source of additional information:

North Fork John Day Ranger District
P.O. Box 158
Ukiah, OR 97880
(541) 427-3231

**Notes on the trail:** Return down the paved road 0.1 mile to gravel Frazier Station Road. Turn right and ride 0.5 mile to a trail crossing the road (this intersection is 0.1 mile beyond a cattle guard). Turn right to follow the trail. Immediately arrive at an intersection and turn right to follow signed Lehman Trail. In 0.8 mile, after a couple of steep climbs, another intersection is reached. Stay to the right to remain on the OHV route. One more mile of pedaling brings you to a gravel road. Turn right onto the road, then immediately bear left to regain the trail. In 0.7 mile, the trail comes close to a gravel road and a double-track comes in from the right—stay to the left to continue on the trail. The trail meets an old road in another 0.5 mile—bear right onto it. Turn right in 0.5 mile at a "Trail" sign. Immediately cross an old road, then a double-track. The riding is easier through this area as you follow a ridge and then enjoy a short descent through the woods. Enter a clearing and arrive at an intersection of trails. Turn right onto signed Butcher Knife Trail. This trail crosses an old road in 0.7 mile, then arrives at a gravel road in another 0.3 mile. Turn right onto the gravel road and then immediately turn left to regain the trail. Soon you pop out into a high exposed area where the trail becomes faint. Follow the faint trail as it curves around to the right and begins to descend (the trail becomes a very rough and rocky double-track here). Arrive at an intersection after about 1.5 miles of downhill riding (Line Creek Trail goes left here). Bear right to remain on unsigned Butcher Knife Trail. Climb for about 0.3 mile to an intersection where a trail heads downhill (to the left). Turn onto this trail and ride 0.2 mile to a road. Turn left onto the road, cross a cattle guard, then turn right to regain the trail. Two miles of excellent downhill single-track deposits you onto a rocky road. Pedaling again, enter a clear-cut and look to the left to regain the trail. Turn onto the trail and travel another 0.3 mile to an intersection of roads. Turn left and follow a gravel road out to the paved entrance road to Lehman Hot Springs. If you are spent, turn right and ride back to your car on the pavement. Otherwise, cross the

# RIDE 29 • Lehman Hot Springs

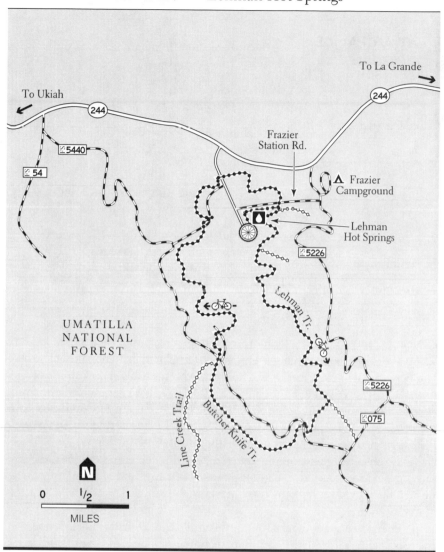

To La Grande

To Ukiah

244

244

Frazier
Station Rd.

5440

54

Frazier
Campground

Lehman
Hot Springs

5226

Lehman Tr.

UMATILLA
NATIONAL
FOREST

5226

075

Line Creek Trail

Butcher Knife Tr.

N

0    1/2    1

MILES

paved road and pick up a single-track. This trail crosses a small wood bridge, then climbs steeply. After crossing the second of two cattle guards on this segment of trail, you will arrive at unsigned Frazier Station Road. Turn right and ride out to your vehicle at Lehman Hot Springs.

# RIDE 30 · Copple Butte Trail

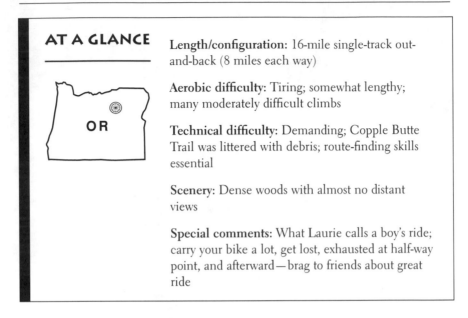

**AT A GLANCE**

OR

**Length/configuration:** 16-mile single-track out-and-back (8 miles each way)

**Aerobic difficulty:** Tiring; somewhat lengthy; many moderately difficult climbs

**Technical difficulty:** Demanding; Copple Butte Trail was littered with debris; route-finding skills essential

**Scenery:** Dense woods with almost no distant views

**Special comments:** What Laurie calls a boy's ride; carry your bike a lot, get lost, exhausted at half-way point, and afterward—brag to friends about great ride

Copple Butte Trail is a seldom traveled single-track in north central Oregon. It is in the Heppner Ranger District of the Umatilla National Forest. The region is a veritable mecca for elk hunters, who probably follow this trail the most. Actually, we wondered if Copple Butte Trail didn't get more traffic from elk than from hunters. Cow pie slalom gates kept us on our toes and indicated that the trail was also popular with cattle.

Loggers had been spending a good amount of time on Copple Butte Trail. Their work had left sections of the trail tangled with debris and crisscrossed with skid roads. We got a solid upper-body workout hefting and dragging our bikes through the wreckage. Keeping track of where the trail went was another aspect of our adventure.

In general, we spent more time on this trail than we had expected, and the trip was much harder than any map reconnaissance would have suggested. (Obviously, you can't glean details about trail conditions or the difficulty of a particular route from a map, but we found ourselves trying.) Luckily, we were riding Copple Butte Trail on a Sunday. The loggers had the day off, so we weren't breathing diesel exhaust or hearing shouts of *timber!* We found that the trail conditions improved as we got deeper into the route. The trail was in good shape and fun to ride on after the first several miles.

Perhaps conditions will have improved by the time you make a trip into this neck of the woods. We've detailed some "hell ride" experiences in other books, only to have our descriptions called into question. Now and then, someone comes along and asks us why we panned their favorite single-track. The ranger

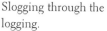
Slogging through the logging.

district is planning to make repairs to Copple Butte Trail, but call ahead and find out if they have been completed. For now, we'll say this ride ain't half bad.

This out-and-back trip is 16 miles long (8 miles each way). It is a rather long ride with a good deal of moderately difficult climbing. We found the ride taxing. Dense woods preclude any distant views.

**General location:** The trailhead is about 40 miles west of Ukiah.

**Elevation change:** The ride begins at 4,740' near Martin Prairie. The high point of the ride, at Copple Butte, is 5,440'. The elevation at the turnaround point is 5,120'. Ups and downs add about 1,500' of climbing to the trip. Total elevation gain: 2,520'.

**Season:** We recommend that you plan on riding here in the summer or fall. The trails in the area are often too wet for early spring riding (especially Martin Prairie Trail). If you would like to ride here in the spring, call ahead to check on the condition of the trails, and consider starting the ride at the Copple Butte Trailhead (off of Forest Service Road 5350). Wear hunter orange if you pedal here in the mid- to late fall.

# RIDE 30 · Copple Butte Trail

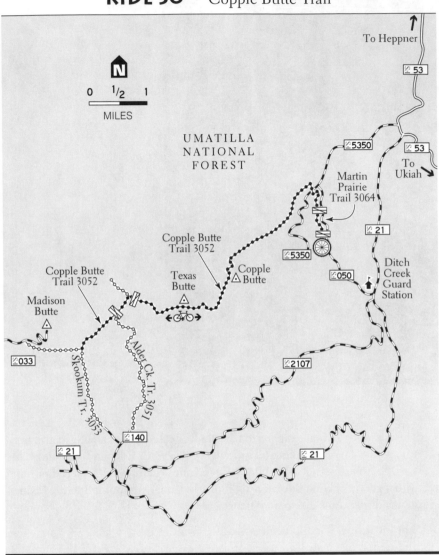

**Services:** There is no water on this ride; bring all you will need with you. You can purchase gas and limited groceries in Ukiah. All services are available in Pendleton and La Grande.

**Hazards:** Debris from logging operations may obscure obstacles in the trail. Low traffic volumes contribute to the accumulation of forest litter on areas of the trail not impacted by logging.

**Rescue index:** You can summon help in Ukiah.

**Land status:** Umatilla National Forest.

**Maps:** We recommend that you carry the district map of the Heppner Ranger District. It is the best map for this ride, but its depiction of Copple Butte Trail is incomplete. USGS 7.5 minute quads: Madison Butte, Arbuckle Mountain, and Summerfield Ridge.

**Finding the trail:** At the intersection of OR 244 and US 395 (1 mile west of Ukiah), head west on paved FS 53. In 23 miles, turn left onto gravel FS 21. Drive 3.3 miles to FS 050 on the right. Turn onto FS 050 (a rough narrow road). Immediately pass Ditch Creek Guard Station (on the right). The road ends in about 0.5 mile; there is enough room to park a few vehicles here. Pull well off of the road—do not block the road or the gate at the end of the road. Backtrack and park farther away from the trailhead if all available parking is taken (not a likely scenario, unless it's hunting season).

## Source of additional information:

Heppner Ranger District
P.O. Box 7
Heppner, OR 97836
(541) 676-9187

**Notes on the trail:** Finding your way on Copple Butte Trail may be a challenge. In the fall of 1997, the first few miles of the trail were in disrepair from logging operations. Carry the recommended map and a compass.

Go through the barbed wire gate at the end of FS 050. (Leave gates as you find them—close them behind you if they were closed.) Follow the faint double-track (Martin Prairie Trail 3064) through the meadow. Go through another barbed wire gate in 0.5 mile, then bear right in 0.2 mile onto a sandy double-track. Turn left when you arrive at a more substantial road (at a sign on the left, facing away from you, for Martin Prairie). You soon come to a **T** intersection at a major road (unsigned FS 5350) and another sign for Martin Prairie. Turn left onto FS 5350, then immediately turn right to access Copple Butte Trailhead. Here, at the time of our visit, the trail had been completely rubbed out. If repairs have been made, follow Copple Butte Trail 3052. If not, go straight up the hill, following a skid road that climbs to the west-southwest. Turn left (south) onto a faint, overgrown trail at the top of the hill. You are now on Copple Butte Trail. The single-track enters another logging operation after about 1 mile. (Again, the trail was gone.) Continue straight through the disruption to a wire fence. Turn left to parallel the fence. This will bring you to a gate and back to the trail. Pass through the gate to continue on Copple Butte Trail (now marked by light-gray, diamond-shaped markers attached to trees). Arrive at a road in 0.3 mile, turn right, then immediately left to regain the trail. Here, Copple Butte Trail climbs steeply through the woods, then passes through another logging operation. You come to a road and an old clear-cut at the far end of the logging operation (these landmarks are 0.6 mile from the last road crossing). Cross the road and enter the clear-cut. The trail stays to the left-hand side of the clear-cut and reenters the woods on the far side of the clearing.

From this point on, Copple Butte Trail was unaffected by ongoing logging operations. The trail travels through dense woods for 0.7 mile to signed Copple Butte. It is another mile to signed Texas Butte. The trail is overgrown with grass at Texas Butte. To find the trail, head south from a sign that reads "Texas Butte." Pick up the trail at a tree marked with a light-gray diamond. Soon you will come to another open area on a hillside. The trail fades out again. Look for a tall evergreen tree (with a dead top) marked with a gray diamond; regain the trail near this tree. Ride 1.2 miles to an intersection of trails at some tank traps and a barbed-wire gate. Go through the gate and turn left to follow the trail uphill. In 0.5 mile you will reach another gate at a signed intersection. Continue straight (right) to remain on Copple Butte Trail. In 1 mile you will come to the intersection of Copple Butte Trail and Skookum Trail. Turn around and return the way you came.

We turned around at the intersection of Copple Butte Trail and Skookum Trail. A look at the district map shows Copple Butte Trail continuing west from our turnaround point toward Madison Butte. A recreation opportunity guide for Copple Butte Trail (available from the Heppner Ranger District) indicates that there are good views from Madison Butte. Skookum Trail and nearby Madison Butte Trail are delineated on the district map and they are described briefly in district R.O.G.s. These and other area trails may be of interest to intrepid mountain bicyclists.

## RIDE 31 · Mt. Fanny

**AT A GLANCE**

**Length/configuration:** 21-mile combination on single-track and gravel roads; 9.4-mile loop and 11.6-mile out-and-back (5.8 miles each way)

**Aerobic difficulty:** A tough ride that gains over 2,700' of elevation

**Technical difficulty:** Difficult; some steep, rocky climbs and descents

**Scenery:** Some views into Eagle Cap Wilderness and Grande Ronde Valley

**Special comments:** These single-tracks are prone to windfalls; call ahead with inquiries about trail conditions

Planning a trip to northeastern Oregon? The La Grande Chamber of Commerce has something you may find interesting. Area agencies and bike groups have joined forces to put together a package of recommended cycling routes. The packet is entitled "Northeast Oregon See and Do Adventures." It contains detailed descriptions of four mountain bike rides and four road bike routes in Union County. Each ride is depicted separately in a slim (fits easily into your jersey pocket), shiny (won't disintegrate when damp) pamphlet. You can pick them up at the La Grande Chamber of Commerce or at local bike shops.

Of the four mountain bike routes offered, we chose to explore Mt. Fanny. The trip is demanding, and there are limited views of the Grande Ronde Valley and the Eagle Cap Wilderness from Forest Service Road 6220. Strong intermediate cyclists and expert riders will appreciate this 21-mile trip. It consists of a 9.4-mile loop and an 11.6-mile out-and-back spur (5.8 miles each way).

Most of the riding is on dirt and gravel roads in fair to good condition. The single-track (5.7 miles) varies in its condition. When we did this ride (in the fall of 1997) Indian Creek Trail was strewn with windfalls. It also passed through some boggy spots and included a couple of steep rocky stretches (walk or carry your bike through these sensitive areas). We have been told that the trail has since been cleared of downed trees, and that it will receive ongoing maintenance. Bell Creek Trail is a popular ORV route. It is in good shape with lots of roots in its tread. We enjoyed climbing up this challenging trail. Another highlight was a rapid, but bumpy, descent on FS 6220 back to the trailhead. Hold on tight!

**General location:** The trailhead is located approximately 23 miles east of La Grande.

**Elevation change:** The ride begins at 5,840'. The high point of the ride (6,910') is reached after a little more than 4 miles of pedaling. The low point of the trip is 5,630'. It occurs at the intersection of Indian Creek Trail and Bell Creek Trail. Ups and downs along the route add about 400' of climbing to the outing. Total elevation gain: 2,750'.

**Season:** The best time to ride here is in August and September. The trails have dried out, the bugs are less intense, and hunting season has yet to begin.

**Services:** Gas and limited groceries can be found in Cove. All services are available in La Grande.

**Hazards:** There is one particularly rough section of downhill on Indian Creek Trail. It is steep, rocky, and ditch-like; walk your bike down. Watch for vehicular traffic and other recreationists on the roads and trails. Be especially careful when descending back to the trailhead on FS 6220. The road is rough with rocks, and it contains some blind corners.

**Rescue index:** You may be able to obtain emergency assistance at Moss Springs Campground (near the trailhead). The nearest pay phone is in Cove. Emergency services are located in La Grande.

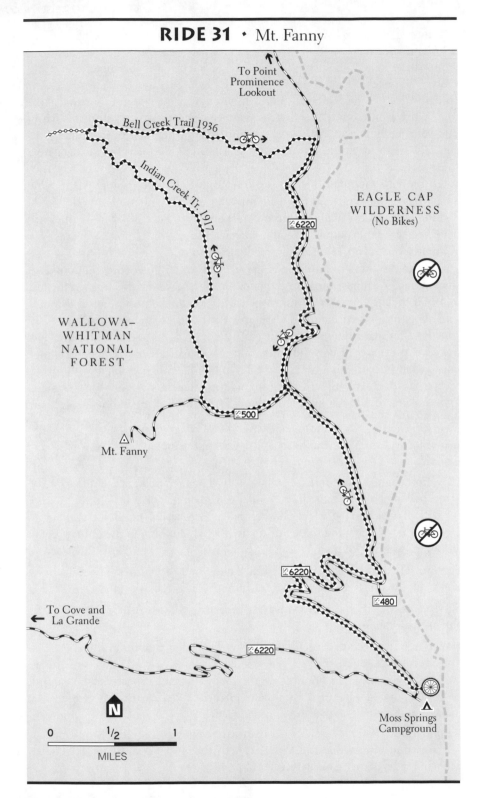

Top of Bell Creek Trail.

**Land status:** Wallowa-Whitman National Forest.

**Maps:** The district map for the La Grande Ranger District is a good guide to this ride. The "Northeast Oregon See and Do Adventures" packet contains a pamphlet describing this and other area rides. USGS 7.5 minute quad: Mt. Fanny.

**Finding the trail:** From La Grande, follow OR 82 east for 1.5 miles to Island City. Continue straight at the stoplight onto OR 237 toward Cove. Drive 13.5 miles to Cove. In Cove, turn left onto French Street (at the church, across from the high school). Follow this road (it becomes a gravel road) for 8.6 miles to Moss Springs Campground on the right. Drive past the campground entrance and take the next left at a sign for Loree's Corral and Moss Creek Campground. Here, park on the right at the start of unsigned FS 6220.

**Sources of additional information:**

La Grande Ranger District
3502 Highway 30
La Grande, OR 97850
(541) 963-7186

La Grande/Union County Chamber of Commerce
1912 Fourth Street, Suite #200
La Grande, OR 97850
(800) 848-9969

**Notes on the trail:** From the trailhead, ride up unsigned FS 6220. After 4 miles the climbing gets easier and there are views on the right into the Eagle Cap Wilderness (just beyond a faint intersection where FS 480 goes right). It is about 2 miles from this landmark to FS 500 (there are signs pointing left for "KTVR Transmitter" and "Mt. Fanny"). Turn left onto FS 500. After 1 mile (at a low point in the road), turn right onto Indian Creek Trail 1917. (Trail 1917 is marked with a yellow survey marker and a sign that reads "This trail open to hiking and mountain biking.") The first mile of Trail 1917 goes through the Indian Creek Natural Research Area. There are some boggy, fragile areas here; please stay on the trail, walking or carrying your bike through these sections. Reach a **T** intersection after 3.3 miles on Indian Creek Trail. Here, turn right onto Bell Creek Trail 1936. In 2.4 miles, arrive at unsigned FS 6220. Turn right and follow this road back to the trailhead.

A side trip to Point Prominence Lookout provides outstanding views into the Eagle Cap Wilderness and adds 4.6 miles to this ride. At the intersection of Bell Creek Trail 1936 and FS 6220, turn left and pedal 2 miles to FS 800. Turn right onto FS 800 and ride to the lookout. (FS 800 is a very rough road; we stashed our bikes in the woods and walked to the lookout.) Call out to the person manning the lookout and ask if you can climb up to take in the view. Return down FS 800 and turn left onto FS 6220. Follow FS 6220 back to your car.

## RIDE 32 · Point Prominence

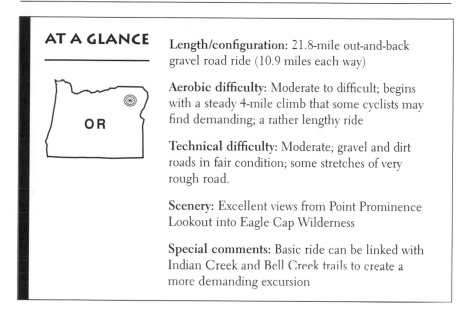

**AT A GLANCE**

**OR**

**Length/configuration:** 21.8-mile out-and-back gravel road ride (10.9 miles each way)

**Aerobic difficulty:** Moderate to difficult; begins with a steady 4-mile climb that some cyclists may find demanding; a rather lengthy ride

**Technical difficulty:** Moderate; gravel and dirt roads in fair condition; some stretches of very rough road.

**Scenery:** Excellent views from Point Prominence Lookout into Eagle Cap Wilderness

**Special comments:** Basic ride can be linked with Indian Creek and Bell Creek trails to create a more demanding excursion

If you arrive in La Grande only to find that the trails in the area are too wet to ride, this road trip is a good option. It's a moderately difficult, 21.8-mile out-and-back route (10.9 miles each way). The length of the ride and the road conditions (rough at times) make it best suited to intermediate and advanced riders. Strong, energetic beginners can attempt the route and turn around if they find it too demanding.

Most of this trip is on Forest Service Road 6220. The first four miles of FS 6220 are in fair condition with some areas where the tread is composed of large, loose gravel. This is not much of a problem while climbing, but it makes the return descent a little sketchy. After climbing for four miles, FS 6220 gains a ridge to traverse over rolling terrain. Here, the riding surface is smooth, if somewhat sandy in places; more of a compacted dirt, four-wheel-drive road. A short spur road, FS 800, branches off of FS 6220 and leads out to Point Prominence Lookout. This road is composed of fist-sized rocks that make travel by bicycle extremely difficult. We parked our bikes at the bottom of this road and hiked to the lookout.

Give a shout to the person manning the lookout and ask if you can climb up. The view from the top into the Eagle Cap Wilderness is outstanding.

**General location:** The trailhead is approximately 23 miles east of La Grande.

**Elevation change:** The ride begins at 5,840' and reaches a high point of 6,745' at Point Prominence Lookout. Ups and downs on the route add an estimated 300' of elevation to the outing. Total elevation gain: 1,205'.

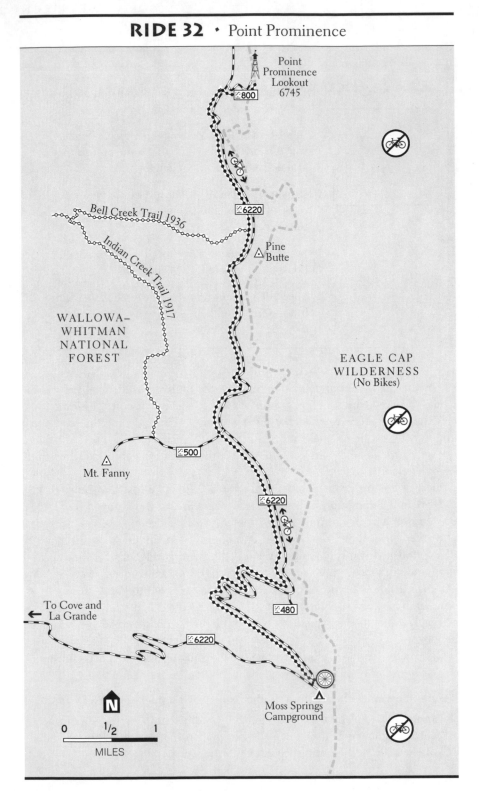

Point
Prominence
Lookout
6745

△800

△6220

Bell Creek Trail 1936

Indian Creek Trail 1917

Pine
Butte

WALLOWA–
WHITMAN
NATIONAL
FOREST

EAGLE CAP
WILDERNESS
(No Bikes)

△500

Mt. Fanny

△6220

To Cove and
La Grande

△480

△6220

N

0    1/2    1

MILES

Moss Springs
Campground

Eagle Cap Wilderness from Point Prominence Lookout.

**Season:** This is a good summertime ride, but you can ride here from the spring through the fall. Insects can be a nuisance in the spring, and traffic from hunters can make the area rather busy in the late fall.

**Services:** There is no water on this ride. Bring all you will require with you. Gas and limited groceries can be obtained in Cove. All services are available in La Grande.

**Hazards:** There are some blind corners and areas of coarse, loose gravel on the roads. Watch for traffic and control your speed on the return descent.

**Rescue index:** You may be able to obtain help in an emergency at Moss Springs Campground (near the trailhead). The nearest pay phone is in Cove. Emergency services are located in La Grande.

**Land status:** Wallowa-Whitman National Forest.

**Maps:** The district map for the La Grande Ranger District is a good guide to this ride. USGS 7.5 minute quad: Mt. Fanny.

**Finding the trail:** From La Grande, follow OR 82 east for 1.5 miles to Island City. Continue straight at the stoplight onto OR 237 toward Cove. Drive 13.5 miles to Cove. In Cove, turn left onto French Street (at the church, across from the high school). Follow this paved road (it soon turns to gravel) for 8.6 miles to Moss Springs Campground on the right. Drive past the campground entrance and take the next left at a sign for Loree's Corral and Moss Creek Campground. Here, park on the right at the start of unsigned FS 6220.

**Source of additional information:**

La Grande Ranger District
3502 Highway 30
La Grande, OR 97850
(541) 963-7186

**Notes on the trail:** From the trailhead, ride up unsigned FS 6220. Stay on this main road for 10.6 miles to FS 800 on the right. (You will pass FS 500 after 5.8 miles, and Bell Creek Trail after pedaling a total of 8.6 miles.) Hide your bike in the woods and walk up FS 800 to the lookout. Return the way you came.

For a longer, more demanding ride, combine this trip with Indian Creek and Bell Creek trails. For connections, see "Notes on the trail" for Mt. Fanny (Ride 31).

## RIDE 33 · Tenderfoot Wagon Trail

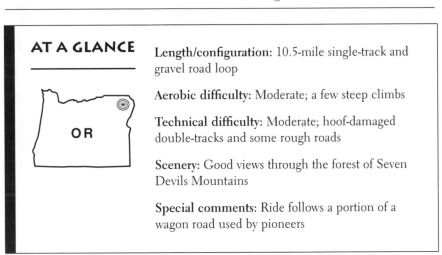

**AT A GLANCE**

OR

**Length/configuration:** 10.5-mile single-track and gravel road loop

**Aerobic difficulty:** Moderate; a few steep climbs

**Technical difficulty:** Moderate; hoof-damaged double-tracks and some rough roads

**Scenery:** Good views through the forest of Seven Devils Mountains

**Special comments:** Ride follows a portion of a wagon road used by pioneers

This 10.5-mile loop is moderately difficult. Tenderfoot Wagon Trail climbs steeply at first, but gets easier as it contours up the hillside. The trail contains some bumpy, hoof-damaged segments. The circuit drops rapidly for 0.4 mile on Big Sheep Cutoff Trail, then continues to descend for 2.4 miles on a rough gravel road. Next, a short pedal on pavement brings you to Forest Service Road 023. This double-track climbs (at times steeply) back to the trailhead at Salt Creek Summit. FS 023 is in poor condition, with rocky and soft stretches.

This ride follows a 3.6-mile segment of the Tenderfoot Wagon Trail; it is well maintained and amply signed. The trail travels through an area devastated by the 1989 Canal Burn, a lightning-caused fire that ravaged a huge portion of the Wallowa-Whitman Forest. There are good views from the path of the Seven

Riding through the
canal burn.

Devils Mountains in Idaho. Early pioneers used this route and installed more
than three miles of "corduroy"—logs laid side by side to span boggy areas.
Remnants of this wooden roadbed can still be seen today.

**General location:** Salt Creek Summit is located approximately 18 miles southeast of Joseph.

**Elevation change:** The loop begins at 6,000' and climbs to a high point of
6,400' in the first 3 miles. A low point of 5,400' occurs where FS 023 crosses Big
Sheep Creek. Ups and downs add an estimated 300' of climbing to the ride.
Total elevation gain: 1,300'.

**Season:** The route is generally free of snow from June through October. Parts of
Tenderfoot Wagon Trail may be boggy, especially in the spring.

**Services:** There is no potable water on the ride. All services are available in
Joseph.

**Hazards:** Portions of Tenderfoot Wagon Trail are obscured by tall grasses. Ruts
and remnants of the corduroy are hidden from view; these obstacles can launch
an unsuspecting cyclist right off the bike. Watch for traffic on the roads. The left

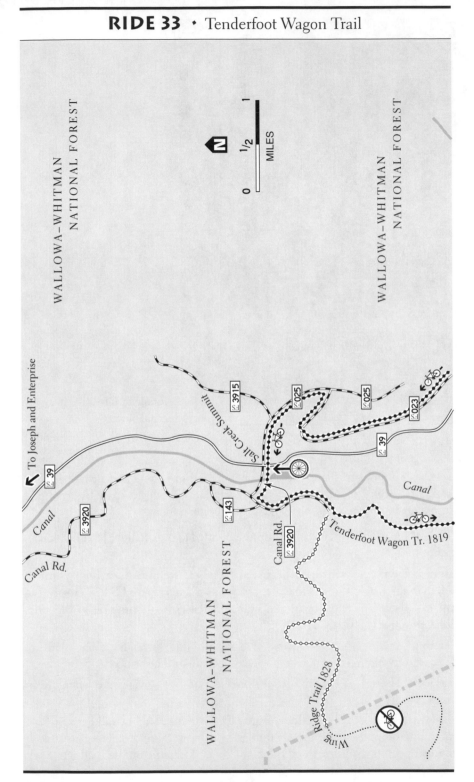

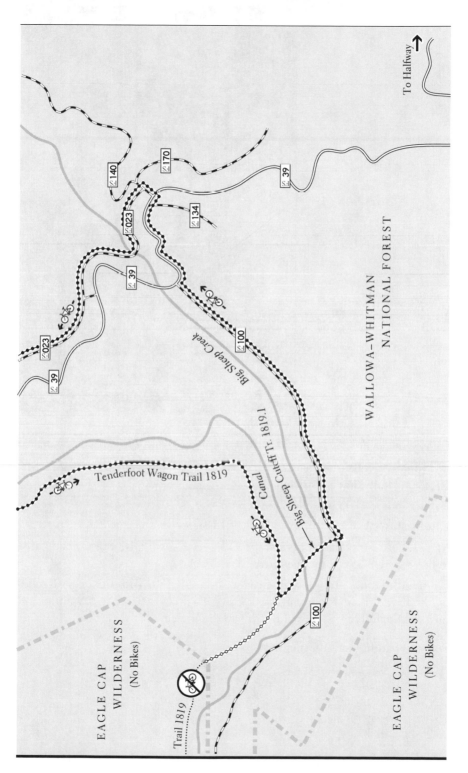

Tenderfoot.

turn onto FS 140 from paved FS 39 should be approached with caution—oncoming traffic has a restricted view.

**Rescue index:** Help is available in Joseph.

**Land status:** Wallowa-Whitman National Forest.

**Maps:** The district map for the Wallowa Valley Ranger District is a good guide to this ride. USGS 7.5 minute quad: Lick Creek.

**Finding the trail:** From Joseph, head east on OR 350. Turn right after 8 miles onto FS 39/Wallowa Mountain Road. Drive 9.5 miles to Salt Creek Summit and turn right onto FS 3920/Canal Road. Park on the left.

**Source of additional information:**

Wallowa Valley Ranger District
88401 Highway 82
Enterprise, OR 97828
(541) 426-5546 (Visitors Center)
(541) 426-4978

**Notes on the trail:** From the parking area, turn left to cross the bridge over the canal. Continue straight (left) up road-like Tenderfoot Wagon Trail 1819. Continue straight where indistinct FS 143 goes right. Cross a boggy area and arrive at a **Y** intersection where Tenderfoot Wagon Road goes left and Wing Ridge Trail 1828 goes right. Turn left, following the sign for Tenderfoot Wagon Road. Turn left when you reach Big Sheep Cutoff Trail 1819.1. Cross three bridges over Big Sheep Creek and pass a corral before turning left onto FS 100. FS 100 deposits you at paved FS 39. Turn right and descend on FS 39 for 0.5 mile to FS 140, a dangerous intersection on the left. FS 140 is hard to see—look for it after passing FS 134 (on the right). Turn left onto FS 140 and immediately turn left onto FS 023. (FS 023 is easy to miss; you have gone too far if you come to FS 170 on the right.) Follow the rough road past the boulders that block access to this portion of the road. Descend and then swing hard to the right; crossing the bridge over Big Sheep Creek. Push your bike across the clearing and turn right when you arrive at the road. Climb steeply to a road that comes in from the left (it accesses FS 39). Bear right to remain on FS 023. Stay on the main road where another road comes in from the left. You will come to a **T** intersection in 2.2 miles. Turn left onto FS 025. Follow the main road (stay left) to FS 39 at Salt Creek Summit. Cross the paved road to reach your vehicle.

## RIDE 34 · Sugarloaf/Deadman Trails

| **AT A GLANCE** | **Length/configuration:** 6.7-mile single-track and gravel road loop |
|---|---|
| **OR** | **Aerobic difficulty:** Moderate, with a steep, 1.2-mile climb to a lookout |
| | **Technical difficulty:** Tough; rocks and roots lie in wait |
| | **Scenery:** Panoramic view of Eagle Cap Wilderness and the Wallowa Mountains from Russel Mountain Lookout |
| | **Special comments:** Bone up on your bike-handling skills with a round of "Dodge the Cow Patties" |

Cow Poop Loop.

We nicknamed this 6.7-mile ride "Cow Poop Loop." Much of the route follows dusty, hoof-worn cow paths through woods and grassy meadows. Technical, rocky ups and downs will have all but superheroes dabbing.

The trip begins with three miles of gravel roads. A quick descent leads into an easy to moderately difficult climb on Forest Service Road 66—the road is in good condition. The climbing becomes moderately difficult to steep on degraded FS 450. This pull lasts for 1.2 miles and ends at the Russel Mountain Lookout. Climb up the tower for a panoramic view of the surrounding countryside. Prominent to the north are snow-capped peaks in the Eagle Cap Wilderness. To the east are Hells Canyon and the distant Seven Devils. Badlands-like scenery stretches out to the south. Fish Lake lies to the southwest, the Wallowa Mountains to the west.

**General location:** The ride begins near Fish Lake, approximately 20 miles north of Halfway. (The small town of Halfway is a remote community in northeastern Oregon. It is east of Baker City; near the Snake River and the Wallowa Mountains.)

**Elevation gain:** The loop starts at 6,800' and quickly drops to the low point of the ride—6,720'. Russel Mountain, at 7,487', is the high point of the trip. Undulations on the circuit add about 100' of climbing to the loop. Total elevation gain: 867'.

**Season:** Snow may linger at higher elevations into the late spring. The meadows often remain boggy until later in the summer. The fall is an excellent time for visiting the region.

# RIDE 34 · Sugarloaf/Deadman Trails

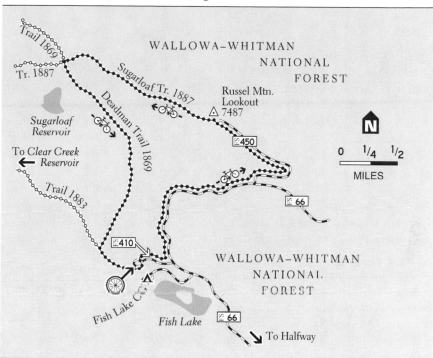

**Services:** There is no water on this ride. Water, food, gas, lodging, pay phones, and limited groceries are available in Halfway.

**Hazards:** Treacherous rocks and roots are encountered on this ride. Control your speed and watch for loose gravel and rocks while descending. You may encounter traffic on the roads.

**Rescue index:** Help is available in Halfway.

**Land status:** Wallowa-Whitman National Forest.

**Maps:** The district map of the Pine Ranger District is a good guide to this ride. USGS 7.5 minute quads: Deadman and Cornucopia.

**Finding the trail:** From the main intersection in downtown Halfway, follow OR 413 (East Pine Road) north through town. Turn right in 0.4 mile onto County Road 1009 (the sign points right to Fish Lake). Turn left onto gravel CR 999 after 3.2 miles (a sign points left to Fish Lake). Follow this road (FS 66, once it enters the national forest) for 16.2 miles; you will pass Fish Lake Campground on the left. Drive 0.1 mile past the entrance to Fish Lake Campground and turn left onto FS 410. Proceed to the end of the road, where there is a parking area for Deadman Canyon.

**Source of additional information:**

Pine Ranger District
General Delivery
Halfway, OR 97834
(541) 742-7511

**Notes on the trail:** Ride back down the road and turn left onto FS 66. Follow this main road to the crest of a hill and turn left onto FS 450. The Russel Mountain Lookout Tower stands at the end of FS 450. Continue straight onto the single-track (unsigned Sugarloaf Trail 1887). The trail descends to a large alpine meadow. Continue in a northwesterly direction across the meadow. The path fades in and out — look for the wooden posts that mark the trail. The route becomes obvious again at the western end of the clearing. Climb up the hill to reenter the woods. Shortly, you arrive at another meadow and a **T** intersection with a sign for Sugarloaf Trail. Turn left and follow the cow path down the draw (you are now on unsigned Deadman Trail 1869). Stay downhill on the main trail. You will pass a couple of signs — one for Sugarloaf Trail and one for Sugarloaf Reservoir. Soon the path reenters the woods and takes you through more rocky areas and meadows. At the intersection where a trail goes right, toward Clear Creek Reservoir, continue straight (left). The trail becomes a rough road that drops steeply. Pass around the gate near the bottom of the hill, and turn left to reach your vehicle.

You can add 6 miles to your ride with a side trip to Clear Creek Reservoir.

## RIDE 35 · Horse Lake/Buck's Crossing

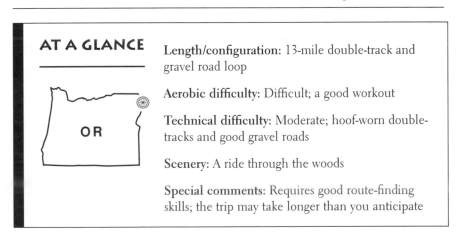

**AT A GLANCE**

**Length/configuration:** 13-mile double-track and gravel road loop

**Aerobic difficulty:** Difficult; a good workout

**Technical difficulty:** Moderate; hoof-worn double-tracks and good gravel roads

**Scenery:** A ride through the woods

**Special comments:** Requires good route-finding skills; the trip may take longer than you anticipate

OR

This is a 13-mile loop for strong intermediate and advanced cyclists. It is not a scenic trip, but it is a good workout. Horse Lake and Buck's Crossing trails are hoof-worn double-tracks used mostly by cattle and equestrians. Gravel roads account for about one-third of the circuit, and they are in good shape. Finding your way on this route is a challenge; at one point the trail fades away completely. The loop includes steep climbs and descents.

**General location:** This ride starts at Fish Lake, approximately 20 miles north of Halfway. (Halfway is a remote, small town in northeastern Oregon.)

**Elevation change:** The ride begins at 6,660' and climbs to a high point of 6,960' at the intersection of Forest Service Road 66 and FS 450. From here, the route descends to a low point of 5,600' at Lake Fork Creek. The route then climbs back to 6,720'. Undulations on the trip add about 300' of climbing to the excursion. Total elevation gain: 1,720'.

**Season:** It is possible to ride here from the late spring through the fall. The trails are less dusty early in the riding season.

**Services:** There is no potable water on the ride. Water, food, gas, lodging, pay phones, and limited groceries are available in Halfway.

**Hazards:** Loose rocks and soft soil are common on the roads and single-track trails. There are some steep descents that are very rocky—walk your bike down. Watch for cars on the forest roads.

**Rescue index:** Help is available in Halfway.

**Land status:** Wallowa-Whitman National Forest.

**Maps:** The district map for the Pine Ranger District is a good guide to this route. USGS 7.5 minute quad: Deadman Point.

**Finding the trail:** From the main intersection in downtown Halfway, follow OR 413 (East Pine Road) north through town. Turn right in 0.4 mile onto County Road 1009 (the sign points right to Fish Lake). Turn left onto gravel CR 999 after 3.2 miles (a sign points left to Fish Lake). Follow this road for 16.2 miles to Fish Lake Campground, on the left. (The road's designation changes to FS 66 where it enters the national forest.) Turn left into the campground. Park on the left side of the entrance road, across from the vault toilets.

## Source of additional information:

Pine Ranger District
General Delivery
Halfway, OR 97834
(541) 742-7511

**Notes on the trail:** Due to the number of unsigned intersections found on this loop, a bicycle odometer is recommended for this ride. All mileage notes in the description below are cumulative.

Ride out of the campground and turn left onto FS 66. In 2.4 miles, turn right onto FS 475. Follow this rough new road a short distance to its end at a blazed trail. Follow this trail into the woods and to the right. Turn left when the trail ends at an old double-track (2.6 miles). You are now on unsigned Horse Lake Trail 1873. Stay to the right at the next **Y** intersection (3.6 miles). Continue

Horse Lake Trail.

straight and downhill at the signs for Horse Lake and Buck's Crossing trails (5.8 miles). You will soon come upon Horse Lake Cow Camp, where you will see a couple of log structures. If you ride into the center of camp you have gone too far. As you approach the buildings, look to the right for the trail—it passes between two halves of a sawn log at 6.1 miles. Bear right and follow this trail south along dry Horse Lake. At the south end of the lake, the trail gets very rocky and starts to veer to the left. Look for a faint trail to the right at 6.3 miles. Turn onto this trail and descend through a boulder field. Walk your bike down a couple of steep rocky pitches and out onto a hillside where several cow paths branch off. Below you is a large open area with two signs on a post. Choose whichever cow path looks most desirable and descend to the signpost. The signs are at 6.5 miles and mark Buck's Crossing and Lake Fork trails. Continue straight (toward Little Elk Road) and cross Lake Fork Creek. The trail fades out on the other side of the creek. Climb the hillside, bearing left on a faint cow path. You reenter open woods as you ascend higher, then you arrive at a canal at 6.6 miles. Get your feet wet crossing the canal and continue to push your bike up the pathless hillside. Go up steeply, bearing left a little. You will come to a double-track at 6.8 miles; turn left onto it. This double-track passes through

# RIDE 35 • Horse Lake/Buck's Crossing

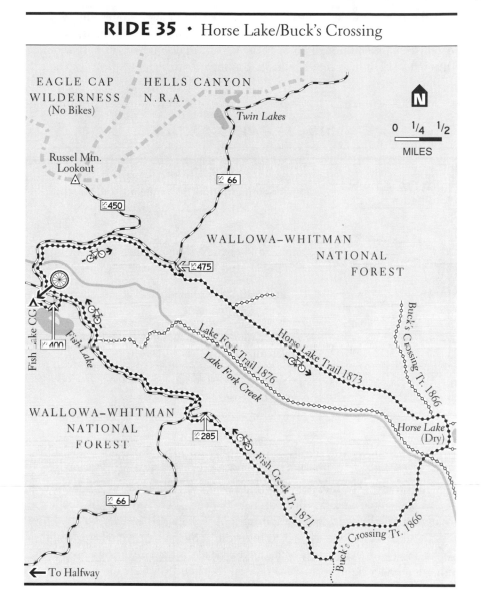

heavier woods and through open areas and crosses several creeks. Buck's Crossing Trail is signed at 7.5 miles. Continue on the now faint double-track; soon the trail begins to climb and crosses more creeks. At the next open area (8.2 miles), you will pass another sign for Buck's Crossing Trail. Bear to the right to go through a gate in a barbed-wire fence. Go left and steeply uphill after passing through the gate, until you reach a double-track. A sign at this road denotes Fish Creek Trail 1871 and points right for FS 66. Turn right and climb. The riding gets more demanding and the scenery gets prettier. Go through many more barbed-wire gates, following the main road. Turn left at 9.9 miles onto a more traveled double-track. Cross a crude bridge over a creek at 10.4 miles, then follow the main road through an open area. Turn right onto FS 66 at 10.6 miles. Turn left at 12.9 miles into Fish Lake Campground.

## RIDE 36 · WINDY RIDGE

**AT A GLANCE**

OR

**Length/configuration:** 17.8-mile out-and-back on single-track, double-track, and gravel roads (8.9 miles each way)

**Aerobic difficulty:** Moderate to difficult; many ups and downs

**Technical difficulty:** Moderate to advanced; varied road and trail conditions

**Scenery:** Wonderful vistas across and into Hells Canyon and Imnaha River Canyon

**Special comments:** A wonderful place that is not easily accessed—thank goodness

Windy Ridge is a 17.8-mile out-and-back trip suited to strong intermediate and advanced cyclists. It is a great ride, with wonderful views and good single-track cycling. The outing begins on the edge of Hells Canyon along Summit Ridge. There are some excellent vistas to the east. The Seven Devils feel close enough to touch, and there are glimpses of the Snake River far below. From Windy Ridge Trail, your view is to the west of Sleepy Ridge and the Wallowa Mountains. The scenery gets better as you head north. The grassy slopes at the turnaround offer sightings into the layered Imnaha River Canyon.

The first 1.6 miles twist and turn over Summit Ridge Trail. Summit Ridge Trail is a double-track that passes through a burned-out "matchstick forest." The road gets rougher and rockier as it rolls up and down along Summit Ridge. Next comes Windy Ridge Trail, an old road that is closed to motorized vehicles. The trail is about half single-track and half double-track. Trail conditions vary. Some stretches are rocky, hoof-worn, and rooty; some segments are great. There are some steep climbs, but the majority of the ascents are only moderately difficult. The return trip is more demanding.

The ride is hard to get to. Hat Point Road begins in Imnaha and climbs the cliffs of the Imnaha River Canyon. The road is steep—especially the first four miles. The roads are in good shape, except for the last few miles, where high

# RIDE 36 · Windy Ridge

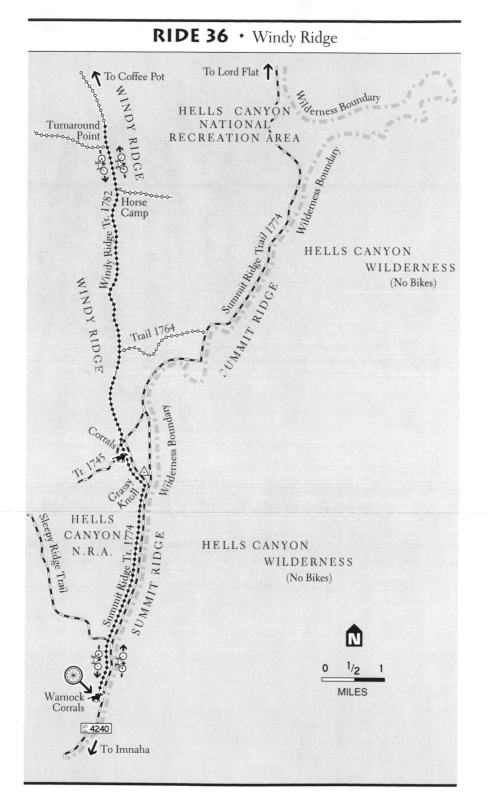

To Coffee Pot

WINDY RIDGE

Turnaround
Point

Windy Ridge Tr. 1782

Horse
Camp

WINDY RIDGE

Trail 1764

Corrals

Tr. 1745

Grassy
Knoll

Wilderness Boundary

Sleepy Ridge Trail

HELLS
CANYON
N.R.A.

Summit Ridge Tr. 1774

SUMMIT RIDGE

Warnock
Corrals

4240

To Imnaha

To Lord Flat

Wilderness Boundary

HELLS CANYON
NATIONAL
RECREATION AREA

Wilderness Boundary

Summit Ridge Trail 1774

SUMMIT RIDGE

HELLS CANYON
WILDERNESS
(No Bikes)

HELLS CANYON
WILDERNESS
(No Bikes)

N

0   1/2   1
MILES

Imnaha River Canyon
from Windy Ridge Trail.

clearance is recommended. The return drive down Hat Point Road is extremely hard on brakes. At some point during your visit, climb the lookout at Hat Point—the view is top-drawer.

**General location:** Warnock Corrals are approximately 25 miles southeast of Imnaha. (Imnaha is a sleepy little town in northeastern Oregon, northeast of Joseph and near Hells Canyon.)

**Elevation change:** The ride begins at 6,720' and rolls up and down to reach a low point of 5,840' at the turnaround point. Undulations on the route add an estimated 800' of climbing to the trip. Total elevation gain: 1,680'.

**Season:** The relatively high elevation and remoteness of the ride combine to make this a good summer trip. The early fall (before hunting season) is a quiet time on these ridges.

**Services:** There is no water on the ride. Bring all you will need for your stay in the Hells Canyon National Recreation Area. Gas and limited supplies can be found in Imnaha. All services are available in Joseph.

**Hazards:** Trail hazards include roots, rocks, soft spots, steep drop-offs, tall grass, and bumpy sections. The roads can be soft and contain areas of rocks and ruts. Watch for traffic on the roads.

**Rescue index:** There is a pay phone in Imnaha. Emergency services are available in Enterprise.

**Land status:** Hells Canyon National Recreation Area, Wallowa-Whitman National Forest.

**Maps:** The district map for the Hells Canyon National Recreation Area is a good guide to this ride. USGS 7.5 minute quad: Sleepy Ridge.

**Finding the trail:** In Imnaha, continue straight onto Forest Service Road 4240/Hat Point Road where Lower Imnaha Road goes left. Follow this main road for 20.9 miles to the intersection with FS 315 (the spur road to Hat Point Lookout) on the right. Stay to the left and drive another 4.2 miles on FS 4240 to Warnock Corrals. Proceed to the north end of the clearing, where the road reenters the woods and becomes a four-wheel-drive road. Park in a grassy area on the right or left.

**Source of additional information:**

Hells Canyon National Recreation Area
88401 Highway 82
Enterprise, OR 97828
(541) 426-5546 (Visitors Center)
(541) 426-4978

**Notes on the trail:** Climb up the road to enter the woods. The road's designation changes here to Summit Ridge Trail 1774. Continue straight where Sleepy Ridge Trail goes left. Turn left toward Windy Ridge at the next intersection, where Summit Ridge Trail continues straight toward Lord Flat. You are now on Windy Ridge Trail 1782. Follow the double-track for 0.7 mile to the end of the road, at some corrals. The trail becomes single-track here. You will enter a campsite in another 1.9 miles. Continue straight where Trail 1764 goes right. The path is obvious for another 2.5 miles, then it fades out near a camp and some pine trees. Find the trail by continuing straight (north) along the grassy ridge. Look for a young pine tree. The trail passes just to the right of the tree. Proceed for about 0.5 mile to a small weathered sign on the left. It is illegible except for an arrow that points west. Park your bike and walk farther north for views of the Imnaha River Canyon. Return the way you came.

# RIDE 37 · Imnaha River Trail

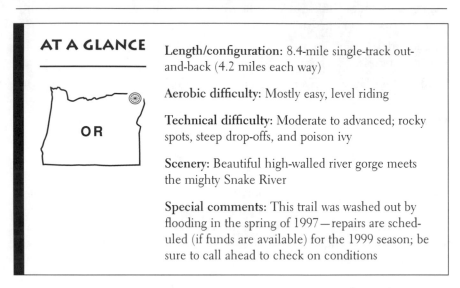

**AT A GLANCE**

**Length/configuration:** 8.4-mile single-track out-and-back (4.2 miles each way)

**Aerobic difficulty:** Mostly easy, level riding

**Technical difficulty:** Moderate to advanced; rocky spots, steep drop-offs, and poison ivy

**Scenery:** Beautiful high-walled river gorge meets the mighty Snake River

**Special comments:** This trail was washed out by flooding in the spring of 1997—repairs are scheduled (if funds are available) for the 1999 season; be sure to call ahead to check on conditions

Hells Canyon is an arid world of sun-baked, terraced rock and sagebrush. This area feels more like the Canyonlands of Utah than the Pacific Northwest. Imnaha River Trail winds through a beautiful high-walled gorge to the Snake River at Eureka Bar. Foundations and mine shafts are all that is left of the historic mining town of Eureka. Con artists created an elaborate scam to lure investors to the valueless mines. A stern-wheel riverboat was used to service the site; a fact that's hard to believe when you look at the Snake's treacherous waters.

This is an 8.4-mile out-and-back single-track ride (4.2 miles each way). The terrain is fairly level, but advanced technical skills are needed for the rocky ups and downs. There are some steep drop-offs, and brush (including lots of poison ivy) encroaches on the trail.

The journey to reach the start of this trail is as much of an adventure as the ride itself. Forest Service Road 4260 is 13 miles of rugged, one-lane gravel road. It is steep, rocky, twisty, and narrow, and has virtually no pullouts. Plan on camping—the trailhead at Cow Creek is a good location and offers excellent swimming in the Imnaha.

**General location:** Cow Creek Bridge is located approximately 20 miles north of Imnaha. (Imnaha is a tiny community in northeastern Oregon; it's northeast of Joseph, near Hells Canyon.)

**Elevation change:** The ride begins at 1,200' and reaches 900' at Eureka Bar. There are many lesser hills to climb on the way to and from the Snake River, adding about 500' of climbing to the trip. Total elevation gain: 800'.

**Season:** This is a good early and late season trip. Winters are generally mild, while summers are hot and dry. The access road to the ride, and the Imnaha River Trail should be avoided when wet.

# RIDE 37 · Imnaha River Trail

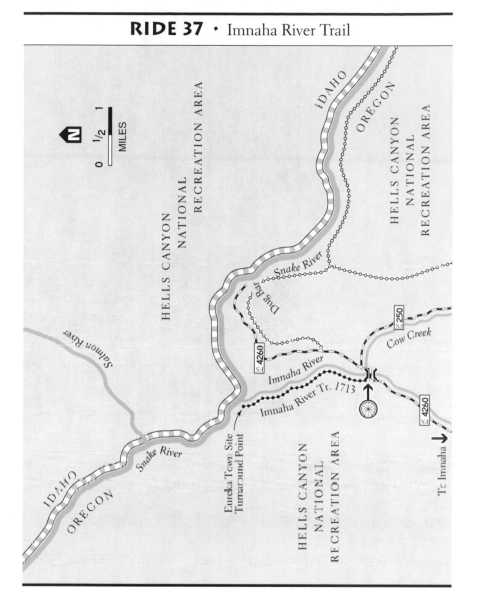

**Services:** There is no potable water here—bring all you will need. Gas and limited supplies can be found in Imnaha. All services are available in Joseph.

**Hazards:** Poison ivy thrives along the trail; there are times when touching it is unavoidable. The tread is narrow, and plant material obscures some obstacles. The trail is rocky and drops off steeply to the side in places. Thorns are a problem; use thorn-resistant tubes or a preferred antipuncture technology. Rattlesnakes are common in Hells Canyon. The drive to the trailhead is treacherous. Area rangers warn that the road can become impassable during bad weather.

Imnaha River Trail.

**Rescue index:** Be prepared for any emergency—you are a long way from assistance. The nearest pay phone is in Imnaha. Emergency services are in Enterprise.

**Land status:** Hells Canyon National Recreation Area, Wallowa-Whitman National Forest.

**Maps:** USGS 7.5 minute quads: Cactus Mountain and Deadhorse Ridge.

**Finding the trail:** Flooding in 1997 destroyed the Imnaha River Trail. Repairs are scheduled to take place in 1999 (if funds are available). Be sure to make inquiries about conditions before you go; it's a long way to drive to find that the trail is closed.

From Joseph, drive west and north on OR 350/Little Sheep Creek Highway to Imnaha (about 30 miles). In Imnaha, turn left onto Lower Imnaha Road. The pavement ends 6 miles outside of Imnaha. Follow the signs for Thorn Creek and Dug Bar (the road becomes Dug Bar Road/FS 4260 here). You will arrive at Cow Creek Bridge in 13 miles. Do not cross the bridge; instead, continue straight to reach the trail on the left. Park on the right.

**Source of additional information:**

Hells Canyon National Recreation Area
88401 Highway 82
Enterprise, OR 97828
(541) 426-5546 (Visitors Center)
(541) 426-4978

**Notes on the trail:** From the parking area, follow the path uphill to reach the signed trailhead for Imnaha River Trail 1713. Follow the single-track downstream to the confluence of the Snake and Imnaha Rivers. A rocky trail goes left toward the foundation of the Eureka Mill; you can see the mill on the hillside above the Snake. Return the way you came.

# BEND AND CENTRAL OREGON

Bend, central Oregon's largest city, is the headliner for recreation in the region. Fun-loving people come here to ski, hike, shoot rapids, and take part in more activities than you could imagine. The area's lineup of festivals, events, shindigs, and bazaars goes on and on. From rock hound powwows to bike races, from snowboard championships to classical concerts, you name it, it's celebrated here with gusto.

Nestled at the foot of the Cascades, central Oregon is a playground surrounded by natural beauty. Volcanoes have played the largest role in the shaping of the region. The remnants of eruptions that occurred over 45 million years ago dominate the landscape. These cataclysmic events deposited layer after layer of volcanic pumice and ash. We encounter these materials today as we ride the trails. When conditions are dry, the pumice in the soil gets ground into a fine powder. This material is deep like sand, but lighter. With practice, you can ride right through this thick dust. These soft conditions are less of a problem early in the season, before the soils become thoroughly dry.

Perhaps a parallel can be drawn between the quality of the bicycling in Bend and the number of bike shops in town. This place offers some great riding, and a lot of people are enjoying the trails (and keeping their mechanics busy). Bend's bike shops are top-notch. The nice folks who work at these stores are riders, and they know a ton about the biking found here. While doing some business with them, you may wish to make some inquiries about the trails in the area.

A great source of information about mountain bike opportunities in Bend is the local ranger station. It's located on US 97, the main highway through town. In 1997, at the time of our last visit, a pass was required for parking at many developed national forest trailhead facilities in Oregon. This fee program is part of a Regional Fee Demonstration Project being tested at various sites throughout the country. You can purchase a pass at the ranger station. (In 1997 the pass was good in eight national forests in Oregon and Washington.) While you're buying your pass, pick up a copy of the district mountain bike route guide, and ask about trail conditions. (We would also recommend purchasing and carrying the Bend District Map.)

Sisters is a town located 21 miles northwest of Bend. In the summer, Sisters is a busy place; it entertains visitors with its western atmosphere, big summer events, and shopping. The place is also becoming increasingly popular among mountain bikers. Like the trails near Bend, the single-track around Sisters is benefiting from the activities of local riders and the hard work of district forest rangers. Head in any direction from Sisters and you'll find excellent riding.

Broken Top, Three Sisters, Mt. Washington, and Mt. Jefferson dominate the western horizon in central Oregon. These impressive giants present themselves as you drive into the region. Ten miles northwest of Sisters is the less imposing landmark, Black Butte. Standing apart, Black Butte doesn't compete with the Cascades in height or bulk. Yet, surrounded by lower, forested lands, this dark-hued symmetrical cone is distinctly recognizable. A view of it, and one of its snow-capped neighbors, will instantly provide you with an idea of your general location. Knowing a bit about the lay of the land won't necessarily keep you from getting lost, but it could prove a handy supplement to other route-finding aids you choose to rely on (like guidebooks).

North of Black Butte is Green Ridge and the Metolius River. The Metolius is famous for its trout fishing. Green Ridge isn't famous for its mountain biking, but you will find good gravel-road riding there (and on Black Butte). A lookout tower on the ridge provides an outstanding view of the area, and the camping along the Metolius is very pleasant. A section of the Metolius-Windigo Trail surmounts Green Ridge. Cyclists considering this trail should keep in mind that it is popular with equestrians and often very soft. Other single-track options in the area include rides at nearby Suttle Lake and Cache Mountain.

Traveling west from Sisters brings you into the McKenzie District of the Willamette National Forest. The area is home to some incredible single-track pedaling. The McKenzie River National Recreation Trail is one of the finest riverside routes in the Pacific Northwest. It parallels the tumultuous river for 27 miles, stumbles past waterfalls, and tests the mettle of hardened riders.

Twenty miles to the east of Sisters is Redmond. Just a few miles north of Redmond is Smith Rock State Park. This park was created to preserve the towering red rock formations of the Crooked River Canyon. The canyon's rock spires and vertical faces are impressive. Climbers began to visit the area in the 1940s. In the last 20 years, the park has gained an international reputation among rock climbers for its demanding routes. Skilled climbers visit the park to challenge the upper limits of the sport of rock climbing, others come to sight-see, or to marvel at the gymnastic feats of others. If you visit the park, bring your bike along. While "The Rock" is not laced with mountain bike routes, a couple of good rides can be accessed from the park.

Most of the riding in Central Oregon is in the Deschutes National Forest. The ranger districts throughout the forest have done a great job developing and maintaining their respective trail networks. The involvement of private citizens has helped them get their work done. The Central Oregon Trail Alliance (COTA) is a regional mountain bike trail advocacy group that promotes responsible riding and trail access for bicyclists. This group's collaborative involvement with land management agencies has been an important factor in the ability of managers to keep trails open. COTA's commitment to volunteer trail maintenance has been a big help to forest service crews charged with keeping area trails maintained. These cooperative efforts have been realized at an opportune time; when budget cuts and belt-tightening are hitting home at ranger stations throughout the region. COTA is also involved in community education projects. They get the word out to bike riders, both young and old, that it is important to tread lightly, use common sense, and extend courtesy to others sharing the trails.

## RIDE 38 · Phil's, Jim's, and Kent's Trails

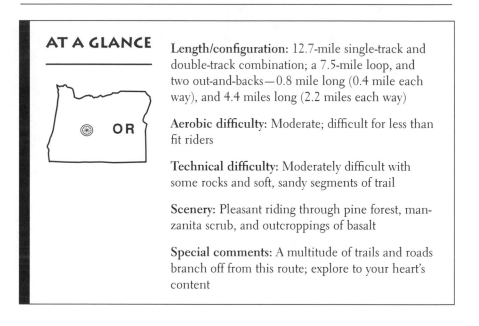

**AT A GLANCE**

**Length/configuration:** 12.7-mile single-track and double-track combination; a 7.5-mile loop, and two out-and-backs—0.8 mile long (0.4 mile each way), and 4.4 miles long (2.2 miles each way)

**Aerobic difficulty:** Moderate; difficult for less than fit riders

**Technical difficulty:** Moderately difficult with some rocks and soft, sandy segments of trail

**Scenery:** Pleasant riding through pine forest, manzanita scrub, and outcroppings of basalt

**Special comments:** A multitude of trails and roads branch off from this route; explore to your heart's content

We're impressed with the network of single-track around Bend. The trails around Bend just seem to get better all the time. Since our last visit in 1993, more trails have been developed and improvements have been made to existing trails. Local forest service rangers and the citizens of the region do a phenomenal job of working together to keep their area trails well-maintained.

Phil's Trail has long been a local favorite. It is also famous with visiting trail bicyclists. Many consider it a "must do" when in Bend. In years past, making a loop with Phil's Trail involved a good deal of double-track pedaling. Some of those road-miles have been replaced with single-track, and now several fun side trails branch off from the loop.

The ride we describe is 12.7 miles long. Strong riders will find it a moderately difficult outing. It includes a 7.5-mile loop and two out-and-back spurs. The

Basalt outcrops along Phil's Trail.

spurs are 0.8 mile out-and-back (0.4 mile each way), and 4.4 miles out-and-back (2.2 miles each way). The longer spur heads west from the far end of the loop; it follows Jim's Trail. The loop portion follows Phil's Trail, Kent's Trail, and some old double-tracks. The climbing is fun, and the trip's single-track downhills are sure to get you grinning. The single-track is in good condition with some rock obstacles and some sandy corners.

**General location:** The trailhead is approximately 3 miles west of Bend.

**Elevation change:** The elevation at the start of the loop is 3,880'. The high point of the ride is 4,815'. Ups and downs add about 400' of climbing to the trip. Total elevation gain: 1,335'.

**Season:** Because of soil conditions and the route's relatively low elevation, this is often a good early season outing. Some of the best riding in this region is in the spring, before the area's pumice soils gets too dry and soft.

**Services:** There is no water on this ride. Water and all services are available in Bend.

**Hazards:** There are some rocky, soft, and forest-littered areas on both the roads and the trails. The rangers at the Bend Ranger District ask that you ride this popular route in a clockwise direction to reduce user conflict. Cyclists descending too fast on the single-track are their main concern. Please control your speed and watch for others sharing the trail.

**Rescue index:** Help is available in Bend.

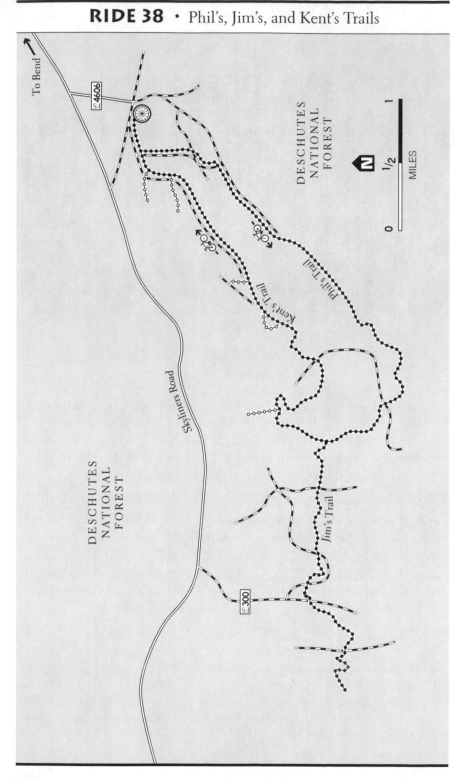

To Bend

FS. 4606

DESCHUTES
NATIONAL
FOREST

N

0    1/2    1
MILES

Phil's Trail

Kent's Trail

Jim's Trail

Skyliners Road

DESCHUTES
NATIONAL
FOREST

FS. 300

**Land status:** Deschutes National Forest.

**Maps:** Check out "Mountain Biking Central Oregon," a map by Fat Tire Publications. It delineates Phil's Trail and was the best representation of the route at the time of our research. The Bend Ranger District "Mountain Biking Route Guide" and the district map of the Bend Ranger District are good resources. USGS 7.5 minute quad: Bend.

**Finding the trail:** A trailhead parking pass was required when we rode here in 1997. They were available for purchase at the offices of the Bend Ranger District.

In downtown Bend, travel west on Franklin Street (follow the "Tour Route" signs). Shortly, Franklin becomes Riverside Boulevard and winds past Drake Park. Continue in a westerly direction as Riverside becomes Galveston Street. Galveston crosses a bridge over the Deschutes River, passes several bike shops, and deposits you at a four-way stop at 14th Street. Continue straight (west) toward Tumalo Falls. The road soon becomes Skyliners Road. Proceed down this road for 2.7 miles to a paved road on the left (at a "bike symbol" sign on the right side of Skyliners Road). Turn left onto this unsigned road (Forest Service Road 4606) and drive 0.4 mile to a road crossing. Turn right onto the cinder road and park on the left side in a pullout.

**Sources of additional information:**

Bend Ranger District
1230 N.E. 3rd Street, Suite A-262
Bend, OR 97701
(541) 388-5664

Bend Chamber of Commerce (Central Oregon Welcome Center)
63085 N. Highway 97
Bend, OR 97701
(541) 382-3221

Central Oregon Trail Alliance (COTA)
1293 N.W. Wall Street #72
Bend, OR 97701
(541) 385-1985
COTA is a regional mountain bike trail advocacy group that is actively involved in trail access issues throughout central Oregon. They promote responsible riding and encourage involvement in volunteer trail maintenance projects. You can join this nonprofit, regional member chapter of the International Mountain Bicycling Association by sending $10 to the above address.

**Notes on the trail:** Phil's Trail Loop is designated Forest Service Mountain Bike Route 24.5. The route is described in the Bend Ranger District "Mountain Biking Route Guide," and it is marked in the field with brown Carsonite signs. The forest service does a good job of replacing signs that go missing, but you may encounter some unmarked intersections.

Coasting down Phil's Trail.

Head west on the cinder road. Turn left in 0.2 mile at the Carsonite sign, and left again in another 0.2 mile at another sign. In another 0.4 mile, turn right at a sign, then immediately left at a **Y** intersection (no sign here in the fall of 1997). Shortly (in 0.2 mile), turn right onto a cinder road. The cinder road ends in 0.6 mile. Continue straight to follow a trail (this trail soon becomes a double-track). Look to the left in 0.3 mile for a single-track (Phil's Trail) marked with a sign reading "This trail is maintained by COTA and USDA Forest Service—closed to all motorized vehicles." Turn left onto the trail. It crosses a double-track in 1.5 miles. It is 0.7 mile from this road crossing to an intersection of trails. (Unsigned Jim's Trail is to the left; unsigned Kent's Trail is straight ahead.) Turn left. Stay on the single-track, crossing several lesser double-tracks to reach a major gravel road (after 1.5 miles on Jim's Trail). Bear left on the gravel road and immediately turn right to regain the trail. The climbing becomes more technical and you will cross a double-track before you reach a rocky high point. (This high point is 0.7 mile from the gravel road.) Turn around and return the way you came. When you get back to the intersection of Jim's, Phil's, and Kent's Trails, turn left. Bear right in 0.5 mile where a secondary trail branches off to the left. In another 0.8 mile, continue straight to cross a native surface road. Stay right at a **Y** in the trail (0.4 mile from the last road crossing) to take the easier way down a hill. A double-track goes left in 0.2 mile—continue straight to remain on the trail. Ride through a burned area that has young trees growing in it. The trail you are on becomes a double-track as you reenter the woods. Here, a side trail branches off to the left. Continue straight to stay on the double-track. From this landmark it is 1.2 miles to another intersection where a trail comes in hard from the left—continue straight on the double-track. Shortly, another intersection is reached—go straight (stay on the main double-track). Turn right when you arrive at the cinder road. Pedal 0.2 mile to the trailhead.

## RIDE 39 · Shevlin Park

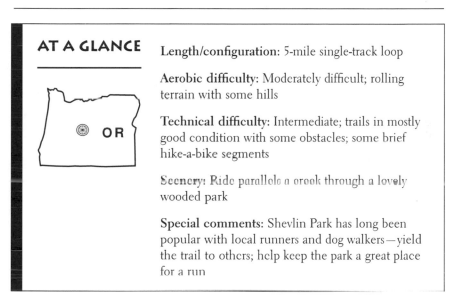

**AT A GLANCE**

**Length/configuration:** 5-mile single-track loop

**Aerobic difficulty:** Moderately difficult; rolling terrain with some hills

**Technical difficulty:** Intermediate; trails in mostly good condition with some obstacles; some brief hike-a-bike segments

**Scenery:** Ride parallels a creek through a lovely wooded park

**Special comments:** Shevlin Park has long been popular with local runners and dog walkers—yield the trail to others; help keep the park a great place for a run

Residents of Bend are lucky. They have miles of recreational trails to enjoy; many are just a hop, skip, and jump away. Some of the closest paths are the trails that run through Shevlin Park. Their proximity helps make them popular with working people. The trails are perfect for a lunch-hour workout or quick early-evening romp. They are especially popular with local runners.

As mountain bike routes, the trails in Shevlin Park are rather short; a five-mile, creekside loop. The riding in Shevlin Park is mostly moderately difficult. There are some short, challenging climbs and some exposed aspects along narrow sections of trail. The trails are in mostly good condition. One notable exception is a rocky, degraded descent that cyclists should walk (or carry) their bikes down. If you ride this hill, you'll be skidding, and that's not good.

Tumalo Creek flows through the middle of Shevlin Park. On either side of the creek are hills dotted with old and young fir trees, manzanita, and sage. The trails roll up and down over shallow bluffs and weave their way through large granite boulders.

**General location:** Shevlin Park is about 4 miles west of downtown Bend.

**Elevation change:** The ride begins at 3,640' and reaches a high point of 3,840'.

# RIDE 39 · Shevlin Park

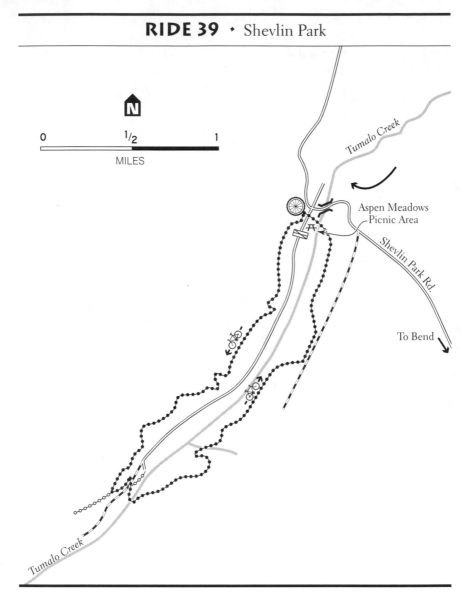

Ups and downs on the route add an estimated 300' of climbing to the loop. Total elevation gain: 500'.

**Season:** The trails in Shevlin Park are usually rideable from the spring through the fall. Stay off of the trails when they are wet.

**Services:** There are vault toilets near the start of the ride. All services are available in Bend.

**Hazards:** You can expect to meet others on these trails—stop and let them pass.

Shevlin Park creek crossing.

When approaching from behind, warn others of your approach, and don't wait until you are right on top of them. Ask for permission to pass. There are some rocky stretches of trail. Minimize your impact by walking your bike down degraded segments of the trails.

**Rescue index:** There is a pay phone at the trailhead. Emergency services are located in Bend.

**Land status:** Bend Metro Parks and Recreation.

**Maps:** A good map for this ride is titled "Mountain Biking Central Oregon." It is published by Fat Tire Publications and is available at area bike shops. USGS 7.5 minute quads: Bend and Shevlin Park.

**Finding the trail:** In Bend, at the intersection of Greenwood Avenue/US 30 and 3rd Street/US 97, follow Greenwood Avenue west. In 0.5 mile, Greenwood Avenue becomes Newport Avenue. Continue west as Newport Avenue becomes Shevlin Park Road (after 1.8 miles). At 4.4 miles, just after crossing unsigned Tumalo Creek, turn left into the parking area at Shevlin Park. Make this turn with care. This intersection presents drivers with a restricted view of oncoming traffic.

## Sources of additional information:

Bend Metro Park and Recreation District
200 N.W. Pacific Park Lane
Bend, OR 97701
(541) 389-7275

Shevlin Park District Office/Aspen Hall
(541) 388-5435

**Notes on the trail:** Ride southwest up the paved road leading into the park. Take a right onto the trail (just before a gate). Stay on the main trail—it hugs the hillside and roughly parallels the creek. (The creek is to your left; below you and often out of sight.) After 2.4 miles, turn hard to the left onto a double-track-like trail. (You have missed this turn if you pass through an opening in a barbed wire fence at a big ponderosa pine.) The double-track-like trail leads down to an intersection of many trails at another large pine. This tree has a yellow and black "State Game Refuge" sign on it. Take the trail that goes hard right. This trail leads to a one-log bridge that spans Tumalo Creek. Carry your bike across the bridge, then carry it up a very steep trail that leads to the ridge top. Ride northeast along the ridge for 0.3 mile, then walk or carry your bike down a degraded section of trail. Cross another footbridge at the bottom of the hill. It is 0.6 mile from this creek crossing to an intersection with a dirt road. Turn left onto the road. Follow the road for just 0.2 mile, turning left to regain the trail. Turn left in 0.8 mile to cross a huge one-log bridge spanning Tumalo Creek. Pass through Aspen Meadows Picnic Area to access the park entrance road and your vehicle.

## RIDE 40 · Deschutes River Trail

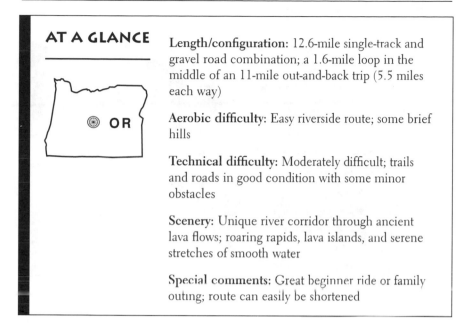

**AT A GLANCE**

**Length/configuration:** 12.6-mile single-track and gravel road combination; a 1.6-mile loop in the middle of an 11-mile out-and-back trip (5.5 miles each way)

**Aerobic difficulty:** Easy riverside route; some brief hills

**Technical difficulty:** Moderately difficult; trails and roads in good condition with some minor obstacles

**Scenery:** Unique river corridor through ancient lava flows; roaring rapids, lava islands, and serene stretches of smooth water

**Special comments:** Great beginner ride or family outing; route can easily be shortened

For years, all manner of runners, equestrians, sight-seers, dog walkers, and hikers have enjoyed the Deschutes River Trail. As mountain biking grew in popularity, the trail became a favorite of bike riders. Everyone appreciated the trail's great scenery, easy terrain, and its high fun factor. Unfortunately, increased use brought increases in user conflicts. To reduce the discord, the Bend Ranger District developed an alternate route for bicyclists.

In our opinion, shared use is best. Sharing trails promotes mutual understanding and a respect for the needs of others. However, there are times when separate trails make sense, especially when the alternative is an outright ban on bikes.

The forest service bike route takes riders away from some good and scenic single-track, but all is not lost. The designated route includes some single-track, and most of the route's road miles are closed to vehicular traffic.

Perhaps it is best to think of the alternate route as a concession that in the long run is good for mountain biking. Land managers fill a tall order as they strive to keep divergent interests satisfied. When mountain bikers get involved, yet remain flexible, they deliver a positive message about our sport.

The route we describe is a 12.6-mile combination. Basically, it is an 11-mile out-and-back (5.5 miles each way) and a 1.6-mile loop. The loop portion of the trip is encountered near Dillon Falls (roughly midway on the out-and-back). This ride is an extension of Designated Forest Service Route 2.3 (a 6.2-mile outing). The designated mountain bike route is extended by following a less busy

Deschutes River Trail.

segment of the Deschutes River Trail. Remember, bikes *always* yield to horses and hikers.

Craggy lava rocks line the river and provide perches for viewing Dillon and Benham Falls. The single-track to Benham Falls passes by some beautiful sections of the river and through some lovely meadows. At times the Deschutes is a cauldron of roiling water, but come around a bend, and it has been transformed into a lazy waterway.

The trails and roads are in good condition with some short, fun technical sections that wiggle through basalt outcroppings. Parts of the trail were formed by closing old double-tracks to vehicular traffic. Dozens of tank traps were dug, one after another. These whoop-de-does have been worn down to a fun size. We aren't much at catching air; we got giggly simply coasting over them.

**General location:** The ride begins at the Lava Island Falls parking area, approximately 8 miles southwest of Bend.

**Elevation change:** The ride begins at 3,960' and reaches a high point of 4,150'. Undulations add an estimated 300' of climbing to the ride. Total elevation gain: 490'.

**Season:** The spring and fall are nice times of the year for a visit. The parking areas at the trailhead and viewpoint can be busy with pedestrian and motorized traffic in the summer.

**Services:** There is no water available on the ride. All services are available in Bend.

# RIDE 40 • Deschutes River Trail

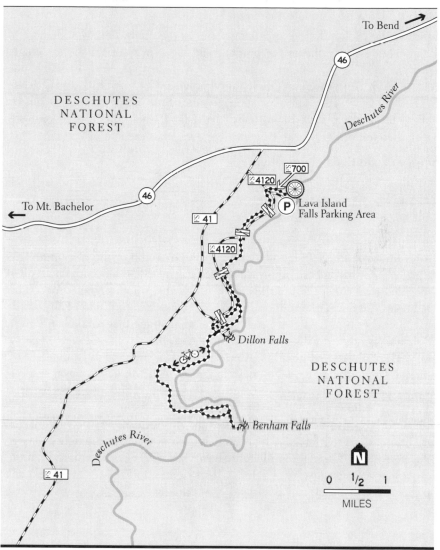

**Hazards:** Control your speed and be courteous (slow down, pull over, say hello). The trail is heavily used; watch for others who may be around the next bend and out of view.

**Rescue index:** Help can be found in Bend.

**Land status:** Deschutes National Forest.

**Maps:** Several useful maps delineate the riding that is available along the Deschutes River. They are all good resources. They include: The Bend Ranger

District "Mountain Biking Route Guide," the district map of the Bend Ranger District, and a map by Fat Tire Publications, "Mountain Biking Central Oregon." USGS 7.5 minute quad: Bend.

**Finding the trail:** A trailhead parking pass was required when we rode here in 1997. They were available for purchase at the offices of the Bend Ranger District.

From Bend, drive west on OR 46 (also known as Century Drive and Cascade Lakes Highway). Turn left after about 7 miles onto Forest Service Road 41. Follow the signs to Lava Island Falls/Lava Island Rock Shelter (left onto FS 4120, then left onto FS 700). Park in the gravel lot at the end of FS 700.

**Source of additional information:**

Bend Ranger District
1230 N.E. 3rd Street, Suite A-262
Bend, OR 97701
(541) 388-5664

**Notes on the trail:** Start by riding up FS 700, then follow the Carsonite signs for route 2.3. Much of the riding is on FS 4120 and side trails that branch off of this gated road. After the fourth gate, turn left onto another gravel road. This road takes you down toward the river and a day-use area for Dillon Falls. At the next intersection of roads, turn right onto a single-track that parallels the river. (This trail is marked with a bollard that reads "Hiker Trail—Slough Meadow 1.6.") The trail passes through a camp in 1.6 miles, then splits in another 1.2 miles. Take the trail to the left to stay along the river. You will arrive at an overlook for Benham Falls in another 0.4 mile. Turn around and return the way you came. (For variety, go left at the first intersection on the return—this takes you over some whoops.) When you get back to the roads, head into the parking area for Dillon Falls. Look for a trail that parallels the river—it is to the right of a large interpretive sign. Once again, the route is marked with Carsonite signs for route 2.3. Follow the signs back to FS 4120. Turn right onto FS 4120 and backtrack on the designated route to Lava Island Falls parking area.

## RIDE 41 · Tumalo Falls

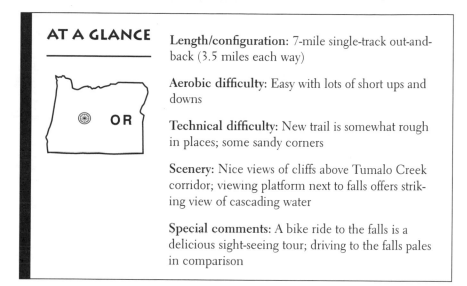

**AT A GLANCE**

**Length/configuration:** 7-mile single-track out-and-back (3.5 miles each way)

**Aerobic difficulty:** Easy with lots of short ups and downs

**Technical difficulty:** New trail is somewhat rough in places; some sandy corners

**Scenery:** Nice views of cliffs above Tumalo Creek corridor; viewing platform next to falls offers striking view of cascading water

**Special comments:** A bike ride to the falls is a delicious sight-seeing tour; driving to the falls pales in comparison

Riding to Tumalo Falls used to involve pedaling Forest Service Road 4603. It was an easy ride, but the road was washboarded and busy with cars kicking up dust. A new trail has been built, making for a much more pleasant trip. The ride is a 7-mile out-and-back excursion (3.5 miles each way).

Tumalo Creek Trail heads into the woods (from a new trailhead facility), then pops out onto a hillside. The surrounding area was devastated by the 1980 Bridge Creek Fire, but the forest is well into its healing process. Young trees and low manzanita bushes cover the slope. On its way to the falls, the trail hugs the hillside, offering lovely views of the rimrock cliffs that dominate the scenery to the north. Tumalo Falls tumbles over this same escarpment. The torrent can be admired from below or from a viewing platform at the top of the 90-foot falls.

Portions of Tumalo Creek Trail are wide and road-like, other sections are winding single-track. The trail is new with some rough areas and sandy sections; it should improve with time and traffic. Energetic beginners (with some single-track experience) should be able to enjoy this ride.

**General location:** The ride starts about 12 miles west of downtown Bend.

**Elevation change:** From the trailhead at 4,760', the trail ascends to a high point of 4,980'. The turnaround point (at the falls) is at 4,960'. Undulating terrain adds about 200' of climbing to the ride. The path to the viewing platform (at the top of the falls) is approximately 0.4 mile long. It climbs roughly 150'. Total elevation gain: 440' (path to platform not included).

**Season:** This ride can be enjoyed from the late spring through the fall.

# RIDE 41 · Tumalo Falls

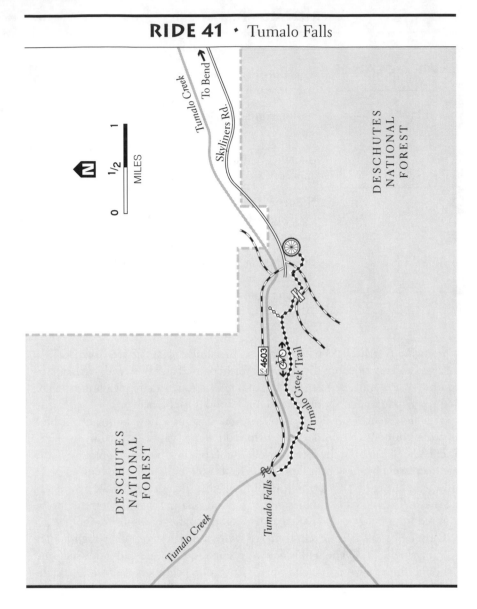

**Services:** There is no water on this trip. There are pit toilets at the trailhead and falls. All services are available in Bend.

**Hazards:** Watch for sandy spots, particularly at the base of hills and in corners. There are a couple of log footbridges that may be slick when wet. Tumalo Creek Trail is used by cyclists as a part of some longer loops. It contains blind corners where your approach, or the approach of others, may go undetected. Keep your speed under control and be mindful that there may be someone around the next bend.

A cool day on
Tumalo Creek Trail.

**Rescue index:** Help can be found in Bend.

**Land status:** Deschutes National Forest.

**Maps:** This trail is delineated on "Mountain Biking Central Oregon," a map by Fat Tire Publications. USGS 7.5 minute quad: Tumalo Falls.

**Finding the trail:** A trailhead parking pass was required when we rode here in 1997. They were available for purchase at the offices of the Bend Ranger District.

In Bend, travel west on Galveston. Galveston becomes Skyliners Road at 14th Street. Continue straight (west) onto Skyliners Road and follow it for 9.7 miles to the trailhead and parking on the left (marked on the right side of Skyliners Road with a "trailhead" sign and an arrow pointing left).

**Source of additional information:**

Bend Ranger District
1230 N.E. 3rd Street, Suite A-262
Bend, OR 97701
(541) 388-5664

**Notes on the trail:** The trail enters the woods (near the pit toilet) and crosses a dirt road. Follow the trail to a green gate, ride around the gate and up the road. Turn right at the next road (at a bollard/signpost directing you toward Tumalo Falls). The remaining intersections are marked with signposts that will direct you to Tumalo Falls. At the falls, turn around and return the way you came.

## RIDE 42 · Skyliners Loop

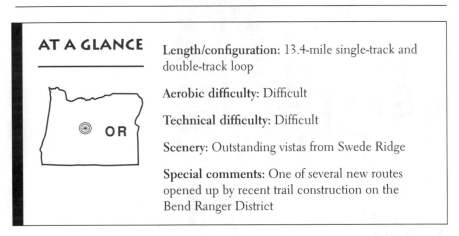

**AT A GLANCE**

**Length/configuration:** 13.4-mile single-track and double-track loop

**Aerobic difficulty:** Difficult

**Technical difficulty:** Difficult

**Scenery:** Outstanding vistas from Swede Ridge

**Special comments:** One of several new routes opened up by recent trail construction on the Bend Ranger District

New stretches of single-track, old logging roads, and old trails come together to form this demanding 13.4-mile loop. The loop passes three shelters that are popular in the winter with cross-country skiers. We plied this loop on a blustery fall day. It was comforting to come across the shelters and their stock of cord wood. To cold backcountry skiers, the shelters and their wood stoves must be an even more welcome sight.

The mountain bike loop begins at a trailhead near the end of Skyliners Road. A new trail, Tumalo Creek Trail, connects this trailhead with the bottom of South Fork Trail (near Tumalo Falls). For years, locals have enjoyed descending (and ascending) on South Fork Trail. Speaking with rangers at the Bend Ranger District, we were told about some problems associated with downhill bike traffic on South Fork Trail. The trail is popular with equestrians and hikers, and the actions of a few inconsiderate bike riders have resulted in some dangerous situations. The rangers asked us to use South Fork Trail as an uphill route.

In the past, we had only descended on South Fork Trail; it was fun and fast. We thought the trail would make for a grueling hump of a climb. We rode up the trail and were pleased to find the climb very enjoyable. It had its tough spots, but it was pleasantly rideable—a gratifying challenge.

# RIDE 42 · Skyliners Loop

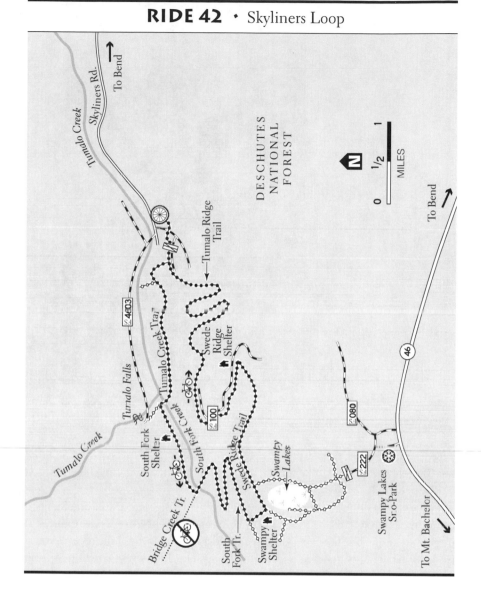

South Fork Trail leads up to Swampy Lakes Shelter. Here, you pick up Swede Ridge Trail, which crosses over to the lovely Swede Ridge Shelter. The terrain on the ridge is rolling; some easy climbing and some fun descents. We'd heard that there are great views from Swede Ridge. Snow was falling lightly as we traversed the ridge, but we did get some views of the rocky cliffs above Tumalo Creek. Even these broken views were impressive. The scenery on a clear day must be outstanding.

A cold day at Swede
Ridge Shelter.

From Swede Ridge Shelter we dropped gently on a rough gravel road that tied
into Tumalo Ridge Trail. The loop was completed with a switchbacking descent
on this new trail.

The ride was difficult, but not as hard as we had expected. It included a good
deal of moderately difficult climbing. The tread of the new trails was somewhat
rough and sandy, but these conditions should improve as the trails receive more
use. The older trails and roads contained obstacles like forest litter, roots, and
rocks.

**General location:** The trailhead is approximately 12 miles west of downtown
Bend.

**Elevation change:** The loop begins at 4,760' and reaches a high point of 5,920'
on Swede Ridge. Ups and downs on the ride add about 500' of climbing to the
trip. Total elevation gain: 1,660'.

**Season:** The trails on this ride are usually rideable by late spring or early summer. We recommend that you call ahead to make inquiries about the trail conditions before planning an early season ride. The trails near Swampy Lakes can
be damp for some time following the melt.

**Services:** No potable water on the ride. All services are available in Bend.

**Hazards:** Watch for others around blind corners. Control your speed on the descents—play it safe and be considerate of other trail users. Do not skid. If you cannot negotiate a descent without locking your brakes, get off your bike and walk it down that section of trail. Expect obstacles like roots, rocks, and sandy sections of trail.

**Rescue index:** Help is available in Bend.

**Land status:** Deschutes National Forest.

**Maps:** "Mountain Biking Central Oregon," by Fat Tire Publications, is a good map for this ride. USGS 7.5 minute quad: Tumalo Falls.

**Finding the trail:** A trailhead parking pass was required when we rode here in 1997. They were available for purchase at the offices of the Bend Ranger District.

In Bend, travel west on Galveston. Galveston becomes Skyliners Road at 14th Street. Continue straight (west) onto Skyliners Road and follow it for 9.7 miles to the trailhead and parking on the left (marked on the right side of Skyliners Road with a "trailhead" sign and an arrow pointing left).

**Source of additional information:**

Bend Ranger District
1230 N.E. 3rd Street, Suite A-262
Bend, OR 97701
(541) 388-5664

**Notes on the trail:** The trail enters the woods (near the pit toilet) and crosses a dirt road. Follow the trail to a green gate. Ride around the gate and up the road. Turn right at the next road (at a bollard/signpost directing you toward Tumalo Falls). Continue straight at the next intersection to remain on Tumalo Creek Trail; follow the signpost for Tumalo Falls (a single-track goes right here). The riding has been road-like, but it soon changes to single-track. The trail crosses a log footbridge, then intersects South Fork Trail. Turn left and begin the climb on South Fork Trail (follow the signpost for OR 46). Pass South Fork Shelter after 0.2 mile on South Fork Trail. From the shelter, pedal 1.2 miles to an intersection. Turn left to cross a footbridge over the creek. (The trail that goes right/straight heads toward Bridge Creek/Tum Lake—no bikes allowed.) Climb for 1.6 miles to a large sign on the left for "City of Bend Watershed." Turn left at this intersection and ride a short distance to the Swampy Lakes Shelter. Turn left at the shelter onto a trail marked with a Carsonite sign (the sign is labeled with a bicycle symbol and an arrow pointing left). In 0.5 mile, turn left at a **Y** intersection (don't follow the Carsonite sign at this intersection—it points down the trail that goes right). Shortly, notice blue diamond-shaped markers placed at intervals on trees marking the trail. This trail intersects with a road near Swede Ridge Shelter. Turn left onto the road and descend gently. The road becomes more double-track-like after 1.3 miles, then climbs a bit to reach the first of several signposts that mark this portion of the bike route. Eventually, the double-track-like road becomes a trail (Tumalo Ridge Trail). It passes through areas of young pine trees and manzanita bushes, then reenters the woods. Next, the trail switchbacks down a hillside and passes the road (trail) that goes toward Tumalo Falls. Continue straight, backtracking to the trailhead at Skyliners Road.

## **RIDE 43** · Tangent/Quarry Site 1041 Loop

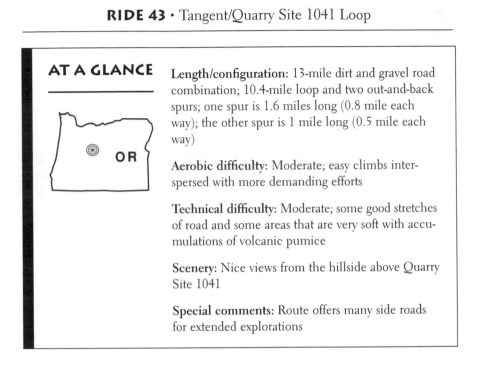

**AT A GLANCE**

**Length/configuration:** 13-mile dirt and gravel road combination; 10.4-mile loop and two out-and-back spurs; one spur is 1.6 miles long (0.8 mile each way); the other spur is 1 mile long (0.5 mile each way)

**Aerobic difficulty:** Moderate; easy climbs interspersed with more demanding efforts

**Technical difficulty:** Moderate; some good stretches of road and some areas that are very soft with accumulations of volcanic pumice

**Scenery:** Nice views from the hillside above Quarry Site 1041

**Special comments:** Route offers many side roads for extended explorations

This 13-mile ride is moderately difficult. It involves a 10.4-mile loop and two short out-and-back spurs. The climbing on the circuit is mostly easy, with several uphills that will require a more concerted effort. The road conditions vary greatly over the course of the ride. Forest Service Road 4615 is in good condition. It is made of crushed volcanic cinders and compacted dirt. Most of the remaining miles are on dirt roads, and some stretches are very thick with volcanic pumice. These soft sections are loose and make pedaling difficult; you may have to push your bike through some of these areas.

The view from Quarry Site 1041 is the highlight of this trip. A short scramble up a steep hillside reveals a lovely view of the surrounding forests and mountains. Broken Top and Mt. Bachelor are prominent in the west. Look southeast for Lava Butte and Newberry Crater.

**General location:** This ride starts at the Virginia Meissner Sno-Park, approximately 13 miles west of Bend.

**Elevation change:** From the trailhead at 5,400', you travel over rolling terrain to 5,540' at the quarry site. Undulations on this portion of the loop add about

# RIDE 43 · Tangent/Quarry Site 1041 Loop

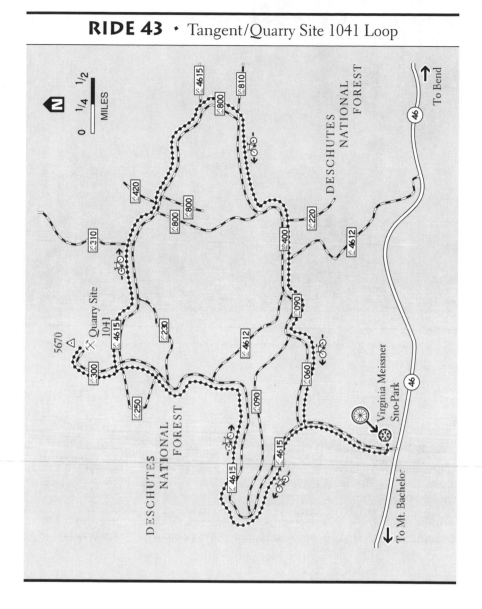

350' of climbing to the ride. Descend rapidly from the quarry, to a low point of 4,720', before pedaling back to the trailhead. Total elevation gain: 1,170'.

**Season:** Roads at these elevations may not be free of snow until late in the spring. This is a good summer ride.

**Services:** There is no water on the route. Water and all services can be obtained in Bend.

**Hazards:** Expect some traffic on the roads. Control your speed on the descent

Broken Top from the hill above Quarry Site 1041.

from the quarry and watch for changing road conditions; soft spots can cause handling problems.

**Rescue index:** Help can be found in Bend.

**Land status:** Deschutes National Forest.

**Maps:** The district map of the Bend Ranger District is a good guide to this ride. USGS 7.5 minute quads: Benham Falls, Wanoga Butte, Shelvin Park, and Tumalo Falls.

**Finding the trail:** From Bend, drive west on OR 46 (Century Drive Highway/Cascade Lakes Highway) for 13 miles to signed FS 4615. Turn right and travel 0.1 mile on FS 4615; park in the Virginia Meissner Sno-Park, on the right.

**Source of additional information:**

Bend Ranger District
1230 N.E. 3rd Street, Suite A-262
Bend, OR 97701
(541) 388-5664

**Notes on the trail:** The Bend Ranger District has developed designated mountain bike routes throughout the forest. Pick up their "Mountain Biking Route Guide" at the ranger station. This particular route is marked with Carsonite signs that show a bike symbol, a directional arrow, and the number 52.5.

Turn right out of the Sno-Park onto FS 4615. Stay on FS 4615 for 4.7 miles to the intersection with FS 300. Continue straight onto FS 300 and follow this road to its terminus at Quarry Site 1041. Park your bike and hike up the hill for good views. Cycle back down FS 300 to FS 4615 and turn left (east). Descend on FS 4615 for 2.9 miles to the third FS 800 entrance. This entrance for FS 800 is on the right; it comes just after the terrain levels out, climbs a bit, and levels out again. Turn right onto FS 800. After pedaling for 1.2 miles on FS 800, turn left onto FS 400. Continue straight on FS 400 where FS 220 goes left. In another 0.4 mile, you will reach an intersection where an unmarked road comes in from the left. Follow the mountain bike route sign that directs you straight, onto unsigned FS 4612. Proceed down FS 4612 for 0.2 mile to signed FS 090 on the left (where FS 4612 continues straight). Turn left onto FS 090. Cycle on FS 090 for 0.5 mile, then turn left onto signed FS 060. Stay on FS 060 for 1 mile to its intersection with signed FS 4615. Turn left onto FS 4615 to return to the Sno-Park.

## RIDE 44 · Ridge Trail Loop

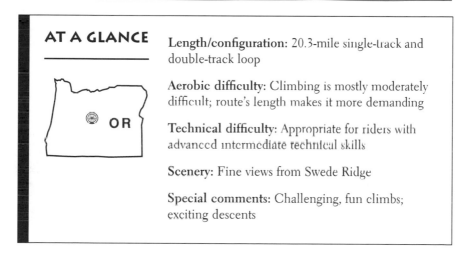

**AT A GLANCE**

**Length/configuration:** 20.3-mile single-track and double-track loop

**Aerobic difficulty:** Climbing is mostly moderately difficult; route's length makes it more demanding

**Technical difficulty:** Appropriate for riders with advanced intermediate technical skills

**Scenery:** Fine views from Swede Ridge

**Special comments:** Challenging, fun climbs; exciting descents

OR

This 20.3-mile loop is a mix of challenging climbs and exhilarating descents. The trip begins on a nice stretch of single-track, the new Tumalo Ridge Trail. The climb up this trail is moderately difficult; it involves several long traverses across an open hillside. An old logging road links Tumalo Ridge Trail with Swede Ridge Shelter. The shelter is a comfortable place for lunch, or for kicking back and enjoying the scenery. (We've been told the views are excellent from Swede Ridge; we encountered overcast conditions when we rode here.)

Swede Ridge Trail is picked up at the Swede Ridge Shelter. This trail works its way over to another shelter at Swampy Lakes. The "ridge riding" over to

Juanita Edwards and
Dan Smithey riding on
the Swampy Lakes trails.

Swampy Lakes involves some stiff climbs and good descents. The trails in the
Swampy Lakes area are less demanding. They lead out to native surface and
crushed cinder forest roads. The roads signal the end to the single-track portion
of the trip, but not an end to the fun. Some climbing (mostly easy) brings you to
some exhilarating downhill stretches.

The roads on the route are in fair to good condition with some washboarding
and ruts. The roads and trails contain some soft sections that can pose problems
if they are entered with abandon. The new Tumalo Ridge Trail contains rough
areas that should improve with use. Older trails on the circuit contain some roots
and rocks. Both the trails and roads on this loop can see accumulations of forest
litter.

**General location:** The trailhead is about 12 miles west of downtown Bend.

**Elevation change:** The loop begins at 4,760'. The high point of the trip is
obtained on Swede Ridge (5,920'). Ups and downs on the ride add about 800' of
climbing to the outing. Total elevation gain: 1,960'.

**Season:** June through October. Call ahead for trail conditions when planning a
ride here. The trails around Swampy Lakes can take a while to dry out in the
spring.

# RIDE 44 · Ridge Trail Loop

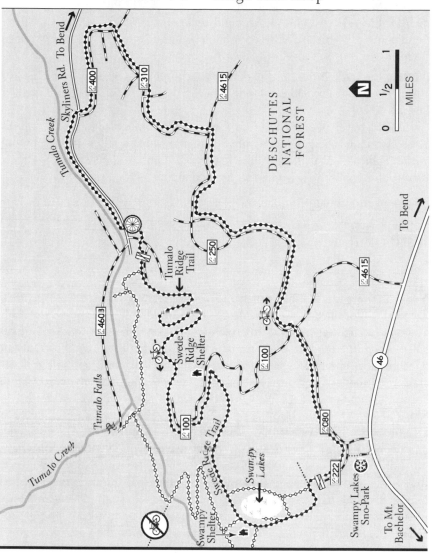

**Services:** There is no water on this ride. Water and all services are available in Bend. You pass a Dairy Queen on the way to (and from) the trailhead.

**Hazards:** The route requires route-finding skills. Carry the recommended maps, a compass, and allow yourself plenty of time to complete the loop. The roads and trails followed contain obstacles like rocks, roots, ruts, and forest litter. Watch out for soft sections of tread that can cause handling problems.

**Rescue index:** Help is available in Bend.

**Land status:** Deschutes National Forest.

**Maps:** "Mountain Biking Central Oregon," by Fat Tire Publications is a good map for this ride. We also recommend that you carry the district map of the Bend Ranger District. USGS 7.5 minute quads: Tumalo Falls and Wanoga Butte.

**Finding the trail:** A trailhead parking pass was required when we rode here in 1997. They were available for purchase at the offices of the Bend Ranger District.

In Bend, travel west on Galveston. Galveston becomes Skyliners Road at 14th Street. Continue straight (west) onto Skyliners Road and follow it for 9.7 miles to the trailhead and parking on the left (marked on the right side of Skyliners Road with a "trailhead" sign and an arrow pointing left).

**Source of additional information:**

Bend Ranger District
1230 N.E. 3rd Street, Suite A-262
Bend, OR 97701
(541) 388-5664

**Notes on the trail:** The trail enters the woods (near the pit toilet) and crosses a dirt road. Follow the trail to a green gate. Ride around the gate and up the road. Continue straight at the next intersection (do not turn right toward Tumalo Falls). Soon, the road becomes a single-track. Tumalo Ridge Trail ascends an open hillside, climbing a series of long switchbacking traverses. The trail re-enters the woods after the switchbacks, then passes through open areas before becoming more road-like. Follow the road (Forest Service Road 100) to Swede Ridge Shelter (4.9 miles into the ride). Ride past the shelter a short distance to a saddle and several cross-country ski route signs. Turn right (west) onto single-track Swede Ridge Trail. In 1.8 miles, you'll arrive at an intersection. Turn right (the trail to the left is marked by a Carsonite sign labeled with a bicycle symbol). In 0.5 mile, you come upon Swampy Lakes Shelter. Continue straight at this intersection (the trail to the right leads to South Fork Trail). There are many intersecting trails in this cross-country ski area, several are marked with signs for Swampy Sno-Park (a parking area for the ski trails). Follow the signs for Swampy Sno-Park. (The Sno-Park is about 2.4 miles southeast of Swampy Shelter.) FS 222 and FS 080 intersect just north of Swampy Sno-Park. Turn left (northeast) onto FS 080 and ride 1.6 miles to FS 4615. Turn left onto FS 4615 and pedal 4.2 miles to FS 310 on the left. Turn onto FS 310; stay on this main double-track for 2.1 miles to FS 400. Turn left onto FS 400 and follow it for 1.2 miles to Skyliners Road. Turn left onto the pavement and ride 1.7 miles back to the trailhead on the left.

The district map indicates that it may be possible to cut a couple of miles off of this loop (at the expense of some single-track riding). Take FS 100 to FS 4615 (go straight at Swede Ridge Shelter instead of turning onto Swede Ridge Trail). We did not ride this shortened route, but it looks like a workable option.

## RIDE 45 · Cultus Lake Loop

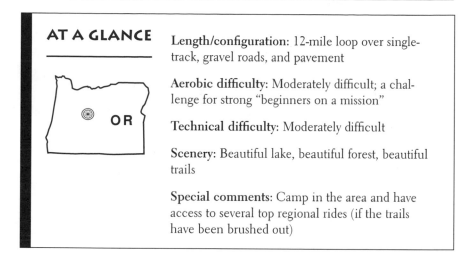

**AT A GLANCE**

**Length/configuration:** 12-mile loop over single-track, gravel roads, and pavement

**Aerobic difficulty:** Moderately difficult; a challenge for strong "beginners on a mission"

**Technical difficulty:** Moderately difficult

**Scenery:** Beautiful lake, beautiful forest, beautiful trails

**Special comments:** Camp in the area and have access to several top regional rides (if the trails have been brushed out)

The rangers at the Bend District warned us—Lemish Lake Loop and Charlton Lake Loop trails had not been cleared. These relatively distant trails are low on the district's list of maintenance priorities. Too bad for us, we had heard that they were treasures. We discussed our options and decided to check out the shorter of these loops anyway. Maybe there wouldn't be too many blow-downs. We drove to the Lemish Lake Loop trailhead and headed off up the trail. Thirty windfalls in the first mile convinced us to turn around and cut our losses. Well, while we were in the area we could at least check out Cultus Lake Loop—the ranger said it had been cleared.

After completing the 12-mile ride around Cultus Lake, we felt like our trip to this corner of the forest had been well rewarded. Cultus Lake Loop is reason enough to plan a trip to this neck of the woods.

There is a wee bit of pavement and a few miles of gravel at the start of the ride. The rest of the fun is on single-track. The first section, Deer Lake Trail, takes you past Little Cultus Lake, then around the west flank of Cultus Mountain to Deer Lake. The trail here is superb, with a smooth tread and some sweet, mild descents through the woods. Deer Lake Trail ties into Cultus Lake Trail. There is a nice beach at primitive West Cultus Lake Campground; it's a great spot for a break. The view across the lake is nice, especially to the southeast, where Cultus Mountain rises from the water's edge.

The character of Cultus Lake Trail changes as you near the north side of the lake. There are a couple of very brief demanding climbs, and obstacles start showing up in the trail. Tire blockers on this stretch include roots, rocks, and large log waterbars. The trail is quite firm through this area, but sandy conditions can develop when the trail is very dry.

The pedaling on this trip is not too demanding. It begins with some descending, then some easy to moderately difficult climbing on gravel roads. The single-track starts out easy, but it gets harder. The demanding hills you do come across are very brief.

**General location:** The trailhead is approximately 40 miles southwest of Bend and about 30 miles northwest of La Pine.

**Elevation change:** The ride begins at 4,690' and reaches a low point of 4,520' in the first mile of the circuit. The high point of the ride (5,000') is obtained near the halfway point; near Deer Lake. Ups and downs add about 300' of climbing to the trip. Total elevation gain: 780'.

**Season:** The late spring and the fall are great times for a ride here. The lakes and trails are at their busiest in the summertime. However, a cool dip after a hot ride can make up for this shortcoming. This place is more remote than other Bend Ranger District playgrounds. The trails in the area may see less maintenance (or receive attention later in the season) than others on the district. Call ahead to check on conditions; ask whether the trails have been cleared of windfalls.

**Services:** Water can be obtained seasonally at Cultus Lake Campground. Food, lodging, water, and a pay phone are available at Cultus Lake Resort. All services are available in La Pine, Sunriver, and Bend.

**Hazards:** Watch for fast-moving vehicles on the roads. The trails contain obstacles like rocks, roots, and large log waterbars. These are popular hiking and equestrian trails; control your speed and extend courtesy to others.

**Rescue index:** There is a pay phone at the Cultus Lake Resort. Emergency services are located in Bend.

**Land status:** Deschutes National Forest.

**Maps:** The district map of the Bend Ranger District is a good guide to this ride. The map shows Cultus Lake Trail briefly entering the Wilderness Area north of Cultus Lake. This portion of trail has been rerouted to avoid the Wilderness Area. USGS 7.5 minute quads: Crane Prairie Reservoir and Irish Mountain.

**Finding the trail:** From locations to the north, travel south from Bend on US 97 for approximately 14 miles. Turn right (west) on South Century Drive toward Sunriver. Follow this main road as it curves through Sunriver and becomes Spring River Road, then Forest Service Road 40. In about 20 miles, FS 40 intersects Cascade Lakes Highway/FS 46. Turn left onto FS 46 and drive 1.2 miles to FS 4635 on the right. Turn onto FS 4635 (toward Cultus Lake Resort/Cultus Lakes). You will pass the entrance road to Cultus Lake Resort after 1.7 miles on FS 4635. Continue straight past the resort (the road designation changes to FS 100). In another 0.1 mile, park in a pullout on the right (across from a day-use picnic area and beach).

From locations to the south, drive north from La Pine on OR 97 for approximately 2.5 miles and turn left onto Burgess Road (signed for Crane Prairie/Wickiup Reservoir/Cascade Lakes Highway). Stay on this main road for

Beach at West Cultus Lake Campground.

10.8 miles to its junction with South Century Drive/FS 42. Turn left on FS 42 and drive 9 miles to Cascade Lakes Highway/FS 46. Turn right onto FS 46 and proceed 6.3 miles to FS 4635 on the left. Turn left on FS 4635 (toward Cultus Lake Resort/Cultus Lakes). Follow FS 4635 for 1.7 miles to the entrance road for Cultus Lake Resort. Continue straight onto FS 100. Drive 0.1 mile and park on the right in a day-use parking pullout across from a picnic area and beach. If this parking area is full, drive farther north on FS 100. There is more day-use parking near Cultus Lake Campground.

### Source of additional information:

Bend Ranger District
1230 N.E. 3rd Street, Suite A-262
Bend, OR 97701
(541) 388-5664

**Notes on the trail:** The Bend Ranger District has developed a "Mountain Biking Route Guide" for the district. You can pick up this handout at the ranger station in Bend. Cultus Lake Loop is designated route number 47.5.

The Three Sisters Wilderness lies to the west and north of the single-track portion of this loop. Bikes are not allowed in designated wilderness areas.

Return down the pavement on FS 4635 for 1.1 miles to FS 4630 on the right. Turn onto gravel FS 4630. In 1.7 miles, continue straight (toward Little Cultus Lake/FS 4636) onto FS 600 where FS 4630 goes left. Turn right onto FS 640 at the next intersection; follow the signs for Deer Lake Trail 6 and Bike Route 47.5.

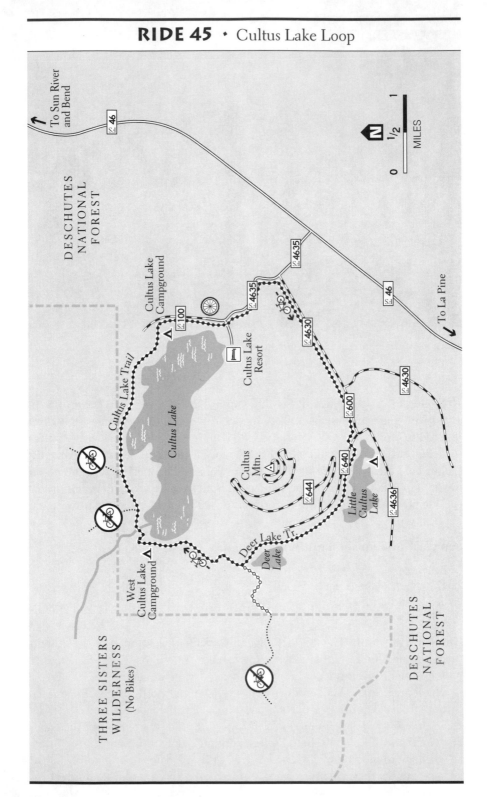

After 0.3 mile on FS 640, bear left at a wide area in the road onto Deer Lake Trail. Follow the single-track along the shore of Little Cultus Lake, then through the woods to Deer Lake (follow the Carsonite bike route signs). After 1.7 miles on Deer Lake Trail, continue straight at a sign-in box and a trail that accesses the wilderness area. In another 0.4 mile, you come upon four bollards and a trail on the left. A double-track (straight ahead) is blocked by windfalls. Turn left onto the trail. Cross a bridge over a creek, then turn right toward Cultus Lake. Just over a mile of fun coasting brings you to another intersection. Turn left toward Cultus Lake onto a wide, road-like trail. Shortly, trails break off to the right to access primitive West Cultus Lake Campground; follow the main road/trail north, bypassing the campground and keeping the lake in view. The road-like conditions give way to single-track at a beachside campsite marked with a flagpole. A trail comes in hard from the left here, and there is a multitude of signs on trees to the right; continue straight. The trail will climb a steep, short hill and then curve left to briefly move away from the lake. In another 0.5 mile, cross a big one-log bridge, then bear right to remain on track. Stay on Cultus Lake Trail where secondary trails branch off toward the lake (to the right) or wilderness (to the left). Near the end of the trail, you will have your choice of going left to a trailhead or right to Cultus Lake Campground. Take your pick, both lead out to FS 100. Turn right when you get to FS 100 and ride back to your vehicle.

For a longer option, ride up to the top of Cultus Mountain. Your district map (Bend) delineates the route well.

This area offers some good, longer single-track opportunities. We have heard good things about Lemish Lake Loop and Charlton Lake Loop. Make inquiries as to trail conditions when considering these trails; windfalls can be a problem. Herculean mountain bicyclists might consider an overnighter (two or more days) that would involve linking trails in the Cultus Lakes area with Waldo Lake Trail.

# RIDE 46 · Peter Skene Ogden Trail

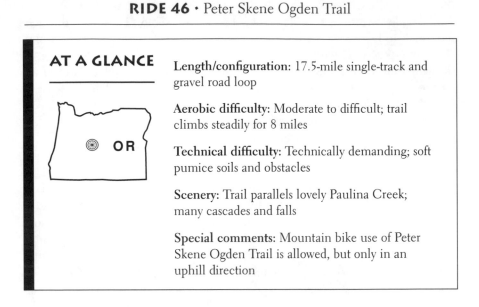

**AT A GLANCE**

**Length/configuration:** 17.5-mile single-track and gravel road loop

**Aerobic difficulty:** Moderate to difficult; trail climbs steadily for 8 miles

OR

**Technical difficulty:** Technically demanding; soft pumice soils and obstacles

**Scenery:** Trail parallels lovely Paulina Creek; many cascades and falls

**Special comments:** Mountain bike use of Peter Skene Ogden Trail is allowed, but only in an uphill direction

This is one of those very satisfying rides that give you a lot for what you put in to it. The Peter Skene Ogden Trail parallels scenic Paulina Creek. The stream cascades into inviting pools and forms beautiful waterfalls. Once at Paulina Lake, you can muse on mountain peaks while enjoying refreshments at Paulina Lake Lodge. The dirt road descent is fast and exhilarating.

We recommend this 17.5-mile loop to strong intermediate cyclists and advanced cyclists. The trail climbs for eight miles, gaining over 2,000 feet of elevation. The surface is soft with accumulations of pumice dust. What would be a moderately difficult climb on a compacted dirt trail is challenging here. There are a few steep pitches and some intricate pedaling through rocky terrain, but most everything is rideable. The descent on forest roads is also technically demanding. The roads contain ruts, soft sections, and washboarding.

**General location:** The trailhead is approximately 25 miles south of Bend.

**Elevation change:** The ride begins at 4,280' and reaches a high point of 6,340' at Paulina Lake. Ups and downs add an estimated 200' of climbing to the circuit. Total elevation gain: 2,260'.

**Season:** The route is generally free of snow from July through October.

**Services:** Water can be obtained seasonally at the Ogden Group Camp and Paulina Lake Campground. Food, lodging, limited groceries, and a pay phone can be found at the Paulina Lake Lodge. All services are available in Bend.

**Hazards:** Soft sections on the dirt roads make the descent somewhat dangerous; control your speed. Wide tires are recommended because of the soft conditions encountered along the route. Watch for traffic on the roads.

**Rescue index:** Help can be found in Bend.

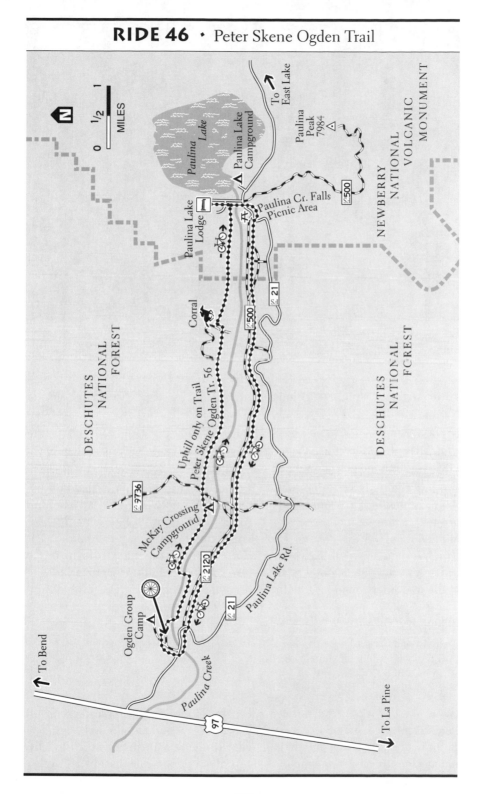

Paulina Creek.

**Land status:** Deschutes National Forest and Newberry National Volcanic Monument.

**Maps:** The district map for the Bend Ranger District is a suitable guide to the route. Its only shortcoming: the trail is shown to cross the creek more than once. USGS 7.5 minute quads: Paulina Peak and Finley Butte.

**Finding the trail:** From locations to the north, travel south from Bend on US 97 for approximately 22 miles to Forest Service Road 21/Paulina Lake Road (on the left). From locations to the south, drive north from La Pine on US 97 for about 6 miles to FS 21/Paulina Lake Road (on the right). Turn east onto FS 21, which is signed here for Newberry Crater, Paulina Lake, and East Lake. In 2.8 miles, turn left onto a gravel road at a sign for Ogden Group Camp. Bear right at the next intersection (at a trailhead sign) and park in the large gravel lot.

**Source of additional information:**

Fort Rock Ranger District
1230 N.E. 3rd Street, Suite A-262
Bend, OR 97701
(541) 388-5664

**Notes on the trail:** Uncontrolled speed by mountain bikers descending on Peter Skene Ogden Trail has created safety concerns and erosion problems. The result is a Forest Service prohibition on downhill use of the trail by cyclists. This management decision is supported by local mountain bike groups and other forest users. Respect the policy—it is better than an outright ban on mountain bikes. Besides, riding the trail uphill gives you time to enjoy the beauty of Paulina Creek.

Walk your bike up the railroad tie steps at the National Recreation Trail sign and cross the log bridge to begin riding on the trail. The beginning of the route is marked with horseshoe symbol signs on trees. You will arrive at a soft double-track after pedaling 0.8 mile. Turn right onto the road to ride toward the boulders that close the road to most vehicles. At the boulders, turn left onto another road and ride 0.2 mile to Paulina Creek. Cross a bridge to the north side of the creek and continue up the trail (on single-track again). The trail passes through McKay Crossing Campground in another 1.8 miles. Cross unsigned FS 9736 to continue on the trail. You will pass by an especially lovely series of waterfalls in another 2 miles, then arrive at a **Y** intersection. Continue straight (left) to follow the more rideable trail. You will come to another intersection in 0.5 mile. Continue straight where a path goes right to a footbridge over the creek. You will enter a horse camp and reach a road in 0.7 mile. Turn left onto the road and pedal a short distance to a trail on the right (just before a corral). Turn onto this trail. Continue straight onto a gravel road when you reach the eastern trailhead, near Paulina Lake. Pedal a short distance to a paved road and turn left. Follow the road to Paulina Lake Lodge. Turn around at the lodge and return the way you came. Cross the concrete bridge that spans the headwaters of Paulina Creek. This will bring you to FS 21. Turn right onto FS 21 and pedal 0.3 mile to the Paulina Creek Falls Picnic Area. Turn right and ride through the parking area to a faint trail at a small section of fence. Ride between the fence posts to a sign pointing left for Paulina Falls Trail. Turn left to access unsigned FS 500. Follow the old roadbed and the telephone poles downhill. Stay on FS 500 where side roads branch off. Cross FS 9736. Bear left when you reach unsigned FS 2120 (a cinder road). FS 2120 takes you back to paved FS 21. Turn right onto the pavement and ride to the entrance of Ogden Group Camp. Turn right and pedal back to your vehicle.

While in the area, you may wish to ride Newberry Crater Rim Trail. A trail brochure from the Fort Rock Ranger District describes this "more difficult" 20-mile loop as "the ultimate high-country trail for this area." This ride was recommended to us by area rangers and bike shop employees, but we got snowed out. The loop is delineated in "Mountain Biking Central Oregon," a map by Fat Tire Publications.

## RIDE 47 · Sisters Mountain Bike Trail/Eagle Rock Loop

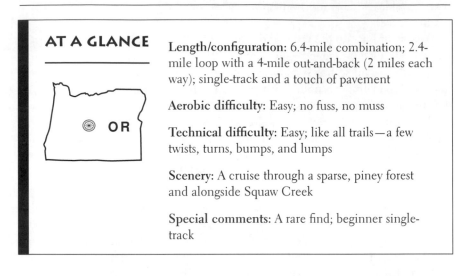

**AT A GLANCE**

**Length/configuration:** 6.4-mile combination; 2.4-mile loop with a 4-mile out-and-back (2 miles each way); single-track and a touch of pavement

**Aerobic difficulty:** Easy; no fuss, no muss

**Technical difficulty:** Easy; like all trails—a few twists, turns, bumps, and lumps

**Scenery:** A cruise through a sparse, piney forest and alongside Squaw Creek

**Special comments:** A rare find; beginner single-track

Over the past several years, Sisters' reputation as a destination for mountain biking has steadily grown. Lately, several easy trails have been added to the mix. This is a pleasant surprise, as beginners and families are often pointed in the direction of less than exciting rides. Ask about beginner riding opportunities at most ranger stations and you hear a common refrain. Something along the lines of, "Just head out into the woods and choose any old road." Yes, the opportunities for forest road explorations are nearly limitless, but where can a novice find a gentle introduction to the joys of single-track pedaling? Sisters comes to mind.

The Sisters Mountain Bike Trail is the result of some hard work by members of the community and the Forest Service. Kirk Metzger (Sisters Ranger District) and Brad Boyd (Eurosports Sporting Goods) were key players in the effort to get these trails developed. In communities throughout the country, people like Kirk and Brad are making good things happen for trails. We often take the trails we ride on for granted, but there is a story, and a lot of sweat behind every mile.

Eagle Rock Loop is one of two routes that make up the Sisters Mountain Bike Trail. Eagle Rock Loop is short and easy. The other route, Peterson Ridge Loop, is longer and moderately difficult. (Peterson Ridge Loop is described later, Ride 48.) Both rides begin in the center of town, at Village Green Park. Rent a bike (and a helmet), fill your water bottle, and off you go on an exciting adventure.

A short pedal through town leads to the trailhead for Sisters Mountain Bike Trail. Eagle Rock Loop travels through a dry landscape of sand, rock, and sparse ponderosa pines. Shade and water make the short paralleling of Squaw Creek the scenic highlight of the outing.

Eagle Rock Loop covers a total of 6.4 miles. The ride combines a 2.4-mile loop with an out-and-back spur. The out-and-back portion is four miles long (two miles each way).

Eagle Rock Loop.

Gaps between old double-tracks have been bridged with new single-track trails. Logs, large rocks, and mounds of soil have been carefully placed to give the double-track sections a trail-like feel. The circuit includes 0.8 mile of pavement.

The first part of the trip climbs very gently. You know you've climbed because the return from the far end includes a little coasting. While the terrain is technically easy, this *is* mountain biking; there are obstacles to surmount. Portions of the tread are bumpy with rocks, there are mounds of dirt to be negotiated, and there are a couple of footbridges to cross. The route snakes through trees and squeezes through logs. Dry spells and lots of traffic can leave portions of the trail soft and sandy.

**General location:** The ride starts in Sisters.

**Elevation change:** The ride begins at 3,185' and reaches a high point of 3,350'. Total elevation gain: 165'.

**Season:** This ride can be enjoyed from the early spring through the late fall.

**Services:** You will find all services in Sisters (except public laundry facilities).

# RIDE 47 · Sisters Mountain Bike Trail/Eagle Rock Loop

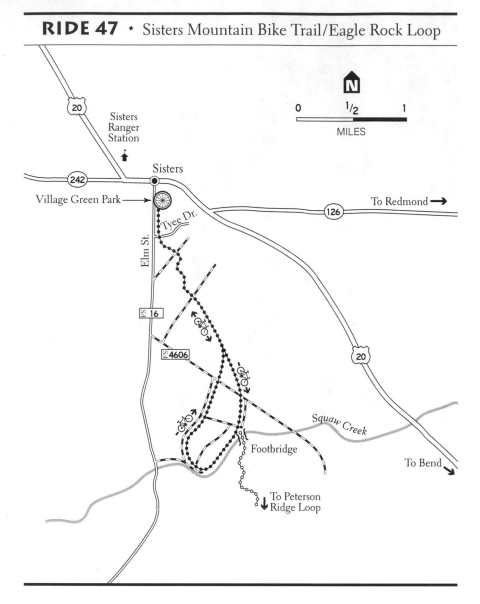

Public rest rooms and drinking water are available at Village Green Park.

**Hazards:** Watch for sandy sections of trail, especially in corners. Control your speed and watch for others using the trail. Be mindful of vehicular traffic in town and where the single-track crosses forest roads.

**Rescue index:** Help can be found in Sisters.

**Land status:** City of Sisters and the Deschutes National Forest.

**Maps:** The handout from the Sisters Ranger District titled "Sisters Bike Trail" describes the ride and includes a map of the route. "Mountain Biking Central Oregon," a map by Fat Tire Publications, delineates the ride. USGS 7.5 minute quad: Sisters.

**Finding the trail:** On Main Street/US 20 in Sisters, turn south onto Elm Street/Forest Service Road 16. Proceed on Elm Street for 2 blocks to Village Green Park on the left. Park your car at the park.

**Source of additional information:**

Sisters Ranger District
P.O. Box 249
Sisters, OR 97759
(541) 549-2111

**Notes on the trail:** Head south from the park on Elm Street. Near the edge of town (at Tyee Drive), bear left onto signed Sisters Mountain Bike Trail. At intersections, follow the Carsonite signs that mark the route. After a couple of wood footbridges, the route follows a rough double-track signed FS 930. Turn right onto single-track after 0.3 mile on FS 930. Immediately cross FS 4606 to follow a double-track. Turn left onto another double-track in 0.3 mile. This will bring you to a larger wood bridge at Squaw Creek. Do not cross the bridge, instead, turn right and parallel the creek. Follow the Carsonite signs as the route utilizes single-tracks, then double-tracks, then dirt roads. When you get back to FS 930, turn left and cross the small footbridge. Return the way you came to your parked vehicle at Village Green Park.

## RIDE 48 · Sisters Mountain Bike Trail/Peterson Ridge Loop

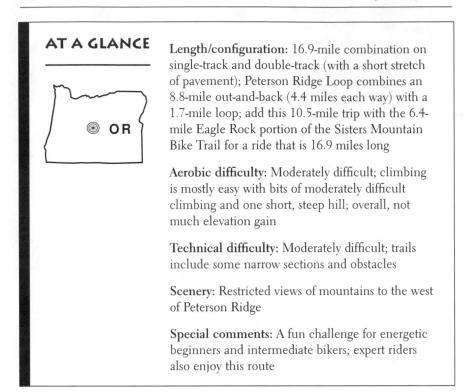

**AT A GLANCE**

**Length/configuration:** 16.9-mile combination on single-track and double-track (with a short stretch of pavement); Peterson Ridge Loop combines an 8.8-mile out-and-back (4.4 miles each way) with a 1.7-mile loop; add this 10.5-mile trip with the 6.4-mile Eagle Rock portion of the Sisters Mountain Bike Trail for a ride that is 16.9 miles long

**Aerobic difficulty:** Moderately difficult; climbing is mostly easy with bits of moderately difficult climbing and one short, steep hill; overall, not much elevation gain

**Technical difficulty:** Moderately difficult; trails include some narrow sections and obstacles

**Scenery:** Restricted views of mountains to the west of Peterson Ridge

**Special comments:** A fun challenge for energetic beginners and intermediate bikers; expert riders also enjoy this route

In the last chapter we explored the "easy" part of the Sisters Mountain Bike Trail, Eagle Rock Loop. This chapter is devoted to its harder cousin, Peterson Ridge Loop. Peterson Ridge Loop is a 16.9-mile outing. (It is an extension of Eagle Rock Loop.) Peterson Ridge Loop involves an 8.8-mile out-and-back (4.4 miles each way) and a 1.7-mile loop. Combining this 10.5-mile trip with the 6.4-mile Eagle Rock Loop makes for a 16.9-mile outing.

This route includes some moderately difficult climbing and one short, steep hill that could pose climbing and descending problems for novices. Energetic beginners might enjoy Peterson Ridge Loop, but they may wish to test their strengths and weaknesses on Eagle Rock Loop first.

Peterson Ridge Loop includes all and more of the technical aspects of Eagle Rock Loop. Expect obstacles like rocks, narrow sections of trail, localized sandy conditions, and roots. There is one brief, steep hill on this ride. It requires good bike-handling skills; push your bike up it. On the return, walk your bike down it.

Skidding is very hard on trails. It is important that trail bicyclists learn to descend hills without locking their brakes. Practice on dirt and gravel roads. Learn to shift your weight back (farther back as the pitch of the descent increases). Experts can descend very steep pitches without skidding; they get their weight well back, and they are adept at modulating their brakes. Seek advice and

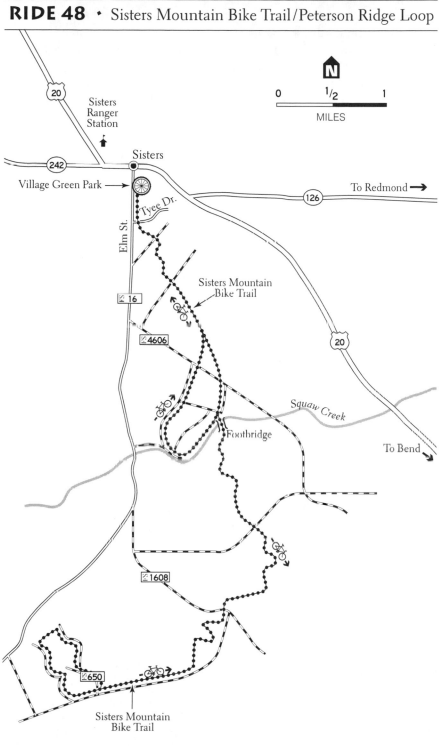

Sisters Ranger Station

Sisters

Village Green Park →

To Redmond →

Tyee Dr.

Elm St.

FS 16

FS 4606

Sisters Mountain Bike Trail

Squaw Creek

Footbridge

To Bend ↘

FS 1608

FS 650

Sisters Mountain Bike Trail

0    ½    1
MILES

information, and don't be put off from riding single-track. Just be ready to walk your bike down hills that are beyond your ability to negotiate without skidding.

This circuit travels past some interesting rock formations and through some areas of old-growth juniper. The southern most portion of the trip traverses Peterson Ridge; a high area in this relatively low section of the forest. The ridge provides some limited views to the west of peaks and glaciers in the Three Sisters Wilderness.

**General location:** The ride starts in Sisters.

**Elevation change:** The route begins at 3,185'. The high point, on Peterson Ridge, is 3,840'. Ups and downs add about 100' of climbing to this ride. Total elevation gain: 755'.

**Season:** These trails are usually accessible from the spring through the fall.

**Services:** Public rest rooms and drinking water are available at Village Green Park. All services (except public laundry facilities) are available in Sisters.

**Hazards:** Dry weather and heavy use can contribute to make sections of the roads and trails sandy. Watch for these conditions, especially in corners. Check your speed on the single-track and watch for other trail users who may be approaching from around blind corners. Ride defensively and predictably through town. Some of the forest roads you encounter on this ride remain in use by motorists. Be mindful of traffic and approach road crossings with care.

**Rescue index:** Help is available in Sisters.

**Land status:** City of Sisters and the Deschutes National Forest.

**Maps:** The Sisters Ranger District Handout titled "Sisters Bike Trail" describes this ride and includes a map of the route. We found the district map of the Sisters Ranger District to be a helpful resource. A map by Fat Tire Publications, "Mountain Biking Central Oregon," delineates the ride. USGS 7.5 minute quads: Three Creek Butte and Sisters.

**Finding the trail:** On Main Street/US 20 in Sisters, turn south onto Elm Street/Forest Service Road 16. Proceed on Elm Street for 2 blocks to Village Green Park on the left. Park your car at the park.

**Source of additional information:**

Sisters Ranger District
P.O. Box 249
Sisters, OR 97759
(541) 549-2111

**Notes on the trail:** Some intersections on the Sisters Mountain Bike Trail are well signed, others are not. Riders with developed route-finding skills may wish to rely only on the recommended maps and a compass as directional aids.

Head south from the park on Elm Street. Near the edge of town (at Tyee Drive), bear left onto signed Sisters Mountain Bike Trail. At intersections, follow the Carsonite signs that mark the route. After a couple of wood footbridges,

Peterson Ridge Loop.

the route follows a rough double-track signed FS 930. Turn right onto a single-track after 0.3 mile on FS 930. Immediately cross FS 1606 to follow a double-track. Turn left onto another double-track in 0.3 mile. This will bring you to a larger wood bridge at Squaw Creek. Cross the bridge and follow the trail to the right. Shortly, bear left onto a double-track. This double-track soon becomes more trail-like. The route crosses a red gravel road onto signed FS 115 (this landmark is 1.6 miles beyond the crossing of Squaw Creek). After 0.3 mile on FS 115, turn left onto a trail (easy to miss) and cross an irrigation ditch. Climb steeply and cross a second, smaller ditch. Follow the trail as it rolls up and down and slowly gains elevation. (This segment of the route alternately follows single-tracks, then old double-tracks.) Cross FS 1608 to pick up a twisty section of single-track. In 0.7 mile, a Carsonite sign directs you right onto a double-track. In another mile, ride around a pile of rocks to continue on the double-track. In 0.3 mile, turn right at a Carsonite sign onto a double-track (trail-like) that takes you past some rock outcroppings. In another 0.7 mile, turn right onto a single-track. Shortly, make another right turn, this time onto a double-track. In 0.5 mile, the trail bears left onto signed FS 650. Turn left at the next **T** intersection (near the pile of rocks you rode around earlier) and backtrack to the bridge over

Squaw Creek. Cross the bridge and turn left to parallel the creek. Follow the Carsonite signs as the route utilizes single-tracks, then double-tracks, then dirt roads. When you get back to FS 930, turn left and cross a small footbridge. Backtrack on this portion of the Sisters Mountain Bike Trail to Elm Street. Follow Elm Street to Village Green Park and your vehicle.

## RIDE 49 · Upper Three Creek Lake Sno-Park/Short Loop

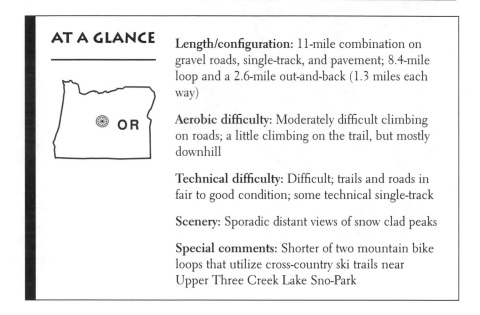

**AT A GLANCE**

**Length/configuration:** 11-mile combination on gravel roads, single-track, and pavement; 8.4-mile loop and a 2.6-mile out-and-back (1.3 miles each way)

**Aerobic difficulty:** Moderately difficult climbing on roads; a little climbing on the trail, but mostly downhill

**Technical difficulty:** Difficult; trails and roads in fair to good condition; some technical single-track

**Scenery:** Sporadic distant views of snow clad peaks

**Special comments:** Shorter of two mountain bike loops that utilize cross-country ski trails near Upper Three Creek Lake Sno-Park

In the winter, it's easy to tell who the Nordic skiers are in central Oregon. Their toothy grins give them away. What's the source of this inextinguishable bliss? A drive on the region's mountain roads provides a clue. Every byway seems to include a Sno-Park. Sno-Parks are trailheads for winter recreation sites. In the Bend/Sisters area, these cross-country ski trail networks are ubiquitous.

Nordic trails are often fashioned from old logging roads. Some Nordic trails make good mountain biking routes. They can be especially good if they tie into single-track trails. The cross-country trails near Three Creek Lake provide a link to a notable piece of single-track—the Metolius/Windigo Trail. Two popular loops originate at the Upper Three Creek Lake Sno-Park. This chapter describes the shorter, easier loop. The next chapter explores the more challenging circuit.

This trip is 11 miles long. It consists of an 8.4-mile loop and a 2.6-mile out-and-back (1.3 miles each way). There are 0.4 mile of pavement, 2.3 miles of single-track, and 8.3 miles of dirt and gravel roads.

The roads are in good condition with some sand and rocks. The single-track portion of the ride explores a small section of the Metolius/Windigo Trail. Here,

Watching the bikes take a break.

the trail is in mostly good condition, but it does contain one short, steep section that is heavily eroded. Abrupt drop-offs and narrow, ditch-like conditions characterize this technical stretch. (Reduce your impact on this damaged portion of single-track—walk or carry your bike down.)

The scenery found in this part of Oregon is incredible. Driving into Sisters, you can't help but be taken by the beauty that surrounds you. Around each bend in the road is another view of giant snow-capped volcanoes and shimmering snowfields. The scenery is so awesome that one tends to start taking grandeur for granted.

This bike route offers riders scenic tidbits. Most of the time you are in the woods, but there are clearings that offer glimpses of distant mountains. Perhaps this "portioned landscape" helped us appreciate the vistas that were available. While the scenery didn't give us goose bumps, we did enjoy what we saw. Most memorable were views of Broken Top and Three Sisters from the forest roads early in the ride. At Jeff View Shelter we had a good look at Mt. Washington. It was a clear day, and Mt. Jefferson could be seen far to the north.

**General location:** Upper Three Creek Lake Sno-Park is about 11 miles south of Sisters.

**Elevation change:** The trailhead is at 5,120'. The high point of the circuit (6,340') is obtained near Park Meadow Trailhead. Undulations over the course of the ride add about 300' of climbing to the trip. Total elevation gain: 1,520'.

**Season:** Give the single-track plenty of time to dry out before attempting to ride on the Metolius/Windigo Trail. This is a good destination for summer and fall excursions. The cross-country trails/forest roads in the area can be approached earlier in the season.

**Services:** All services (except public laundry facilities) are available in Sisters.

**Hazards:** Watch for vehicles on the roads. Expect obstacles like rocks, roots, forest litter, and sandy patches on the trails and roads. A short section of the Metolius/Windigo Trail is steep and degraded. Hikers and horses may be encountered on the Metolius/Windigo Trail. Watch for them, especially on the stretch between Park Meadow Trailhead and the Snow Creek tributary. This section of trail is popular with equestrians and hikers accessing the backcountry.

**Rescue index:** Help is available in Sisters.

**Land status:** Deschutes National Forest.

**Maps:** We consider the district map of the Sisters Ranger District the best map for this loop. The map is especially handy when you are trying to figure out the area's spider web of forest roads. USGS 7.5 minute quads: Broken Top, Three Creek Butte, and Trout Creek Butte.

**Finding the trail:** On Main Street/US 20 in Sisters, turn south onto Elm Street/Forest Service Road 16. Follow this road for 10.7 miles to FS 1620 and Upper Three Creek Lake Sno-Park on the left (1.3 miles past Lower Three Creek Lake Sno-Park). Park in Upper Three Creek Lake Sno-Park.

**Source of additional information:**

Sisters Ranger District
P.O. Box 249
Sisters, OR 97759
(541) 549-2111

**Notes on the trail:** Turn left out of the Sno-Park onto FS 16. Shortly, turn right onto FS 700 at a sign for "Nancy and Warren Loop Trails" and "Three Creek Lake." Stay on FS 700 where side roads branch off. In 3.9 miles, turn right onto FS 16. Follow FS 16 for 0.5 mile, then turn right at a sign for Park Meadow Trailhead. Follow a native surface road through an open area to Park Meadow Trailhead. (The road to the trailhead is actually the beginning leg of Trail 99 — the Metolius/Windigo Trail.) Continue on the road as it twists its way downhill and becomes more trail-like. Arrive at a small creek (a tributary of Snow Creek) marked by several signs for "Snow Creek Nordic Trail" and "Three Creek Lake." Cross the creek and arrive at an intersection of trails near a sign-in box for Three Sisters Wilderness (no bikes in designated wilderness areas). Turn right to follow poorly marked Trail 99. (The trail is signed with a small red, white, and blue National Scenic Trail marker that is attached to a tree.) The trail descends and parallels the creek, immediately re-crosses the creek, then drops steeply through ditch-like conditions. (Carry or walk your bike down this section of single-track to avoid damaging the trail further.) Pass near the creek again, then climb briefly before arriving at an intersection with several signs for "Three Creek Trail."

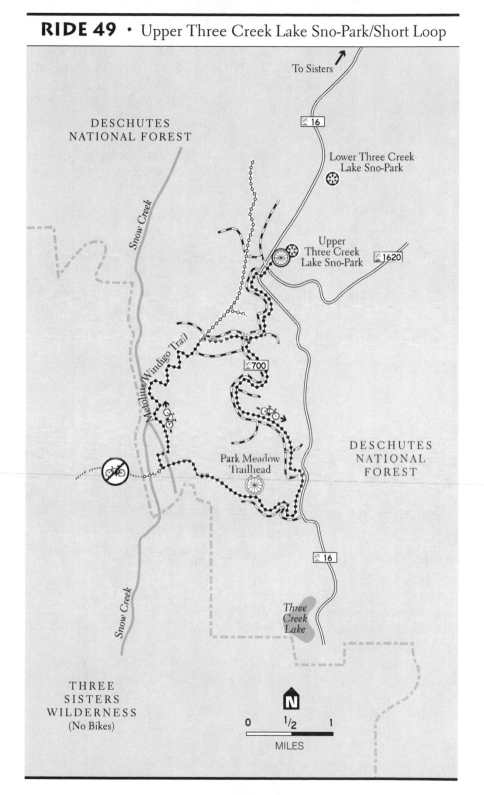

To Sisters

FS 16

DESCHUTES
NATIONAL FOREST

Lower Three Creek
Lake Sno-Park

Snow Creek

Upper
Three Creek
Lake Sno-Park

FS 1620

Metolius/Windigo Trail

FS 700

Park Meadow
Trailhead

DESCHUTES
NATIONAL
FOREST

FS 16

Snow Creek

Three
Creek
Lake

THREE
SISTERS
WILDERNESS
(No Bikes)

N

0    ½    1
MILES

Continue straight. In 0.3 mile, turn right onto a double-track signed for "Warren's and Nancy's Loop." (This turn is 8.9 miles into the ride.) Stay on this double-track until you reach FS 700. Turn left onto FS 700 and backtrack to your vehicle.

## RIDE 50 · Upper Three Creek Lake Sno-Park/Long Loop

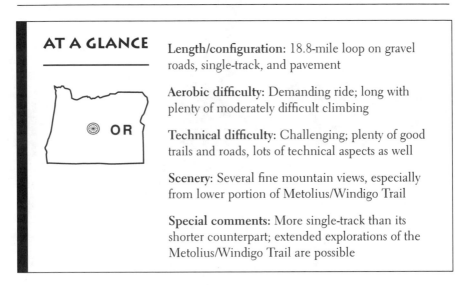

**AT A GLANCE**

**Length/configuration:** 18.8-mile loop on gravel roads, single-track, and pavement

**Aerobic difficulty:** Demanding ride; long with plenty of moderately difficult climbing

**Technical difficulty:** Challenging; plenty of good trails and roads, lots of technical aspects as well

**Scenery:** Several fine mountain views, especially from lower portion of Metolius/Windigo Trail

**Special comments:** More single-track than its shorter counterpart; extended explorations of the Metolius/Windigo Trail are possible

This is the longer Upper Three Creek Lake Sno-Park Loop. This long-winded title of a ride is an 18.8-mile loop. It includes 4.1 miles of pavement, 7.8 miles of dirt and gravel roads, and 6.9 miles of single-track. This circuit is similar to the shorter "Three Creek" Loop, but it adds several miles of single-track, and several road miles to the mix.

The scenery on this trip is very fine, with particularly lovely views of Middle and North Sister from the Metolius/Windigo Trail. This scenery presents itself where the trail gains a ridge and proceeds through stands of large ponderosa pines. Soon, the forest gives way to open areas choked with manzanita bushes. Even though we weren't far from civilization, we enjoyed a feeling of remoteness while riding on this trail.

Length, technical difficulties, and significant climbs add up to make this a demanding loop. It begins and ends with a moderately difficult climb on forest roads. There is a lot of descending on the Metolius/Windigo Trail, but it climbs some, too. Parts of the trail are steep, rocky, and sandy. On the ridge, the trail is narrow with encroaching vegetation. Technical aspects include exciting descents through soft and rough conditions.

It is possible to enjoy further explorations of the rugged and challenging

Stunning backdrop on the "Upper Three Creek Long Loop."

Metolius/Windigo Trail. You may wish to consider a car shuttle ride between Park Meadow Trailhead and either Cow Campground or Cold Springs Campground. This trail can also be connected with the Sisters Mountain Bike Trail. Be advised that the Metolius/Windigo Trail is technically demanding and, at times, hard to follow. Seek out current information from local bike shops and the Sisters ranger station. Carry the district map, a compass, and be prepared to spend some time getting unlost.

**General location:**  Begins at Upper Three Creek Lake Sno-Park, about 11 miles south of Sisters.

**Elevation change:**  Begins at 5,120' and reaches a high point of 6,340' near Park Meadow Trailhead. The low point (4,120') is obtained on Forest Service Road 1514. Ups and downs on the loop add approximately 500' of climbing to the trip. Overall elevation gain: 2,720'.

**Season:**  The upper end of the Metolius/Windigo Trail can remain damp until late June or early July. Call ahead and inquire about trail conditions. The cross-country trails/forest roads and the lower reaches of the Metolius/Windigo Trail are often ready for traffic earlier in the spring.

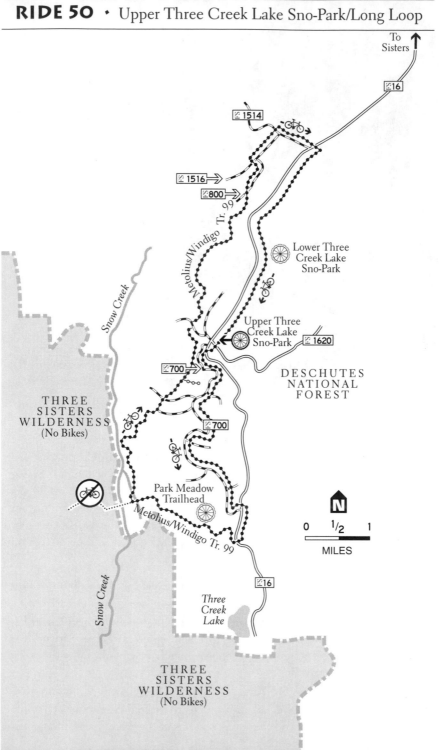

**Services:** There is no potable water on this ride. All services (except public laundry facilities) are available in Sisters.

**Hazards:** Ride defensively and predictably on the roads; especially paved FS 16. You will encounter obstacles on the trails like rocks, roots, sand, and abrupt drop-offs. Walk your bike down the trail where it is most severely eroded. Hikers and equestrians are often encountered on the Metolius/Windigo Trail. Control your speed on descents and watch for others around blind corners.

**Rescue index:** Help can be obtained in Sisters.

**Land status:** Deschutes National Forest.

**Maps:** The best map is the district map of the Sisters Ranger District. It isn't perfect, but it is useful in delineating the area's maze of forest roads. USGS 7.5 minute quads: Broken Top, Three Creek Butte, and Trout Creek Butte.

**Finding the trail:** On Main Street/US 20 in Sisters, turn south onto Elm Street/FS 16. Follow FS 16 for 10.7 miles to FS 1620 and Upper Three Creek Lake Sno-Park on the left. (This Sno-Park is 1.3 miles beyond Lower Three Creek Lake Sno-Park.)

## Source of additional information:

Sisters Ranger District
P.O. Box 249
Sisters, OR 97759
(541) 549-2111

**Notes on the trail:** Follow the "Notes on the trail" for Ride 49/Upper Three Creek Lake Sno-Park/Short Loop. When you reach the double-track signed for "Warren and Nancy's Loop" (8.9 miles into the ride), continue straight on the single track (follow the signs for "Sno-Park"). In 0.4 mile, notice a faint trail that goes right at an intersection indicated by two blue diamond-shaped markers on a tree. Continue straight on the main trail. Soon, the trail begins to roll up and down. Each successive climb becomes more difficult. In 0.7 mile, the trail bends left and intersects a double-track-like trail. (If you would like to bail out of the ride, turn hard to the right onto the double-track and descend. Stay to the right at the next two intersections to arrive back at your parked car.) For those continuing on with the long loop, bear left onto the double-track. Shortly, the double-track climbs steeply up a sandy slope and deposits you at a **Y** intersection. This intersection is dotted with markers: orange diamonds and black arrows. Turn right onto the single-track and climb to pass between two large ponderosa pines. Here, the trail is marked with yellow diamonds. In 3.2 miles the trail dumps you out onto an old double-track (FS 800). Continue downhill (bear right) onto the double-track (still following yellow diamonds). Turn right when you reach a major gravel road (FS 1516). Turn right at the next intersection onto FS 1514. Turn right when you get to paved FS 16. Climb 3.7 miles to the Upper Three Creek Lake Sno-Park.

# RIDE 51 · Suttle Tie Trail/Suttle Lake Loop Trail

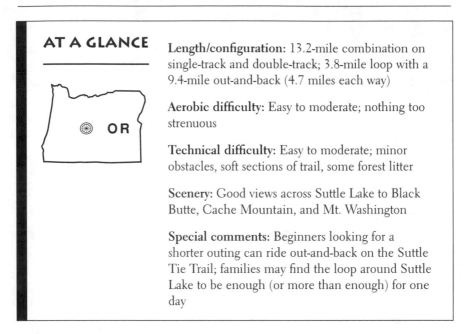

**AT A GLANCE**

**Length/configuration:** 13.2-mile combination on single-track and double-track; 3.8-mile loop with a 9.4-mile out-and-back (4.7 miles each way)

**Aerobic difficulty:** Easy to moderate; nothing too strenuous

**Technical difficulty:** Easy to moderate; minor obstacles, soft sections of trail, some forest litter

**Scenery:** Good views across Suttle Lake to Black Butte, Cache Mountain, and Mt. Washington

**Special comments:** Beginners looking for a shorter outing can ride out-and-back on the Suttle Tie Trail; families may find the loop around Suttle Lake to be enough (or more than enough) for one day

Trail crews with the Sisters Ranger District have been busy developing a trail resource known as "Roads to Trails." First, old double-tracks are closed to vehicles, then the crews work the tread of the roads to provide a more trail-like feel. Some new sections of single-track are then built. These new pieces of trail are used as links between the old double-tracks. The results have been impressive, especially the Suttle Tie Trail. This route includes some good single-track, and the double-track sections themselves seem a lot like trails. Forest vegetation is encroaching on the old roads, and bicyclists seem to be choosing the same lines of travel. In time, you won't be able to tell that this route followed roads at all.

Suttle Tie Trail creates a link between riding opportunities on the flanks of Black Butte and the single-track that encircles Suttle Lake. Combining Suttle Tie Trail and Suttle Lake Loop Trail makes for a 13.2-mile excursion. The ride is a combination of a 3.8-mile loop and a 9.4-mile out-and-back leg (4.7 miles each way). The riding is easy with some short, moderately difficult hills on Suttle Tie Trail. On the return, these hills provide for some mildly exciting descents. Suttle Lake Loop Trail hugs the shoreline of the lake and gains small increments of elevation as it rolls over footbridges and through small drainages.

Sandy conditions, rocks, roots, and forest litter add some difficulty to the riding, but in general, these obstacles are not too technically demanding. Beginners and families may find the trip too long. An easier option is riding only the lake loop. Suttle Tie Trail is more difficult, but energetic beginners may appreciate its challenges. They can approach it as an out-and-back trip, leaving the loop around the lake for another day.

# RIDE 51 · Suttle Tie Trail/Suttle Lake Loop Trail

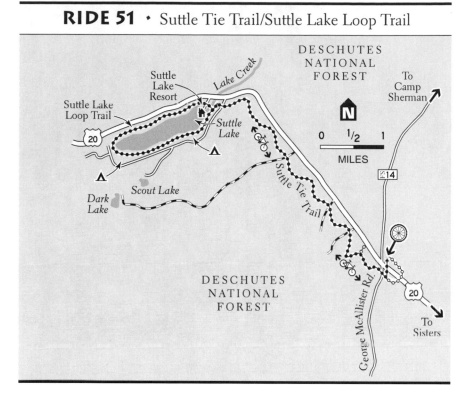

Suttle Tie Trail parallels US 20, but the highway is hidden from view. However, traffic noise is often audible. Suttle Tie Trail is more exciting than the loop trail around Suttle Lake, but the lake is the scenic highlight of the ride. The north shore provides good views of Black Butte, Cache Mountain, and Mt. Washington. Fishing gear, bait, and boats are available for rent at the resort at the east end of the lake. There are several campgrounds on the south shore. Some offer beachside sites (if you're lucky enough to snag one). Last but not least on the list of things to like about Suttle Lake—swimming after a hot summertime ride.

**General location:** The trailhead is just off US 20, approximately 10 miles northwest of Sisters.

**Elevation change:** The ride begins at 3,325' and reaches a high point of 3,440' at Suttle Lake. Ups and downs on Suttle Tie Trail add about 300' of climbing to the tour. Total elevation gain: 415'.

**Season:** Suttle Tie Trail is usually rideable in the early spring. The single-track around Suttle Lake may require several more weeks before it is sufficiently dry.

**Services:** Water is available seasonally at the campgrounds around Suttle Lake. Suttle Lake Resort sells bait, tackle, and ice. The resort rents foot-powered

Suttle Lake Loop Trail.

paddleboats and fishing boats. All services (except public laundry facilities) are available in Sisters.

**Hazards:** Suttle Lake is a popular warm weather destination. Watch for people strolling on the trail and fishing from the bank. Sections of the trails are very soft with fine gravel and sand. Watch for these hazards and consider walking your bike through them. Control your speed on the trails, particularly around the lake and on the Suttle Tie Trail return; someone may be around the next corner. Exercise caution where the route crosses roads; your line of sight, and that of motorists, may be restricted. Some road crossings are not obvious from the trail; you may not notice that you are approaching a road. Be careful crossing US 20.

**Rescue index:** There is a pay phone at the start of the ride, and at Suttle Lake Resort. Emergency services are located in Sisters and Bend.

**Land status:** Deschutes National Forest.

**Maps:** The Suttle Lake Loop Trail is shown on the district map of the Sisters Ranger District. Suttle Tie Trail is not delineated on this map. A good map for the entire route, "Mountain Biking Central Oregon," is available at area bike shops. USGS 7.5 minute quads: Black Butte and Three Fingered Jack.

**Finding the trail:** From Sisters, drive north on US 20. After 9.5 miles, turn right onto unsigned Forest Service Road 14. (This intersection is just beyond mile marker 91, and it is signed for Camp Sherman.) Immediately turn right into a forest information pull-out and parking area. If this parking area is full, park on the opposite side of FS 14, in a large gravel pull-out.

## Source of additional information:

Sisters Ranger District
P.O. Box 249
Sisters, OR 97759
(541) 549-2111

**Notes on the trail:** Check carefully for traffic, then walk (or ride) your bike across US 20 to paved George McAllister Road. There is a "Suttle Tie Trail" trailhead sign on the right. Here, turn right onto the double-track trail. The route alternates between old double-tracks and stretches of single-track. Nearing the lake, the trail crosses several gravel roads, then a paved road. Stay on the main trail to parallel Lake Creek. You will soon arrive at a trailhead interpretive sign for Suttle Tie Trail (near a large footbridge spanning Lake Creek). Continue straight and pick up Suttle Lake Loop Trail—it hugs the shoreline. Circle the lake in a clockwise direction. The trail arrives at pavement near Suttle Lake Resort (back at the east end of the lake). Turn left and follow the paved road a short distance to another trail on the right. Turn onto this trail (it heads toward a dam). As you near the dam look left for the large footbridge spanning Lake Creek. The bridge is marked by a sign for "Suttle Lake Loop Trail #90." Cross the bridge. Turn left onto Suttle Tie Trail and backtrack to your car.

## RIDE 52 · Green Ridge Lookout Loop

**AT A GLANCE**

**Length/configuration:** 34.4-mile combination on gravel and paved roads; the ride involves a 31.2-mile loop and a 3.2-mile out-and-back (1.6 miles each way)

**Aerobic difficulty:** Difficult; long steady climb to the ridge

**Technical difficulty:** Easy; gravel and dirt roads in mostly good condition

**Scenery:** Excellent views from the lookout of Mt. Jefferson and the Metolius River Basin

**Special comments:** Green Ridge is traversed by a portion of the Metolius/Windigo Trail; we found it too soft to ride (even downhill), but wet weather is said to improve the tread

This 34.4-mile road loop includes a short out-and-back to Green Ridge Lookout Tower. The ride is difficult due to its length and the long, steady climb to Green Ridge. Still, it is not technically demanding and could be tackled by determined intermediate cyclists. The trip follows gravel and dirt roads for 22.8 miles and pavement for 11.6 miles. Clear days allow good views of Three Sisters, Mt. Washington, Three Fingered Jack, Mt. Jefferson, and the Metolius River Basin.

A segment of the Metolius/Windigo Trail traverses Green Ridge. We attempted to descend off of the ridge on this trail; picking it up south of the lookout. In places, the trail was difficult to follow. It was also very soft with pumice dust; a common problem in regions with volcanic soils. Deep pockets of dust can accumulate, especially during periods of dry weather and high traffic (the trail is popular with equestrians and cyclists). Local riders attempt the trail in the spring or following periods of rain. We backtracked to forest roads for our departure off of the ridge top.

**General location:** This ride begins near the headwaters of the Metolius River, approximately 17 miles north of Sisters.

**Elevation change:** The elevation at the start of the ride is 2,960'. The high point is on Forest Service Road 600, at 4,860'. Ups and downs contribute about 1,000' of climbing to the tour. Total elevation gain: 2,900'.

**Season:** The roads are generally free of snow from late May through the middle of October.

# RIDE 52 · Green Ridge Lookout Loop

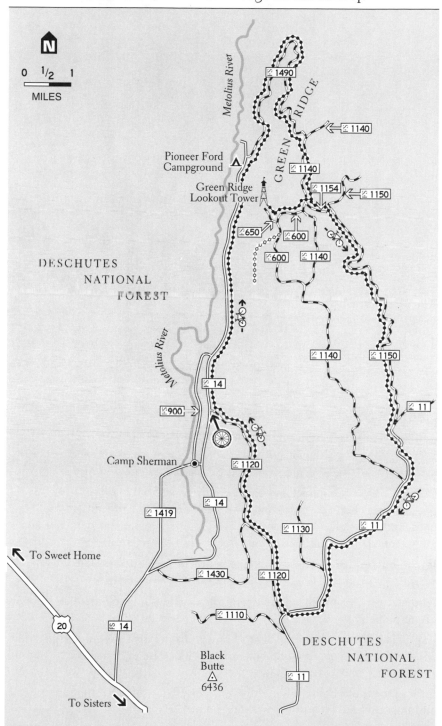

Climbing to
Green Ridge.

**Services:** There is no water on this ride. Water is available seasonally at camp-grounds along the Metolius River. A pay phone can be found in Camp Sherman. Food, lodging, groceries, and gas can be obtained in Sisters.

**Hazards:** Watch for traffic, and be especially careful while riding on the paved roads. If you choose to ride down the Metolius/Windigo Trail, control your speed and be ready for soft conditions. This trail is popular with horseback riders. Anticipate others approaching from around blind corners.

**Rescue index:** The nearest pay phone is in Camp Sherman. Help is available in Sisters.

**Land status:** Deschutes National Forest lands and public right-of-way through private property.

**Maps:** The district map of the Sisters Ranger District is a good guide to this ride. USGS 7.5 minute quads: Little Squaw Back, Black Butte, Prairie Farm Spring, and Candle Creek.

**Finding the trail:** From Sisters, drive north on US 20. After 9.4 miles, turn right onto unsigned FS 14 (just beyond mile marker 91). FS 14 is a paved two-lane road marked with a sign reading "Metolius River—5, Camp Sherman—5." Stay to the right in 2.7 miles, remaining on FS 14. (Follow the sign that directs you to the campgrounds.) Continue on FS 14 for another 4.6 miles and turn right onto FS 1120. Take the next right, onto a double-track. Park on the right.

**Source of additional information:**

Sisters Ranger District
P.O. Box 249
Sisters, OR 97759
(541) 549-2111

**Notes on the trail:** Ride back to FS 14 and turn right. After nearly 6 miles of pavement, turn right onto red cinder FS 1490. (You come to this turn after passing Pioneer Ford Campground.) Remain on FS 1490 as spur roads branch off. After attaining the ridge, you will arrive at a **T** intersection. Turn right onto FS 1140. In another 1.5 miles, bear right, remaining on FS 1140 where FS 1154 goes left. (You will return to this intersection after visiting the lookout.) Ride 0.2 mile farther on FS 1140 and turn right onto FS 600. Stay on FS 600 for 1.3 miles to FS 650. Turn right onto FS 650 and descend to the lookout tower. Turn around at the lookout and return the way you came, to the intersection of FS 1140 and FS 1154. Turn right onto FS 1154 (toward US 20). Turn right onto FS 1150 (again, toward US 20) in 0.7 mile. Follow FS 1150 for 6.8 miles to a stop sign and paved FS 11. Continue straight onto FS 11. After 5.8 miles on FS 11, turn right onto cinder FS 1120. Remain on FS 1120 to reach your vehicle on the left.

## RIDE 53 · Cache Mountain Loop

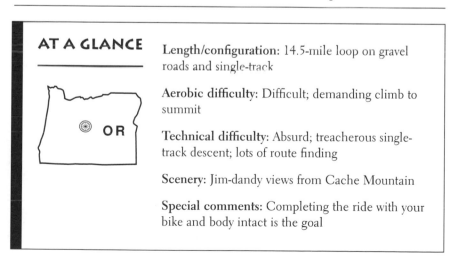

**AT A GLANCE**

**OR**

**Length/configuration:** 14.5-mile loop on gravel roads and single-track

**Aerobic difficulty:** Difficult; demanding climb to summit

**Technical difficulty:** Absurd; treacherous single-track descent; lots of route finding

**Scenery:** Jim-dandy views from Cache Mountain

**Special comments:** Completing the ride with your bike and body intact is the goal

Three Fingered Jack
from Cache Mountain.

In Sisters, inquiries about local rides had us heading for Cache Mountain. We'd been told that a demanding road climb would take us to the summit of Cache Mountain, then we could enjoy an exciting single-track descent off of the top. The ride lived up to its billing, but the descent was a little too thrilling for our blood.

The climb up Cache Mountain begins with grades that provide a nice warm-up. As you approach the top, the roads become rougher and the climbing gets more demanding. Attaining the summit is a relief. It is good to be done with the climb, and the views from the top seem to confirm your good judgment in choosing this ride. Hold on Einstein, don't go congratulating yourself just yet; check out the single-track descent off of the mountain first. It's so torturous that you may be tempted to blame the selection of this ride on your riding partner. Then again, we know some nut cases who enjoy challenges of this type.

We found ourselves wondering, "Who laid out this trail?" Perhaps this route isn't the result of any design process. Maybe it's a bootleg downhill mountain bike route or a motorcycle trail. Could it have been built by equestrians who were mad at their horses?

The worst trail conditions occur during the first 1.5 miles of the descent, then the trail improves. Up high, the single-track is very steep; rain and run-off flow straight down the gut. This results in tire-grabbing, ditch-like conditions. These conditions result in mountain bike guidebook authors being thrown ass over teakettle. What's that you say, you're beginning to like the sound of this ride?

The loop is 14.5 miles long. Most of the riding (11.1 miles) is on forest roads. The single-track is a 3.4-mile descent. The roads are in mostly good condition, but they begin to break up near the top of the mountain. These soft conditions make the climbing difficult.

The vista from the top of Cache Mountain is worth climbing for. While the view is not a complete 360-degree panorama, it comes close. Even with less than ideal conditions we could make out cloud-shrouded snowfields on Middle and North Sister. Panning north we picked out more snowy peaks, including Mt. Washington, Three Fingered Jack, and Mt. Jefferson. Down below, at the foot of Cache Mountain, sat Link Creek Lakes Basin, a dozen or so tiny lakes and boggy meadows cradled between Little Cache Mountain, Hayrick Butte, and Hogg Rock.

Staying on track during the descent isn't easy; there are a lot of turns at unmarked intersections. Non-daredevils and the directionally challenged can return from the mountain top by backtracking on the forest roads they climbed on. Missy Giove and her friends can take the trail.

**General location:** The trailhead for this ride is at Scout Lake, approximately 15 miles northwest of Sisters.

**Elevation change:** The loop begins at 3,700' at Scout Lake. The high point of the trip is atop Cache Mountain at 5,580'. Ups and downs add about 500' of climbing to the trip. Overall elevation gain: 2,380'.

**Season:** Depending on snow, the roads on this ride can be followed year round (as an out-and-back trip). Avoid the trail when it is wet.

**Services:** Water is available seasonally at Scout Lake. All services are available in Sisters (except public laundry facilities).

**Hazards:** The upper portion of the single track is eroded. Its tread is narrow and in places it is **V**-shaped. You can easily catch your tire in a rut and lose control. Roots, rocks, and sand are encountered on the ride. Control your speed and watch for others on the trails and roads.

**Rescue index:** Help is available in Sisters. There is a pay phone at Suttle Lake Resort (at the east end of the lake).

**Land status:** Deschutes National Forest.

**Maps:** The trail is delineated on "Mountain Biking Central Oregon," a map by Fat Tire Publications. The district map of the Sisters Ranger District is a helpful guide to roads and landmarks in the area. (The trail is not indicated on the district map.) USGS 7.5 minute quads: Black Crater, Little Squaw Back, and Black Butte.

**Finding the trail:** From Sisters, drive north on US 20 for approximately 13

# RIDE 53 · Cache Mountain Loop

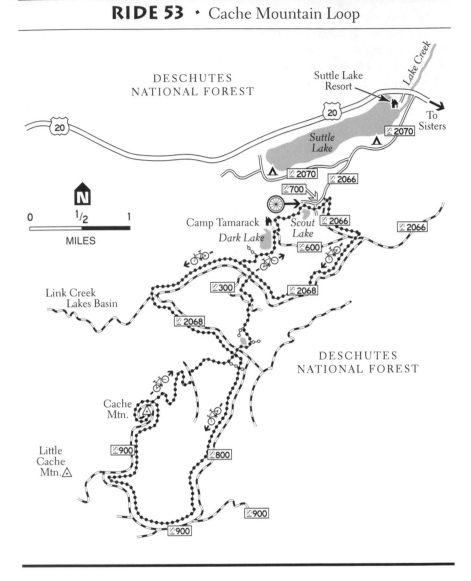

miles to Forest Service Road 2070 (signed for Suttle Lake Campgrounds). Turn left onto FS 2070 and drive 1.3 miles to FS 2066. Turn left onto FS 2066. In 0.5 mile, bear right onto FS 700 where FS 2066 goes left (follow the paved road). Shortly, arrive at Scout Lake and park your vehicle.

## Source of additional information:

Sisters Ranger District
P.O. Box 249
Sisters, OR 97759
(541) 549-2111

**Notes on the trail:** Head out paved FS 700. In 0.2 mile, turn right and climb on FS 2066. Continue straight past the entrance road to Camp Tamarack (FS 600). In another 0.2 mile, make a hard right onto FS 2068. Follow FS 2068 for 4.1 miles to a red gravel road on the right (signed FS 800). Turn right onto FS 800 and pedal 1.8 miles to signed FS 900. Bear right onto FS 900 and climb for 1.3 miles to a **T** intersection (you will pass several side roads, stay on the main road). Turn right to remain on FS 900. Travel another 1.1 miles to an unmarked trail on the right. This is the single-track that descends off the mountain. Note its location, then continue up FS 900 for another 0.2 mile to the top of Cache Mountain. Trees block the view from the summit. The best views are obtained just below the summit, at the last bend in the road. After sight-seeing, return down the road and turn left onto the trail. (To avoid the trail, return the way you came on the forest roads, or use your district map to find an alternate road route back to Scout Lake.) Trail riders: in 1 mile, turn left onto a double-track, then immediately turn right to regain the trail. In another 0.4 mile, the trail passes through an area dense with young evergreen trees, then curves to the right into a more open area with some distant views. Here, look left for a faint path. Turn left onto the indistinct trail. (If you miss this turn you will come out onto FS 800. See accompanying map.) Soon, the trail crosses FS 2068, then passes a tiny lake and arrives at an intersection of trails. Turn left at this junction. Then, in 0.2 mile, bear right where a trail comes in hard from the left. (Follow the white poles downhill.) Shortly, turn left and follow an overgrown double-track (FS 300) downhill; follow the yellow squares. In 0.7 mile, turn left onto a major gravel road, unsigned FS 2068. Follow the road a short distance to a faint trail on the right. This trail enters the woods at an area of recent logging activity. Get on the trail, then immediately bear left to follow a skid road a short distance to another faint trail on the right. Follow this indistinct trail down into a wooded gulch. Stay right and downhill at the next intersection where a trail goes left and climbs. Follow the main trail around the east side of Dark Lake to FS 600 and the entrance gate for Camp Tamarack. Turn right onto FS 600 and pedal a few yards to a trail on the left (near a couple of hitching posts). Follow this new single-track through an area that was recently logged. The trail curves left and passes above the camp's corrals. Bear right to stay on the single-track where a double-track continues straight. Stay right at the next two intersections to arrive back at Scout Lake. Ride around the lake to your car.

## RIDE 54 · McKenzie River National Recreation Trail

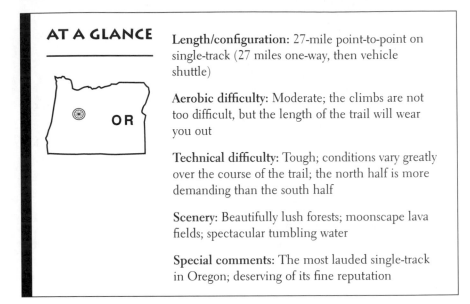

**AT A GLANCE**

**Length/configuration:** 27-mile point-to-point on single-track (27 miles one-way, then vehicle shuttle)

**Aerobic difficulty:** Moderate; the climbs are not too difficult, but the length of the trail will wear you out

**Technical difficulty:** Tough; conditions vary greatly over the course of the trail; the north half is more demanding than the south half

**Scenery:** Beautifully lush forests; moonscape lava fields; spectacular tumbling water

**Special comments:** The most lauded single-track in Oregon; deserving of its fine reputation

We spoke with hundreds of people about mountain biking opportunities in Oregon. The most common response to our inquiries about where to ride, was the McKenzie River Trail. Regardless of where we were, in Portland or Grants Pass, Eugene or Baker City (Seattle or Boise), people wanted to let us know that this trail was a must for our book. When we got to central Oregon, we rode the McKenzie River Trail. It really is a treasure.

The upper McKenzie is a spectacular whitewater river originating in the high Cascades. The 27-mile-long McKenzie River National Recreation Trail 3507 closely follows the river and passes through many contrasting environments. The northern end traverses an area of recent volcanic activity. The riding is extreme as the path crosses lava flows and skirts the eastern shore of beautiful Clear Lake. Beyond the lake, the trail passes two magnificent waterfalls before entering Tamolitch Valley. The river flows underground through much of the valley and then emerges from the base of a cliff (dry Tamolitch Falls), forming an azure, crystalline pool. The variety of environments is less dramatic in the remaining miles of the ride—just more great single-track, lush forest, and tumbling water.

The northern half of the trail is technical and demanding with narrow, twisty sections over razor-edged lava rock. Steep ups and downs near Sahalie and Koosah Falls are real skill-testers. South of Tamolitch Falls, the riding gets progressively easier. Beginners may wish to start at Paradise Campground and ride out and back in either direction.

Log bridge on McKenzie
River National
Recreation Trail.

**General location:** The southern terminus of the trail is 1.5 miles east of the tiny community of McKenzie Bridge, on OR 126 (approximately 50 miles east of Eugene).

**Elevation change:** The Santiam Wagon Road Trailhead is at 3,200'. The southern trailhead is at 1,450'. There are uphill stretches along the course of the descent. There is approximately 700' of climbing between the Santiam Wagon Road Trailhead and Trail Bridge Campground. There is about 400' of climbing between Trail Bridge and the southern trailhead. Total elevation gain: 1,100' (riding north to south only).

**Season:** Rhododendrons, dogwoods, and many species of wildflowers put on a good show of color in the spring and early summer. The trail is popular with hikers, and the highway can become busy with vacationers during the summer. Avoid the trail when it is wet; phone ahead to check on conditions.

**Services:** Water is available seasonally at Coldwater Cove, Trail Bridge, and Paradise campgrounds. Food, lodging, gas, and a pay phone can be found in McKenzie Bridge. All services are available in Springfield and Eugene.

**Hazards:** Creating a loop by using the highway is not recommended. Traffic travels at high speeds, and there are narrow bridges and blind corners to contend with. A possible exception is the stretch of highway from the southern trailhead to Paradise Campground—it has a wide shoulder. The trail crosses lava flows near Clear Lake and Tamolitch Falls. The tread is coarse and narrow, and pedaling over the lava requires good bike-handling skills. A fall here can cause nasty cuts. The trail contains some steep drop-offs, especially near the waterfalls.

**Rescue index:** Help is available at the McKenzie Ranger Station during regular office hours. There is a pay phone at the intersection of Forest Service Road 730 and FS 655 (at the north end of Trail Bridge Reservoir). Assistance can also be found in McKenzie Bridge.

**Land status:** Willamette National Forest.

**Maps:** We highly recommend the Willamette National Forest color map/brochure of the McKenzie River National Recreation Trail. USGS 7.5 minute quads: McKenzie Bridge, Belknap Springs, Tamolitch Falls, Echo Mountain, Clear Lake, and Santiam Junction.

**Finding the trail:** From Interstate 5 in Eugene/Springfield, take Exit 194 and follow OR 126 east. Drive approximately 50 miles to the community of McKenzie Bridge. Continue east on OR 126 for another 1.8 miles to a parking area on the left for the trail's southernmost trailhead. Eleven parking areas dispersed along OR 126 provide additional access points to the trail. The northern terminus of the trail is at the Santiam Wagon Road Trailhead. To reach it, drive 21.3 miles north of McKenzie Bridge on OR 126 and turn right onto a gravel road marked with a large sign for the McKenzie River Trail. Proceed a short distance down the road to parking on the left and the trailhead on the right.

From locations to the east, follow either OR 126 or OR 242 from Sisters. Take OR 126 to access the Santiam Wagon Road Trailhead. Take OR 242 for a scenic drive to the southern trailhead.

**Source of additional information:**

McKenzie Ranger District
57600 McKenzie Highway
McKenzie Bridge, OR 97413
(541) 822-3381

**Notes on the trail:** Numerous access points along the trail create a myriad of opportunities for out-and-back or shuttle rides. Loops are possible, but they involve pedaling on the narrow highway. Because we had only one vehicle at our disposal, we rode on the highway to make a loop. From the southern trailhead, we rode uphill on the highway to Trail Bridge Campground and then back to our vehicle on the single-track. The next day, we formed another loop by riding up the highway from Trail Bridge to the northern trailhead at the Old Santiam Wagon Road. The climbing on the highway was easy, but somewhat dangerous. The shoulder ends after Paradise Campground.

The upper portion of the trail was closed to bicycles for several years, but it is open again. The Forest Service does stress that the trail was designed as an

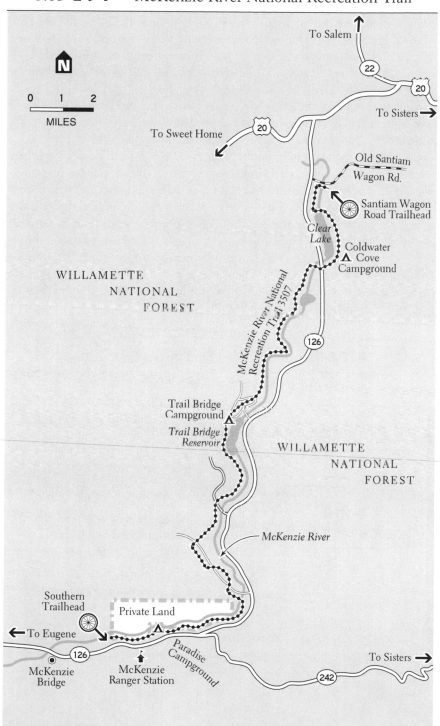

**N**

0 1 2
MILES

To Salem

22

20

To Sisters →

To Sweet Home

20

Old Santiam
Wagon Rd.

Santiam Wagon
Road Trailhead

Clear
Lake

Coldwater
△ Cove
Campground

WILLAMETTE
NATIONAL
FOREST

McKenzie River National
Recreation Trail 3507

126

Trail Bridge
Campground

Trail Bridge
Reservoir

WILLAMETTE
NATIONAL
FOREST

McKenzie River

Southern
Trailhead

Private Land

← To Eugene

126

McKenzie
Bridge

McKenzie
Ranger Station

Paradise
Campground

To Sisters →

242

easy, slow-paced recreational trail and that mountain bikers must practice trail etiquette and tread lightly—good advice. A high potential for user conflict exists from Trail Bridge Reservoir south. The area is popular with hikers, and there are some straight stretches of trail where cyclists tend to ride too fast. Slow down and anticipate others approaching from around the next bend. Be mindful that this trail is open to pedestrians and bicyclists only, so trail deterioration will be blamed on inappropriate bike handling. No skidding!

Most of the intersections on McKenzie River Trail are signed. You should have little difficulty finding your way, especially if you refer to your map. We came across a couple of unsigned intersections on the stretch from Trail Bridge Reservoir south. About 4 miles south of the reservoir you will cross a log bridge over signed Deer Creek, then the trail crosses a paved road. From this road crossing, it is 1.7 miles farther along the trail to an unsigned gravel spur road. Turn left onto the spur road and ride toward a locked gate. Go around the gate and immediately bear left onto the trail as it heads into the woods. The trail crosses another log bridge in 1.2 miles, then the trail splits at an unsigned **Y** intersection. Take either trail; both lead to a nearby unsigned road. Turn left onto the road and follow it over a bridge to the eastern side of the river. Turn right onto the trail, paralleling the highway. The remainder of the trail is well marked.

## RIDE 55 · Burma Road/Smith Rock State Park

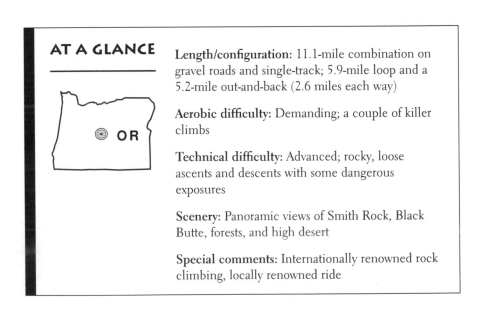

**AT A GLANCE**

**Length/configuration:** 11.1-mile combination on gravel roads and single-track; 5.9-mile loop and a 5.2-mile out-and-back (2.6 miles each way)

**Aerobic difficulty:** Demanding; a couple of killer climbs

**Technical difficulty:** Advanced; rocky, loose ascents and descents with some dangerous exposures

**Scenery:** Panoramic views of Smith Rock, Black Butte, forests, and high desert

**Special comments:** Internationally renowned rock climbing, locally renowned ride

Climbing Burma Road.

East of the town of Terrebonne, giant rock pillars rise abruptly from the valley floor. Climbers come from all over the world to scale these rocks. Smith Rock State Park is known for both its novice routes and its expert-only faces; it is considered one of the best rock climbing areas in the United States. It is also the starting point for a good mountain bike ride.

As you enter the park, you may notice a road that is etched across the flank of a nearby mountain. This is Burma Road, and yes, it is as steep as it looks. Thankfully, the arduous climb up Burma Road is not too long, and it takes you to a lovely overlook. You are about 300' higher than "The Summit" (at 3,230', the tallest peak in the park). You may wish to bring a pair of binoculars with you on the ride.

This trip covers a total of 11.1 miles. It is suited to strong cyclists with good technical skills. The route involves a 5.9-mile loop and a 5.2-mile out-and-back (2.6 miles each way). Gravel and dirt roads comprise 6.2 miles of the ride, while 4.9 miles are on single-track.

The ride begins with a steep drop on a rocky service road, then you wind along the canyon floor on a nice stretch of trail. At the base of a rocky bluff, bikers become climbers—you will need to briefly carry your bike up a steep, slippery section of trail. Once atop the basalt rim, the mile-long grunt up Burma Road begins. The road is soft and covered in coarse gravel. It is a challenge to stay on your bike. From the crest, the road dives steeply, and its surface changes to rutted dirt. Most of the elevation you gained climbing Burma Road is lost in one quick mile. From this low point, you climb on a dirt road through Sherwood

Canyon. At the top of the canyon you pick up a single-track. It contours around a mountainside to swing you back to the overlook at Burma Road. There are some off-camber sections with loose conditions and rocks, but generally the path is very pleasant. The descent down Burma Road is wild; staying in control was our main concern. The trip ends with a return cruise through the park's bottomlands and a steep pull back out of the canyon.

**General location:** Smith Rock State Park is located approximately 9 miles north of Redmond (about 25 miles north of Bend).

**Elevation change:** The trailhead for the ride is at 2,850'. The route immediately drops to a low point of 2,660' (at the footbridge across the Crooked River). From here the route climbs to 3,500' at the top of Burma Road. The road then drops to 2,900', then proceeds to 3,670'. From this high point, the route descends back to the footbridge at the Crooked River (2,660'), before climbing back up to the trailhead. Undulations on the route add about 200' of climbing to the excursion. Total elevation gain: 2,000'.

**Season:** The roads followed on this trip are suitable for year-round travel. The trails can stand some moisture, but stay off of them when they are saturated. During extended periods of hot, dry weather and heavy use, the roads and trails in the area can become soft and dusty. We met some riders who said that the region's trails are improved by dust-settling showers. It was a hot, dry day, but we received some rain through the night. The following day, we tried to ride on nearby Gray Butte, but found the trails had become too soft with sticky mud. After soaking rains, we would recommend giving the trails in the area some time to dry.

**Services:** Water, toilets, and a pay phone are available in Smith Rock State Park (day-use fee required). The park's facilities also include a hike-in campground (with solar showers). All services are available in Redmond and Bend.

**Hazards:** Smith Rock State Park is a popular spot for rock climbers, hikers, and shutterbugs. Take your time and use caution on the park trails. Stop and yield the trail to people accessing climbs, hiking, or strolling through the park. Many of the roads and trails on this route are steep and technically demanding. There are soft spots, loose rocks, and drop-offs. Cleated bike shoes can make the ride's hike-a-bike sections especially treacherous; particularly the scramble up and down the section of trail at the park's basalt rim (near the base of Burma Road).

**Rescue index:** There is a pay phone at the day-use area. Emergency services are located in Redmond and Bend.

**Land status:** Lands administered by Smith Rock State Park and Crooked River National Grassland.

**Maps:** Carry "Mountain Biking Central Oregon," a map by Fat Tire Publications (available at area bike shops). A map of Smith Rock State Park is available at the day-use parking area; it details the trails and landmarks found within the park's boundaries. USGS 7.5 minute quads: O'Neil, Redmond, Gray Butte, and Opal City.

**Finding the trail:** From Redmond, drive north on OR 97 (follow the signs for Madras/Portland). You will enter the small town of Terrebonne in about 5 miles. At the flashing yellow light, turn right (east) toward Smith Rock State Park. From Madras, drive south on OR 97 for approximately 28 miles to Terrebonne. Turn left (east) at the flashing yellow light toward Smith Rock State Park.

In 0.5 mile, turn left onto N.E. 1st Street/N.E. Wilcox Avenue. Drive 1.9 miles to Crooked River Drive. Turn left and remain on Crooked River Drive for 1 mile to reach the day-use parking area for Smith Rock State Park.

## Sources of additional information:

Smith Rock State Park
9241 N.E. Crooked River Drive
Terrebonne, OR 97760
(541) 548-7501

Crooked River National Grassland
813 S.W. Highway 97
Madras, OR 97741
(541) 416-6640
(541) 475-9272

**Notes on the trail:** From the toilets/recycle center, go toward the rim of the canyon and bear right. Shortly, at a viewpoint/low stone wall, turn left onto a service road and ride down to the canyon floor. Cross the footbridge over the Crooked River and turn right onto a single-track. After about a mile you will come to an intersection at a sign-in box and a rescue basket/backboard. Turn left to climb steeply up a slippery trail. Several trails branch off from the main trail; follow the main trail to the top of the basalt rim. Once on top, ride out to a gravel road and turn left. Immediately turn left onto another gravel road (Burma Road) that parallels a canal. Stay on this road as it swings right and then begins to climb steeply (the road becomes rocky and rutted). Burma Road switchbacks left, then meets a green metal gate. Pass around the gate and climb another 0.5 mile to the top of the hill. Stay on the main road; cresting the hill and descending for 1 mile to a double-track that goes hard right. (You will be cruising downhill on a straight stretch of road as you approach this intersection—Black Butte is in the distance, directly in front of you. You will arrive at the intersection just before the road you are on starts to curve right.) Turn hard right onto the double-track (northeast) and begin the climb up Sherwood Canyon. In 1 mile, bear right onto another road. Immediately pass through a low point in the road and climb up to a T intersection. Turn right and head to a metal gate at a wire fence. Pass through the gate and bear right. Climb over rolling terrain to a Y intersection; stay right on the main road. In 1 mile, turn right onto a trail that crosses the road. (If you miss this turn you will immediately arrive at a gravel road and a double-track that goes hard right.) Follow the trail through the junipers and bear right to remain on the main single-track. Stay on the main trail as it contours around the mountain. Pass through a gate in about 1 mile. In another 0.4 mile,

# RIDE 55 · Burma Road/Smith Rock State Park

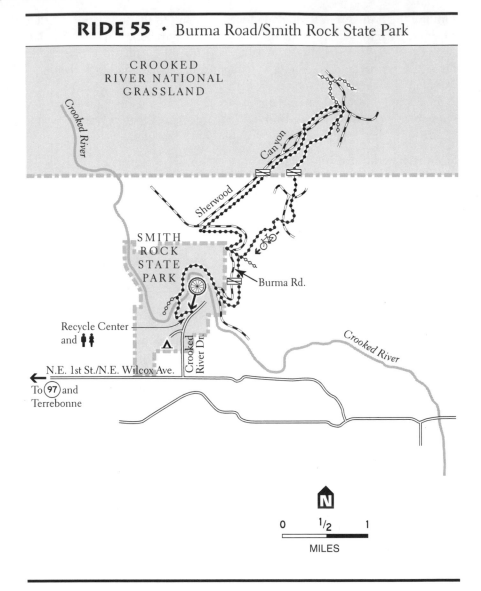

CROOKED
RIVER NATIONAL
GRASSLAND

Crooked River

Canyon

Sherwood

SMITH
ROCK
STATE
PARK

Burma Rd.

Crooked River

Recycle Center
and

Crooked River Dr.

N.E. 1st St./N.E. Wilcox Ave.

To 97 and
Terrebonne

N

0    1/2    1
MILES

continue straight to cross a road onto a double-track. Climb briefly on the double-track, then bear left onto a single-track. The trail climbs steeply, passing
some nice rocks, then meets a double-track. Cross the double-track and follow
the trail as it twists and descends steeply. This technical stretch of trail is followed
by more contouring on good trail. In 0.6 mile, bear right onto another trail,
which leads out to the viewpoint at Burma Road. Turn left onto Burma Road
and backtrack to return the way you came.

## RIDE 56 · Gray Butte Loop

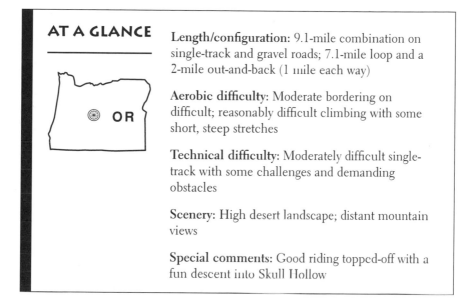

**AT A GLANCE**

**Length/configuration:** 9.1-mile combination on single-track and gravel roads; 7.1-mile loop and a 2-mile out-and-back (1 mile each way)

**Aerobic difficulty:** Moderate bordering on difficult; reasonably difficult climbing with some short, steep stretches

**Technical difficulty:** Moderately difficult single-track with some challenges and demanding obstacles

**Scenery:** High desert landscape; distant mountain views

**Special comments:** Good riding topped-off with a fun descent into Skull Hollow

Gray Butte Loop is a 9.1-mile ride near Smith Rock State Park. The outing involves a loop of 7.1 miles, and a 2-mile out-and-back (1 mile each way). The trip includes five miles of single-track. The ride begins with a good warm-up, then moves into moderately difficult to strenuous climbing on gravel roads. After three miles of roads, you get on single-track. Here, the route continues to climb, traversing around the west flank of Gray Butte. This stretch provides views of familiar landmarks like Black Butte, Green Ridge, and Three Sisters.

Highlighting the excursion is an exhilarating single-track descent off of Gray Butte into Skull Hollow. The route dodges trees, banks past rocks, and swoops through swales. The trail leads the way, but it's up to you to negotiate its sandy corners, rocky sections of tread, and occasional steep drops (fun stuff).

For a longer ride, you can link Gray Butte Loop with a segment of Ride 55/Burma Road. As you pedal around Gray Butte, a high trail comes into view. It traverses a ridge above Sherwood Canyon. This exposed trail heads west to an impressive overlook of Smith Rock State Park. From the overlook, you can back-track on the ridge trail, or drop into Sherwood Canyon and climb on a double-track back to Gray Butte Loop. Either way, this is a nice way to extend the trip.

**General location:** The trailhead is Skull Hollow Campground in the Crooked River National Grassland, about 15 miles northeast of Redmond.

**Elevation change:** Begins at 3,000' and reaches a high point of 4,100' on Gray Butte. Ups and downs add about 300' of climbing to the trip. Total elevation gain: 1,400'.

**Season:** This route can usually be approached late in the spring through the

# RIDE 56 · Gray Butte Loop

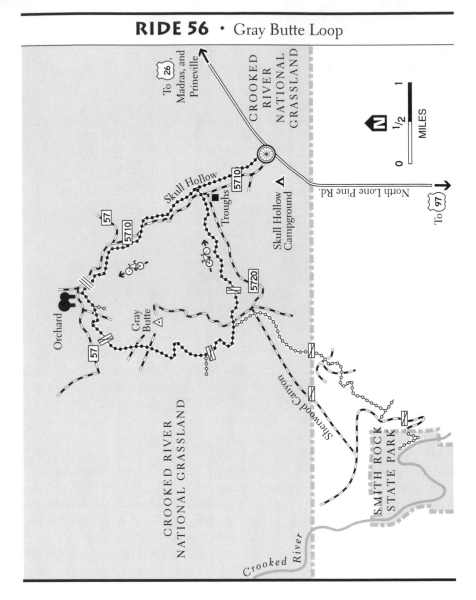

fall. Stay off of the single-track during periods of wet weather or in the early spring when it is still damp from snowmelt. When wet, the soils on Gray Butte turn into sticky mud. This gumbo will clog your drive train, tires, and brakes. Your bike will stop functioning, and you will trash a nice trail.

**Services:** There is no water on this ride. Water can be obtained at Smith Rock State Park (there is a day-use fee). You can also purchase showers at the park. All services are available in Redmond.

**Hazards:** The roads and trails on this ride include obstacles like rocks, ruts, and sand. There is one extra-steep segment of trail (6.8 miles into the ride, just beyond a wire gate). Be careful riding down (or walking your bike down) this rocky, ditch-like section. Watch for vehicles on the roads, and other trail users on the single-track.

**Rescue index:** There is a pay phone at Smith Rock State Park. Help can be found in Redmond.

**Land status:** Crooked River National Grassland.

**Maps:** A map by Fat Tire Publications, "Mountain Biking Central Oregon," is a good guide to this ride. USGS 7.5 minute quad: Gray Butte.

**Finding the trail:** From Redmond, drive north on US 97 for about 3 miles to O'Neil Highway (at Prineville Junction). Turn right (east) onto O'Neil Highway toward Prineville. Follow O'Neil Highway for approximately 5 miles to North Lone Pine Road on the left. From Prineville, drive west on O'Neil Highway for approximately 14 miles to North Lone Pine Road on the right.

Turn north onto North Lone Pine Road. Stay on North Lone Pine Road for 5.5 miles to gravel Road 5710 on the left. Turn onto Road 5710 and park on the right in a pull-out. If you are camping, drive a short distance up Road 5710 and turn left to park in Skull Hollow Campground.

**Source of additional information:**

Crooked River National Grassland
813 S.W. Highway 97
Madras, OR 97741
(541) 416-6640
(541) 475-9272

**Notes on the trail:** The route passes through several gates. Leave gates as you find them—close them behind you if they were closed.

Ride up Road 5710. In 1 mile, continue straight at a couple of water troughs and Road 5720 on the left. In another 1.4 miles, bear left onto Road 57. Climb a little more, then descend over a cattle guard to a left-hand curve in the road near an old orchard, some poplar trees, and a couple of double-tracks. Bear left to remain on Road 57, then immediately turn left onto a single-track that climbs moderately. (This turn is 0.6 mile from the intersection of Roads 57 and 5710.) In 0.2 mile, bear left onto a wider trail that is improved with stretches of gravel. Stay on the main trail where side trails branch off. Cross a double-track, follow a switchback to the right, then arrive at a green metal gate. (You will arrive at the gate after 1 mile of single-track pedaling.) Pass through the gate and continue up the trail. The trail passes some double-tracks that head toward the summit. Then you will arrive at a faint trail (marked by a signpost missing its sign) and another gate. Continue straight to pass through the gate. In 0.8 mile, stay left to cross a road, regaining the trail on the other side. (Longer option: don't cross the road here. Instead, bear right onto a single-track that leads to a saddle and the trail above Sherwood Canyon. For more information see "Notes on the trail" for Burma Road [Ride 55].) Back to the basic route: the trail descends for 0.3 mile,

Single-track on
Gray Butte Loop.

passes through a wire gate (6.8 miles into the ride), and arrives at a section of trail that is steep, rough, and somewhat ditch-like. Skilled riders should be able to roll through this section without locking their brakes. Walk your bike down the trail if you are unsure about your abilities to negotiate this section without skidding. In another mile, the trail merges with Road 5720. Continue downhill, turning right onto Road 5710 and backtracking to your car.

## **RIDE 57** · Round Mountain

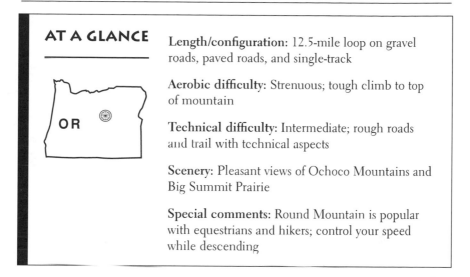

**AT A GLANCE**

**Length/configuration:** 12.5-mile loop on gravel roads, paved roads, and single-track

**Aerobic difficulty:** Strenuous; tough climb to top of mountain

**Technical difficulty:** Intermediate; rough roads and trail with technical aspects

**Scenery:** Pleasant views of Ochoco Mountains and Big Summit Prairie

**Special comments:** Round Mountain is popular with equestrians and hikers; control your speed while descending

This 12.5-mile loop is physically demanding. The ride begins with one mile of pavement and then moves to dirt and gravel forest roads. These climb steeply at times, especially as you get closer to the top of the mountain. The roads are in fair shape. Rocks and ruts make the steeper parts more difficult. The descent from the mountain is on Round Mountain National Recreation Trail 805, a dirt single-track in good condition. The most technically demanding portion of the trip is a one-mile stretch of rough rock on Trail 805.

You obtain a nice view of the Ochoco Mountains and the surrounding countryside from the summit of Round Mountain. To the east is Big Summit Prairie. This huge grassy area is a privately owned cattle ranch. Numerous creeks drain this high prairie. Cottonwoods line the waterways and add splashes of color to the fall landscape.

**General location:** The loop begins near Walton Lake Campground, approximately 30 miles east of Prineville.

**Elevation change:** The ride starts at 5,360' and reaches 6,753' at the top of Round Mountain. There are some downhills on the way to the summit and some uphills on Trail 805. These undulations add about 500' of climbing to the ride. Total elevation gain: 1,893'.

**Season:** Warm sunny days and cool nights are typical of this region in the summer. The early fall (before hunting season) is also an excellent time for a visit. Snow and mud often create impassable conditions during the winter and spring. The soils comprising the Round Mountain Trail are vulnerable to erosion, and when they are wet they stick to mountain bike tires like glue. If the single-track is damp, return the way you came.

# RIDE 57 · Round Mountain

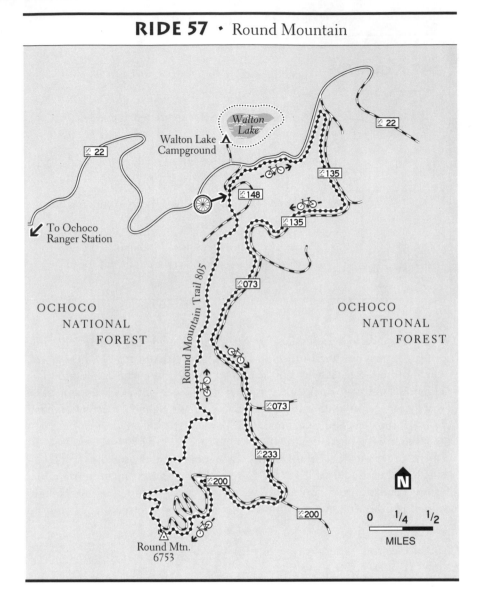

**Services:** Water is available seasonally at Walton Lake Campground. Food, lodging, gas, and groceries can be obtained in Prineville.

**Hazards:** The beginning of the trip is on paved Forest Service Road 22. This road sees a moderate amount of vehicular traffic from loggers and other forest users. Round Mountain Trail drops steeply at first; walk your bike down the switchbacks in the trail. You will come to a dilapidated footbridge after the switchbacks. It is tilted and slippery; walk your bike across it. A 1-mile stretch of rocky trail occurs near the end of the ride; again, walking may be necessary.

Round Mountain bike toss.

Control your speed while descending on Round Mountain Trail—it is popular with hikers and equestrians.

**Rescue index:** Help may be available at the Ochoco Ranger Station during regular business hours. If the ranger station is closed, you may be able to obtain assistance at the nearby Forest Service housing area, located behind the ranger station. Aid can be found in Prineville.

**Land status:** Ochoco National Forest.

**Maps:** The district map for the Prineville Ranger District shows the roads followed on this route, but not Round Mountain Trail. The forest map for the Ochoco National Forest includes the trail, but not all of the roads. Carry both maps. USGS 7.5 minute quad: Ochoco Butte.

**Finding the trail:** From Prineville, travel east on US 26 for about 15 miles, to County Road 23. Turn right onto CR 23, toward the Ochoco Ranger Station and the Ochoco Campground. After 9 miles, you will come to the intersection of CR 23, FS 22, and FS 42 (0.3 mile past the ranger station). Turn left onto FS 22, toward Walton Lake, where FS 42 goes right, toward Lookout Mountain. Stay on FS 22 for 7 miles to Walton Lake Campground (on the left). Pass the campground and continue straight on FS 22 for 0.1 mile to FS 148. This gravel road is marked by a hiking sign for Trail 805. Turn right and proceed up FS 148 for 0.4 mile to a parking area on the right for Trail 805.

## Source of additional information:

Prineville Ranger District
P.O. Box 490
Prineville, OR 97754
(541) 416-6500

**Notes on the trail:**  From the parking area, return the way you came on FS 148 (downhill) to FS 22. Turn right onto FS 22 and climb on pavement to signed FS 135. Turn right onto FS 135. Take note of the orange diamond-shaped symbols on trees that line the road. The next 4.5 miles of the ride are marked with these orange diamonds. The route stays on FS 135 for 2.2 miles and then follows FS 073 and FS 233. These roads are unsigned; at intersections, choose the road marked by the orange diamonds. After 4.5 miles of dirt and gravel roads, you will reach unsigned FS 200. This gravel road is marked with a sign to your right that reads "Road Closed 1 Mile Ahead—Local Traffic Only." Turn right and climb on FS 200. Stay on this switchbacking road to the top of the mountain. Just before the top, at the last switchback on FS 200, you will pass Round Mountain Trail 805 on the right (north). Visit the summit and return down FS 200, then turn left onto Round Mountain Trail 805. Continue on this trail back to your vehicle.

The Walton Lake Campground is a great base of operations for exploring miles of nearby roads and trails. There is a path around the small lake; children enjoy riding on this loop.

# EUGENE/OAKRIDGE

The neighboring cities of Eugene and Springfield are located in the south-ernmost portion of the Willamette Valley, about 100 miles south of Portland. Lane County, where Eugene and Springfield are located, is bounded on the west by the Pacific Ocean and by the Cascades on the east. Lane County is the most popular cycling destination in Oregon; the riding here is diverse and excellent. Touring is tremendously popular, and the region plays host to some of the best mountain biking in Oregon.

Eugene is home to the University of Oregon, and it is a center of bicycling culture. Riding a bike is a very popular way to get around in Eugene; the city's public buses are even outfitted with bike racks. The number of bicycle clubs, bike advocacy groups, and alternative transportation organizations found here is mind boggling. Group rides, tours, races, clinics, and bike festivals are com-monplace events. Eugene is alive with active, bike-riding people.

Single-track experiences in Eugene are rather limited (but not unheard of). The good stuff is in Oakridge, about 40 miles southwest of Eugene on OR 58. The riding is so good in Oakridge that mountain bikers from Eugene give little thought to how far away it is; they just load up their cars and go. The opportu-nities around Oakridge are gaining a national reputation. Lovers of challenging single-track are making Oakridge a vacation destination. Oakridge locals are get-ting used to seeing lycra-clad geeks wandering the aisles of their grocery stores.

Like many communities throughout the Pacific Northwest, Oakridge's econ-omy is tied to the timber industry. In the last ten years or so, timber harvests have slowed dramatically. Lots of people have lost jobs, and towns like Oakridge have undergone some big changes. Of course, not everyone is (or was) employed by the timber industry, but the jobs of nearly everyone in mill towns are linked to the ups and downs of timber.

For decades, tourism has meant a lot to the economy of Oregon. Bicycling is a significant, seasonal component of that industry. In Oakridge, bicycle tourism plays a small role in the local economy. Like other tourists, bicyclists spend money, and towns like Oakridge are benefiting from the increased interest in mountain biking. There is little hope, however, that mountain biking will pro-duce the economies of scale that an industry like timber generated.

## RIDE 58 · South Hills Ridgeline Trail

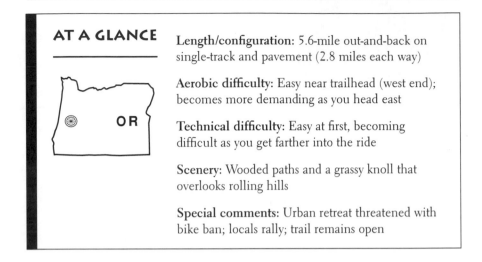

**AT A GLANCE**

**Length/configuration:** 5.6-mile out-and-back on single-track and pavement (2.8 miles each way)

**Aerobic difficulty:** Easy near trailhead (west end); becomes more demanding as you head east

**Technical difficulty:** Easy at first, becoming difficult as you get farther into the ride

**Scenery:** Wooded paths and a grassy knoll that overlooks rolling hills

**Special comments:** Urban retreat threatened with bike ban; locals rally; trail remains open

Bicycles are a part of everyday life in Eugene. You see lots of people riding, the city is laced with dedicated bike lanes, and there are tons of excellent bike shops. Local clubs lead rides and hold races regularly. All of the community's public buses are outfitted with bike racks. Bus routes include destinations like Oakridge and McKenzie Bridge (places with great trails).

Like most cities, Eugene's in-town single-track is limited. One of the city's few bikeable trails is the South Hills Ridgeline Trail. Recently, it looked like bikes would be banned from this local favorite. Mountain bikers rallied to keep it open. They attended meetings, made "public comment," and wrote letters. Perhaps more importantly, they involved themselves in the upkeep of the trail, and they spread the word about responsible riding (tread lightly and extend common courtesy to others).

The mountain bikers who worked to keep Ridgeline Trail open were successful. They demonstrated that the great majority of mountain bikers ride responsibly. They also established the fact that mountain bikers are eager to work with land managers and other user groups to rectify problems that can arise with shared use.

Eugene's Ridgeline Trail is a 5.6-mile out-and-back ride (2.8 miles each way). While short, it packs in a lot of good stuff, and regardless of its length, local riders are glad to have a place to ride. Advanced beginners can enjoy riding out and back on the first mile or so of the trail. Here, the trail is quite mellow as it rolls along through dense woods and over a few tree roots. Stronger riders can venture farther, onto a short stretch of paved road, then up some switchbacks to a grassy hillside. The hill provides some distant views of rolling terrain to the south. The far end of the trail drops down a technical series of switchbacks. Climbing back up is a true test of strength and bike-handling skills. The more

Eugene's Ridgeline Trail.

distant reaches of the trail (farther from the trailhead) include obstacles like roots, rocks, sandy corners, and good-sized waterbars.

**General location:** The South Hills Ridgeline Trail is in Eugene, on the south side of town.

**Elevation change:** The trailhead is at approximately 850'. The high point (1,100') is obtained after pedaling 2 miles. The east end of the trail (the turn-around point) is at roughly 780'. Undulations over the course of the trip add about 200' of climbing to the ride. Total elevation gain: 770'.

**Season:** Depending on the weather, this trail can be ridden year-round. If the trail is wet, stay off. Summers are typically the driest time of the year.

**Services:** There is no water on this ride. All services are available in Eugene.

**Hazards:** This is a very popular trail. Ride at a casual pace and yield the trail to all you meet. Expect obstacles like roots and rocks in the first mile, and more challenging impediments as you travel farther. The route follows Dillard Road for 0.8 mile (0.4 mile going out, 0.4 mile on the return). Ride defensively and predictably on this paved thoroughfare. There are some steep hills and some ditch-like trail conditions on this ride. Walk your bike down the trail if you

## RIDE 58 · South Hills Ridgeline Trail

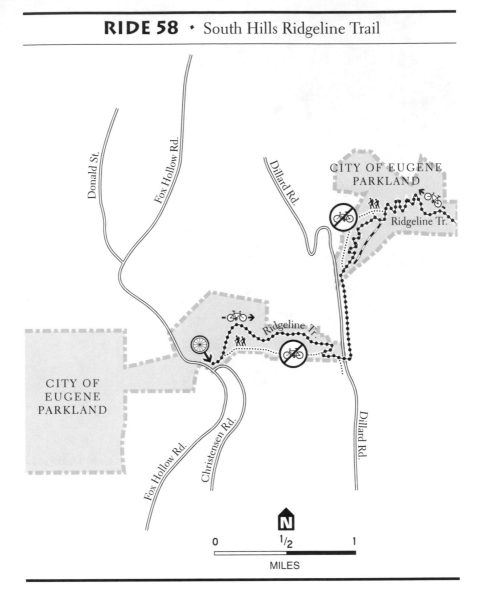

cannot negotiate it without locking your brakes (no skidding). Poison oak borders portions of the trail.

**Rescue index:** Emergency services are available in Eugene.

**Land status:** City of Eugene Parks and Recreation.

**Maps:** We were able to obtain a photo copy of a trail map titled "South Hills Ridgeline Trail Map and Guide." The map was developed by the City of Eugene Parks, Recreation, and Cultural Services. USGS 7.5 minute quad: Creswell.

**Finding the trail:**  From Interstate 5 in Eugene, take Exit 194 for I-105. Follow I-105 west for several miles, crossing the Willamette River and entering downtown Eugene. Follow the signs for Jefferson Street. Take Jefferson Street South for 0.5 mile to 13th Avenue. Turn left onto 13th Avenue and drive 0.6 mile to Pearl Street (the street after Oak Street). Turn right (south) onto one-way Pearl Street. After 0.4 mile, Pearl Street's designation changes to Amazon Parkway— continue south. In about 1 mile, you will come to a stop sign at 29th Avenue; continue straight on Amazon Parkway. In 0.2 mile, turn right onto Hilyard Street. In 0.3 mile, turn left on West Amazon Drive. (You will pass East Amazon Drive, then come to your turn for West Amazon Drive.) In 0.8 mile, turn right onto Fox Hollow Road. Climb up Fox Hollow Road for 2.2 miles to the trailhead and parking area for Ridgeline Trail on the left (at the intersection of Fox Hollow Road and Christensen Road).

## Sources of additional information:

City of Eugene Public Works Maintenance
1820 Roosevelt Boulevard
Eugene, OR 97402
(541) 682-4800

Disciples of Dirt (Mountain Bike Club)
P.O. Box 12122
Eugene, OR 97440
(541) 895-5169

**Notes on the trail:**  At the bollards, head up a short steep hill to begin the ride. Continue straight where a hiking trail goes up some wood stairs to the right (no bikes). Stay on the main trail for 0.9 mile to a couple of switchbacks. At the second switchback, stay left to remain on the trail that is open to bikes (the trail that goes straight is closed to bikes). Shortly, continue straight where a trail goes hard to the right. You will soon arrive at a sign for Ridgeline Trail. Bear left at the sign to follow a ditch-like trail down to paved Dillard Road. (Be careful not to roll out onto Dillard Road.) Check for traffic, then turn left onto Dillard Road. Pedal the pavement for 0.4 mile to a sign for Ridgeline Trail on the right (beneath some powerlines). Turn right and pass through a **V**-shaped gate. Bear left after the gate to climb steeply. (As you climb, you will pass a hiking trail that goes left; stay right to remain on the trail that is open to bikes.) Several switchbacks bring you to an open summit; continue straight. It is 0.1 mile from the hilltop to an intersection of trails at a wood post set in concrete (no sign at the time of our research). Turn right at the post onto a faint trail and descend to a double-track. Turn left onto the double-track and climb up to another wood post (no sign) at an intersection. Turn right and descend down a switchbacking trail. At the base of the hill, the trail travels through a low area, then over a rooty hillock. Bear right when you arrive at a sign for Ridgeline Trail, then follow a double-track downhill. At a chain across the road, turn around and return the way you came.

## RIDE 59 · Row River Trail

**AT A GLANCE**

**OR**

**Length/configuration:** 21-mile paved path out-and-back (10.5 miles each way)

**Aerobic difficulty:** Easy; mostly level

**Technical difficulty:** Easy; paved cruise

**Scenery:** Trail rolls past farms and alongside Dorena Lake

**Special comments:** A good trail for beginners and families

The Row River Trail is an example of a relatively recent trend—fashioning public trails out of old railroad beds. Rip up the tracks and ties, smooth the surface a bit, and you've got yourself a trail. Actually, getting a rail-trail built is a lot of work. The planning and design of these trails is an incredibly involved process, and the construction of the trail and its facilities costs a lot of money. Some rail-trails are left as gravel paths, but many of them are paved (to the delight of in-line skaters and bike-riding families).

Rail-trails are easy trails. Obviously, they follow a route once used by trains, and trains are lousy climbers. Nearly level terrain is commonplace on rail-trails; you will rarely encounter a grade greater than 5%.

The Oregon Pacific and Eastern Railroad Line was built in 1902. It hauled lumber from Culp Creek Mill and ore from the Bohemia Mines to the City of Cottage Grove. In the 1970s, the line's two-mile-per-hour steam engine was used to pull a passenger excursion train called the "Goose." In 1993, the railroad was abandoned and the Bureau of Land Management obtained the right-of-way. In 1994, the bureau built the Row River Trail as a non-motorized recreational trail. The paving of the trail was completed in 1997.

Cottage Grove is known as the "Covered Bridge Capital of Oregon." The region's five covered bridges were built at the turn of the century. Steel was scarce, so the bridges were crafted from the finest timber, then roofed to protect them from rain and ruin. Mosby Creek Covered Bridge is at the western end of the trail (where we start the ride). Two others, the Currin and Dorena bridges, can be visited by taking short side trips from the bike path.

The people of Cottage Grove take great pride in their community, and in the things that make it special. Locals have adopted portions of the path, taking responsibility for minor repairs and the general upkeep of its facilities. We were impressed with the lack of litter along the trail and the path's simple good looks.

# RIDE 59 · Row River Trail

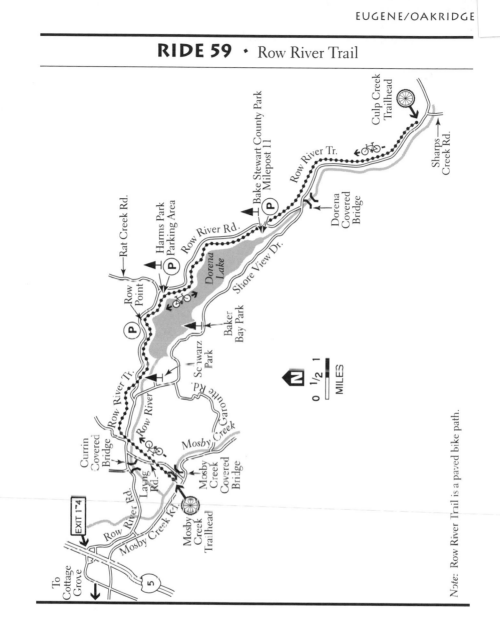

Culp Creek Trailhead

Sharps Creek Rd.

Row River Tr.

Bake Stewart County Park Milepost 11

Dorena Covered Bridge

Rat Creek Rd.

Harms Park Parking Area

Row River Rd.

P

Dorena Lake

Shore View Dr.

Row Point

P

Baker Bay Park

Schwarz Park

Caroune Rd.

N

0  1/2  1
MILES

Row River Tr.

Row River

Currin Covered Bridge

Laying Rd.

Mosby Creek

Mosby Creek Covered Bridge

EXIT 174

Row River Rd.

Mosby Creek Rd.

Mosby Creek Trailhead

To Cottage Grove

5

*Note: Row River Trail is a paved bike path.*

---

The first several miles of the trail meander through rural farm country. Apple and pear trees and burgeoning blackberry thickets line the route. The trail follows along the north shore of Dorena Lake for five miles, then through more rural countryside as it passes behind the community of Dorena. The backdrop for this ride is never spectacular, but the scenery is pleasant and often interesting.

The Row River Trail is 12.5 miles long. We turned around (in a driving rain) after following the trail for 10.5 mile—making for a 21-mile round-trip. The route is paved and the pedaling is easy.

**General location:** Mosby Creek Trailhead is located approximately 7 miles east of Cottage Grove.

**Elevation change:** The ride begins at approximately 750' and climbs to a high point of 950' at Sallee Road (our turnaround point). Additional ups and downs add about 100' of climbing to the ride. Total elevation gain: 300'.

**Season:** Year-round.

**Services:** All services can be found in Cottage Grove.

**Hazards:** The trail crosses secondary roads and the arterial Row River Road several times; exercise caution at these intersections. Slow down and signal your approach when coming upon other trail users. If you elect to visit the Currin or the Dorena covered bridges, ride predictably and defensively on the roads. Be especially careful on Row River Road; traffic moves at a good clip and motorists may not expect to see cyclists.

**Rescue index:** Help can be found in Cottage Grove.

**Land status:** Lands administered by the Bureau of Land Management.

**Maps:** A BLM handout and map entitled "Row River Trail, A Multi-Use Recreation Trail," is available at the BLM offices in Eugene and at the US Forest Service Cottage Grove Ranger Station (in Cottage Grove). USGS 7.5 minute quads: Cottage Grove, Culp Creek, Blue Mountain, and Dorena Lake.

**Finding the trail:** From Interstate 5, take Exit 174 and head east on Row River Road. In approximately 4 miles, turn right onto Layng Road. (Layng Road is not signed as Layng Road, it is marked with a sign that directs you right/south toward Mosby Creek Road. Look for the Currin Covered Bridge; it is at this intersection.) In 1.2 miles, cross Mosby Creek Covered Bridge. After the bridge, immediately turn right and park at the Mosby Creek Trailhead.

The trail can be accessed at several places other than the Mosby Creek Trailhead. There are 4 access points and parking areas on the north shore of Dorena Lake.

**Sources of additional information:**

Bureau of Land Management
Eugene District Office
P.O. Box 10226
Eugene, OR 97440
(541) 683-6600

Cottage Grove Ranger District
78405 Cedar Park Road
Cottage Grove, OR 97424
(541) 942-5591

**Notes on the trail:** Turn right onto the Row River Trail and follow the trail to its eastern terminus at the Culp Creek Trailhead. Return the way you came (or turn around when you have had one-half of your paved path fun limit).

Paved pedaling on
Row River Trail.

You can visit Currin Covered Bridge by turning left (north) at the first road crossing west of the Mosby Creek Trailhead (turn onto Layng Road). You will arrive at the bridge after 0.6 mile on Layng Road. Dorena Covered Bridge is in the small community of Dorena. You will pass to the north of this community after 9.6 miles on the Row River Trail. At a sign for Dorena, turn right toward a school, and pedal out to Row River Road. Turn right onto Row River Road and ride approximately 1 mile to the bridge (at the intersection of Row River Road and Shore View Drive/Government Road).

# RIDE 60 · Brice Creek Trail

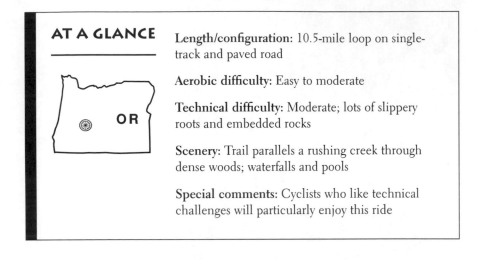

**AT A GLANCE**

**Length/configuration:** 10.5-mile loop on single-track and paved road

**Aerobic difficulty:** Easy to moderate

**Technical difficulty:** Moderate; lots of slippery roots and embedded rocks

**Scenery:** Trail parallels a rushing creek through dense woods; waterfalls and pools

**Special comments:** Cyclists who like technical challenges will particularly enjoy this ride

In the early 1900s, gold miners followed part of Brice Creek Trail to access the Bohemia Mining District. The area bustled with hopeful prospectors in search of their fortunes. Lund Park, now a dispersed camping area near the middle of the trail, was once a place of commerce. Here, miners en route to their claims found overnight accommodations and purchased provisions. In the late 1980s the trail was rebuilt for recreational use; the area bustles once again. Today, hikers and bikers strike it rich on Brice Creek Trail.

Brice Creek Trail is part of a 10.5-mile loop. The route is made up of 5.5 miles of single-track, and 5 miles of paved forest road. The path rises and falls as it travels beside the rushing water of Brice Creek. The elevation gained on this route is not huge, but because of the trail's technical aspects, we recommend this outing to intermediate and advanced riders. Even experts will find themselves creeping along over portions of Brice Creek Trail. The technical challenges include roots, rocks, cliffs, and poison oak. When these hindrances are wet (often), they are treacherous. There is not much traction to be found on slick logs and moss-covered rocks.

Cyclists should take a break once in a while to appreciate the scenic sights along the creek. The creek's waterfalls and rocky pools may even entice a sweaty cyclist to take a dip. The last mile of the trail runs beside a flume that once carried water to generate electricity in Lund Park. A five-mile downhill cruise on paved Forest Service Road 22 completes the journey.

**General location:** The trailhead is located approximately 25 miles southeast of Cottage Grove.

**Elevation change:** The route begins at 1,375' and reaches a high point of 1,840' near the end of the trail. Ups and downs on the route add an estimated 150' of climbing to the ride. Total elevation gain: 615'.

Riding upstream on
Brice Creek Trail.

**Season:** This route is open year-round. Due to its popularity with hikers, the trail is best ridden on a weekday. Try to ride the trail when it is relatively dry (though the trail does drain very well).

**Services:** There is no potable water on this ride. All services are available in Cottage Grove.

**Hazards:** Watch for, and give way to, other trail users; the trail is open to equestrians. There are rocks, roots, poison oak, and cliff experiences along Brice Creek Trail. Walk all creek crossings. Expect some traffic on FS 22.

**Rescue index:** Emergency services are located in Cottage Grove.

**Land status:** Umpqua National Forest.

**Maps:** A useful map for area bike routes is titled "Bike Routes: Oakridge/Upper Willamette." It is available at area bike shops and ranger stations. This route is also delineated on the Umpqua National Forest map. USGS 7.5 minute quad: Rose Hill.

**Finding the trail:** From Interstate 5, take Exit 174 for Cottage Grove/Dorena. Head east toward Dorena Reservoir. Continue on Row River Road, passing

# RIDE 60 · Brice Creek Trail

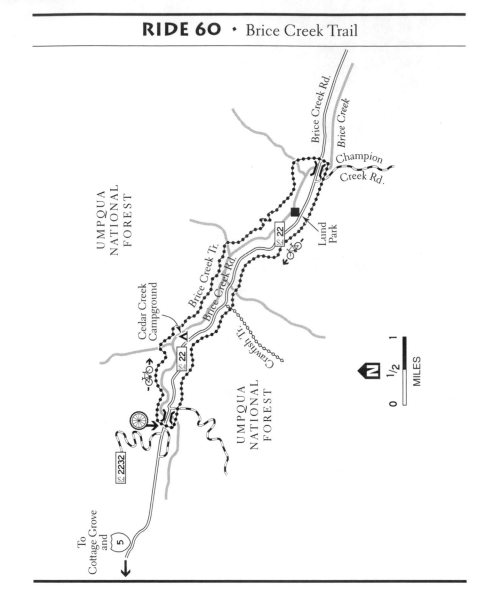

Dorena Reservoir and driving through the small communities of Dorena and Culp Creek. Note your mileage as you pass the Culp Creek Post Office; it is 4.2 miles from this landmark to the junction of Layng Creek Road and Brice Creek Road. Stay right onto Brice Creek Road; follow it for 3.3 miles. Park in the pull-out on the left at signed Brice Creek Trailhead (just before a bridge over the creek).

**Source of additional information:**

Cottage Grove Ranger District
78405 Cedar Park Road
Cottage Grove, OR 97424
(541) 942-5591

**Notes on the trail:** From the parking area, follow Brice Creek Trail upstream. The trail is well marked with signs and arrows. Continue to the trail's end at paved FS 22. Turn right and cross the bridge over Brice Creek. Follow paved FS 22 for 5 miles to your vehicle.

If you prefer, you can avoid riding on FS 22 by returning the way you came on Brice Creek Trail.

## RIDE 61 · Goodman Trail

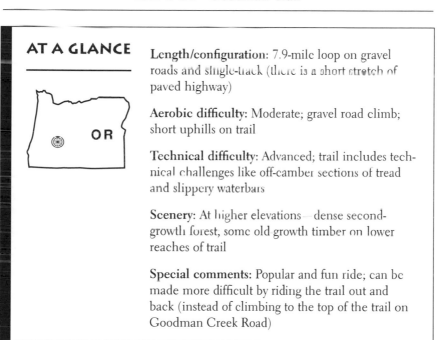

**AT A GLANCE**

**Length/configuration:** 7.9-mile loop on gravel roads and single-track (there is a short stretch of paved highway)

**Aerobic difficulty:** Moderate; gravel road climb; short uphills on trail

**Technical difficulty:** Advanced; trail includes technical challenges like off-camber sections of tread and slippery waterbars

**Scenery:** At higher elevations—dense second-growth forest, some old-growth timber on lower reaches of trail

**Special comments:** Popular and fun ride; can be made more difficult by riding the trail out and back (instead of climbing to the top of the trail on Goodman Creek Road)

Goodman Trail is one of the first single-track riding opportunities for cyclists driving east from Eugene, and it is subsequently a popular path. Some riders enjoy the challenge of climbing up the trail, then turning around at the top (where it intersects with Goodman Creek Road). We describe a moderately difficult alternative—a 7.9-mile loop. It involves climbing on gravel Goodman Creek Road to the top of the trail, then descending on the single-track.

# RIDE 61 · Goodman Trail

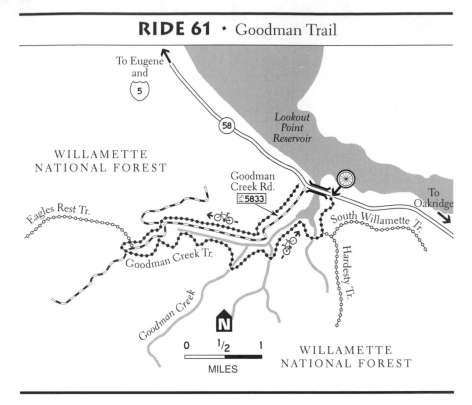

The loop begins with a very brief stretch (0.2 mile) on busy OR 58. This is followed by several miles of easy to moderately difficult climbing on Goodman Creek Road. The terrain on Goodman Trail can be characterized as rolling. It's mostly downhill, but it includes some short, moderately difficult climbs. The single-track includes technical roots, waterbars, rocks, switchbacks, exposed drop-offs, and some steep and tricky downhills.

This trail has seen many hours of volunteer maintenance from local riders. Maintenance and construction projects by both volunteers and Forest Service crews have been important to the upkeep of this well-used single-track. Boggy conditions continue to be problem on some sections of the path. Local trail advocates would like to see the trail realigned around these wet areas.

The technical aspects of the trail are made more hazardous when the trail is damp; obstacles like wooden waterbars, roots, and forest litter become slick. This creates treacherous conditions on switchbacks and where the trail is canted or steep. Windfalls can be a problem on this ride.

**General location:** The trailhead is approximately 25 miles east of Eugene (about 14 miles west of Oakridge).

**Elevation change:** The ride begins at roughly 950' and climbs to a high point

Densely wooded
Goodman Trail.

of approximately 1,600'. Undulations over the course of the loop add about 400' of climbing to the ride. Overall elevation gain. 1,050'.

**Season:** Stay off of the trail when it is wet. The late fall and winter are generally the wettest times of the year. We recommend this trail as a weekday, summertime ride.

**Services:** There is no potable water on this loop. You can get drinking water at Hampton Campground (5 miles east of the trailhead on OR 58). All services are available in Eugene. Food, gas, lodging, and groceries can be obtained in Oakridge.

**Hazards:** The ride begins on a busy highway; OR 58. Use extreme caution riding or walking your bike along the shoulder of the highway. You may come upon hikers as you descend on the single-track—this is especially likely as you near the completion of the loop. The ride ends on a portion of Hardesty Mountain Trail, which is very popular with hikers. Watch for other trail users as you come around blind corners. Keep your speed in check. Do not skid. The trail contains obstacles like roots and waterbars; they become slippery when wet. Watch for obstructions; especially where the trail is steep or canted.

**Rescue index:** Help is available in Eugene. There is a pay phone several miles west of the trailhead, on OR 58. It is at a truck scale on the north side of the highway. (Do not block the scale with your parked vehicle.)

**Land status:** Willamette National Forest.

**Maps:** The district map of the Lowell Ranger District is a good guide to this ride. A useful map for area bike routes is titled "Bike Routes: Oakridge/Upper Willamette." It is available at local bike shops and ranger stations. USGS 7.5 minute quad: Mount June.

**Finding the trail:** From locations to the west and Interstate 5, take Exit 188 for OR 58/Willamette Highway/Oakridge. (Exit 188 is about 5 miles south of Eugene.) Follow OR 58 east for about 20 miles to a large gravel pullout and the trailhead on the right. (This parking area is 0.2 mile east of the intersection with Goodman Creek Road/Forest Service Road 5833.)

From locations to the east, drive west from Oakridge on OR 58. In approximately 15 miles, turn left into the parking area and trailhead (just west of milepost 21).

**Source of additional information:**

Lowell Ranger District
60 South Pioneer Street
Lowell, OR 97452
(541) 937-2129

**Notes on the trail:** Ride or walk your bike out to the highway. (Keep an eye out for traffic turning off the highway into the parking area.) Here, you must make a decision about how best to get 0.2 mile west to Goodman Creek Road/FS 5833. (There is a shoulder on both sides of the highway.) You can wait for traffic to clear, cross the highway, then turn left to walk or ride your bike (with the flow of traffic) 0.2 mile to FS 5833 on your left—you will have to cross the highway again to access FS 5833. Your other option is to remain on the south side of the highway, turning left to walk or ride your bike against the flow of traffic for 0.2 mile to FS 5833 on the left. Once on FS 5833, pedal up the road. You will arrive at a **Y** intersection after 2.6 miles on FS 5833, bear left to remain on FS 5833. In another 0.7 mile, turn left onto unsigned Goodman Trail (across from a spur road/parking lot that accesses Eagles Rest Trail). Goodman Trail intersects with Hardesty Trail after 4.1 miles. Turn left onto Hardesty Trail and ride another 0.3 mile to your vehicle.

## RIDE 62 · Hardesty Trail

**AT A GLANCE**

**Length/configuration:** 6.1 miles of single-track (two-car shuttle); can be approached as an extremely demanding 16.5-mile loop

**Aerobic difficulty:** Moderately difficult with shuttle; excruciating when configured as part of a loop

**Technical difficulty:** For experts; very steep descent on technical single-track

**Scenery:** Beautiful forest; limited ridge views

**Special comments:** Hard on brakes

Built in 1910, Hardesty Trail is one of the oldest trails on the Lowell Ranger District. The builders of the trail must have been a hardy lot, as the route tackles Hardesty Mountain with a minimum of switchbacks and traverses. A fire lookout was built atop the mountain in 1920. Today, all that remains of the lookout are some concrete footings; even the view is gone as trees have grown up and cut off the vistas.

Most mountain bikers who ply this trail approach it as a two-car shuttle ride. Another option is to create a loop using the South Willamette Trail, OR 58, gravel forest roads, and the Hardesty Trail. It is also possible to ride out-and-back on the trail. However you approach it, this trail presents some difficulties. As a shuttle ride, you have to deal with the logistics of ferrying vehicles about. Making a loop involves riding on a busy highway and a long climb up a steep grade. As an out-and-back you will undoubtedly find it necessary to push your bike uphill for several miles.

We recommend this ride as a shuttle, but with some reservations. For one thing, the gravel roads are hard on vehicles. The grades are steep and the last couple of miles are narrow and require high clearance. Second, the end of the road (at the upper trailhead for Hardesty Trail) provides little room to park, especially if others have preceded you and taken what parking space is available. Turning around at the end of the road is also a problem.

It is important that riders appreciate that this is a popular hiking trail. At one time, this area was under consideration for designation as a wilderness area. The effort failed, but hikers and conservationists still hold the region dear. Understand that people enjoy this place as a retreat. Remain in control at all times, anticipating that you may be approaching someone hidden from your view.

Lush vegetation along
Hardesty Trail.

Hardesty Trail is 6.1 miles long. This piece of single-track is for experts only—people who can descend steep, technical pitches without skidding. The trail is rugged and exposed with steep drop-offs, ditch-like conditions, roots, rocks, and sand. Negotiating the upper reaches of the trail involves some climbing (before the trail descends off of the mountain).

Higher sections of the trail traverse an open hillside where there are some distant views of forested ridges to the west. Farther along, the trail passes through fern-carpeted stands of old-growth timber. Stopping to enjoy your surroundings will give your brakes a chance to cool and your hands time to uncramp.

**General location:** The ride begins about 25 miles east of Eugene (approximately 14 miles west of Oakridge).

**Elevation change:** The following information describes the elevation change for riding the trail from south to north (shuttling to the top). The southern end of Hardesty Trail (at the end of Forest Service Road 550) is at 3,550'. The high point of the ride (4,250') is obtained in the next 0.7 mile. The trail ends at the northern trailhead (at OR 58) at 950'. Ups and downs add about 200' of climbing to the ride. Total elevation gain: 900'.

# RIDE 62 · Hardesty Trail

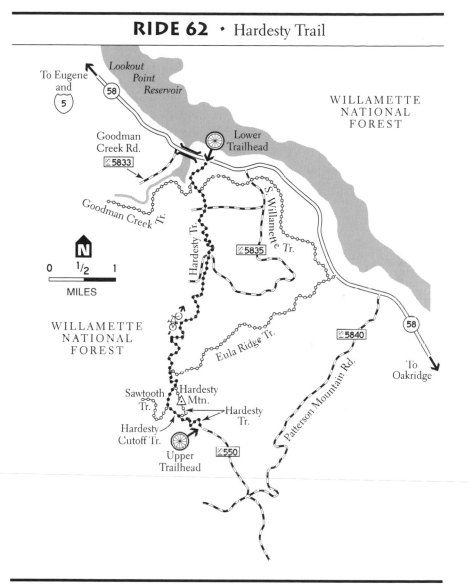

**Season:** You can plan on riding here from the late spring through the early fall. Stay off of the trail when it is wet.

**Services:** There is no water on this ride. Water can be obtained at Hampton Campground (5 miles east of the lower trailhead, on OR 58). Food, lodging, gas, and groceries are available in Oakridge. All services are available in Eugene.

**Hazards:** Trail conditions vary greatly from one moment to the next; remain alert. Just when you think things are mellowing out, the trail surprises you with unexpected difficulties. Control your speed, don't skid, and watch for others enjoying the trail. The bottom reaches of the trail can be busy with hikers accessing South Willamette Trail. In places, poison oak grows beside the trail.

**Rescue index:** Emergency services are located in Eugene. There is a pay phone several miles west of the trailhead, on OR 58. It is at a truck scale on the north side of the highway. (Do not block the scale with your parked vehicle.)

**Land status:** Willamette National Forest.

**Maps:** The district map of the Lowell Ranger District is a good guide to this ride. A map titled "Bike Routes: Oakridge/Upper Willamette" is available at area bike shops and ranger stations; it is a handy resource for cyclists interested in exploring the region. USGS 7.5 minute quad: Mount June.

**Finding the trail:** From locations to the west and Interstate 5, take Exit 188 for OR 58/Willamette Highway/Oakridge. (Exit 188 is about 5 miles south of Eugene.) Follow OR 58 east for about 20 miles to a large gravel parking area on the right. (This parking area is 0.2 mile east of Goodman Creek Road/FS 5833.) Park one vehicle here (at the lower trailhead for Hardesty Trail).

From locations to the east, drive west from Oakridge on OR 58. Turn left into a large gravel parking area after approximately 15 miles (just west of milepost 21). Park one vehicle here (at the lower trailhead for Hardesty Trail).

Continue east on OR 58 in the other vehicle for 3.8 miles to Patterson Mountain Road/FS 5840. Turn right and climb on FS 5840 (at intersections, stay on the main road). After 5 miles on FS 5840 you will arrive at Patterson Saddle. Turn hard to the right onto FS 550. Drive 1.7 miles to the end of the road at the upper trailhead for Hardesty Mountain Trail. Park your vehicle. (Park in a fashion that will allow room for others to park and turn around.)

**Source of additional information:**

Lowell Ranger District
60 South Pioneer Street
Lowell, OR 97452
(541) 973-2129

**Notes on the trail:** Pedal up signed Hardesty Trail 3469. You will arrive at an intersection of trails in 0.5 mile. Continue straight onto Hardesty Cutoff Trail 3469A. (Hardesty Trail goes hard to the right and climbs to the summit; Hardesty Cutoff Trail is the easier route.) In 0.2 mile, continue straight where a trail goes hard to the left for Eagles Rest/Mt. June/Sawtooth Rock. Pedal 0.2 mile to yet another intersection where Hardesty Cutoff Trail and Hardesty Trail meet up again; continue straight. Continue straight when you meet Eula Ridge Trail 3463 (on the right, 0.3 mile from the last intersection). In 2.5 miles, turn right onto a double-track marked with a hiker symbol sign. When the road swings right (in 0.2 mile—at a bench), continue straight to regain the trail. Follow the trail steeply downhill (through 10 closely spaced switchbacks). This steep pitch is followed by more descending (not as steep), then the trail crosses a road. From this road crossing, it is 0.5 mile to an intersection. Go left to remain on Hardesty Trail (South Willamette Trail 3465 goes right). Continue straight at the next intersection (Goodman Trail goes left). The trail ends at the lower trailhead. Drive back to the upper trailhead and fetch your other rig.

If you are hungry for pain and suffering, you may wish to consider this trail as part of a loop. We have not attempted this feat. Take OR 58 east from the lower trailhead, climb up FS 5840 and FS 550, then follow Hardesty Trail; you are looking at a 16.5-mile excursion. You may wish to cut some of the highway miles from the loop by following South Willamette Trail (see recommended maps). We know not of the condition or difficulty of this trail.

## RIDE 63 · Flat Creek Trail/Dead Mountain

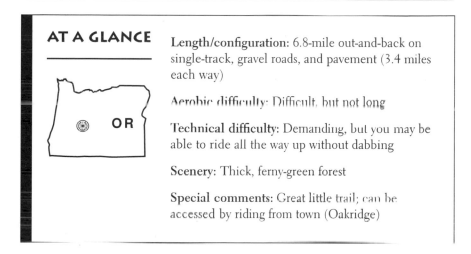

**AT A GLANCE**

**Length/configuration:** 6.8-mile out-and-back on single-track, gravel roads, and pavement (3.4 miles each way)

**Aerobic difficulty:** Difficult, but not long

**Technical difficulty:** Demanding, but you may be able to ride all the way up without dabbing

**Scenery:** Thick, ferny-green forest

**Special comments:** Great little trail; can be accessed by riding from town (Oakridge)

Flat Creek Trail is only 2.4 miles long, but it's a sweet little path. While short, it gains a lot of elevation—it is a pretty hard ride. The trail passes through stands of tall firs. The dense trees check any views, but we didn't mind. We were content to enjoy the woods and concentrate on the challenges beneath our tires.

If you happen to arrive in Oakridge in the early afternoon, you can choose a campsite, pitch your tent, and enjoy this ride—all before dinner. If you camp at Salmon Creek Falls Campground (or at a dispersed site along the creek), you can ride from your site and add a few miles to the trip we describe. Another option involves linking the top of the trail with forest roads that lead to the summit of Dead Mountain.

The basic route is a 6.8-mile out-and-back ride (3.4 miles each way) beginning and ending at the Rigdon/Oakridge Ranger Station. The ranger station is a convenient starting point. You can purchase maps, pick up the district's ride guides, and then head out to the trail.

The ride includes 0.8 mile of pavement, 1.2 miles of gravel road, and 4.8 miles of single-track. The gravel road is in fair condition with some loose gravel

# RIDE 63 · Flat Creek Trail/Dead Mountain

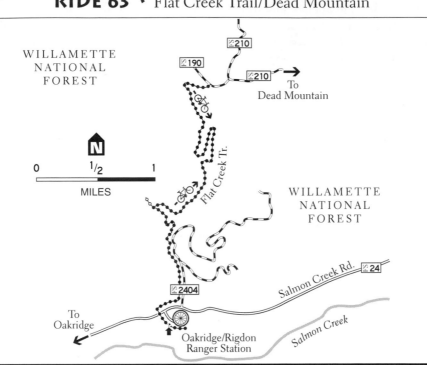

and washboarding. The trail is great. Steep climbing and technical turns characterize the first part of the trail. Roots and rocks make the going tricky and fun. This lower portion includes "breathers," or easier stretches between the hard parts. Later, the grades become gentle.

The return descent is a hoot. Some of the curves and narrow sections come up pretty fast, posing problems if you miss your line. When wet, the trail does not hold up well to traffic. Call ahead and inquire about trail conditions before planning a ride here, and please don't skid around the switchbacks.

**General location:** This ride starts in Oakridge.

**Elevation change:** The trip begins at the ranger station at 1,300'. The high point of the ride (3,040') occurs at the turnaround point—at the top of Flat Creek Trail. Total elevation gain: 1,740'.

**Season:** Wet weather can be a limiting factor from the late fall through the early spring. The trail is often dry by late spring. Windfalls can be a problem; call ahead and ask to speak with the trail coordinator or a recreation specialist—they should know if the trail is dry and whether it has been cleared.

**Hazards:** Roots, rocks, sandy conditions, narrow sections of trail, and tight switchbacks increase the risk on this path. A mistake could result in a good tumble.

There is a tendency to go fast on the return descent. This is not often a problem—if you have a clear line of sight. However, it is difficult to anticipate some of the curves in the trail. Entering a turn too fast can result in riding off the trail, skidding, or surprising someone who is climbing. Take it easy. There are some patches of poison oak bordering the route.

**Rescue index:** The ride begins and ends at the Rigdon/Oakridge Ranger Station. This is a good place to seek help.

**Land status:** Willamette National Forest.

**Maps:** The district map of the Oakridge Ranger District is a good guide to this ride. USGS 7.5 minute quad: Westfir East.

**Finding the trail:** From OR 58 in Oakridge, turn north at the stoplight (at the Sentry Market) onto Crestview Street. Drive up the hill and over a bridge spanning a railroad yard. At a **T** intersection, turn right onto First Street. Pass through town (leaving town, the road designation changes to Salmon Creek Road/Forest Service Road 24.) Turn right in 1.9 miles onto the access road that leads into the Rigdon/Oakridge Ranger Station. Stay to the left and park in the large parking lot.

**Source of additional information:**

Oakridge Ranger District
P.O. Box 1410
Oakridge, OR 97463
(541) 782-2283

Group ride on Dead Mountain Trail.

**Notes on the trail:** Head back out to Salmon Creek Road/FS 24. Turn right onto FS 24 and pedal 0.2 mile to FS 2404 on the left. Ride up FS 2404. Continue straight (left) where a side road goes right in 0.4 mile. The trailhead for Flat Creek Trail will be on your left in another 0.2 mile. You will arrive at a **Y** intersection after 0.4 mile on the trail; stay to the right to remain on Flat Creek Trail. The trail ends at FS 190 in another 2 miles. Turn around and return the way you came.

You can follow forest roads to the top of nearby Dead Mountain. Inspect the district map for connections. Personally, we did not proceed past the intersection of Flat Creek Trail and FS 190.

## RIDE 64 · Blair Lake Loop

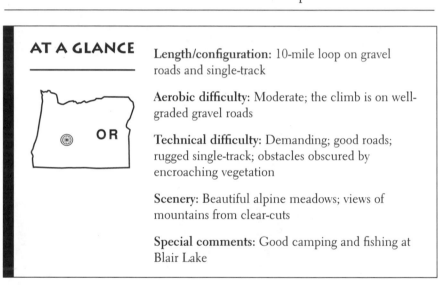

**AT A GLANCE**

**Length/configuration:** 10-mile loop on gravel roads and single-track

**Aerobic difficulty:** Moderate; the climb is on well-graded gravel roads

**Technical difficulty:** Demanding; good roads; rugged single-track; obstacles obscured by encroaching vegetation

**Scenery:** Beautiful alpine meadows; views of mountains from clear-cuts

**Special comments:** Good camping and fishing at Blair Lake

Blair Lake Trail is often overlooked. It's a bit of a trek from Oakridge, and the single-track is only 2.4 miles long. Still, the place has an isolated feeling, and the ride takes you to a lovely alpine meadow. If you spend the night at Blair Lake, you are likely to have the campground to yourself. (On a holiday weekend, or during the Oakridge Fat Tire Festival, maybe not.) If you enjoy fishing, you will appreciate that Blair Lake is stocked with trout.

The loop begins with 7.6 miles of gravel roads. A quick drop from the campground leads to an easy to moderately difficult six-mile climb. Segments of the climb pass through clear-cuts, offering open views across the forest to distant mountains (and other clear-cuts). Blair Lake Trail is picked-up at Spring Prairie, a huge glade carpeted with bear grass. We visited the area in the fall and found the place delightful. We could only imagine what Spring Prairie is like in the

View from Forest Service Road 730.

spring; our guess—fields and hillsides washed with spikes of white flowers. If you venture up the road a bit, just beyond the turnoff for Blair Lake Trail, you come to an opening and a view to the northwest of Three Sisters and Mt. Jefferson.

We found the descent on Blair Lake Trail complicated by encroaching huckleberry bushes and windfalls. Wear tights and long sleeves if you would like to protect your skin from scratches. This trail is also made more difficult by bear grass encroaching onto the tread. The route crosses a couple of bear grass meadows where it is difficult to keep your wheels rolling. The trail is completely obscured by the grass, and the path's many obstacles cannot be seen. The advancing vegetation was beginning to make route-finding difficult too. At least the roads are in good shape.

**General location:**  Blair Lake is approximately 18 miles northwest of Oakridge.

**Elevation change:**  Blair Lake sits at an elevation of 4,760'. The ride descends to 4,360' near the intersection of Forest Service Road 1934 and FS 730. A high point of 5,530' is attained at Spring Prairie. Ups and downs over the course of the ride add about 200' of climbing to the trip. Total elevation gain: 1,370'.

**Season:**  This ride passes through open sunny areas that support a wide variety of wildflowers, but put off riding here until the late spring or early summer. The flowers will still be good, and the trail will have had a chance to dry out. In the spring, the lower reaches of Blair Lake Trail are very wet. Here, the trail travels through a boggy meadow surrounding the lake. Mosquitoes can be bothersome; they are less of a problem in the late summer and fall.

# RIDE 64 · Blair Lake Loop

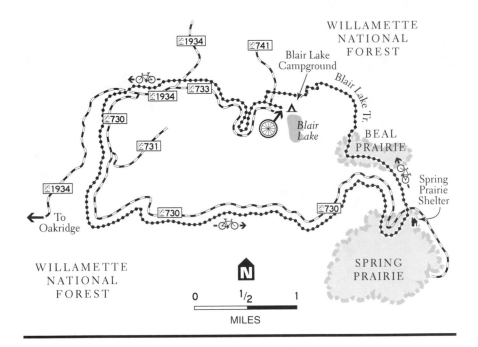

**Services:** Water can be obtained seasonally in Blair Lake Campground (from a hand pump). Food, gas, groceries, and lodging can be found in Oakridge. All services are available in Eugene and Springfield.

**Hazards:** Plants encroach upon the trail and restrict your ability to see obstacles like rocks, roots, endo holes, drop-offs, and narrow sections of tread. Watch for vehicular traffic on the roads.

**Rescue index:** Help can be found in Oakridge.

**Land status:** Willamette National Forest.

**Maps:** The forest service map titled "Bike Routes: Oakridge/Upper Willamette" is a good guide to this ride. USGS 7.5 minute quads: Blair Lake and Huckleberry Mountain.

**Finding the trail:** From OR 58 in Oakridge, turn north at the stoplight (at the Sentry Market) onto Crestview Street. Drive up the hill and over a bridge spanning a railroad yard. At a **T** intersection, turn right onto First Street. Pass through town (leaving town, the road designation changes to Salmon Creek Road/FS 24). Continue on FS 24 for approximately 9 miles and turn left onto FS 1934. Follow gravel FS 1934 for 7.3 miles and turn right onto FS 733. Drive to the end of the road to Blair Lake Campground.

**Source of additional information:**

Oakridge Ranger District
P.O. Box 1410
Oakridge, OR 97463
(541) 782-2283

**Notes on the trail:** From the campground, ride back down FS 733. In 1.5 miles, continue straight (left) onto FS 1934. In 0.4 mile, turn left onto signed FS 730. Stay on this main road for 5.6 miles to reach Spring Prairie Shelter on the right and Blair Lake Trail 3553 on the left. Turn left and follow the trail down into the woods. In 0.3 mile, the trail enters a bear grass meadow. After traversing the meadow the trail emerges onto a rocky slope and then goes back into the woods. Once out of the woods again, the trail switchbacks through an open area. Be alert here for a large rock drop-off that is hidden by bear grass. Nearing Blair Lake, the trail becomes obscured. Follow the posts marked with orange diamonds. The trail ends at a gravel road (FS 741). Turn left and follow the gravel road for 0.2 mile to FS 733. Turn left onto FS 733 and ride 0.5 mile to Blair Lake Campground.

## RIDE 65 · Larison Rock Trail

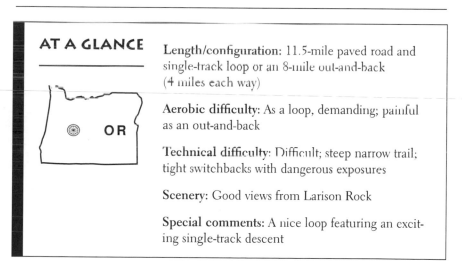

**AT A GLANCE**

**Length/configuration:** 11.5-mile paved road and single-track loop or an 8-mile out-and-back (4 miles each way)

**Aerobic difficulty:** As a loop, demanding; painful as an out-and-back

**Technical difficulty:** Difficult; steep narrow trail; tight switchbacks with dangerous exposures

**Scenery:** Good views from Larison Rock

**Special comments:** A nice loop featuring an exciting single-track descent

If you're inclined toward inclines, you may fancy approaching this trail head on, as an eight-mile out-and-back trip (four miles each way). Leave your skinny-legged friends at home, though; this single-track rises very steeply from the get-go. Much of the trail is rideable, but there are several stretches that will require pushing your bike. A more sensible approach involves riding on forest roads

# RIDE 65 · Larison Rock Trail

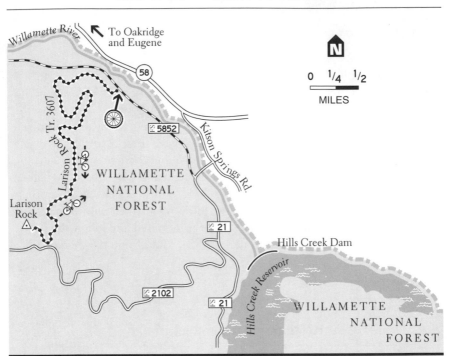

(most of them paved) to the top of the trail, then descending on the single-track. This makes for a difficult 11.5-mile loop.

Parts of the trail are narrow and steep with rocks and roots protruding from the tread. Tight switchbacks with menacing exposures keep you on your toes. Walk your bike down sections of the trail that are beyond your ability to roll through. Locking your brakes to complete a switchback is not an option; it is too hard on the trail. Besides, if a local sees you skidding, his reaction may compromise your safety.

A side trail near the top of Larison Rock Trail leads to the route's namesake. A scramble up the rock puts you in the catbird seat—stretching out below you is a beautiful landscape. We understand that the view from this promontory used to be even better, but trees have grown up to obscure some of the scenery to the north. We didn't have a crystal clear day when we visited, but the forested mountains to the south and west are lovely. Look to the southeast and see if you can make out Diamond Peak. We hear it is visible on a clear day.

**General location:** The ride starts near Oakridge, approximately 40 miles east of Eugene.

**Elevation change:** The trailhead is at 1,200'. The high point is 3,600' at Larison Rock. Total elevation gain: 2,400'.

Ken Ely sampling
some sweet
Oakridge single-track.

**Season:** This trail is open year-round, but should be avoided during wet periods. The path is often wet during the winter and spring.

**Services:** There is no water on this ride. Food, gas, groceries, and lodging are available in Oakridge. All services in Eugene and Springfield.

**Hazards:** Control your speed on the descent, watch for obstacles, and anticipate others approaching from around blind corners. Equestrians and hikers also enjoy this narrow trail. If you decide to climb on the trail, keep your eyes and ears open for descending cyclists.

**Rescue index:** Help can be found in Oakridge.

**Land status:** Willamette National Forest.

**Maps:** The district map of the Rigdon Ranger District is a good guide to this ride. USGS 7.5 minute quad: Oakridge.

**Finding the trail:** From the stop light in Oakridge, drive east on OR 58 for 1.7 miles to Kitson Springs Road. Turn right (south) onto Kitson Springs Road, toward Hills Creek Dam. Proceed for 0.5 mile to Forest Service Road 21 (Rigdon Road). Turn right onto FS 21, cross the bridge over the river, and turn right onto

FS 5852 (South Bank Road). Follow FS 5852 for 1.8 miles to the trailhead, on the left. Park on the right side of the road or continue farther along FS 5852 to locate alternative parking.

**Source of additional information:**

> Rigdon Ranger District
> P.O. Box 1410
> Oakridge, OR 97463
> (541) 782-2283

**Notes on the trail:** Follow FS 5852 back out to FS 21. Turn right onto FS 21 and pedal 0.8 mile to FS 2102 on the right. Head up FS 2102; you will arrive at the upper trailhead for Larison Rock Trail in 4.3 miles. Turn right onto the trail, then immediately turn left onto a side trail that heads to Larison Rock. After visiting the rock, return the way you came to the main trail. Turn left and descend for 3.4 miles on Larison Rock Trail.

## RIDE 66 · Larison Creek Trail

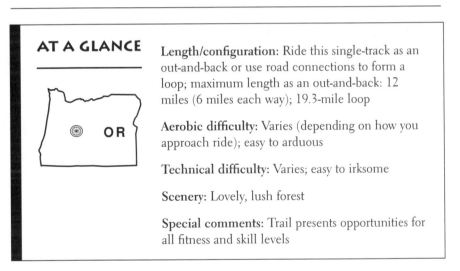

**AT A GLANCE**

**Length/configuration:** Ride this single-track as an out-and-back or use road connections to form a loop; maximum length as an out-and-back: 12 miles (6 miles each way); 19.3-mile loop

**Aerobic difficulty:** Varies (depending on how you approach ride); easy to arduous

**Technical difficulty:** Varies; easy to irksome

**Scenery:** Lovely, lush forest

**Special comments:** Trail presents opportunities for all fitness and skill levels

Larison Creek Trail provides a setting for all manner of mountain bicyclists. Although it gains 1,400' in its six-mile length, most of this elevation gain comes in the trail's last few miles. Beginners can enjoy the lower reaches of the trail, turning around when they feel the terrain is becoming too difficult. Intermediate bikers can test their abilities with climbs and technical terrain encountered farther along. Experts can pedal (and push their bikes) to the top of the trail, then turn around and return the way they came to form a 12-mile out-and-back ride. A longer option involves following paved and gravel roads to

# RIDE 66 · Larison Creek Trail

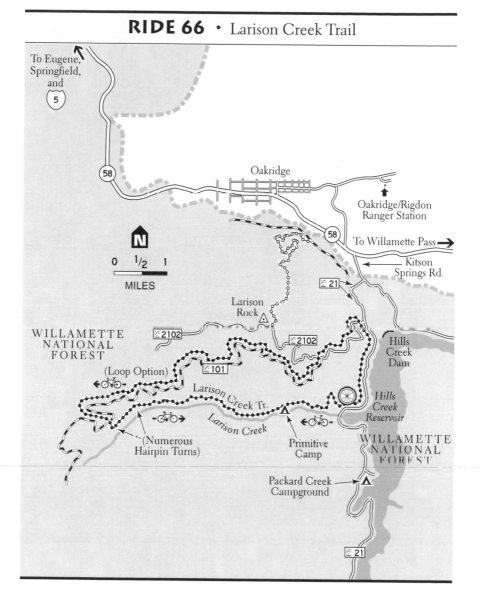

the top of Larison Creek Trail, then descending on the single-track to close the loop.

The lower section of the trail rolls up and down, paralleling Larison Creek and traveling below a canopy of young firs, cedars, and maples. Those not accustomed to riding on single-track may have difficulty with tree roots here. After passing a dispersed camp, 1.5 miles up the trail, the riding becomes more difficult. There are plenty of short, steep ups and downs, and roots are laced across areas of the trail. This is fun, technical single-track.

Larison Creek Trail.

Hanging moss, stands of old-growth timber, and the bubbling of Larison Creek combine to give this place an enchanted feel. An illusion-crushing clear-cut signals the approach of the really steep climbing. Here we found ourselves pushing our bikes several times, but much of the climb was rideable. This steeper section includes areas loose with gravel and sand. Watch out for these hazards as you descend back from the top. Take it easy around the switchbacks, too.

The paved and gravel roads on this ride (if you choose the loop option) are in fair condition and include some moderately difficult to steep climbing. The easiest road riding is on Forest Service Road 21. It is a paved arterial that parallels the shore of Hills Creek Reservoir. Watch for logging trucks and other traffic on the roads. Watch for pedestrians on Larison Creek Trail; it is a popular hike. Stay off of the trail when it is wet, and please tread lightly.

**General location:** This ride begins near the Hills Creek Reservoir, approximately 6 miles south of Oakridge.

**Elevation change:** The ride begins at 1,600' and reaches a high point of 3,000' at the top of Larison Creek Trail. Total elevation gain for the 12-mile out-and-back: 1,400'. Opting for the loop adds roughly 500' of climbing to this base figure. Total elevation gain for the loop: 1,900'

**Season:** The trail is open year-round, but it is usually too wet for mountain biking in the winter and spring.

**Services:** There is no potable water on this ride. Water can be obtained seasonally at Packard Creek Campground (a couple of miles south of the trailhead on FS 21). Food, lodging, groceries, gas, and espresso can be found in Oakridge. All services are available in Eugene and Springfield.

**Hazards:** The trail includes obstacles like slippery roots, rocks, gravel, and sand. Watch for loose conditions when descending on the trail, and approach exposed switchbacks with care. Anticipate others approaching from around blind corners. Ride defensively and predictably on the roads.

**Rescue index:** Help can be found in Oakridge.

**Land status:** Willamette National Forest.

**Maps:** The district map of the Rigdon Ranger District is a good guide to this route. USGS 7.5 minute quads: Oakridge and Holland Point.

**Finding the trail:** From the stop light in Oakridge, drive east on OR 58 for 1.7 miles to Kitson Springs Road. Turn right (south) onto Kitson Springs Road, toward Hills Creek Dam. Proceed for 0.5 mile to FS 21 (Rigdon Road). Turn right onto FS 21. Follow FS 21 for 3.3 miles to the trailhead parking area on the right.

**Source of additional information:**

Rigdon Ranger District
P.O. Box 1410
Oakridge, OR 97463
(541) 782-2283

**Notes on the trail:** From the parking area, follow Larison Creek Trail 3646 upstream. Pass a primitive campsite and a pit toilet at 1.5 miles (a good turnaround point for beginners). The trail becomes more challenging after you pass the campsite. Push on to the top of the trail at its intersection with FS 101, or turn around when you have had enough hiking with your bike.

For the loop option, follow FS 21 north for 2.3 miles to FS 2102. Turn left onto FS 2102 and pedal 2.2 miles to FS 101. Turn left onto FS 101 and ride 8.8 miles to Larison Creek Trail on the left. Descend on the trail to your vehicle.

## RIDE 67 · Middle Fork Willamette Trail

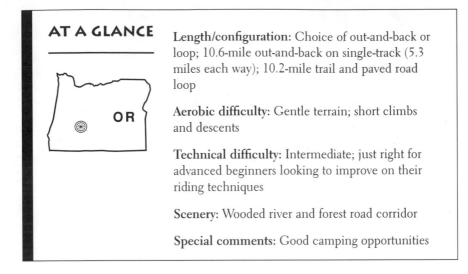

**AT A GLANCE**

**Length/configuration:** Choice of out-and-back or loop; 10.6-mile out-and-back on single-track (5.3 miles each way); 10.2-mile trail and paved road loop

OR

**Aerobic difficulty:** Gentle terrain; short climbs and descents

**Technical difficulty:** Intermediate; just right for advanced beginners looking to improve on their riding techniques

**Scenery:** Wooded river and forest road corridor

**Special comments:** Good camping opportunities

The Middle Fork Willamette Trail is a long piece of single-track. It follows the Middle Fork of the Willamette River for 27 miles. The trail's upper reaches begin below peaks in the Cascade Range; near the river's headwaters at Timpanogas Lake. It ends at Sand Prairie Campground; just a mile from where the river flows into Hills Creek Reservoir. The higher portions of the trail are demanding and technical. We explored the lowest five miles of the trail. Here, the pedaling is easy and the route contains few difficult obstacles.

Beginning at Sand Prairie Campground and riding out and back on the trail makes for a 10.6-mile trip (5.3 miles each way). While the elevation gain is not very significant, you will be climbing as you pedal away from the campground. If you get tired, you have the option of turning around at any time or bailing out onto paved Forest Service Road 21 (the road parallels the trail). Creating a loop by first following FS 21, then descending on the trail is another approach. You can ride up on the road and access the trail in a number of places. The longest possible loop is 10.2 miles long (this supposes that you are limiting your travels to the lower, easier section of the trail).

Those interested in camping will have little difficulty finding a site to their liking. Sand Prairie Campground offers shady, developed sites, vault toilets, and piped water. Folks interested in a more private setting can choose from many fine dispersed sites bordering the river and trail.

**General location:** The ride begins at Sand Prairie Campground, approximately 14 miles south of Oakridge.

**Elevation change:** The trail's low point is 1,560' at Sand Prairie Campground. The high point, 1,800', is obtained at the intersection of the trail and FS 21

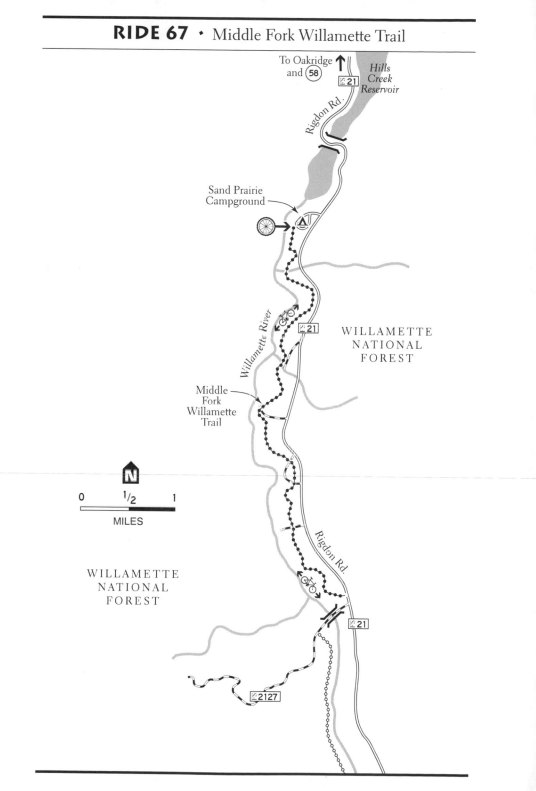

To Oakridge
and (58)

Hills
Creek
Reservoir

Rigdon Rd.

21

Sand Prairie
Campground

WILLAMETTE
NATIONAL
FOREST

21

Willamette River

Middle
Fork
Willamette
Trail

N

0     1/2     1
MILES

WILLAMETTE
NATIONAL
FOREST

Rigdon Rd.

21

21

2127

A mellow pedal
on the Middle Fork
Willamette Trail.

(near the intersection of FS 21 and FS 2127). Undulations in the trail add about 200' of climbing to an out-and-back excursion. Total elevation gain: 440'.

**Season:** The lower elevations of the Middle Fork Willamette Trail can be enjoyed from the early spring through the late fall. Stay off the trail when it is wet.

**Services:** Water is available seasonally at Sand Prairie Campground. Food, gas, lodging, and groceries can be obtained in Oakridge. All services are available in Eugene and Springfield.

**Hazards:** The trail contains obstacles like roots, narrow sections of tread, rocks, small drop-offs, short, steep hills, and areas that are soft with sand and gravel. Although these conditions may sound daunting, the trail is actually quite mild. This is a good introduction to some of the fun that single-track trails offer. Give it a go, take your time, and walk your bike where you encounter conditions that make you uncomfortable. If you choose to ride on FS 21, watch for logging trucks and other vehicular traffic—ride predictably and defensively (stay to the right and ride single-file).

**Rescue index:** Help is available in Oakridge.

**Land status:** Willamette National Forest.

**Maps:** The district map of the Rigdon Ranger District is suitable as a guide to this ride. The trail has been realigned in places. Some of these reroutes are not reflected on the district map. USGS 7.5 minute quad: Warner Mountain.

**Finding the trail:** From the stoplight in Oakridge, drive east on OR 58 for 1.7 miles to Kitson Springs Road. Turn right (south) onto Kitson Springs Road, toward Hills Creek Dam. Proceed for 0.5 mile to FS 21 (Rigdon Road). Turn right onto FS 21 and drive 11.7 miles to Sand Prairie Campground. Turn right into the campground. Stay to the right through the campground to arrive at a small day-use parking area near a group picnic area and 2 utility buildings.

**Source of additional information:**

Rigdon Ranger District
P.O. Box 1410
Oakridge, OR 97463
(541) 782-2283

**Notes on the trail:** Access signed "Middle Fork Trail" at the wood guardrail (at the end of the parking area). Follow the trail upriver. The path travels through a narrow corridor bounded by the river and FS 21. At times, the route follows old roads and passes through dispersed campsites. Staying on course may require some poking about, but you should have little difficulty finding your way. If you get tired and would like to return to the campground on FS 21, turn left (east) onto one of the many double-tracks that cross the trail (most head out to the pavement). The lower portion of the Middle Fork Willamette Trail is 5.3 miles long. It terminates at FS 21. Turn around and return the way you came.

To create a loop with FS 21 and the Middle Fork Willamette Trail, ride out of the campground to FS 21. Turn right onto FS 21 and pedal 4.7 miles to the signed "Middle Fork Trail" on the right. (This intersection is 0.5 mile beyond milepost 16). Turn onto the trail and follow it back to your vehicle at Sand Prairie Campground.

# RIDE 68 · Moon Point/Youngs Rock Trail

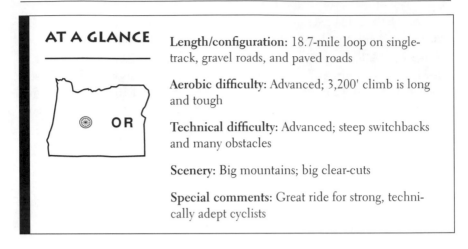

**AT A GLANCE**

**Length/configuration:** 18.7-mile loop on single-track, gravel roads, and paved roads

**Aerobic difficulty:** Advanced; 3,200' climb is long and tough

**Technical difficulty:** Advanced; steep switchbacks and many obstacles

**Scenery:** Big mountains; big clear-cuts

**Special comments:** Great ride for strong, technically adept cyclists

Moon Point/Youngs Rock Trail requires a lot of stamina and technical skill. We recommend this ride for strong mountain bikers. The route begins with a 9.6-mile ascent on gravel roads. The climb is not a total grunt, in fact, three miles are actually easy to moderate. One of the rewards for all of this effort is the view from Moon Point. The view is expansive and revealing. Diamond Peak, Sawtooth Mountain, and Dome Rock, compete with huge clear-cuts for your attention.

The next prize on this ride is a five-mile single-track descent on Youngs Rock Trail. This descent is by no means a cruise. It is riddled with tight switchbacks, extremely steep drops, and dangerous exposures.

This route is an 18.7-mile loop. The ride is made up of 9.6 miles of gravel roads, 2.5 miles of paved roads, and 6.6 miles of single-track. The roads are all in good condition. The condition of the single-tracks varies, but for the most part they are in fair condition. The first mile on Moon Point Trail is mostly level, but it is overgrown; vegetation obscures obstacles such as embedded rocks and roots. Parts of Youngs Rock Trail are steep and rocky. The last two miles of the trail descend more moderately through a park-like forest. The ride ends with a couple of miles on paved Forest Service Road 21.

**General location:** The parking area for this route is approximately 20 miles southeast of Oakridge.

**Elevation change:** The ride begins at 1,900' and reaches a high point of 5,100' at Moon Point. Ups and downs add an estimated 150' of climbing to the circuit. Total elevation gain: 3,350'.

**Season:** This route is best ridden from June through October. The ascent can be hot and dusty during the summer months. Stay off the trail when it is wet.

# RIDE 68 · Moon Point/Youngs Rock Trail

**Services:** Water can be obtained seasonally at Campers Flat Campground. You will find gas, food, lodging, and groceries in Oakridge. All services are available in Eugene and Springfield.

**Hazards:** There are many hazards on this route. These include; steep drop-offs, narrow and ditch-like trails, tight switchbacks, dangerous exposures, rocks, roots, and obscured obstacles. Be careful as you scramble up the rocks at Moon Point; cleated bike shoes make lousy climbing shoes. Watch for motor vehicles on all of the forest roads.

Descending on
Youngs Rock Trail.

**Rescue index:** Help can be found in Oakridge.

**Land status:** Willamette National Forest.

**Maps:** The district map of the Rigdon Ranger District is a good guide to this ride. USGS 7.5 minute quad: Warner Mountain.

**Finding the trail:** From the stoplight in Oakridge, drive east on OR 58 for 1.7 miles to Kitson Springs Road. Turn right (south) onto Kitson Springs Road, toward Hills Creek Dam. Proceed for 0.5 mile to FS 21 (Rigdon Road). Turn right onto FS 21 and drive 18 miles to the junction with FS 2129 (on the left). Continue straight to stay on FS 21. In 0.1 mile, turn right and park in the large grassy parking area. This parking area is marked with a sign that reads, "Disperse Host."

**Source of additional information:**

Rigdon Ranger District
P.O. Box 1410
Oakridge, OR 97463
(541) 782-2283

**Notes on the trail:** Skidding around turns is inappropriate; it causes severe trail damage. If you are an expert trials rider, have at the tight switchbacks on Youngs Rock Trail. Everyone else should walk their bikes down them. This may sound severe, but attempting to clean them doesn't cut it—you may clean some of them, but you will miss frequently. When you miss, your foot comes down to catch your fall. Invariably, this damages the hillside above the trail and leads to slope failure (i.e., the trail gets trashed).

Turn left onto FS 21, then immediately turn right onto Youngs Creek Road/FS 2129. In 3 miles, pass Youngs Rock Trail 3685 (on the right). Continue on FS 2129 for another 5.1 miles to the intersection with FS 439. Turn right and follow the sign for Moon Point Trail. Proceed on FS 439 for 1.5 miles to the trailhead for Moon Point Trail 3688. Turn right onto the trail. Reach an intersection of trails in 0.8 mile. A sign on a tree directs you straight to Moon Point and left for Youngs Rock Trail and Campers Flat Campground. Continue straight on Moon Point Trail to arrive at Moon Point in 0.3 mile. Return to the intersection of trails and turn right onto Youngs Rock Trail. The trail climbs briefly and then begins its long descent. In 3.3 miles, cross an unsigned dirt road. Pass a trail on the right in 0.4 mile. In another 0.6 mile, at the next dirt road, go slightly to the right to regain the trail. Cross a double-track in 0.4 mile, following the trail as it gets ditch-like. The trail improves before ending at FS 21. Turn right and follow FS 21 for 2.5 miles to reach your vehicle.

## RIDE 69 · Waldo Lake

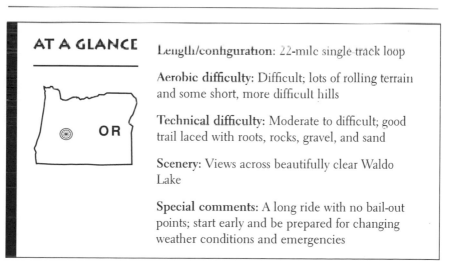

**AT A GLANCE**

**OR**

**Length/configuration:** 22-mile single-track loop

**Aerobic difficulty:** Difficult; lots of rolling terrain and some short, more difficult hills

**Technical difficulty:** Moderate to difficult; good trail laced with roots, rocks, gravel, and sand

**Scenery:** Views across beautifully clear Waldo Lake

**Special comments:** A long ride with no bail-out points; start early and be prepared for changing weather conditions and emergencies

This single-track trip around Waldo Lake is 22 miles long. Depending on your conditioning and technical proficiency, it is a moderately difficult to difficult loop. The trails take you past rocky coves, quiet beaches, meadows,

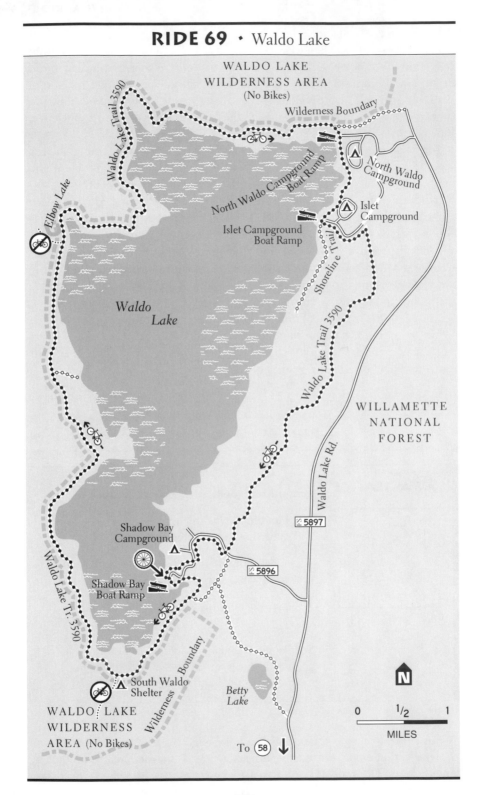

WALDO LAKE
WILDERNESS AREA
(No Bikes)

Wilderness Boundary

Waldo Lake Trail 3590

Elbow Lake

Waldo
Lake

North Waldo Campground
Boat Ramp

North Waldo
Campground

Islet
Campground

Islet Campground
Boat Ramp

Shoreline Trail

Waldo Lake Trail 3590

WILLAMETTE
NATIONAL
FOREST

Waldo Lake Rd.

5897

5896

Shadow Bay
Campground

Shadow Bay
Boat Ramp

Waldo Lake Tr. 3590

South Waldo
Shelter

Betty
Lake

WALDO LAKE
WILDERNESS
AREA (No Bikes)

Wilderness Boundary

To 58

N

0    1/2    1

MILES

Circling Waldo Lake.

campsites, and several smaller lakes and ponds. The view across the water is of forested ridge lines and low mountains. In general, the trail is in good condition.

The trip starts with two easy miles along the lakeshore. Then the trail becomes more demanding, with several steep pitches and a rougher tread. Protruding tree roots, boulders, loose gravel, and sandy conditions are inter-mixed with smooth stretches. This more difficult terrain continues for about five miles. After passing Elbow Lake, the cycling becomes very agreeable, with an improved trail surface and rolling hills. Gentle climbing and good descents characterize the pedaling on the eastern shore.

Please do your part to help keep this fine trail open to mountain bikes. Stay off the trail when it is wet. If you encounter an isolated wet area, carry your bike through it. (Stay on the trail; carrying your bike around wet areas widens the area of impact.) Be courteous and yield the trail to hikers and equestrians. Much of the trail is bounded by the Waldo Lake Wilderness Area; bikes are not allowed in designated wilderness areas.

**General location:** Waldo Lake is about 75 miles southeast of Eugene.

**Elevation change:** The trailhead is at 5,440'. A high point of 5,700' occurs just a few miles from the completion of the loop. There are a lot of ups and downs along the course of the ride, adding about 700' of climbing to the outing. Total elevation gain: 960'.

**Season:** The trails around Waldo Lake are generally clear of snow from June through October. Mosquitoes can be a problem from June through August. The lake is a popular summer destination. Plan on visiting in the fall or on a week-day for a quieter experience.

**Services:** Water can be obtained seasonally at the trailhead. Food, lodging, gas, and groceries are available in Oakridge. All services are available in Eugene.

**Hazards:** Obstacles in the trail can cause handling problems. Common impediments include tight squeezes through boulders; slick roots and rocks; drop-offs; windfalls; and sand. There is about 1 mile of paved road riding on the eastern shore, where you may encounter vehicular traffic. If you run into problems, you could have trouble completing the loop before nightfall. Get an early start, take food and plenty of water, anticipate changes in the weather, and be prepared to make trailside repairs.

**Rescue index:** Help can be found in Oakridge. In an emergency, help may be available at the campgrounds on the eastern side of the lake.

**Land status:** Willamette National Forest.

**Maps:** The district map of the Oakridge Ranger District is a good guide to this ride. USGS 7.5 minute quads: Waldo Lake and Waldo Mountain.

**Finding the trail:** From locations to the west, follow OR 58 east from Oakridge for about 23 miles, to Waldo Lake Road/Forest Service Road 5897 (on the left). From locations to the east, follow OR 58 west from Willamette Pass for about 3 miles to Waldo Lake Road/FS 5897 (on the right). Turn north onto FS 5897 and drive 6.9 miles to FS 5896. Turn left onto FS 5896 toward Shadow Bay. Stay left toward the boat ramp. Park your vehicle in the large gravel parking area above the boat ramp.

### Source of additional information:

Oakridge Ranger District
P.O. Box 1410
Oakridge, OR 97463
(541) 782-2283

**Notes on the trail:** Waldo Lake Trail 3590 heads south from the parking area. Follow the well-marked trail around the lake. There is a tricky intersection near Elbow Lake (about 8 miles into the ride). Do not go left to follow the sign for Waldo Meadows; stay to the right, continuing on Waldo Lake Trail. You will pass through Dam Camp in another 3.3 miles; follow the signs for North Waldo Campground. The trail divides at a trail sign-in box near North Waldo Campground; bear right, following Shoreline Trail. Continue south past the North Waldo Campground boat ramp and stay on Shoreline Trail as it goes through the campground amphitheater. Then walk your bike across a sandy beach and continue on Shoreline Trail past Islet Point. Turn left onto the paved road at the Islet Campground boat ramp. After 0.5 mile on pavement, turn right onto signed Waldo Lake Trail. Follow the path through the woods for 4.6 miles to unsigned FS 5896 (the first paved road you come to on this section of Waldo Lake Trail). Turn right and follow FS 5896 back to your vehicle.

## RIDE 70 · Summit Lake Trail/Meek Lake Trail

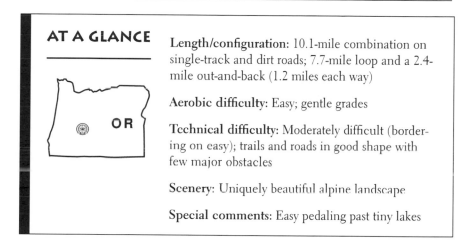

**AT A GLANCE**

**Length/configuration:** 10.1-mile combination on single-track and dirt roads; 7.7-mile loop and a 2.4-mile out-and-back (1.2 miles each way)

**Aerobic difficulty:** Easy; gentle grades

**Technical difficulty:** Moderately difficult (bordering on easy); trails and roads in good shape with few major obstacles

**Scenery:** Uniquely beautiful alpine landscape

**Special comments:** Easy pedaling past tiny lakes

Summit Lake and Meek Lake trails are in the Windy Lakes region of the Deschutes National Forest. Hundreds of tiny alpine lakes dot the area. Small rock outcroppings, dwarf conifers, and multitudes of mushrooms, moss, and ground covers provide this place with an other-worldly feel. The landscape is unusual and beautiful. The gentle nature of the area's single-track is also unique. The paths contain obstacles, but compared to other mountain trails, these are mellow. They roll along over small hills, cross occasional tree roots, and dodge between rocks and logs.

This 10.1-mile ride is a combination of a 7.7-mile loop and a 2.4-mile out-and-back (1.2 miles each way). The trip includes 1.5 miles of dirt road, the rest is single-track. It is an easy ride, but novices may find it a tad long. We rate the technical difficulty of the trail as moderate. Still, we would encourage strong, energetic beginners to try these trails; especially if they are comfortable with pushing their bikes from time to time. Turn around and return the way you came if you find that the riding is becoming too difficult.

**General location:** The ride starts at Summit Lake; approximately 45 miles southeast of Oakridge.

**Elevation change:** The trailhead at Summit Lake is at 5,560'. A high point of

# RIDE 70 · Summit Lake Trail/Meek Lake Trail

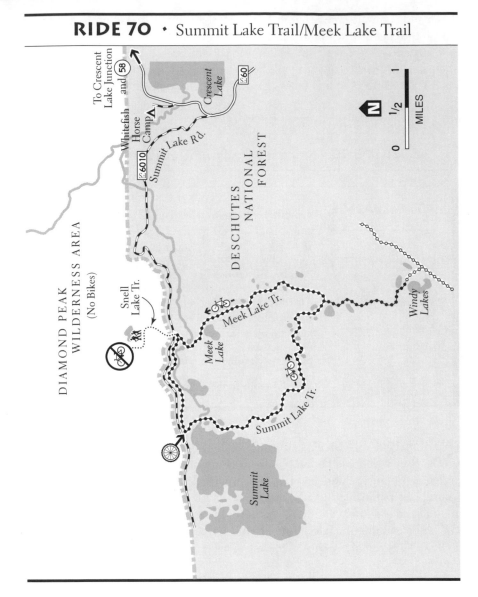

6,140' is obtained at North Windy Lake. Undulations over the course of the circuit add about 300' of climbing to the trip. Total elevation gain: 880'.

**Season:** The trails may not be free of snow until June. The soils in the area are quite sandy, so the trails drain well and dry quickly after rains. However, dry spells and heavy use can promote soft conditions. Mosquitoes can limit your enjoyment of the area in the spring and early summer. The region is quite popular with hikers in the summer. The late summer through the early fall is an ideal time for a visit to the area.

**Services:** There is no potable water on this ride. Drinking water is available seasonally at Crescent Lake Campground and Whitefish Horse Camp. Food, gas, and lodging can be found in Crescent Lake Junction. The nearest supermarkets are in Oakridge. All services are available in Eugene and Bend.

**Hazards:** Obstacles on this route include roots, rocks, and sandy conditions. Be prepared for sudden changes in the weather. Anticipate hikers, horseback riders, and other cyclists approaching from around blind corners. Watch for vehicles on the road.

**Rescue index:** The nearest pay phone is at Crescent Lake Lodge and Resort. The resort is at the north end of Crescent Lake, very near the Crescent Lake Campground. (The entrance road to the campground is off of Forest Service Road 60, just 0.4 mile south of the intersection of FS 60 and Crescent Lake Highway.) You can also find a pay phone at Crescent Lake Junction, on OR 58. There are hospitals in Eugene and Bend.

**Land status:** Deschutes National Forest.

**Maps:** The district map of the Crescent Ranger District is a good guide to this ride. The district's "Mountain Biking Trail Guide" is a valuable resource for cyclists interested in further explorations in the region. You can pick one up at the ranger station in Crescent. (Crescent is on US 97; about 10 miles north of the intersection of US 97 and OR 58.) USGS 7.5 minute quad: Cowhorn Mountain.

**Finding the trail:** Getting to the trailhead is somewhat of a challenge. The access road is narrow, and in places, quite rough; high clearance is recommended.

From locations to the west, head southeast out of Oakridge on OR 58. You will reach Crescent Lake Junction after driving about 34 miles (about 7 miles beyond Willamette Pass). From locations to the east, drive north from Klamath Falls, or south from Bend to the intersection of US 97 and OR 58. Follow OR 58 northwest for approximately 17 miles to Crescent Lake Junction.

In Crescent Lake Junction, drive south on Crescent Lake Highway. In 2 miles, follow the road as it passes over railroad tracks, then curves left. Take the next road to the right; FS 60 (follow the sign for "Campgrounds" and "Camp Makualla"). In 4.7 miles you will pass Tandy Bay (it is on the left). From this landmark it is 0.3 mile to Summit Lake Road/FS 6010 on the right (easy to miss). Turn sharply right and climb up this narrow, sandy road. Pass the trailhead for Meek Lake Trail 43 in 3.8 miles (on the left). In another 1.5 miles, arrive at the trailhead for Summit Lake Trail (after a total of 5.3 miles on FS 6010). Turn left into the lakeside parking area.

## Source of additional information:

Crescent Ranger District
P.O. Box 208
Crescent, OR 97733
(541) 433-2234

A damp day at
North Windy Lake.

**Notes on the trail:** Follow signed Summit Lake Trail for 3.4 miles to its intersection with Meek Lake Trail. Bear right to remain on Summit Lake Trail. You
will arrive at North Windy Lake in another 1.2 miles (signed on its western
shore). Turn around and return to the last intersection. Turn right to follow
Meek Lake Trail for 2.8 miles to FS 6010. Turn left onto the road and ride 1.5
miles to your car at Summit Lake.

There are many riding opportunities in the area. You may wish to extend the
described ride by continuing on Summit Lake Trail to Windy Lakes Trail,
Oldenberg Trail, or both. Please note that bikes are *not* allowed in the nearby
Diamond Peak Wilderness Area.

# OREGON COAST/COASTAL RANGE

The Oregon Coast is 360 miles of beaches, rocky headlands, rainforests, and wildflower-stippled meadows. Sections of the coast offer promontories for watching birds, whales, and other marine life. Nestled along the shore are towns and fishing villages, and each of these communities acts as a gateway to more wilderness beauty.

Following US 101 north out of California brings you into an area known as Oregon's Banana Belt. A sheltering headland protects the area around Brookings (the first town north of the border) from prevailing northwest winds. The climate is so mild that citrus trees and palms are grown here.

Twenty-seven miles north of Brookings is the community of Gold Beach. The 40-minute drive between these two towns can easily turn into a day-long outing. Scenic overlooks from rocky capes and hikes to secluded beaches are strung out along the course of the highway. The scenes you gaze upon have changed very little from those seen by early western explorers.

Searching for golden cities to conquer, the Spanish pilot Bartolome Ferrelo sailed as far north as the southern coast of Oregon in 1542. In 1579, the Englishman Sir Francis Drake challenged Spain's claim to the coast by sailing north to the Rogue River (near present-day Gold Beach). "Thicke and stinking fogges" caused him to give up his search for a passage back to the Atlantic.

The hope of a northwest passage lingered and fueled more explorations. James Cook searched the northern waters of the Pacific in the late eighteenth century. Stopping in the Orient on the way home to England, his men made a monumental discovery: they could sell their makeshift bedding of sea otter pelts to the Chinese—for a small fortune! To Europeans, the value of the Pacific Coast was forever changed; the great tide from the West had begun.

Today, the coastal strip is thinly populated; only a few of its towns approach 10,000 residents. Timber, fishing, and the millions of dollars generated by tourism stoke the region's economy. US 101 is the conduit for tourists and their credit cards.

For most of its length, US 101 hugs the coast. This road is a favored destination for touring bicyclists. Thousands enjoy all or part of the Oregon Coast Bike Route annually. What draws these riders is the natural beauty of the Pacific, the excellent camping, and the state's welcoming approach to cycling. These same qualities make the area attractive to mountain bikers.

State parks and excursions on private property (with permission) provide some opportunities for mountain bike riding along the coastline. Inland from the coast are miles of river-level trails and forest roads. State and national forests offer the greatest selection of all-terrain rides.

The Siskiyou National Forest surrounds the Klamath Mountains along the southern coast of Oregon. The Klamath Mountains are the most severe subgroup of mountains within the Coastal Range. Good access into these steep peaks can be found in Brookings and Gold Beach.

Farther north, the Siuslaw National Forest covers over one-half million acres between Coos Bay and Tillamook. This large holding within the Coastal Range contains miles of gravel roads that have seldom, if ever, been explored by bicycle.

The ocean has a moderating effect on the weather along the coast. Clear, cool summers are the rule. Rain and fog are common from November until May, but pleasant, sunny winter days are not unheard of.

## RIDE 71 · Lower Rogue River Trail

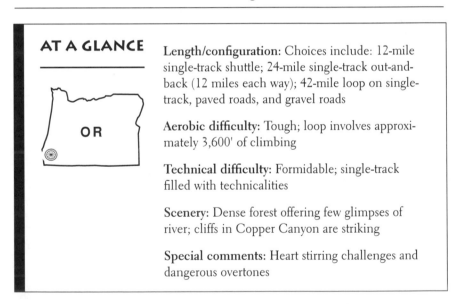

**AT A GLANCE**

**Length/configuration:** Choices include: 12-mile single-track shuttle; 24-mile single-track out-and-back (12 miles each way); 42-mile loop on single-track, paved roads, and gravel roads

**Aerobic difficulty:** Tough; loop involves approximately 3,600' of climbing

**Technical difficulty:** Formidable; single-track filled with technicalities

**Scenery:** Dense forest offering few glimpses of river; cliffs in Copper Canyon are striking

**Special comments:** Heart stirring challenges and dangerous overtones

In the late 1800s, the Rogue River Trail was an important transportation link between the coast at Gold Beach and inland settlements. After the construction of other roads, this route was all but abandoned. Today, it is a well-maintained recreational trail that rambles through a dense, temperate rainforest. Sightings of the Rogue from the trail are few. The view of the river from the cliffs in Copper Canyon is a memorable exception.

Ancient cedar on the Lower Rogue River Trail.

Cycling this 12-mile Lower Rogue River Trail is a demanding experience. Much of the single-track is rideable, though some parts can be a real struggle. The path is a technical challenge, with roots, rocks, scree slopes, steep climbs and descents, narrow cliff experiences, lots of small creek crossings, and scratchy, encroaching vegetation. There are also plenty of hike-a-bike stretches. This route is just the ticket for strong, experienced, and slightly demented cyclists.

After pedaling and pushing your bike for 12 miles, you must decide whether to return on the trail or loop back on paved and gravel roads. Beaten up by the single-track, we chose the roads. It made for a long day (42 miles), but making a loop was probably less taxing than riding back on the trail. Any way you approach it, this is a tough ride.

**General location:** The trailhead is on the north side of the Rogue River, 16 miles east of Gold Beach.

**Elevation change:** Starts at 540' and drops to 160' in 3.7 miles. The high point of the trail, 780', occurs shortly after Schoolhouse Creek (about 6 miles into the trip). The small town of Agness (elevation 200') marks the end of the single-track portion of the circuit. Lower Rogue River Trail contains innumerable climbs and descents that are shorter than those described above. We estimate that the trail rises and falls enough to add over 1,000' of climbing to the ride. The return to the trailhead on the roads is all up and down. From Agness, rolling terrain takes you to a bridge that crosses the Illinois River at 160'. Shortly after crossing the river, you will commence a long climb to 840'. This climb is followed by a

4-mile descent and many lesser hills. The loop closes with another longer climb—300' in 1 mile. Undulations add about 1,000' of climbing to the road riding. Total elevation gain: 3,600'.

**Season:** This tour can be fun year-round if the trail is dry. Much of the single-track is covered with leaves and other forest litter. When wet, the surface is fragile and extremely slick and should be avoided. Wood ticks are a problem in the spring and summer.

**Services:** There is no potable water on this ride. There is a small store in Agness that maintains a limited inventory of groceries. All services are available in Gold Beach.

**Hazards:** You should consider tackling the Lower Rogue River Trail only if you are fit and possess advanced bike-handling skills; this is a long and demanding ride with no bail-out options. Turn around before passing Schoolhouse Creek if you are getting tired. The narrow trail drops off steeply in places and contains many obstacles to a safe passage. Wood ticks, poison oak, and rattlesnakes are additional concerns (we're not kidding). In Agness, the trail deposits you onto a street. The first house on the right had a couple of mean, unchained dogs protecting it.

**Rescue index:** Help can be found in Gold Beach.

**Land status:** Siskiyou National Forest lands and public right-of-way through private property.

**Maps:** The district map of the Gold Beach Ranger District is a good guide to this ride. USGS 7.5 minute quads: Quosatana Butte, Signal Buttes, Agness, Soldier Camp Mountain, and Brushy Bald Mountain.

**Finding the trail:** From Gold Beach and US 101, turn east onto Jerrys Flat Road. (Jerrys Flat Road meets the highway just south of the bridge over the Rogue River.) Drive east for 9.6 miles, then turn left to cross the North Bank Bridge at Lobster Bar. Immediately after the bridge, turn right onto Forest Service Road 3533/North Bank Road. Stay on the main road and follow the signs to the Lower Rogue River Trail. After 5.8 miles on FS 3533 you will come to a **Y** intersection at a clearing. There is a sign here that points the way toward the Lower Rogue River Trail. Park on the right at this intersection, next to the big log.

**Source of additional information:**

Gold Beach Ranger District
29279 Ellensburg Avenue
Gold Beach, OR 97444
(541) 247-3600

**Notes on the trail:** From the parking area and trailhead, follow the signs to access the Lower Rogue River Trail 1168. Stay left where side trails descend to summer homes along the river. After about 10 miles, the trail crosses a fence (by means of some wooden steps) and comes to a gravel road. Turn left, cross Blue

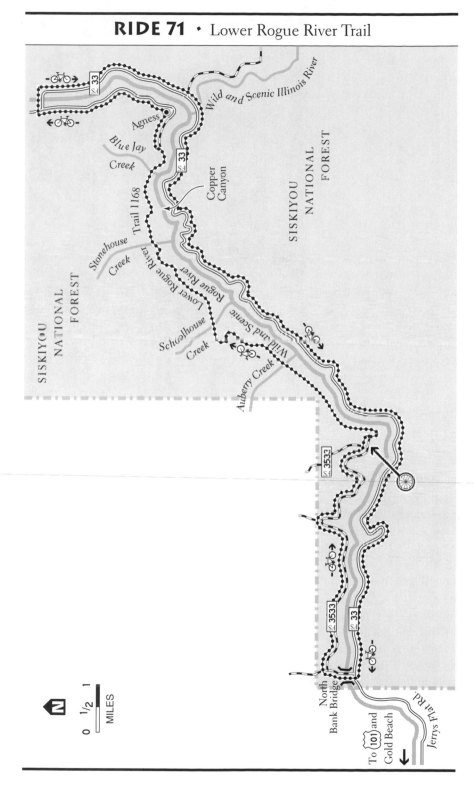

N

0  ½  1
MILES

Wild and Scenic Illinois River

SISKIYOU
NATIONAL
FOREST

Agness

Blue Jay
Creek

S.t. 33

Copper
Canyon

Trail 1168

Stonehouse Creek

Lower Rogue River

Rogue River

SISKIYOU

NATIONAL

FOREST

Wild and Scenic

Schoolhouse
Creek

Auberry Creek

S.t. 3533

S.t. 3533

S.t. 33

North
Bank Bridge

To 101 and
Gold Beach

Jerrys Flat Rd.

Passing through
Copper Canyon.

Jay Creek, and follow the road a very short distance to the trail (signed on the right). Turn right, back onto the trail. Stay left at all side-trails for another 1.3 miles, until you reach the streets of Agness. Stay right at the first **Y** intersection. Soon you will reach pavement and then the Agness Store on the left. Turn left at the Agness Store and follow the road upriver. Follow this road for 3 miles to FS 33. Turn right to cross the bridge over the Rogue River; follow FS 33 toward Gold Beach. Remain on FS 33 for 21 miles to the North Bank Bridge. Turn right to cross the bridge, then immediately turn right onto FS 3533/North Bank Road. Follow the signs to the Lower Rogue River Trail.

This ride can be approached as an out-and-back "all trail" ride, or as a shuttle; leaving a car at the described trailhead, then driving to Agness in a second vehicle to access the trail. You may wish to ride it as a loop, but in a counterclockwise direction (completing the road miles first, then following the trail downstream from Agness).

## RIDE 72 · Siltcoos Lake Trail

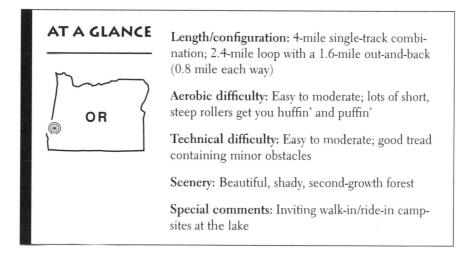

**AT A GLANCE**

**Length/configuration:** 4-mile single-track combination; 2.4-mile loop with a 1.6-mile out-and-back (0.8 mile each way)

**Aerobic difficulty:** Easy to moderate; lots of short, steep rollers get you huffin' and puffin'

**Technical difficulty:** Easy to moderate; good tread containing minor obstacles

**Scenery:** Beautiful, shady, second-growth forest

**Special comments:** Inviting walk-in/ride-in campsites at the lake

This easy to moderately difficult four-mile circuit combines a 2.4-mile loop with a 1.6-mile out-and-back (0.8 mile each way). Energetic beginners should give this trail a whirl; they may find it necessary to push their bikes up some of the hills. Intermediate cyclists will thrill at the challenges this trail throws at them. Seasoned cyclists may be surprised by the amount of fun that is packed into this short ride, which is a mix of twists, turns, bumps, and short, steep, rideable climbs. The compacted dirt and rock trail was in great shape at the time of our initial research. Evergreen needles carpeted the path and hushed our rolling tires. Seeing fresh skid marks on this beautiful trail certainly dampened our mood.

Early accounts of this area speak of trees that were "100 feet to the bottom limbs." The forest was said to be "so open you could ride a saddle horse anywhere." Today the trails to Siltcoos Lake lead through a 50-year-old stand of Sitka spruce, Douglas fir, cedar, and hemlock. Scattered throughout the area are huge stumps where giants once stood. Some of the stumps still contain springboard holes. Fallers inserted planks into these holes and wielded their saws from these precarious perches.

**General location:** The trailhead is on the east side of US 101, approximately 7 miles south of Florence.

**Elevation change:** The ride starts at 280' and climbs to a high point of 540' in the first half mile. The low point of the ride is Siltcoos Lake at 160'. You will ride from the lake to an intersection at 260', then descend back to the lake. The trip ascends once more to 540' before returning to the trailhead. Additional hills along the trail add about 200' of climbing to the ride. Total elevation gain: 940'.

**Season:** The trail is open year-round. Avoid visiting this trail during wet times

# RIDE 72 · Siltcoos Lake Trail

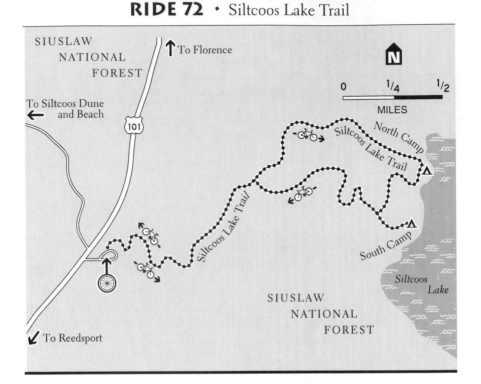

of the year. The trail can be soggy, and mosquitoes are thick in the spring and early summer.

**Services:** There is no potable water on this ride. Water can be obtained at several of the Forest Service campgrounds along US 101. Food, lodging, groceries, and gas are available in Florence.

**Hazards:** The trail is extremely slick when wet. Although the tread holds relatively few obstacles, common trail hindrances (like slippery roots) still occur.

**Rescue index:** Help can be found in Florence.

**Land status:** Siuslaw National Forest.

**Maps:** This trail is not depicted on forest maps. A crude map titled "Siltcoos Lake Trail" may be obtained from the offices of the Oregon Dunes National Recreation Area in Reedsport. USGS 7.5 minute quad: Florence.

**Finding the trail:** From Florence, drive south on US 101 for approximately 7 miles to the parking area for the Siltcoos Lake Trailhead (on the east side of the highway). From Reedsport, travel north for about 13 miles to the Siltcoos Lake Trailhead. The trailhead parking is opposite the Siltcoos Dune and Beach Access Road.

Siltcoos Lake Trail.

**Source of additional information:**

Oregon Dunes National Recreation Area
855 Highway 101
Reedsport, OR 97467
(541) 271-3611

**Notes on the trail:** Follow the trail for 0.8 mile to a **Y** intersection at a huge stump. The intersection is marked with a sign that directs you left for the northern route or right to the southern route. This description covers the northern route. In another mile, you will arrive at some campsites near the lakeshore. After walking down to the water, return to the trail and stay to the left (follow the signs for US 101). The trail crosses a boardwalk over a marsh, then goes up some steep steps before depositing you at a **T** intersection. Turn left at the **T** to visit South Camp. Turn around at South Camp and retrace your path to the last intersection. Continue straight, following the sign for US 101. This route will take you back to the intersection at the big stump. Turn left to return to the parking lot.

## RIDE 73 · North Fork Siuslaw River Loop

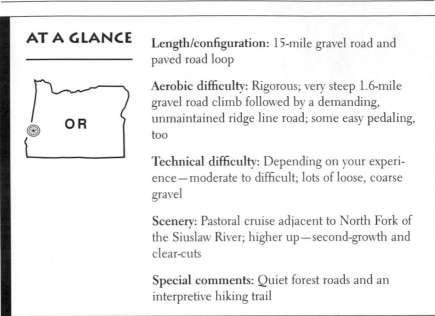

**AT A GLANCE**

**Length/configuration:** 15-mile gravel road and paved road loop

**Aerobic difficulty:** Rigorous; very steep 1.6-mile gravel road climb followed by a demanding, unmaintained ridge line road; some easy pedaling, too

**Technical difficulty:** Depending on your experience—moderate to difficult; lots of loose, coarse gravel

**Scenery:** Pastoral cruise adjacent to North Fork of the Siuslaw River; higher up—second-growth and clear-cuts

**Special comments:** Quiet forest roads and an interpretive hiking trail

This rigorous 15-mile loop begins and ends with easygoing paved cycling along the North Fork of the Siuslaw River. An opportunity for an easy hike through an old-growth forest comes early in the route. This interpretive hike is called the PAWN Trail. PAWN is an acronym for Poole, Akerley, Worthington, and Noland, four families that settled here in the early 1900s. The path is less than a mile in length and takes you past trees that are over 500 years old.

Back on your bike, you take on an uncommonly steep stretch of gravel; a 1.6-mile quadricep tweaker called Elk Tie Road. This is followed by a short, easy climb on lumpy pavement. Vigorous pedaling is again needed as you turn onto unmaintained Cataract Road. This ridge line road climbs and descends many hills. These ups and downs are made more difficult by the road's coarse, loose texture. Paved North Fork Road rolls by pastures, farms, and homes; it is the most heavily traveled road on the loop, but it is far from busy.

**General location:** This ride begins at the North Fork Siuslaw Campground, about 15 miles east of Florence.

**Elevation change:** The trip starts at 260' and reaches a high point of 1,280' in 5 miles. This is followed by ridge riding that adds about 700' of climbing to the loop. When you finally descend from the crest, you lose 800' in about 2 miles. Several miles of easy climbing along the river bring you back to the starting point. Total elevation gain: about 2,000'.

**Season:** These roads can be ridden year-round. The summer is a nice time for a visit, because much of the route is shaded and the river lends a cool atmos-

# RIDE 73 · North Fork Siuslaw River Loop

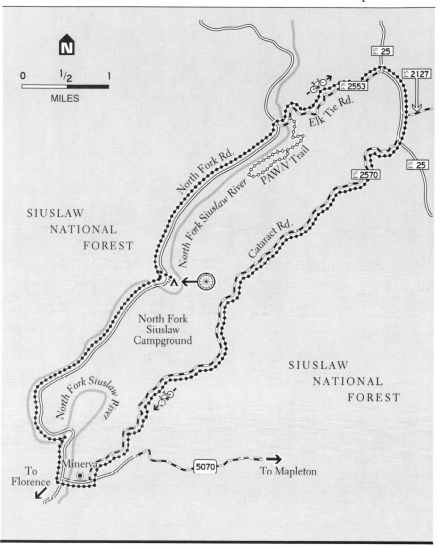

phere to the tour. Native rhododendrons do well on the ridge; they are usually in bloom from mid- to late spring.

**Services:** There is no potable water on this ride. Water, food, lodging, groceries, and gas can be obtained in Florence.

**Hazards:** Some of the pedaling is on one-lane roads with pullouts. Remain alert for motorists, who may not expect to encounter cyclists on these roads. Sections of the roads are rough; keep your speed under control on descents and watch for pockets of loose material.

North Fork
Siuslaw River.

**Rescue index:** Help is available in Florence.

**Land status:** Siuslaw National Forest lands and public right-of-way through private land.

**Maps:** The district map of the Mapleton Ranger District is a good guide to this ride. USGS 7.5 minute quads: Cummins Peak and Tiernan.

**Finding the trail:** From US 101 in Florence, drive east on OR 126 for 1 mile to North Fork Road/County Road 5070 (on the left). Follow North Fork Road for 11 miles to an intersection where CR 5070 goes right, toward Minerva and Mapleton. Continue straight, following the sign for the Upper North Fork. In another 3.2 miles, turn right into the North Fork Siuslaw Campground. The road into the campground is Forest Service Road 715. There is no designated day-use parking, but there is room to park in the campground.

**Source of additional information:**

Mapleton Ranger District
4480 Highway 101 North, Building G
Florence, OR 97439
(541) 902-8526

**Notes on the trail:** Exit the campground and turn right onto the pave
After 2.5 miles, turn right onto signed FS 2553/Elk Tie Road. For some r.....,
the Visitor Map of the Siuslaw National Forest shows this road's designation as
FS 2500 and as FS 653. Immediately after you turn right, you will pass the trailhead for the PAWN Trail on the right. Continue cycling on FS 2553 to a **Y** intersection. Turn right onto FS 25 and stay on it for 0.8 mile to FS 2570/Cataract
Road. Turn right onto FS 2570. Stay on the main road where side roads branch
off. Turn right when you reach pavement; cross a bridge over the river; then turn
right again to follow the sign for the Upper North Fork. Follow this road back to
the campground and your vehicle.

## RIDE 74 · Burnt Timber Mountain

**AT A GLANCE**

**OR**

**Length/configuration:** 10.4-mile gravel road and
paved road loop

**Aerobic difficulty:** Moderately difficult; some brief
steep pitches

**Technical difficulty:** Easy; good gravel and paved
roads

**Scenery:** Lush forests, huge clear-cuts, clear creeks

**Special comments:** Tame road ride

This 10.4-mile loop is moderately difficult. It begins with a three-mile ascent
on a gravel road. This climb is evenly divided between easy, moderately
difficult, and strenuous pedaling. (There are several short downhill stretches as
well.) This leg is followed by 2.3 miles of pavement along a rolling ridge. Back
on gravel, you descend for a mile, climb moderately for 0.2 mile, and then enjoy
a three-mile grin-inducing drop along Bear Creek. The last mile back to your
car is paved and easy. The scenery on this ride varies from beautiful green forests
and lovely creeks to scarred mountains with massive clear-cuts.

**General location:** This ride begins approximately 12 miles east of the coastal
community of Waldport.

**Elevation change:** The circuit starts at 100' and reaches a high point of 1,380'
on Burnt Timber Mountain. Ups and downs along the ride add about 300' of
climbing to the trip. Total elevation gain: 1,580'.

# RIDE 74 · Burnt Timber Mountain

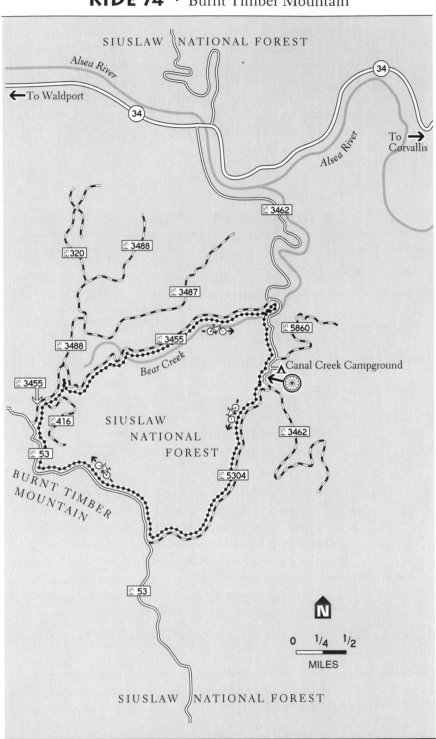

SIUSLAW NATIONAL FOREST

*Alsea River*

←To Waldport

34

34

To → Corvallis

*Alsea River*

3462

3488

320

3487

5860

3488

3455

Canal Creek Campground

*Bear Creek*

3455

416

SIUSLAW NATIONAL FOREST

3462

53

5304

BURNT TIMBER MOUNTAIN

53

N

0    1/4    1/2

MILES

SIUSLAW NATIONAL FOREST

Back road in the Siuslaw
National Forest.

**Season:** This road ride is suitable for year-round use. The winter and spring are typically the wettest seasons of the year.

**Services:** Water is available near the start of the loop at Canal Creek Campground. Food, lodging, gas, and groceries can be obtained in Waldport.

**Hazards:** Control your speed while descending—some corners contain loose gravel. Watch for logging trucks and other motorists.

**Rescue index:** Help can be found in Waldport.

**Land status:** Siuslaw National Forest.

**Maps:** The district map of the Waldport Ranger District is a good guide to this ride. USGS 7.5 minute quads: Cannibal Mountain and Tidewater.

**Finding the trail:** From the intersection of US 101 and OR 34 in Waldport, follow OR 34 east toward Corvallis. After 7 miles, turn right onto Canal Creek Road/Forest Service Road 3462. Proceed down this one-lane paved road for 4 miles to Canal Creek Campground (on the left). Go past the campground and park in the large open area on the left side of FS 3462.

**Source of additional information:**

Waldport Ranger District
1049 S.W. Pacific Highway
P.O. Box 400
Waldport, OR 97394
(541) 563-3211

**Notes on the trail:** Continue south on FS 3462. The road immediately turns to gravel and intersects with FS 5304. Turn right onto FS 5304. Follow the main road to a **T** intersection and pavement, and turn right onto FS 53. After 2 miles on FS 53 you will come to the high point of the ride and to views over clear-cuts. Descend for 0.2 mile to a low point and gravel FS 3455. Turn right onto FS 3455 (an easy turn to miss). Stay on this main road as spur roads branch off. Turn right when you reach pavement, and ride back to your car.

Explorations on side roads can add many miles to this outing. Two note-worthy side roads are FS 3488 and FS 320 (see map). These head down to some stands of old-growth Douglas fir. The trees are not giants, but it is a pleasure to view larger, mature evergreens.

## RIDE 75 · Marys Peak

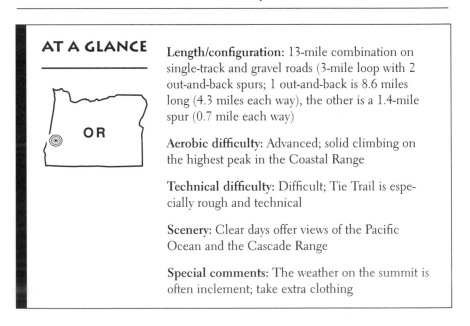

**AT A GLANCE**

**Length/configuration:** 13-mile combination on single-track and gravel roads (3-mile loop with 2 out-and-back spurs; 1 out-and-back is 8.6 miles long (4.3 miles each way), the other is a 1.4-mile spur (0.7 mile each way)

**Aerobic difficulty:** Advanced; solid climbing on the highest peak in the Coastal Range

**Technical difficulty:** Difficult; Tie Trail is especially rough and technical

**Scenery:** Clear days offer views of the Pacific Ocean and the Cascade Range

**Special comments:** The weather on the summit is often inclement; take extra clothing

This 13-mile out-and-back ride (with a short loop) will challenge advanced cyclists with 6 miles of varied single-track riding. A sign at the summit of Marys Peak reads "The Top Of The World." At 4,097 feet, Marys Peak is the

Negotiating
East Ridge Trail.

highest point in the Coastal Range. On clear days (which are rare) you can look
west to the Pacific Ocean or east for a view of the Cascade Range.

The initial miles on Forest Service Road 2005 are a moderately difficult
warm-up. Then you get on East Ridge Trail and climb 1,500' in 2.7 miles to
Marys Peak. This ascent is moderately difficult to strenuous, with some very
steep pitches and some easy breathers. The trail gets rocky in places, but is in
good condition overall. North Ridge Trail and Tie Trail descend from the mountain and reconnect you with East Ridge Trail. Tie Trail is especially rough and
includes some very technical climbing and some unrideable sections.

**General location:** The start of the ride is about 22 miles west of Corvallis.

**Elevation change:** The ride begins at 1,700' and reaches 4,097' atop Marys
Peak. Undulations add about 300' of climbing to the trip. Total elevation gain:
2,697'.

**Season:** It is possible to ride here from spring through autumn. Stay off the trails
when they are wet.

**Services:** Water can be obtained seasonally at the observation point on Marys

# RIDE 75 · Marys Peak

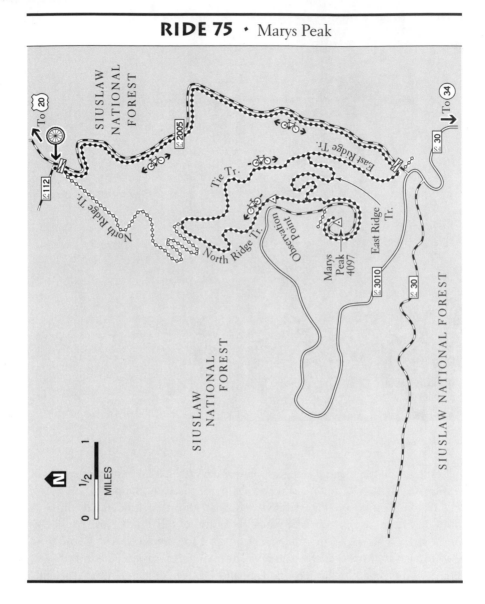

Peak. Food, lodging, gas, and pay phones can be found in Philomath. All services are available in Corvallis.

**Hazards:** Tie Trail includes cliff experiences and some very rocky stretches. Control your speed on the return—watch for other trail users. Sudden changes in the weather are not uncommon on this mountain. Temperatures can be surprisingly cold at the peak; bring extra clothing.

**Rescue index:** Help can be found in Philomath and Corvallis.

**Land status:** Siuslaw National Forest.

**Maps:** A pamphlet titled "Marys Peak—A Place to Discover" can be obtained from the Waldport Ranger District. It is the best map available. USGS 7.5 minute quad: Marys Peak.

**Finding the trail:** From Corvallis, follow US 20/OR 34 west to Philomath. Proceed through town and remain on US 20 toward Toledo/Newport, where OR 34 goes left toward Alsea/Waldport. Turn left onto Woods Creek Road/FS 2005 near milepost marker 48 (about a mile after crossing Marys River). Follow FS 2005 for 7.4 miles to FS 112 (on the right) and a gate across FS 2005. Park in the pull-out on the left.

**Source of additional information:**

> Waldport Ranger District
> 1049 S.W. Pacific Highway
> P.O. Box 400
> Waldport, OR 97394
> (541) 563-3211

**Notes on the trail:** Pedal around the gate and ride up FS 2005. Stay on the main road where trails and side roads branch off. After 3.4 miles on FS 2005, near paved FS 3010, you will arrive at a gate across the road. Go around the gate and immediately turn right onto East Ridge Trail. After 1 mile you will come to an unmarked intersection where unsigned Tie Trail goes right. Stay to the left and switchback uphill, remaining on East Ridge Trail. Carry your bike up some rock steps after another 0.7 mile. It is 0.4 mile from this landmark to another intersection, with 5 railroad tie steps on the left. Carry your bike up the steps. Soon you will emerge from the woods onto a grassy hillside. Proceed across the hillside to a gravel road. Turn left onto the gravel road and ride to Marys Peak. Turn around at the summit and backtrack to the 5 railroad tie steps; turn left and pedal to rest rooms and a parking lot for the observation point. Ride by the rest rooms and across the pavement (stay to the right) to a sign for North Ridge Trail. Bear right onto the trail and reenter the woods. Follow this trail for 0.6 mile to a log bench on the left. Turn right onto unsigned Tie Trail at this faint inter-section (easy to miss). Take Tie Trail to East Ridge Trail. Bear left onto East Ridge Trail and return the way you came.

## RIDE 76 · McDonald Research Forest/McCulloch Peak

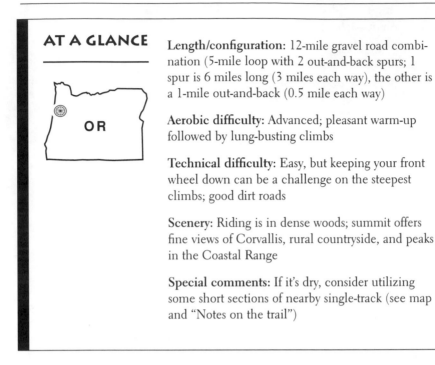

**AT A GLANCE**

**Length/configuration:** 12-mile gravel road combination (5-mile loop with 2 out-and-back spurs; 1 spur is 6 miles long (3 miles each way), the other is a 1-mile out-and-back (0.5 mile each way)

**Aerobic difficulty:** Advanced; pleasant warm-up followed by lung-busting climbs

**Technical difficulty:** Easy, but keeping your front wheel down can be a challenge on the steepest climbs; good dirt roads

**Scenery:** Riding is in dense woods; summit offers fine views of Corvallis, rural countryside, and peaks in the Coastal Range

**Special comments:** If it's dry, consider utilizing some short sections of nearby single-track (see map and "Notes on the trail")

OR

The 7,000-acre McDonald Research Forest is managed by Oregon State University's School of Forestry. The area is, first and foremost, an educational and research facility. Recreational use is allowed, and the forest is very popular with local hikers, joggers, mountain bikers, and equestrians. The forest's managers ask that visitors work to reduce impacts on research projects. The most important way that visitors can help is by staying on roads or on marked trails.

Over 60 miles of well-maintained forest roads and shared-use trails crisscross the area. The route described in this chapter travels on gravel roads for 12 miles. This trip combines a five-mile loop with a six-mile out-and-back spur (three miles each way), and a one-mile out-and-back (0.5 mile each way). It is an intermediate to advanced workout. The first 1.5 miles are a pleasant warm-up; the roads climb easily to moderately. Then the ascent gets steeper, but the terrain is still mostly moderately difficult. This initial climbing is followed by a furious 500-foot drop. Then the real exertion begins. Monster climbs will have you working feverishly to keep your front wheel on the ground. Wipe the sweat from your eyes upon reaching McCulloch Peak and look out over Corvallis and the surrounding rural flatlands. Marys Peak is off to the southwest. The remainder of the circuit is nearly all downhill.

The McDonald Research Forest provides unique opportunities for students and visitors alike. If you would like to learn more about this living laboratory, visit the Peavy Arboretum. (The arboretum is at the northeast end of the forest,

# RIDE 76 · McDonald Research Forest/McCulloch Peak

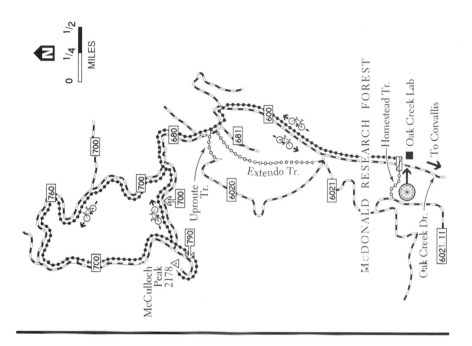

off of OR 99 West, on Arboretum Road.) Several interpretive hiking trails radiate out from Peavy Lodge; Powder House Trail passes by lovely Cronemiller Lake and through stands of old-growth forest. Cultural history brochures and a plant species list are available at the arboretum.

**General location:** The ride begins approximately 6 miles northwest of Corvallis.

**Elevation change:** The ride begins at 500' and climbs to 1,460'. Then you drop to 950' before continuing with the climbing. The high point of the trip is 2,178' at McCulloch Peak. A few short ups and downs add another 100' of climbing to the loop. Total elevation gain: 2,288'.

**Season:** Many of the trails and roads in the forest are open year-round. Some trails are open seasonally, typically April 15 through October 31. Closures can occur at any time due to management activities, special events, and wet conditions. Stay off of the trails when they are wet. Please call the forest's "Trail and Road Condition Report" before planning a visit to the area.

**Services:** There is no potable water available on this ride. All services can be found in Corvallis. Would you be interested in providing a service? Contact the OSU Research Forests Office to volunteer for trail maintenance or to involve yourself with the forest's "Volunteer Trail Patrol."

**Hazards:** The roads on this ride are technically easy, but are often busy with other recreationists. Extend common courtesy; control your speed and announce

Mark Price reaching
the summit of
McCullough Peak.

your presence well in advance of overtaking others. Besides other self-propelled users, these roads are traveled by logging trucks and other authorized vehicles. Watch for loose gravel.

**Rescue index:** Help is available in Corvallis.

**Land status:** OSU Research Forest and private property. The described route passes through a parcel of property owned by Starker Forests; a special land-use permit is required for access to this land. To obtain a permit, please visit the Starker Forests offices at 7240 S.W. Philomath Boulevard in Corvallis, or call (541) 929-2477.

**Maps:** A brochure box at the trailhead is stocked with a McDonald Research Forest Visitor Map and Guide. A detailed topo map of the McDonald and Paul M. Dunn forests may be purchased at the OSU bookstore and local bike shops. It contains directions for other rides in the forests. USGS 7.5 minute quads: Corvallis and Airlie South.

**Finding the trail:** In Corvallis, go west on Harrison Boulevard. Continue straight at the stop sign at S.W. 53rd Street/N.W. Walnut Boulevard. Stay on this road (now Oak Creek Drive) for 1.8 miles to an intersection where Oak Creek Drive goes right and Cardwell Hill Drive goes straight. Turn right to remain on Oak Creek Drive. (Cardwell Hill Drive is marked with a "Dead End" sign at this intersection.) Stay on Oak Creek Drive to the end of the road, at the Oak Creek Laboratory of Biology. Park in the small lot on the left.

**Sources of additional information:**

> Oregon State University Research Forests Office
> 8692 Peavy Arboretum Road
> Corvallis, OR 97330-9328
> (541) 737-4452
> On the Web: http://www.cof.orst.edu/resfor

> Trail and Road Condition Report:
> (541) 737-4434 (recorded message)

> Corvallis Mountain Bike Club
> 5549 S.W. Redtop Place
> Corvallis, OR 97333
> (541) 754-3752

Notes on the trail: Go around the gate and climb up Road 600 for 1.7 miles to a **Y** intersection at a brown information board. Turn left onto Road 680. Stay on the main road as Road 681 goes left. Stay on the main road where Extendo Trail goes left (signaled by a brown Carsonite marker). After passing Extendo Trail, you will come to an intersection with an island of vegetation in the middle of it. This junction is also marked by an evergreen tree marked with pale blue spray paint. Continue straight (left) on the main road. In another 0.5 mile you will come to another intersection with an island of vegetation in the middle. Turn right onto Road 700 and descend sharply for about 1.3 miles. Control your speed and watch for Road 760 on the left. Turn left and climb briskly on Road 760. Stay on Road 760 as side roads branch off. (Road 760 becomes Road 700 after about 2 miles.) After the road levels out some, you will arrive at a major intersection and Road 790 on the right. Turn right and follow Road 790 to McCulloch Peak. Turn around at the summit and return to the last intersection. Turn right onto Road 700. Descend on the main road for 0.8 mile to the intersection of Road 700 and Road 680. Stay to the right, bearing onto Road 680. Backtrack to your vehicle.

You may wish to incorporate some single-track into this ride. The area trails were too muddy when we visited this section of the forest. Check out the map, taking note of Homestead Trail, Extendo Trail, and Uproute Trail. It looks like Homestead and Uproute trails can be linked with Roads 6021 and 6020 to provide an alternate uphill route. Descending on Extendo Trail (open seasonally) is another option. (We have not ridden on these trails.)

## RIDE 77 · McDonald Research Forest/Dan's Trail—Horse Trail

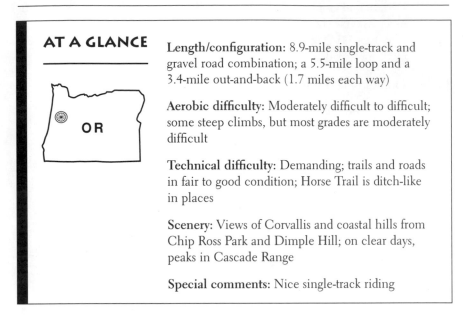

**AT A GLANCE**

**Length/configuration:** 8.9-mile single-track and gravel road combination; a 5.5-mile loop and a 3.4-mile out-and-back (1.7 miles each way)

**Aerobic difficulty:** Moderately difficult to difficult; some steep climbs, but most grades are moderately difficult

**Technical difficulty:** Demanding; trails and roads in fair to good condition; Horse Trail is ditch-like in places

**Scenery:** Views of Corvallis and coastal hills from Chip Ross Park and Dimple Hill; on clear days, peaks in Cascade Range

**Special comments:** Nice single-track riding

This ride begins aggressively with a short, steep climb to a grassy hillside in Chip Ross Park. The hillside is dotted with benches and commemorative plaques; it's a good place to catch your breath. If your riding partners feel it's too early for a break, pretend you're interested in the view or what's written on the plaques. Taking your time to survey the landscape can be rewarding; Three Sisters, Mt. Washington, Three Fingered Jack, and Mt. Jefferson can be viewed here on crystal clear days.

Dan's Trail begins at the McDonald Research Forest boundary. This single-track meanders through damp lowlands and old orchards before climbing to the top of Dimple Hill. Dimple Hill is no giant; it makes for a moderately difficult climb. Dan's Trail is followed by a 1.2-mile descent on gravel roads. This brings you to the top of Horse Trail. Horse Trail starts out with some smooth, exciting switchbacks. Further down, the trail's condition deteriorates. The path becomes ditch-like, but only briefly—the tread improves before the trail comes to an end. The circuit is completed by backtracking to Chip Ross Park on a section of Dan's Trail (not all downhill).

This ride is 8.9 miles long. It consists of a 5.5-mile loop and a 3.4-mile out-and-back (1.7 miles each way). Most of the ride is on single-track. The climbing is moderately difficult, but there are some short, steep pulls. The most technically demanding part of the ride is the descent on Horse Trail. Portions of this trail are in fine condition, others are narrow and technical. You will want to keep your speed under control as you drop on Horse Trail—watch for horseback riders who may be hidden from view. Dan's Trail is a pleasure to ride on; its

Dan's Trail.

higher reaches are smooth and well drained. Its lower reaches, however, travel through wet areas.

The trails in the McDonald Research Forest receive many hours of work from volunteers and forest crews. Improvements like elevated sections of tread, drainage structures, and footbridges have been incorporated into Dan's Trail. Help with maintenance is always appreciated. Call the OSU Research Forests Office for information about upcoming work parties, or to get involved with the forest's "Volunteer Trail Patrol."

**General location:** The route begins in the City of Corvallis Chip Ross Park.

**Elevation change:** The trailhead in Chip Ross Park is at approximately 500'. The high point of the ride is 1,478' on Dimple Hill. Ups and downs over the course of the ride add about 500' of climbing to the trip. Total elevation gain: 1,478'.

**Season:** The lower reaches of Dan's Trail pass through boggy areas, which remain wet for extended periods of time in the spring and following rains. Dan's

Trail has been designated as a seasonal trail; it is typically open from April 15 through October 31 (depending on conditions). Horse Trail is a year-round trail, but it should be avoided when it is wet. A summertime visit is your best bet for finding dry conditions in this part of Oregon. Closures can occur at any time due to management activities, special events, and wet conditions. Before planning a visit to the area, please call the forest's "Trail and Road Condition Report."

**Services:** There is no potable water available on this ride. All services can be found in Corvallis.

**Hazards:** The trails contain obstacles like loose gravel and roots. In places, Horse Trail is narrow, ditch-like, and sandy. Control your speed and watch for other trail users. These trails are popular with equestrians. Encounters with horses require special considerations and care. When approaching horses, stop and dismount to yield the trail. (When approaching from behind, stop well behind of the equestrians and announce your presence; do your best to avoid spooking the animals.) Talk to the riders in a normal tone of voice; ask if their horses are easily spooked and ask for instructions on how the equestrians would prefer you to facilitate passing. Your voice will help the horses recognize you as a human. Although not heavily traveled, you may encounter some vehicular traffic on the roads.

**Rescue index:** Help can be obtained in Corvallis.

**Land status:** City of Corvallis Public Park and OSU Research Forest.

**Maps:** A McDonald Research Forest Visitor Map and Guide can be obtained at the OSU Research Forests Office. The Visitor Map is also available on the ride. You can pick one up at an information sign near the boundary between Chip Ross Park and the research forest. A detailed topo map of the McDonald and Paul M. Dunn forests may be purchased at the OSU bookstore and local bike shops; it contains directions for other rides in the forests. USGS 7.5 minute quad: Corvallis.

**Finding the trail:** In Corvallis, drive north on Tenth Street/Highland Drive. Continue straight on Highland Drive at Walnut Boulevard (at a stoplight). In 0.9 mile, turn left onto Lester Avenue. (The intersection of Highland Drive and Lester Avenue is marked with a small, blue and white sign for Chip Ross Park.) Follow Lester Avenue to its end in Chip Ross Park.

### Sources of additional information:

Oregon State University Research Forests Office
8692 Peavy Arboretum Road
Corvallis, OR 97330-9328
(541) 737-4452
On the Web: http://www.cof.orst.edu/resfor

Trail and Road Condition Report:
(541) 737-4434 (recorded message)

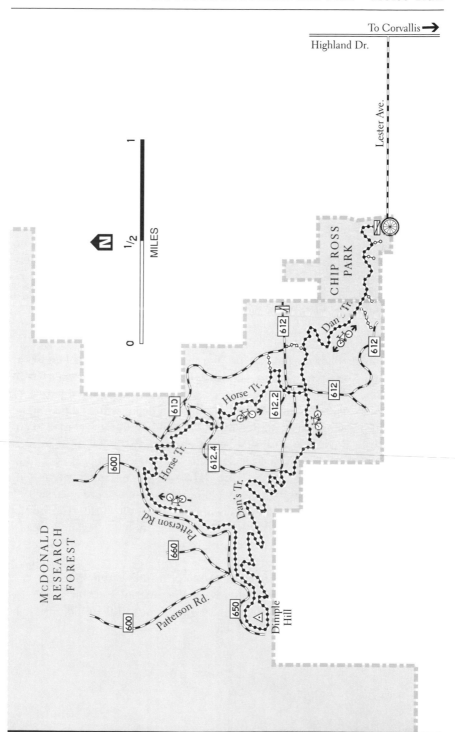

Corvallis Mountain Bike Club
5549 S.W. Redtop Place
Corvallis, OR 97333
(541) 754-3752

**Notes on the trail:** Please help reduce impacts to research in the McDonald Research Forest by staying on roads and designated trails.

The ride begins with a short, stiff climb. If you would like to warm up before getting started with the ride, head back out gravel Lester Avenue. Turn around when you are warmed up.

Start the trip at the yellow gate. Ride uphill (north) on the gravel road. (Immediately, stay right where another road goes left and climbs more steeply.) Follow the main road as it breaks out of the woods onto an open hillside. The road becomes more trail-like as it passes several benches and commemorative plaques. Follow the trail across the hillside. You will arrive at a bench, and a plaque dedicated to Jaycee Joe Beretta after pedaling 0.7 mile. Here, turn right onto a secondary trail (the main trail bears left) and descend to an intersection of several trails. Turn right onto signed Dan's Trail, passing through an opening in a wire fence. You will immediately arrive at a large information sign. (Here, you can pick up a McDonald Research Forest Visitor Map and Guide.) At this sign, take the middle path (of three) to remain on Dan's Trail. Stay on the main trail where side trails branch off. After passing under some power lines you will arrive at an intersection of trails (a trail goes right toward Jackson Creek). Continue straight, following the trail for Dimple Hill. Shortly, the trail crosses a gravel road and passes through an old orchard. Next, the trail passes over a wood bridge spanning a creek, then the trail reaches another road; turn left to regain the trail. After a total of 4 miles of pedaling, the trail deposits you atop Dimple Hill. Continue straight to pick up Road 650. Descend on this gravel road to an intersection with Roads 600 and 660. Turn right onto Road 600. In 0.7 mile, turn right and descend on signed Horse Trail. The trail switchbacks 6 times, then arrives at an intersection. Here, turn right and descend gently on an old double-track. In 0.2 mile, turn right (at an old pear tree) onto an unsigned single-track. (If you miss this trail, the double-track will lead out to Road 610.) In 0.2 mile, turn right onto a gravel road, then immediately turn left to regain the trail. After some switchbacks, the trail enters a more open area where you can see a house below you. Turn right at the next **Y** intersection and descend to Road 612. Turn right onto the gravel road. Bear left at the next intersection to remain on Road 612 (Road 612.2 goes right). Shortly, at the next intersection, continue straight to remain on Road 612 (Road 612.4 goes right.) In 0.1 mile, turn left onto Dan's Trail. Backtrack to your vehicle.

## RIDE 78 · McDonald Research Forest/Vineyard Mountain Loop

---

**AT A GLANCE**

**Length/configuration:** 6.7-mile gravel road loop; longer options available

**Aerobic difficulty:** Easy; rolling terrain and easy sustained grades

**OR**

**Technical difficulty:** Well-maintained gravel roads

**Scenery:** No distant views; dense wooded ridge riding

**Special comments:** Super beginner ride; technically demanding single-track options available (see "Notes on the trail")

---

Dog walkers, joggers, and folks who like easy, gravel road bike rides flock to Lewisburg Saddle. It is the trailhead for a variety of rides, walks, and runs in the area, including the Vineyard Mountain Loop. This loop is an easy 6.7-mile ride, but the terrain is not flat; there is some climbing involved. The first leg, on Davies Road, rolls up and down. A longer, sustained grade is encountered on Nettleton Road. Cyclists looking for a demanding experience can create a long ride by linking Vineyard Mountain Loop with Dan's Trail and Horse Trail.

Vineyard Mountain Loop is technically easy; it travels on well-maintained gravel roads. The route traverses a heavily wooded ridge, so distant views are nonexistent. A trailhead for the Old-growth Trail is passed near the beginning of the ride. A stroll on the trail takes you through a landscape rarely seen today, a stand of Douglas fir old-growth forest (no bikes please—hiking only).

**General location:** McDonald Research Forest is just north of Corvallis.

**Elevation change:** Lewisburg Saddle lies at 960'. The high point of the Vineyard Mountain Loop (1,360') is obtained on Nettleton Road; near its intersection with Road 5010. Undulations over the course of the loop add about 300' of climbing to the circuit. Total elevation gain: 700'.

**Season:** Suitable for year-round travel. Road and trail closures can occur at any time due to management activities, special events, and wet conditions. Before planning a visit to the area, please call the forest's "Trail and Road Condition Report."

**Services:** There is no potable water on this ride. All services are available in Corvallis.

**Hazards:** These roads are popular with all manner of recreationists looking for

# RIDE 78 · McDonald Research Forest/Vineyard Mtn. Loop

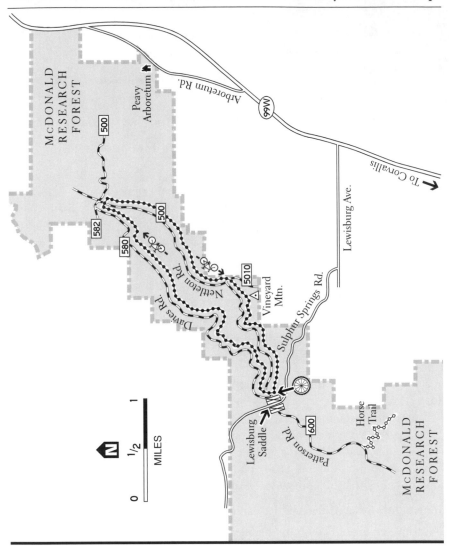

a moment's peace. Give them a break; slow down and warn them of your approach well in advance of overtaking them (try not to startle anyone). Slow down as you approach blind corners. Be prepared to encounter cyclists descending with less forethought than you are being asked to consider. Ride predictably and defensively—travel single-file and stay to the right as you round bends in the road. Yield to logging trucks and other authorized vehicles, which may be encountered on these roads. Observe posted speed limits.

**Rescue index:** Help can be obtained in Corvallis.

Dirt road riding.

**Land status:** OSU Research Forest

**Maps:** A McDonald Research Forest Visitor Map and Guide can be obtained at the OSU Research Forests Office. A detailed topo map of the McDonald and Paul M. Dunn forests may be purchased at the OSU bookstore and local bike shops; it contains directions for other rides in the forests. USGS 7.5 minute quad: Airlie South.

**Finding the trail:** In Corvallis, proceed north on OR 99 West to Lewisburg. Turn left onto Lewisburg Avenue and drive 1 mile to Sulphur Springs Road. Turn right onto Sulfur Springs Road and drive about 2 miles to Lewisburg Saddle. Park at the saddle.

**Sources of additional information:**

Oregon State University Research Forests Office
8692 Peavy Arboretum Road
Corvallis, OR 97330-9328
(541) 737-4452
On the Web: **http://www.cof.orst.edu/resfor**

Trail and Road Condition Report:
(541) 737-4434 (recorded message)

Corvallis Mountain Bike Club
5549 S.W. Redtop Place
Corvallis, OR 97333
(541) 754-3752

**Notes on the trail:** Please help reduce impacts to research in the McDonald Research Forest by staying on roads and designated trails.

Head east and pass around the orange metal gate. Turn left and descend on William A. Davies Road/Road 580. The trailhead for the Old-growth Trail is on the left, 0.4 mile into the ride. (No bikes allowed on the Old-growth Trail.) In another 3 miles, pass signed Poison Oak Road/Road 582 (on the left). After passing Poison Oak Road, you will immediately arrive at a major intersection of roads. Turn right onto signed Harry J. Nettleton Road/Road 500. Road 500 climbs for about 1.6 miles, then levels out before reaching an intersection with Road 5010. (Road 5010 leads to the summit of Vineyard Mountain.) Turn right to remain on Road 500. The ride ends back at Lewisburg Saddle.

If you are interested in a longer option, consider linking this loop with Horse Trail and Dan's Trail. Patterson Road/Road 600 heads west from Lewisburg Saddle; it meets the top of Horse Trail in 1.3 miles. Drop on Horse Trail, then take Dan's Trail to Dimple Hill. At Dimple Hill, head east on Road 600 to return to Lewisburg Saddle. This longer ride can also be started from Chip Ross Park. For directions to Chip Ross Park, and for information that will help you find your way on the trails, see McDonald Research Forest/Dan's Trail—Horse Trail (Ride 77).

## RIDE 79 · Fort Stevens Bicycle Trails

**AT A GLANCE**

**Length/configuration:** 8 miles of paved bike paths (maze of possible routes)

**Aerobic difficulty:** Easy; mostly level

**Technical difficulty:** Easy; paved bike path

**Scenery:** Sandy beaches, historic museum, and a nature trail

**Special comments:** Excellent family ride; Oregon State Law: children under 16 years of age must wear a helmet while riding on a bike

OR

Beachfront parking at Fort Stevens State Park.

Fort Stevens State Park contains an eight-mile network of paved, mostly level bike paths. Prominent in the park is a 600-site campground. Everywhere you look, children are absorbed in lively games and resolutely pumping their bikes around (and around and around) the many campground loops. Exploring this historic park on two wheels is a great family activity. You can have more fun with the clan by enjoying the sandy beaches and good fishing at Coffenbury Lake, hiking a nature trail, or attending an evening program at the campground amphitheater.

Fort Stevens Military Reservation guarded the mouth of the Columbia River from the Civil War through World War II. The fort is a couple of miles north of the campground and features a museum and a self-guided walking tour. The abandoned gun batteries and the commander's station offer good views of the Columbia River and South Jetty. Another historic point of interest is the wreck of the *Peter Iredale*, an English vessel that ran aground in 1906. Its rusting skeleton is embedded in the beach about a mile west of the campground.

**General location:** Fort Stevens State Park is located at the extreme northwest tip of Oregon, approximately 8 miles west of Astoria.

**Elevation change:** The park is quite flat. The trail dips and rises in places to surmount lesser landforms and cross bridges.

**Season:** The park is open year-round. For full-tilt campmania, visit on a summer holiday weekend. Other seasons of the year are less frenzied. The early fall is a good time for a ride in the park.

# RIDE 79 · Fort Stevens Bicycle Trails

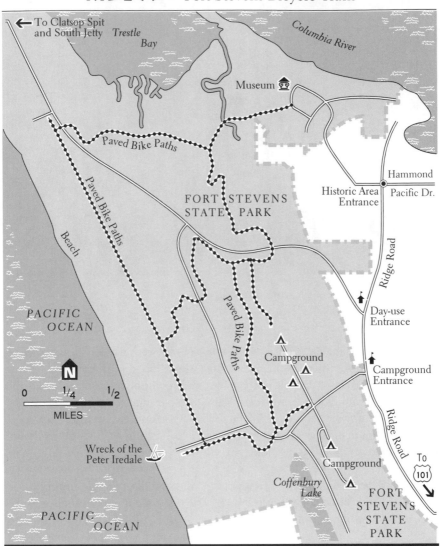

To Clatsop Spit and South Jetty

Trestle Bay

Columbia River

Museum

Paved Bike Paths

FORT STEVENS STATE PARK

Hammond

Historic Area Entrance

Pacific Dr.

Paved Bike Paths

Beach

Ridge Road

PACIFIC OCEAN

Day-use Entrance

N

0   ¼   ½

MILES

Paved Bike Paths

Campground

Campground Entrance

Wreck of the Peter Iredale

Ridge Road

To 101

PACIFIC OCEAN

Coffenbury Lake

Campground

FORT STEVENS STATE PARK

**Services:** Water is available at the campground and at various day-use areas within the park. All services are available in Astoria.

**Hazards:** The roads in the park can get busy, and motorists often drive too fast. Children should be supervised and given instruction on safe cycling. The park's bike safety rules are printed on the trail map available at the campground entrance station. Oregon State Law requires that children under the age of 16 must wear a helmet while riding on a bicycle.

**Rescue index:** Help can be obtained at the campground entrance station or by contacting one of the camp hosts. The park roads are patrolled, and there are pay phones at the entrance station.

**Land status:** State park.

**Maps:** You can obtain a bicycle and hiking trail map at the campground entrance station or at the museum. A flyer for a walking tour is available at the museum. USGS 7.5 minute quads: Warrenton and Clatsop Spit.

**Finding the trail:** From Astoria, follow US 101/Oregon Coast Highway south. The route to Fort Stevens is well marked; follow the signs. You may enter the park at the camping entrance or at either of 2 day-use entrances. The day-use entrances are north of the campground entrance on Ridge Road. There is a day-use fee.

## Sources of additional information:

Fort Stevens State Park
Hammond, OR 97121
(503) 861-1671

Fort Stevens State Park
Historical Area and Military Museum
P.O. Box 138
Hammond, OR 97121
(503) 861-2000

**Notes on the trail:** For those seeking a more difficult riding experience, the woods below the Astoria Column (near Astoria) are home to an extensive network of single-track trails. It is an easy place to get lost—the trails lead in many directions and are unmapped and unsigned. Drop by one of the bike shops in Astoria and see if anyone has produced a map. Perhaps they can set you on course; if not, they can at least sell you a compass and a Power Bar.

# PORTLAND/SALEM

The landscapes of big cities don't often provide ideal conditions for "purist" mountain bikers. It is rare to find trails in urban settings, let alone single-track that is open to bikes. However, people who love to mountain bike will find places to enjoy their bikes. Hopping curbs or running errands, mountain bikes make great town bikes. They're easy to operate, and they afford riders with an upright, "have a look around" posture. Bikes of all kinds are great; the independence and freedom they offer is unique and special. The feeling of the wind in your face is a sensation that can be especially welcome in an urban environment.

Weekend getaways to the mountains and forests are popular with citified aficionados of single-track. During the week, devoted riders will pedal where they can. In Portland, mountain bikers head for Forest Park. This huge wooded corridor sits high on a hillside above the city. It remains largely undeveloped. This natural setting is a favorite of people looking for a little exercise and a brief escape from pavement and traffic. Most of the roads in the park are gravel or native surface, and they are closed to public motor traffic. Rain or shine, the park is busy with lunch-hour athletes, dog walkers, and nature lovers.

Families will find some terrific paved bike paths south of Portland. Tame trails and good camping can be accessed in Champoeg State Heritage Area and at Silver Falls State Park. Champoeg is known as the "birthplace of Oregon government." This historic site is brought to life by the park's living history programs and interpretive displays. Silver Falls is a large, developed park east of Salem. The park's many amenities include a charming log day-lodge, sandy riverside beach and swimming hole, and a great system of hiking trails. The hiking trails access the park's many beautiful waterfalls.

The town of Molalla is located about halfway between Portland and Salem; roughly 15 miles east of Interstate 5. South of town, a corridor of public land has been developed into a fine network of single-track trails and gravel roads. The trails are adjacent to the Molalla River. They have been built through the co-operative efforts of local trail activists, conservationists, and the Bureau of Land Management. Things are looking good for these trails; several ambitious maintenance and construction projects are under way along this stretch of the river.

# RIDE 80 · Forest Park/Leif Erikson Drive

---

**AT A GLANCE**

---

OR

**Length/configuration:** 22.4-mile gravel road out-and-back (11.2 miles each way); longer and shorter rides easily configured

**Aerobic difficulty:** Easy; Leif Erikson Drive contours along a ridge for most of its length

**Technical difficulty:** Easy; fine textured gravel road

**Scenery:** Cool riding under a canopy of big trees; limited views of city and Willamette River

**Special comments:** Easy outing for families or anyone looking to briefly escape the city

---

Portland's Forest Park is a breath of fresh air. At 5,000 acres, it is one of the nation's largest inner-city parks. Closed to private motor vehicles, this woodland is a haven for city dwellers looking for a green place to play. Leif Erikson Drive is the park's most popular route for cyclists and joggers. The road was built in 1915 as part of a land development scheme. Luckily, the project failed and the road was deeded to the city of Portland.

Leif Erikson Drive is a wide, well-maintained, gravel thoroughfare; it winds through the middle of Forest Park for 11.2 miles. From the eastern end of the park at Thurman Road, Leif Erikson Drive climbs gently for just over six miles to Saltzman Road. At Saltzman Road, it drops gently for five miles to its western terminus at Germantown Road. An out-and-back of up to 22.4 miles (that's total mileage) can be enjoyed on this road. The cycling is easy.

The steep hills that border the road are covered with mossy trees and lush ferns. Most of the views through the foliage are distinctly urban; railroad yards and industrial facilities on the Willamette River and the city streets of north Portland. On a clear day, however, the Columbia River, Mt. Hood, and Mt. St. Helens can be spied in the distance.

Bicycles are allowed on some of the other roads in Forest Park; most of these roads surmount the park's steep hillsides. If you have strong legs, intermediate (or better) bike-handling skills, and you're confident that your brakes are in good working order, these routes are worth looking into. Consult the recommended map for ride ideas; the map includes descriptions of the park's bikeable roads.

**General location:** Forest Park is in northwest Portland.

**Elevation change:** The lowest elevation on Leif Erikson Drive (at Thurman

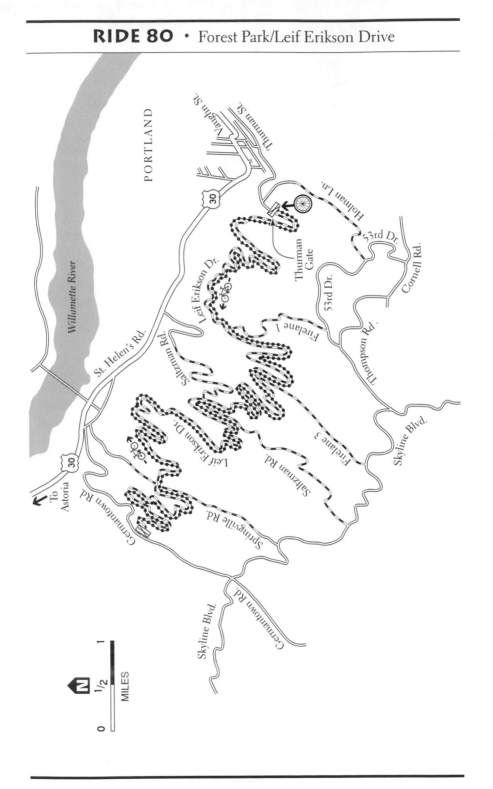

Cruising in Portland's
Forest Park.

Road) is roughly 300'. The high point on the road (approximately 675') is at its intersection with Saltzman Road.

**Season:** This road is suitable for year-round use.

**Services:** There is no potable water on this ride. All services are available in Portland.

**Hazards:** Some of the park's roads are closed to bicycles; ride on designated bike routes only. The park is open to pedestrians, bicyclists, and equestrians. Bike riders are required to yield to all other park users. Control your speed on descents. Alert others of your approach. Private motor vehicles are not allowed in the park, but you may encounter authorized patrol or maintenance vehicles.

**Rescue index:** Help can be found in Portland.

**Land Status:** City of Portland Parks and Recreation Department.

**Maps:** "A Cyclist's Guide to the Trails of Forest Park," published by Bicycle Concepts and Designs, is a good guide to this ride. This map can be purchased at area bike shops. USGS 7.5 minute quads: Portland and Linnton.

**Finding the trail:** From Interstate 405 in Portland, exit onto OR 30 West. From

OR 30 West, exit onto Vaughn Street. Continue a short distance on Vaughn Street, turning left onto 23rd Avenue (at the stoplight). In a couple of blocks, turn right onto Thurman Road. Stay on Thurman Road for 1.4 miles to limited parking at Forest Park's Thurman Road Gate. There are about 10 parking spots; if they are all taken, return down Thurman Road and park curbside.

**Source of additional information:**

> City of Portland Parks and Recreation
> 1120 S.W. 5th Avenue, Room 1302
> Portland, OR 97204-1933
> (503) 823-2223

**Notes on the trail:** Follow the paved road up and around Thurman Gate. When ready, turn around and return the way you came.

## RIDE 81 · Champoeg State Park

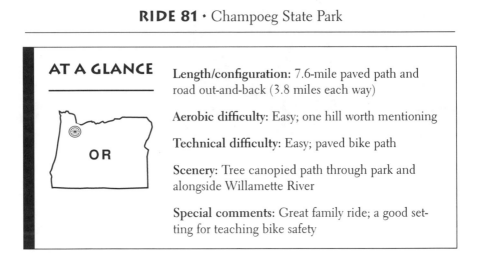

**AT A GLANCE**

**Length/configuration:** 7.6-mile paved path and road out-and-back (3.8 miles each way)

**Aerobic difficulty:** Easy; one hill worth mentioning

**Technical difficulty:** Easy; paved bike path

**Scenery:** Tree canopied path through park and alongside Willamette River

**Special comments:** Great family ride; a good setting for teaching bike safety

Have the rainy-day blues got you down? Well, pack up the kids and the bikes, and hightail it to Champoeg State Park. The paved bike path at Champoeg (sounds like shampoo-egg) makes a good drizzly day destination. Generally, the path is separated from nearby roads, but in places, the route does follow roads and cross intersections. The park provides a controlled setting that is ideal for teaching children the rules of the road and the importance of riding safely.

Prior to the arrival of settlers, the Champoeg Prairie was the home of the Kalapuya Indians. They lived by hunting, fishing, and by gathering foods. Camas bulbs were an important part of the Indian diet. The place name, Champoeg, is thought to be derived from the Kalapuya word for Camas—*Champooick.*

Wooded section of the
Champoeg bike path.

Trappers were some of the first white men to come into the area. When
beaver hats went out of style, the market for the trappers' goods dried up. Most
of the trappers moved on, but some decided to settle here. As farms sprung up,
the settlers felt the need to organize for protection. On May 2, 1843, they agreed
to form a provisional government, the first in the Pacific Northwest.

Historic sites within the park offer glimpses of what life was like on the fron-
tier. Of particular interest is the park's exhibit-filled Visitor Center. Adjacent to
the Visitor Center is the Manson Barn, an original town-site building salvaged
after the flood of 1861. Local historical societies host living history programs and
offer tours of some of the park buildings.

The Champoeg State Park bike path rolls through the park's woodlands and
old pastures, then it follows the Willamette River to connect with the Butteville
General Store. Thick vegetation often obscures views of the river, but benches
and picnic tables have been placed at several of the more scenic spots along the
route. The total mileage for this easy out-and-back excursion is 7.6 miles (3.8
miles each way). There is one significant hill to climb near the east end of the
park (on the approach to and from Butteville). The bike path itself ends after 3.2
miles; the last stretch into Butteville is on paved roads.

The Butteville Store is known as "the oldest operating store in the United States." The store sells refreshments, and its front porch is equipped with a couple of comfy benches that invite you to sit a spell before heading back to the park.

**General location:** The park is approximately 30 miles south of downtown Portland; about 30 miles north of Salem.

**Elevation change:** The ride begins at approximately 180' and reaches a high point of 280' near the intersection of Schuler Road and Butteville Road. Ups and downs on the route add an estimated 100' of climbing to the outing. Total elevation gain: 200'.

**Season:** This route is suitable for year-round travel. Autumn is a quiet time in the park.

**Services:** Water can be obtained at the day-use area or campground in Champoeg State Park. (The campground has showers.) Limited groceries can be found at the Butteville Store. Food, gas, lodging, and groceries can be found in Newburg; 7 miles northwest of the park.

**Hazards:** The route crosses and follows roads; watch for traffic and supervise the riding of children in your party. Oregon law requires children under age 16 to wear helmets while traveling on a bike. Several of the bike path's intersections are blocked by tightly spaced bollards—walk your bike, or slow to a crawl to weave through the bollards. The path crosses a wooden footbridge that can be slippery when wet. (The footbridge is located about midway on the trail.) Control your speed and watch for other trail users and their pets. Poison oak is found throughout the park.

**Rescue index:** Help can be obtained at the campground registration booth or at the camp host campground site. A pay phone is located near the host's site. The nearest hospital is in Newberg.

**Land status:** State Heritage Area and public right-of-way through private property.

**Maps:** A handout for the park is available at the campground entrance station; it includes a map that is suitable as a guide to this ride. However, the map in the guide does not delineate the eastern end of the bike path. We were unable to locate a map that shows the entire route. USGS 7.5 minute quads: Sherwood and Newberg.

**Finding the trail:** From Interstate 5, take Exit 278. (Exit 278 is roughly halfway between Salem and Portland; it is signed for Donald/Aurora/Champoeg State Park.) Head west on Ehlen Road/Yergen Road for 3.5 miles to Case Road. Turn right onto Case Road (follow the signs for the state park). In 1.3 miles the road bears left and its designation changes to Champoeg Road. In another 0.9 mile, turn right at the park entrance. The Visitor Center is on the right as you enter the park. After the Visitor Center, stay left through the park to reach the western end of the bike path (where our ride description begins). If you wish to camp,

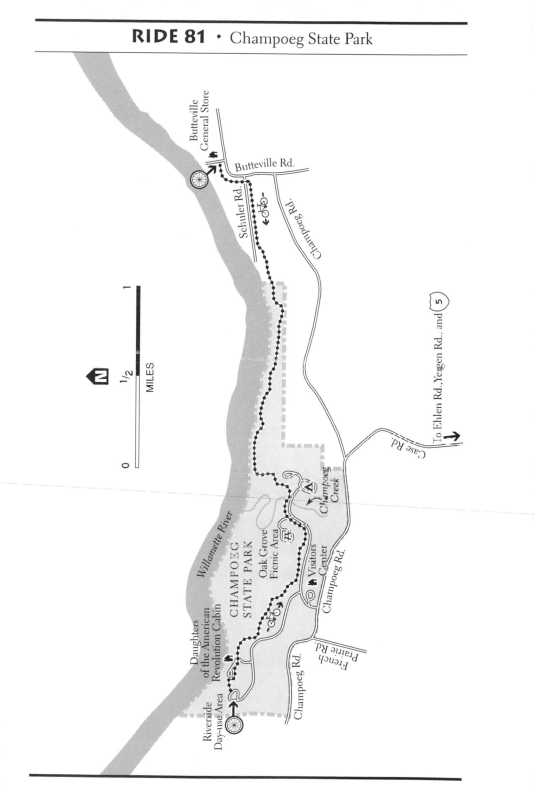

Butteville
General Store

Butteville Rd.

Schuler Rd.

Champoeg Rd.

To Ehlen Rd., Yegen Rd., and (5)

Case Rd.

N

1/2

0

MILES

Willamette River

CHAMPOEG
STATE PARK

Oak Grove
Picnic Area

Champoeg
Creek

Visitors
Center

Champoeg Rd.

French
Prairie Rd.

Champoeg Rd.

Daughters
of the American
Revolution Cabin

Riverside
Day-use Area

stay right after passing the Visitor Center, and drive east through the park to reach the campground entrance station.

**Source of additional information:**

Champoeg State Heritage Area
7679 Champoeg Road N.E.
St. Paul, OR 97137
(503) 678-1251

**Notes on the trail:** We begin the ride at the Riverside Day-use Area parking lot. (This huge parking lot is the western terminus of the bike path.) Head east on the paved bike path. Shortly, you will arrive at a cul-de-sac. Follow the paved road past the Daughters of the American Revolution Cabin. Shortly, continue straight to regain the paved path where the road curves right (south). Stay on the main bike path, passing Oak Grove Picnic Area. Follow the path as it merges with the park's main road to cross a bridge over Champoeg Creek. After the bridge, bear left to regain the bike path. Stay on the paved path for another 1.8 miles to Schuler Road. Turn right onto Schuler Road and pedal 0.4 mile to a **T** intersection at Butteville Road. Turn left (stay on the west side of Butteville Road to pass behind the guard rail) and ride on the shoulder 0.2 mile to the Butteville General Store. Return the way you came.

## RIDE 82 · Molalla River Corridor

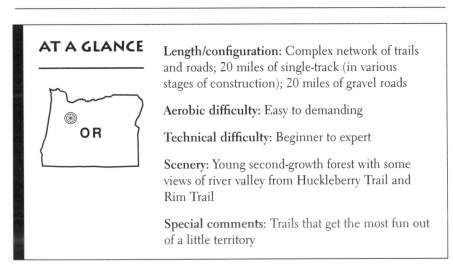

**AT A GLANCE**

**Length/configuration:** Complex network of trails and roads; 20 miles of single-track (in various stages of construction); 20 miles of gravel roads

**Aerobic difficulty:** Easy to demanding

**Technical difficulty:** Beginner to expert

**Scenery:** Young second-growth forest with some views of river valley from Huckleberry Trail and Rim Trail

**Special comments:** Trails that get the most fun out of a little territory

The Molalla River is a source of drinking water for the cities of Molalla and Canby. To protect this resource, and the scenic qualities of the watershed, local citizens formed Molalla RiverWatch. This group has worked hard to care

Fern Creek Trail in the
Molalla River Corridor.

for the area. Local mountain bike and equestrian groups, in cooperation with
the BLM, have spearheaded efforts to identify and improve existing trails, and
develop new single-track trails in the Molalla River Corridor. Many of these
paths have been linked with old roads. These connections have helped create
a network of routes that are suitable for mountain bikers of all skill and fitness
levels.

The efforts of Mark Flint have been instrumental in seeing the Molalla
River Corridor developed and maintained as an outstanding trail resource. He
is a founding member of the Salem-based mountain bike club, The Merry
Cranksters. Mark has lead efforts to foster communication and understanding
between user groups, provided assistance to mountain bike clubs throughout
the Pacific Northwest, and helped create Oregon Mountain Bikers (a
statewide advocacy group). His work to develop shared-use trails in the
Molalla River Corridor has resulted in exciting opportunities for cyclists, hikers, and equestrians.

The trails and roads in the corridor form a complex web of routes. With a limited amount of land to work with, the builders of this system packed a lot of
excitement into a small package. It seems that their goal was not to get trail users

from one point to another, but to allow folks to have a good time while nearly staying put. The paths weave about, climb and fall, then climb and fall, then, well, you get the idea—they cover as much territory as possible. Are you familiar with the saying, "it's not the destination that counts, it's the journey?" As you pedal this network, you may find it a suitable mantra.

Huckleberry Trail (actually an old gravel road) is a central artery running the length of the corridor. In the late 1800s, the road was used by Willamette Valley homesteaders traveling east to gather huckleberries in the Table Rock area. Beginner and intermediate riders can pick up Huckleberry Trail at the Hardy Creek Trailhead, following it upstream for 6.5 miles to connect with the Molalla Forest Road. A side trail near the end of the road leads through a clear-cut to a small waterfall.

A series of loop trails in the northern section of the system are more challenging. Single-tracks are linked with gravel roads to form short circuits that dip, swirl, and get you completely turned around. No worries, mate; you're never far from your home base at the Hardy Creek Trailhead. Just head downhill to reach Huckleberry Trail, then go north until you get your bearings (or see some other interesting trail to explore).

We provide directions to an outing that is quite demanding. If you like to stay on track, follow our directions for a 7.8-mile trip. Strong, adventurous cyclists can use our description to orient themselves to the trails, then head off to do their own route finding. Regardless of your plans, before heading out onto the trails, stuff a trail map and a compass in your jersey pocket.

**General location:** The Molalla River Recreation Corridor is 9 miles southeast of the city of Molalla. Molalla is about halfway between Portland and Salem, about 16 miles east of Interstate 5.

**Elevation change:** There is approximately 700' of elevation change from the Hardy Creek Trailhead to the top of Rim Trail. The trails in the corridor rise and fall repeatedly.

**Season:** Typically, the region begins to experience an extended period of wet weather in the fall. The trails are often dry and ready for traffic by the late spring or early summer. Soils in the area contain high amounts of clay, and a dense, shady canopy helps to maintain these soils in a damp condition for some time following rains. Help keep these trails open to bicycles; stay off them while they are wet. The Huckleberry Trail, a gravel road that runs the length of the corridor, is suitable for year-round riding.

**Services:** There is no potable water available on these trails. There is a vault toilet at the Hardy Creek Trailhead, and 2 composting toilets on Huckleberry Trail. Lodging, food, gas, and groceries can be obtained in Molalla. All services are available in Salem and Portland.

**Hazards:** Some of the trails are technically challenging with soft sections, slick roots, rocks, and forest litter. Many of the single-tracks twist through narrow openings (between trees and rocks) and bump over undulating terrain. Don't

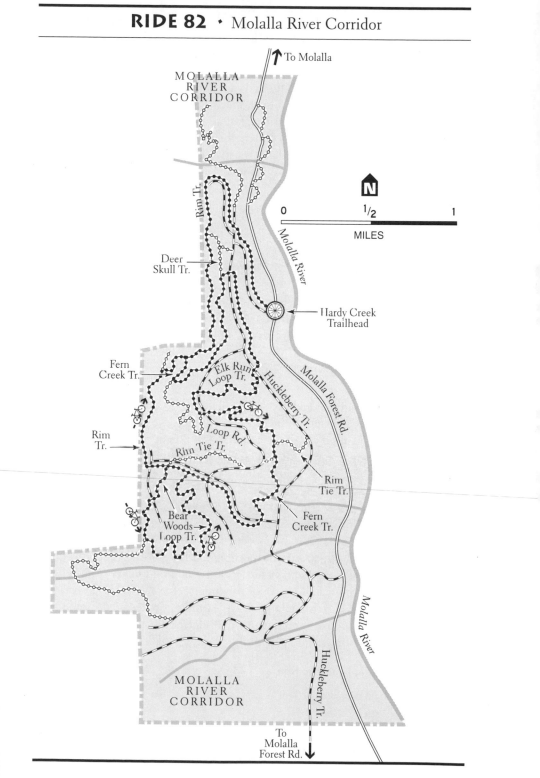

skid; it's too hard on the trails. If you create a loop with Huckleberry Trail and the Molalla Forest Road, watch for traffic; it moves rapidly on the paved road. Respect private property by honoring "No Trespassing" signs. Keep your speed under control and be prepared to meet other trail users who may be hidden from view around blind corners. The trails are popular with equestrians. When approaching horses, stop and dismount to yield the trail. (When approaching from behind, stop well in back of equestrians, announce your presence; do your best to avoid spooking the animals.) Talk to the riders in a normal tone of voice; ask if their horses are easily spooked and for instructions on how the equestrians would prefer you to facilitate passing. Your voice will help the horses recognize you as a human.

**Rescue index:** There is a pay phone at the Dickey Prairie Store. (To reach the store, head back toward Molalla. The store will be to your right, 3.6 miles north of the Glen Avon Bridge.) Help is available in Molalla.

**Land status:** Lands managed by the Clackamas Resource Area of the Salem District of the BLM.

**Maps:** The best map of the trails is titled "Molalla River Corridor Recreational Trail System, A Guide to Singletrack For Mountain Bike Riders." This brochure is provided by the Bike Gallery bike shops. At last count, this outfit had 5 locations in the greater Portland area. We understand that the BLM is developing a map of the trails in the Molalla River Corridor. USGS 7.5 minute quads: Fernwood and Gawley Creek.

**Finding the trail:** From I-5, take Exit 271 (singed for Woodburn and Silverton) and head east on OR 214; follow the signs for Molalla. Continue straight at the first stop light to remain on OR 214. At the next stop light (1.4 miles east of the first stop light), continue straight to follow OR 211 toward Molalla. Stay on OR 211 for 13.4 miles, passing through Molalla to a **Y** intersection (The "Y-Drive-in" is on the right, and the "Y-Market" is on the left at this intersection.) Turn right at the **Y** intersection onto Mathias Road (toward Dickey Prairie). In 0.3 mile, bear left to follow the main road; its designation changes to Feyer Park Road. Pass Feyer Memorial Park in another 1.7 miles, then cross a bridge over the Molalla River to arrive at a **T** intersection. Turn right onto Dickey Prairie Road. In 1.6 miles, bear right at a yield sign to remain on Dickey Prairie Road (the Dickey Prairie Store is just east of this intersection). The road crosses a bridge over the North Fork Molalla River in 3.4 miles. Proceed for another 0.2 mile and turn right to cross the Glen Avon Bridge/South Fork Molalla River. Drive 3.5 miles and turn right to park at the Hardy Creek Trailhead.

### Sources of additional information:

Bureau of Land Management
1717 Fabry Road, S.E.
Salem, OR 97306
(503) 375-5646

Molalla RiverWatch, Inc.
P.O. Box 867
Molalla, OR 97038-0867
(503) 829-6793 (Mountain Bike Patrol)
(503) 829-7858 (voice mail)

The Merry Cranksters Mountain Bike Club of Salem
1783 Cottage Street S.E.
Salem, OR 97302
(503) 589-0330

**Notes on the trail:** At the time of our visit, most of the trails and roads in the Molalla River Recreation Corridor were unsigned. Grant moneys and matching funds have been allocated for the continued development of this trail system; signage upgrades are anticipated. A voluntary pay station is scheduled to be installed near the Hardy Creek Trailhead (just up the trail from the parking area). Please make a donation. Your contribution will go directly to Molalla RiverWatch for the upkeep and improvement of the trails.

Allow yourself plenty of time for finding the route when heading out onto these trails. Reading our directions and orienting yourself will eat up lots of time. Likewise, you will spend a lot of time finding the route if you choose to arm yourself with only a map and compass.

Head up the wide trail/double-track near the two large information signs. Turn right at the **T** intersection (at a composting toilet) onto double-track Huckleberry Trail. Shortly, turn left onto a double-track at a **Y** intersection. (A couple of Carsonite signs mark this intersection; you are heading toward Rim Trail.) After some climbing (0.2 mile), the road curves left and the route changes to an elevated section of single-track; you are now on Rim Trail. Travel on Rim Trail for 0.8 mile (passing the north end of Deer Skull Trail) to Fern Creek Trail on the left. Turn onto Fern Creek Trail. In 0.1 mile, turn left onto Deer Skull Trail (very technical). In 0.5 mile, turn right and drop down to Huckleberry Trail. Turn right onto Huckleberry Trail. (If you want to return to the trailhead at this point, turn left onto Huckleberry Trail to reach the intersection at the composting toilet, then turn right and descend to your car.) Ride south on Huckleberry Trail for 0.5 mile to Elk Run Loop Trail (0.2 mile past Loop Road). Here, turn right onto Elk Run Loop Trail. In 0.5 mile, turn left onto Loop Road. In 0.1 mile, turn left onto Fern Creek Trail. In 0.3 mile, continue straight to briefly access Rim Tie Trail (Rim Tie Trail also goes left here). Shortly, bear left at a **Y** intersection to regain Fern Creek Trail (here, Rim Tie Trail goes right). Fern Creek Trail intersects with Fern Creek Road in another 0.6 mile. Turn right and climb up this rough, steep road. (We had to push our bikes up the first leg of Fern Creek Road.) In 0.3 mile, go straight to continue climbing on the main road (at an intersection of roads). Pass the lower intersection with Bear Woods Loop Trail, then pass Rim Tie Trail on the right. Soon after passing Rim Tie Trail, turn left at the upper Bear Woods Loop Trail intersection. In 0.2 mile, turn left off of Bear Woods Loop Trail onto Rim Trail (Rim

Trail is a double-track here). Immediately turn right to regain a single-track (here, you are staying on Rim Trail, it turns back into a single-track). (Your progress will become impeded if you miss this turn; the double-track becomes overgrown.) You will arrive at a **Y** intersection in 0.2 mile, turn left, back onto Bear Woods Loop Trail. Shortly, turn right to remain on Bear Woods Loop Trail where a faint trail continues straight. After a lot of twists, turns, and challenging obstacles, the trail deposits you back at the road you were climbing on earlier. Turn left onto the road and climb up to Rim Trail. Turn right onto Rim Trail. In 0.5 mile (during a descent), turn right to remain on Rim Trail (where a game trail continues straight). Continue straight where Fern Creek Trail goes right. You are now backtracking on a portion of Rim Trail. Return the way you came to Hardy Creek Trailhead.

We have heard reports that Looney's Trail is a fun and technical piece of single-track at the northern end of the corridor. We understand that you can reach this 6-mile segment of trail by heading north on Huckleberry Trail.

The southern portion of the Molalla River Corridor is slated to see extensive development. Campground construction and linkages to the Table Rock Wilderness Area will help disperse equestrian traffic in the area.

## RIDE 83 · Silver Falls State Park Bike Path

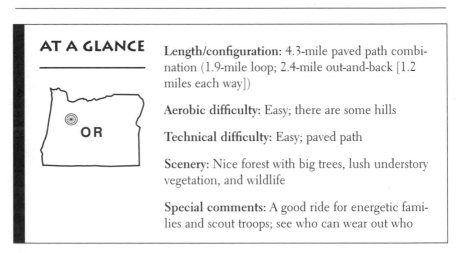

**AT A GLANCE**

**OR**

**Length/configuration:** 4.3-mile paved path combination (1.9-mile loop; 2.4-mile out-and-back [1.2 miles each way])

**Aerobic difficulty:** Easy; there are some hills

**Technical difficulty:** Easy; paved path

**Scenery:** Nice forest with big trees, lush understory vegetation, and wildlife

**Special comments:** A good ride for energetic families and scout troops; see who can wear out who

Silver Falls State Park is a special place. It is the largest and most diverse state park in Oregon. Featured attractions include; designated hiking, biking, jogging, and equestrian trails; a swimming hole, beach, and play area; campgrounds and picnic areas; and a day-lodge loaded with neat interpretive displays, a snack bar, and a cozy fireplace. The fireplace was high on our list of favorites. We were there on a cold, drippy, foggy day in October. We spent more than a few minutes in front of the fire thawing out our frigid digits.

Pedaling through Silver Falls State Park.

This route follows a paved bike path for 4.3 miles. The route consists of a 1.9-mile loop and a 2.4-mile out-and-back (1.2 miles each way). The loop portion of the trip travels through a lovely second-growth forest; we saw a lot of deer on this part of the ride. We were all alone, riding on a paved path through a beautiful forest, deer bounding every which way. It was pleasant, but at the same time, somewhat odd. It felt at once wild and natural, and at the same time contrived.

While visiting the park, you shouldn't miss the main attraction—the waterfalls. Check out all or part of the seven-mile Trail of Ten Falls. You can access this hiking trail near the South Falls Lodge, and at two viewpoints along OR 214.

**General location:** Silver Falls State Park is about 22 miles southwest of Salem.

**Elevation change:** The trailhead for the ride is at approximately 1,500'. Ups and downs on the bike path add up to about 200' of climbing.

**Season:** The State Park is open year-round. The park is busiest on summer holiday weekends. The spring is a nice time for a visit; some of the waterfalls receive their water from snowmelt, these should be raging.

**Services:** Water and snacks can be obtained at South Falls Lodge. The park's facilities include a 105-site campground (with showers), swimming pond, a conference center, and a youth camp. All services are available in Salem.

**Hazards:** Control your speed. Watch out for other people of all ages and stability. Be careful around blind corners; someone may be approaching from the

# RIDE 83 · Silver Falls State Park Bike Path

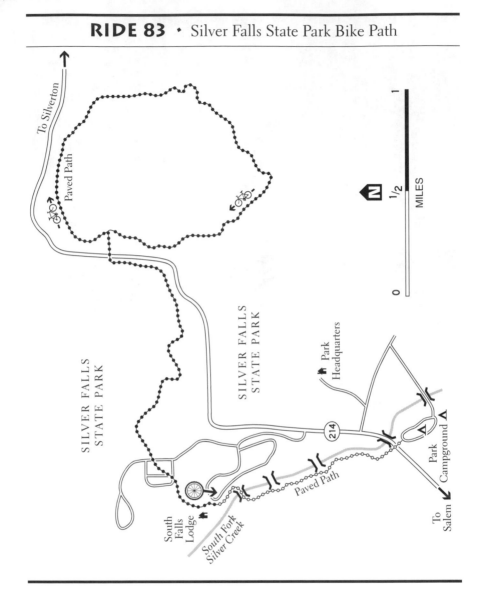

opposite direction. Moss and wet pavement can make for a loss of traction. Use caution at road crossings. Oregon law requires children under the age of 16 to wear helmets while riding on a bike (every rider should wear a helmet).

**Rescue index:** Help can be found at South Falls Lodge. Emergency services are located in Salem.

**Land status:** State park.

**Maps:** A handout titled "Silver Falls State Park Bike Trail" is a good guide to this ride. You can pick one up at South Falls Lodge. USGS 7.5 minute quads: Lyons and Elk Prairie.

**Finding the trail:** From Interstate 5, take Exit 253 (just south of Salem) and follow OR 22/North Santiam Highway southeast. OR 22 intersects with OR 214 in 5 miles. Head east on OR 214 toward Silver Falls State Park. Drive approximately 17 miles to the South Falls Lodge (on the left).

From Silverton, follow OR 214 south for approximately 16 miles to the South Falls Lodge (on the right). Park near the lodge (there is a day-use fee).

**Source of additional information:**

Silver Falls State Park
20024 Silver Falls Highway S.E.
Sublimity, OR 97385
(503) 873-8681

**Notes on the trail:** At South Falls Lodge, head north (away from the big parking lots) and follow the signs that direct you toward the bike path. You will immediately arrive at a small parking lot; ride across it and get on the paved path. Shortly, the path crosses a road. In another 0.8 mile, carefully cross OR 214. Turn left at a T intersection and ride around the loop. Turn left upon completing the loop. Retrace your path back to the lodge.

The paved path also connects with the swimming area and campground (south of the lodge).

# HOOD RIVER/MT. HOOD

For over a century, Mt. Hood has captured the imagination of Americans. After thousands of arduous miles on the Oregon Trail, emigrants came up against one final obstacle: the massive bulk of Mt. Hood. Today, tourists travel around the mountain on highways, and sportsmen and recreation-minded people flock to its slopes. All who behold it are struck by the beauty of this isolated and majestic peak. In Portland, Mt. Hood is visible from every section of the city. The people lovingly refer to it as "our mountain."

Just a couple of hours east of Portland is the town of Hood River. It sits at the foot of Mt. Hood on the banks of the mighty Columbia River. The steady, intense winds that blow up the Columbia Gorge have made Hood River the wind surfing capital of the Northwest. This young recreation-oriented community also enjoys access to some fine single-track mountain biking.

From Hood River, the Mt. Hood Highway climbs away from the Columbia Gorge. The drive up this two-lane highway is a scenic trip. On either side of you are the apple and pear orchards of the wide Hood River Valley. Before you is the shining volcanic cone of Mt. Hood. To the east, high above the roadway, is Surveyor's Ridge. A trail follows the ridge for 17 miles and offers incredible views of the snowfields and glaciers on Mt. Hood. There are a number of excellent loops and longer rides available in this section of the forest. It is an outstanding place to ride a mountain bike.

Still heading south along the highway, the valley narrows rapidly and gives way to evergreen forests. The East Fork Hood River runs beside the highway; good camping and mountain biking can be found on its banks. Connecting the Sherwood and Robinhood campgrounds is East Fork Trail, which parallels the vigorous river and offers cyclists a short, less demanding single-track experience. A hiking trail leads from Sherwood Campground to beautiful Tamanawas Falls.

Climbing higher, the highway brings you to Bennett Pass. A gravel road leads from the pass to a quiet trail that follows Gunsight Ridge to Gumjuwac Saddle. The ridge provides breathtaking vistas of nearby Mt. Hood and distant views of many other Cascade peaks.

South of Barlow Pass, the Mt. Hood Highway meets US 12 and swings west toward Portland. Here you pass the towns of Government Camp and Zigzag. The resort hotel Timberline Lodge is accessed from Government Camp. The lodge sees many visitors in the winter for downhill skiing and snowboarding. In the summer, it is the trailhead for the popular southside climb of Mt. Hood and the Round-the-Mountain Trail. Good camping and gravel road riding can be found below Government Camp at lovely Trillium Lake.

Head south from Government Camp on US 12 to access rides in the Bear Springs Ranger District, or drive west toward Portland and stop in at the ranger station in Zigzag. All of the ranger districts in the Mt. Hood National Forest supply handouts on mountain bike opportunities in their section of the forest.

Due to its proximity to Portland, the Mt. Hood National Forest is a hugely popular destination. The increased use of mountain bikes has not gone unnoticed by the forest's recreation managers. We recommend that you make a visit or phone call before your trip to check on special conditions that could affect your ride. Some trails are closed periodically to reduce erosion or to lessen user conflicts.

## RIDE 84 · Post Canyon/Seven Streams

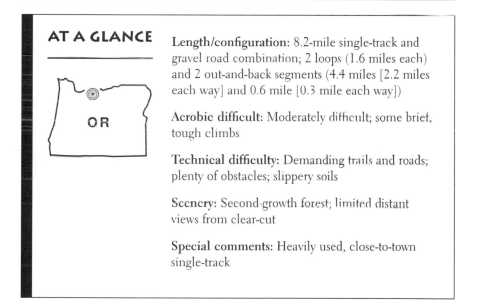

**AT A GLANCE**

OR

**Length/configuration:** 8.2-mile single-track and gravel road combination; 2 loops (1.6 miles each) and 2 out-and-back segments (4.4 miles [2.2 miles each way] and 0.6 mile [0.3 mile each way])

**Aerobic difficult:** Moderately difficult; some brief, tough climbs

**Technical difficulty:** Demanding trails and roads; plenty of obstacles; slippery soils

**Scenery:** Second-growth forest; limited distant views from clear-cut

**Special comments:** Heavily used, close-to-town single-track

Just west of the community of Hood River, sandwiched between suburbs and the national forest, lies the Hood River County Forest. Timber sales on the forest generate huge sums of money for the county. Recently, the managers of the forest decided to sell a large parcel of timber. The resulting clear-cuts would have severely impacted some prime sections of trail. The decision to cut

Exploring near
Hood River.

was met with an outcry of public protest. Since then, trail enthusiasts and the forest's managers have come together to form a compromise. In key areas, selective cutting has replaced the plan to clear-cut—the county makes money, and trail users get to enjoy their trails.

Seven Streams is a demanding 8.2-mile outing; it climbs through Post Canyon and over some adjacent hills. The trip is a grab bag of conditions and difficulties. It is composed of two loops (each of the loops are 1.6 miles long) and two out-and-back segments. The out-and-backs are 4.4 miles long (2.2 miles each way) and 0.6 mile long (0.3 mile each way). The trip involves 4.3 miles of gravel and dirt roads and 3.7 miles of single-track. The roads are in fair condition with some very rough areas where large, loose rocks make climbing a struggle. The trails are similarly variable in their condition. In places, they are smooth and easy to negotiate. In other areas, they are fraught with roots and sandy patches; frequent dips and climbs require excellent bike-handling skills. Both the trails and the roads include areas with high clay content soils; when wet, these soils are very slippery.

This shady, often damp forest is not known for its scenery. Abandoned cars are a problem, and beer can–littered pullouts point to the area's popularity with

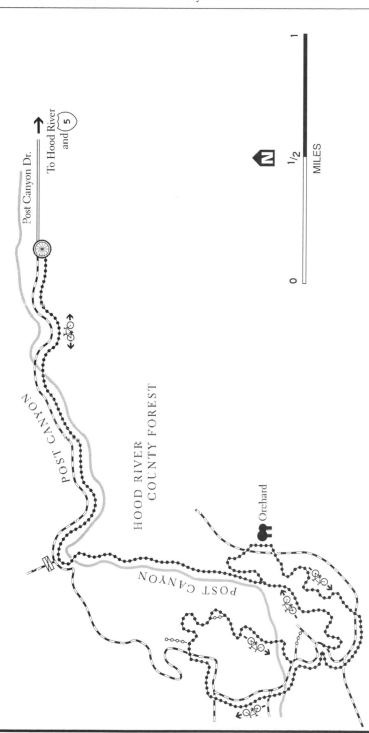

nighttime revelers. The highest elevations of the ride, on a hillside west of Post Canyon, are open and sunny. The contrasting, open character of this clear-cut knob is surprisingly refreshing. On bright days, Mt. Hood and Mt. Adams are within view here.

**General location:** Post Canyon is just west of the city of Hood River.

**Elevation change:** The ride begins at 730' and reaches a high point of 1,490'. Undulations over the course of the circuit add approximately 500' of climbing to trip. Overall elevation gain: 1,260'.

**Season:** The trails and roads in the forest remain open year-round. In this part of the country, wet weather is common from the late fall through the winter. Please stay off of the trails when they are wet. This is an actively managed forest, closures can occur at any time due to management activities, special events, and wet conditions.

**Services:** There is no potable water on this ride. All services are available in Hood River.

**Hazards:** Watch for traffic on the roads and other recreationists on the heavily used trails. Some of the trails on this ride cross steep gullies and negotiate steep drop-offs; obstacles like roots, rocks, slick soils, slippery bridges, and soft conditions are common. The roads can be both slick and rocky. The creek crossings in Post Canyon may be difficult during periods of high water.

**Rescue index:** Help is available in Hood River.

**Land status:** Hood River County Forest.

**Maps:** We found the most useful map for this ride contained in a regional mountain bike guidebook, *The Singletrack Anthology, Hood River* by T. Barnes and K. Reynolds. It is published by Pinnacle Publishing and is available at bookstores and bike shops throughout the region. USGS 7.5 minute quad: Hood River.

**Finding the trail:** From locations to the west, travel east on Interstate 84 and take Exit 62. (This exit is just west of Hood River and signed for US 30/West Hood River/Westcliff Drive.) Turn right onto US 30/Cascade Avenue at the stop sign, then immediately turn right onto Country Club Road. From locations to the east, drive west on I-84 to Exit 62. After exiting the highway, head south over I-84, then turn right onto Country Club Road. From locations in downtown Hood River, drive west through town on Oak Street/US 30. Continue west where Oak Street merges into Cascade Avenue. Turn left in about 1 mile onto Country Club Road. Follow Country Club Road for 1.4 miles to Post Canyon Drive. Turn right onto Post Canyon Drive and proceed 0.6 mile to the end of the pavement. Park on the right side of the gravel road.

**Sources of additional information:**

Hood River County Forestry Department
918 18th Street
Hood River, OR 97031
(541) 387-6888

Hood River Velo (Bicycle Club)
1729 Avalon Court
Hood River, OR 97031
(541) 386-7810
(541) 386-2453

**Notes on the trail:** Head up the gravel road. In 1.2 miles, continue straight (left) on the main road at a **Y** intersection (there is a metal gate at the road to the right). In another 0.1 mile, turn left onto a trail marked by 2 large rocks. (Actually, there are 2 trails to choose from at this intersection; take the right one.) Cross the creek and follow the trail as it travels up the east side of the streambed. Several secondary creeks feed into the main channel; some are spanned by small wood footbridges. You will come to a larger footbridge after a braided section of trail. Take the bridge to avoid another braided section of trail. (This braided section was tangled by windfalls and roots.) In another 0.3 mile you will arrive at an intersection of trails at the top of a short steep rise. Turn hard to the left and climb 0.2 mile to a gravel road. Turn right onto the road (parallel a fenced orchard). In 0.2 mile, turn right onto a trail. Turn right when the trail deposits you back onto the gravel road. Climb for 0.2 mile to a **Y** intersection; turn right to descend on a smoother, native surface road. Stay on the main road, descending to a low point in 0.5 mile. Follow the road as it bears left, then enter a clearing. At a **Y** in the road, stay to the right to climb up a very rough section of road. At the top of the hill, at a **T** intersection, turn right onto a gravel road. In 0.2 mile, turn right onto a single-track and reenter the woods. Immediately, stay right at an intersection of trails. In 0.5 mile (after the trail dips and climbs twice), bear left at a **Y** intersection. (Both trails lead to the same place; the trail on the left descends more gradually and is less ditch-like. If you cannot descend without skidding, walk your bike down the hill.) Continue straight at the next intersection. More ups and downs bring you to a creek crossing (the creek is spanned by 2 planks), then to a **T** intersection at a dirt road (this completes the first loop). Turn left, descending briefly to a low point and a wide trail on the left. Bear right to remain on the main road. Stay right at the next intersection (after climbing over a large waterbar in the road). In 0.1 mile, turn left onto an unmarked single-track trail (easy to miss). Descend for 0.6 mile to a **Y** intersection. Turn left to regain the trail that parallels the creek in Post Canyon. Return the way you came to your vehicle.

## RIDE 85 · Post Canyon/Mitchell Ridge

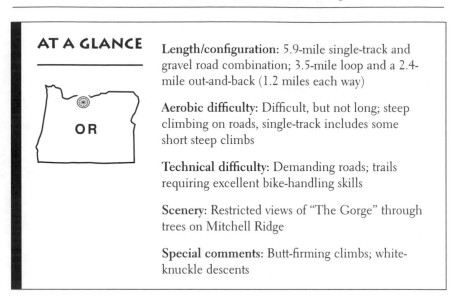

**AT A GLANCE**

**Length/configuration:** 5.9-mile single-track and gravel road combination; 3.5-mile loop and a 2.4-mile out-and-back (1.2 miles each way)

**Aerobic difficulty:** Difficult, but not long; steep climbing on roads, single-track includes some short steep climbs

**Technical difficulty:** Demanding roads; trails requiring excellent bike-handling skills

**Scenery:** Restricted views of "The Gorge" through trees on Mitchell Ridge

**Special comments:** Butt-firming climbs; white-knuckle descents

The Mitchell Ridge ride begins by climbing on a gravel road through a portion of Post Canyon in the Hood River County Forest. This ascent emerges from the woods onto an open hilltop, where a trail is picked up. The single-track rolls up and down (mostly down) to another road and more climbing. Again, the roads lead to single-track. The last stretch of trail includes several precipitous descents on Mitchell Ridge. Peeks at the Columbia River Gorge (from Mitchell Ridge) and glimpses of Mt. Hood and Mt. Adams (from a clear-cut) highlight the scenery on this wooded ride.

This ride is demanding, both physically and technically, but at 5.9 miles, it's relatively short. The circuit consists of a 3.5-mile loop and a 2.4-mile out-and-back (1.2 miles each way). The trip involves 4 miles of dirt and gravel roads and 1.9 miles of single-track. The opening road climb vacillates between gentle gradients and steep pitches. This road is in relatively good condition. Roads followed later in the ride include conditions that vary from coarse rocky surfaces to slick, deeply rutted situations. The trails are technically challenging with extreme conditions. Concentration is required for route finding; numerous side trails branch off from the route.

**General location:** The trailhead in Post Canyon is just west of Hood River.

**Elevation change:** The trip begins at 730'. A high point of roughly 1,500' is attained on Mitchell Ridge. Ups and downs over the course of the ride add about 400' of climbing to the outing. Overall elevation gain: 1,170'.

**Season:** The roads and trails in the forest are usually open year-round, but closures can occur at any time due to management activities, special events, and

Muscling over
Mitchell Ridge.

wet conditions. Please stay off of the trails when they are wet. Wet weather is common in this region from the late fall through the winter.

**Services:** There is no potable water on this outing. All services are available in Hood River.

**Hazards:** The trails on this ride include obstacles like roots, rocks, slick soils, and soft sections of tread. The native surface roads can be slick when wet, and the gravel roads contain ruts and coarse sections of roadbed. Watch for traffic on the roads and other trail users on the well-traveled single-track.

**Rescue index:** Help can be found in Hood River.

**Land status:** Hood River County Forest and Wygant State Park.

**Maps:** A regional mountain bike guidebook for the area, *The Singletrack Anthology, Hood River* by T. Barnes and K. Reynolds, contains a useful map of the trails and roads followed on this ride. USGS 7.5 minute quad: Hood River.

**Finding the trail:** From locations to the west, travel east on Interstate 84 and take Exit 62. (This exit is just west of Hood River and signed for US 30/West Hood River/Westcliff Drive.) Turn right onto US 30/Cascade Avenue at the stop sign, then immediately turn right onto Country Club Road. From locations to the east, drive west on I-84 to Exit 62. After exiting the highway, head south over I-84, then turn right onto Country Club Road. From locations in downtown Hood River, drive west through town on Oak Street/US 30. Continue west where Oak Street merges into Cascade Avenue. Turn left in about 1 mile onto Country Club Road. Follow Country Club Road for 1.4 miles to Post Canyon Drive. Turn right onto Post Canyon Drive and proceed 0.6 mile to the end of the pavement. Park on the right side of the gravel road.

**Sources of additional information:**

Hood River County Forestry Department
918 18th Street
Hood River, OR 97031
(541) 387-6888

Hood River Velo (Bicycle Club)
1729 Avalon Court
Hood River, OR 97031
(541) 386-7810
(541) 386-2453

**Notes on the trail:** Ride up the gravel road. Stay on the main road where roads and trails branch off. After climbing 2.1 miles the road tops out and enters a clearing. Turn left onto a single-track and reenter the woods. Immediately, stay right at an intersection of trails. In 0.5 mile (after the trail dips and climbs twice), bear left at a **Y** intersection. (Both trails lead to the same place; the trail on the left descends more gradually and is less ditch-like. If you can not descend without skidding, walk your bike down the hill.) Continue straight at the next intersection. More ups and downs bring you to a creek crossing (the creek is spanned by 2 planks), then to a **T** intersection at a dirt road. Turn right onto the dirt road and ride into a clearing. At a **Y** in the road, stay right to climb up a very rough stretch of road. At the top of the hill, at a **T** intersection, turn left onto another gravel road. In 0.1 mile, turn right to follow a double-track. The double-track becomes trail-like and immediately enters the woods. Bear right to pick up a single-track. The trail climbs gently for about 50 feet, then levels out. You will immediately arrive at another intersection of trails; continue straight (left) to follow the main trail in a northerly direction through the woods. (Here, a secondary trail goes right; descending in an easterly direction to border the clear-cut you just exited.) In 0.2 mile, bear right to drop in earnest on a single-track where a double-track goes left. (There is a Carsonite "State Park" boundary-marker at this intersection.) At the next intersection of trails (in 0.3 mile), continue straight (right) to descend where a trail goes left into an overgrown area. Shortly, bear left on the main trail to drop down a short, but extremely steep descent (carry your bike down to reduce your impact on the trail). In 0.4 mile, at a high point in a small clearing (marked by a little fire ring), stay right at a **Y** intersection, then immediately stay right at another **Y** in the trail. Pass under

# RIDE 85 · Post Canyon/Mitchell Ridge

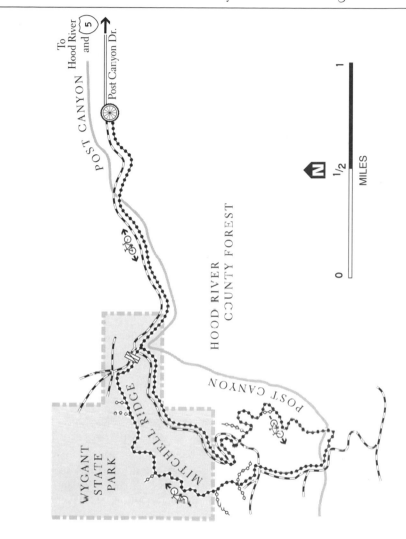

power lines to drop into a clearing at the junction of several roads. Turn hard to the right (pass back under the power lines) and descend on a rutted dirt road. Turn left when you reach the main gravel road in Post Canyon. Descend to your car.

## RIDE 86 · Deschutes River State Recreation Area Bike Path

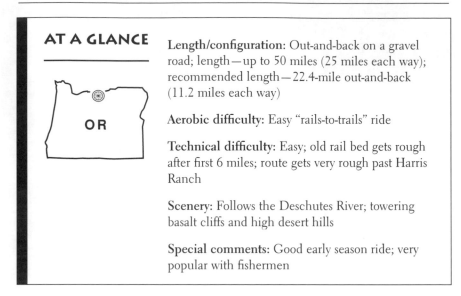

**AT A GLANCE**

**Length/configuration:** Out-and-back on a gravel road; length—up to 50 miles (25 miles each way); recommended length—22.4-mile out-and-back (11.2 miles each way)

**Aerobic difficulty:** Easy "rails-to-trails" ride

**Technical difficulty:** Easy; old rail bed gets rough after first 6 miles; route gets very rough past Harris Ranch

**Scenery:** Follows the Deschutes River; towering basalt cliffs and high desert hills

**Special comments:** Good early season ride; very popular with fishermen

If you've just put your winter toys away and you're ready to pump up the tires on your mountain bike, you should take a look at this early season ride. It's a good warm-up for greater things to come. The Deschutes River State Recreation Area sits at the confluence of the Deschutes and Columbia rivers. One of the features of this park is a gravel "rails-to-trails" bike path; it heads up the east side of the Deschutes. Huge basalt cliffs and dry grassy hillsides line the route. The scenery imparts an almost southwestern feel to the ride.

We arrived at the trailhead to find the parking area full of cars. Riding down the trail, we noticed lots of two-wheeled clunkers stashed beside the path. It didn't take long to figure out that the bikes belonged to the fishermen who were down by the river. Float boats and rafts; waders and lawn chairs; tents and coolers— the trappings of men on a mission. Sitting to eat our lunch at a riverside setting, we soon figured out what all the fuss was about. Every once in a while, a huge steelhead would jump out of the water. They must be fun to wrestle with.

The bike path gains elevation very gently as it heads upriver. There is one short, moderately steep section of trail where the path drops down to cross a creek. The path is quite smooth over its first six miles, then the route gets rougher. We spoke with a park ranger who mentioned that it is possible to ride all the way to Maupin on the old railbed (several hike-a-bike sections). We wouldn't recommend it however, the trail gets rougher as you get deeper into the canyon. A good ride can be had by traveling 11.2 miles to the abandoned Harris Ranch. The return is just downhill enough to take the edge off of the pedaling.

# RIDE 86 · Deschutes River State Recreation Area Bike Path

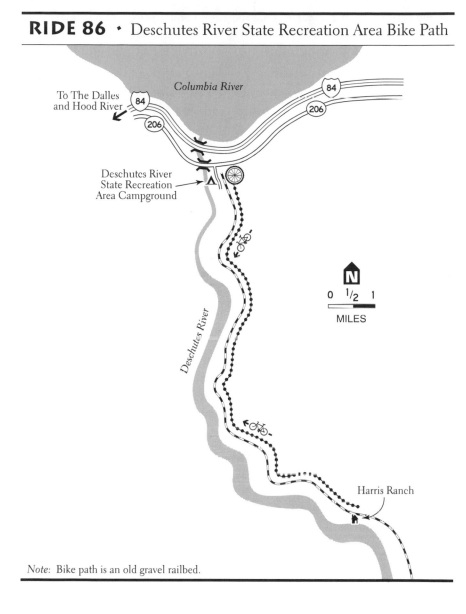

*Note:* Bike path is an old gravel railbed.

**General location:** The trailhead in the Deschutes River State Recreation Area is located approximately 35 miles east of Hood River (about 15 miles east of The Dalles).

**Elevation change:** The ride begins at roughly 80' and reaches a high point approaching 130' at Harris Ranch. Ups and downs on the path add about 150' of climbing to the ride. Total elevation gain: 200'.

**Season:** Year-round, weather permitting. Good wildflowers in the spring.

**Services:** You can obtain water at the recreation area campground. Toilets and a pay phone are also available. All services are located in Hood River.

**Hazards:** The path includes some loose rock and some sandy, soft sections of roadbed. Rattlesnakes reside in the canyon.

**Rescue index:** Help can be summoned at the campground host site. There is a pay phone in the campground. Emergency services are located in The Dalles and Hood River.

**Land status:** Lands administered by the Oregon Parks and Recreation Department, the Oregon Department of Fish and Wildlife, and the Bureau of Land Management.

**Maps:** A handout titled "Deschutes River Campground" contains an adequate guide to the bike path. It is available at the recreation area campground. USGS 7.5 minute quads: Locust Grove, Emerson, Erskine, and Wishram.

**Finding the trail:** Follow Interstate 84 to Exit 97 (about 35 miles east of Hood River). Exit the highway and proceed east on OR 206 for three miles to the Deschutes River State Recreation Area on the right (just over the Deschutes River). Park on the east side of the entrance road, in the dirt pullout marked with a bike symbol sign. Do not block access to the bike path (leave enough room for service trucks or emergency vehicles to access the path). If this parking area is full, proceed south on the paved entrance road; pass by the campground to find additional day-use parking.

### Sources of additional information:

Oregon Parks and Recreation Department
1115 Commercial Street N.E.
Salem, OR 97310-1001
(503) 378-6305

Deschutes River State Recreation Area
89600 Biggs-Rufus Highway
Wasco, OR 97065
(541) 739-2322

Oregon Department of Fish and Wildlife
3701 West 13th Street
The Dalles, OR 97058
(541) 296-4628

Bureau of Land Management
Prineville District Office
P.O. Box 550
Prineville, OR 97754
(541) 416-6700

The Deschutes River
near its confluence with
the Columbia.

**Notes on the trail:** The trails that lead off of the main path are closed to bikes. From the trailhead, head south up the gravel service road (marked with a bike symbol sign). Follow the wide path for 11.2 miles to Harris Ranch. Turn around and return the way you came.

**RIDE 87** · East Fork Trail

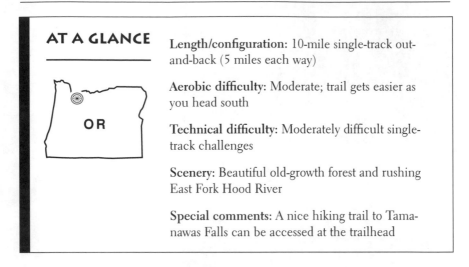

**AT A GLANCE**

**Length/configuration:** 10-mile single-track out-and-back (5 miles each way)

**Aerobic difficulty:** Moderate; trail gets easier as you head south

**Technical difficulty:** Moderately difficult single-track challenges

**Scenery:** Beautiful old-growth forest and rushing East Fork Hood River

**Special comments:** A nice hiking trail to Tamanawas Falls can be accessed at the trailhead

This is a moderately difficult ten-mile out-and-back trip on East Fork Trail. It begins with the ride's most demanding terrain. The pedaling gets much easier near Robinhood Campground (at the south end of the trail). Technical

# **RIDE 87** · East Fork Trail

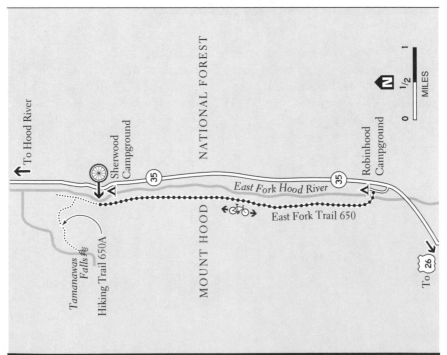

Boardwalk near Robinhood Campground.

challenges include roots, embedded boulders, waterbars, and whoop-dee-doos. The path is in mostly good condition with some sandy sections and wet areas. Since we last rode here, the trail has been rerouted at its north end. This should improve an already fine trail.

This fun, popular route parallels the East Fork Hood River and travels through some nice old-growth forest. Trail 650A to Tamanawas Falls makes for an excellent side trip (no bikes—hiking only).

**General location:** This ride begins near Sherwood Campground, approximately 25 miles south of Hood River on OR 35.

**Elevation change:** The trip begins at 3,000' and reaches 3,550' at Robinhood Campground. Undulations on the route add about 200' of climbing to the ride. Total elevation gain: 750'.

**Season:** The Hood River Ranger District recommends this trail as an early and late season ride. Dry summer conditions turn the soil to dust, which can lead to trenching by mountain bike tires. Call ahead to check on seasonal closure.

**Services:** Water can be obtained seasonally at Sherwood and Robinhood camp-

Footbridge over the East
Fork of the Hood River.

grounds. You can purchase limited groceries at the Mt. Hood Country Store (on OR 35, 13 miles south of Hood River). In the summer and fall, check out the fruit stands that dot the highway near the community of Mt. Hood. All services are available in Hood River.

**Hazards:**  Good bike-handling skills are required to safely negotiate obstacles in the trail. The route includes some wooden bridges that are slippery, especially when wet. Minimize trail damage by walking your bike over the steepest and most fragile segments of the path.

**Rescue index:**  Help can be obtained at the Hood River Ranger Station. (Drive north from the trailhead on OR 35 for 10 miles to the ranger station on the left.) There is a pay phone at the Mt. Hood Country Store (0.2 mile north of the ranger station on OR 35). Emergency services are located in Hood River.

**Land status:**  Mt. Hood National Forest.

**Maps:**  The district map of the Hood River Ranger District is a good guide to this route. USGS 7.5 minute quads: Badger Lake and Dog River.

**Finding the trail:**  From the community of Hood River, follow OR 35 south for

25 miles. Turn right to park in the gravel pullout signed for East Fork Trailhead/Tamanawas Falls (just north of Sherwood Campground).

**Source of additional information:**

Hood River Ranger District
6780 Highway 35
Mt. Hood-Parkdale, OR 97041
(541) 352-6002

**Notes on the trail:** From the parking area, walk your bike to the river and across the footbridge. Turn left onto East Fork Trail 650. Follow the single-track to Robinhood Campground. Turn around and return the way you came.

Beginners can explore this trail by starting at Robinhood Campground and heading north. Keep in mind that you will be descending from Robinhood Campground. Although the riding may seem easy, your return will be uphill. Save something for the second half.

## RIDE 88 · Surveyor's Ridge Trail

**AT A GLANCE**

**Length/configuration:** 20-mile single-track and gravel road loop

**Aerobic difficulty:** Demanding; trail rises and falls continually over its length

**Technical difficulty:** Mixed bag of single-track challenges requiring advanced skills

**Scenery:** Panoramic ridge riding; spectacular views of Mt. Hood

**Special comments:** Great ride; good dispersed camping on ridge

Surveyor's Ridge Trail is 15 miles long and is mostly single-track. Parts of the trail require excellent bike-handling skills, while others are smooth and dreamy. We describe a 20-mile loop that utilizes 12.4 miles of the trail, with a return on paved and gravel roads. Longer and shorter loops are possible. This demanding ridge ride passes through grassy meadows, through stands of heavy timber, and around rocky outcroppings. On clear days, views of the Hood River Valley, Mt. Hood, and Mt. Adams are spectacular. Sunshine or clouds, Surveyor's Ridge will bring a smile to fans of single-track cycling.

Mt. Hood from Surveyor's Ridge Trail.

The trail loses elevation as it heads north, but it undulates continually. Most of the uphills are easy to moderately difficult; there are about 1.5 miles of steep climbing (some sections are unrideable). The trail is in fair to good condition, with some rocky sections, roots, and some soft stretches. Returning on the roads involves mostly moderately difficult to easy climbing.

We enjoy poking around on side roads, looking for great campsites. There are a lot of quiet, dispersed campsites on Surveyor's Ridge; some look out over Mt. Hood. A base camp on Surveyor's Ridge allows you to easily access several fine rides in the area.

**General location:** The trailhead is approximately 30 miles south of Hood River.

**Elevation change:** The southern terminus of the trail lies at 4,200'. The northern end of the trail, for this ride description, is at 3,400'. The path nears 4,300' several times and stays above the 4,000' mark for 10 miles. Ups and downs on the trail add up to about 1,200' of climbing. The road return takes you to the trip's low point, 3,300'. Hills contribute an estimated 1,500' of climbing to the road miles. Total elevation gain: 2,700'.

**Season:** Surveyor's Ridge is usually free of snow from late June through October. Wildflowers are abundant in June and July, especially at the northern end of the trail.

**Services:** There is no potable water on the ride. Water can be obtained seasonally at Sherwood and Robinhood campgrounds. (These campgrounds are on OR

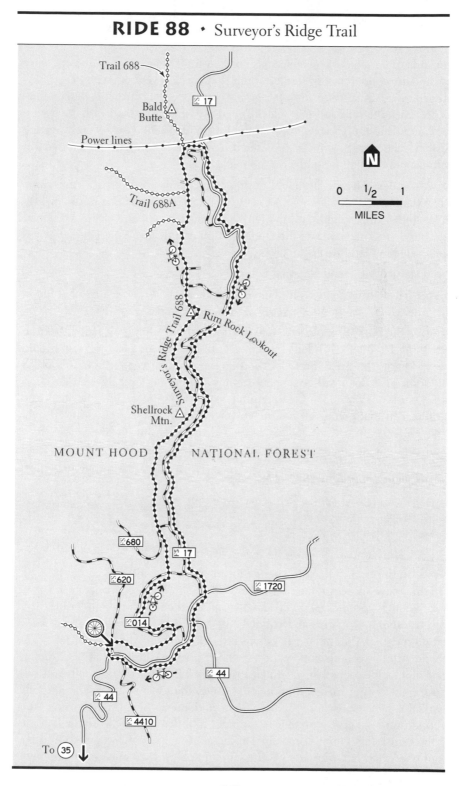

Trail 688

Bald Butte

17

Power lines

Trail 688A

N

0   1/2   1

MILES

Surveyor's Ridge Trail 688

Rim Rock Lookout

Shellrock Mtn.

MOUNT HOOD   NATIONAL FOREST

680

17

620

1720

014

44

44

44

4410

To 35

35; you will pass one or the other on your way to the described trailhead.) All services are available in Hood River.

**Hazards:** The region's volcanic soils contain high amounts of pumice. Heavy use and dry conditions can result in trails that become very soft with deep pockets of pumice dust. Watch for soft segments of trail, especially while descending. Expect rocky terrain and obstacles like exposed roots. There is a barbed wire gate across the trail, 1 mile north of the trail's intersection with Forest Service Road 17. The gate is on a steep descent if you are heading north; approach it with caution. Watch for traffic on the roads.

**Rescue index:** Help is available during regular business hours at the Hood River Ranger Station. (Take FS 44 to OR 35; turn right and drive north for 11.7 miles to the ranger station on the left). There is a pay phone at the Mt. Hood Country Store (just north of the ranger station on OR 35). Emergency services are located in Hood River.

**Land status:** Mt. Hood National Forest.

**Maps:** The district map of the Hood River Ranger District is a good guide to this ride. USGS 7.5 minute quads: Dog River and Parkdale.

**Finding the trail:** From locations to the north, drive south from Hood River on OR 35 for 25 miles. Turn left (1.4 miles south of Sherwood Campground) onto FS 44/Dufur Mill Road. From locations to the south, drive north on OR 35. FS 44/Dufur Mill Road will be on your right, 6.8 miles north of Bennett Pass (2.6 miles north of Robinhood Campground). Follow FS 44 for 3.6 miles to a sign on the right that points left toward Surveyor's Ridge Trail 688. Turn left here onto FS 620; you will immediately arrive at the trailhead for Surveyor's Ridge Trail, on the right. Park on the side of the road.

**Source of additional information:**

Hood River Ranger District
6780 Highway 35
Mt. Hood-Parkdale, OR 97041
(541) 352-6002

**Notes on the trail:** The path goes east from the large trailhead sign at FS 620. The trail passes through Cooks Meadow and then arrives at unsigned FS 014. Turn left to follow the sign for Trail 688. Stay on the road for about 3 miles as it travels through clear-cuts and parallels the buried Dog River Aqueduct. Turn left onto signed Trail 688—just before FS 014 commences a steep climb up to FS 17. At intersections, follow the signs for Surveyor's Ridge Trail 688. After a total of 9.2 miles of pedaling, you pass Rim Rock Lookout on your left. You will cross 2 gravel spur roads in the next 0.6 mile, then you will arrive at a poorly marked **Y** intersection in a grove of old-growth Douglas fir (0.7 mile north of the second spur road crossing). Stay to the right to follow Trail 688. You will come to the next intersection of trails in 1 mile; continue straight where Oak Ridge Trail 688A goes left. Surveyor's Ridge Trail quickly arrives at another unsigned spur road. Cross the road to continue north on Surveyor's Ridge Trail. (The trail is marked by a sign that directs you toward Bald Butte.) Next you will approach 4 huge power line towers and a trailhead sign on your right. Bear right toward the trailhead sign and onto a faint trail that leads out to a dirt road. Turn right onto the road and descend a short distance to a **T** intersection at unsigned FS 630. Turn left and drop down to paved FS 17 (unsigned). Turn right onto the pavement. FS 17 becomes a gravel road in 2.8 miles. It changes back to pavement in 5.5 miles. After following FS 17 for 9 miles, you will come to a **T** intersection where FS 1720 goes left toward Knebal Springs Campground. Turn right here to stay on FS 17 (a sign directs you right toward FS 44). In 0.4 mile, FS 17 intersects with FS 44. Continue straight onto FS 44 toward OR 35. You will remain on FS 44 for 1.6 miles. Pass FS 4410 (which goes left to High Prairie) and take the next right onto FS 620 to reach your vehicle.

## RIDE 89 · High Prairie Loop

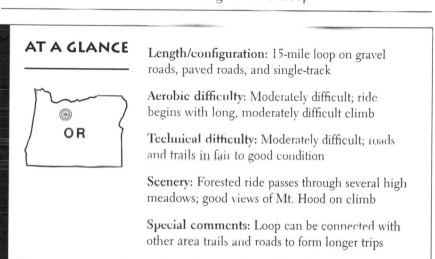

**AT A GLANCE**

**Length/configuration:** 15-mile loop on gravel roads, paved roads, and single-track

**Aerobic difficulty:** Moderately difficult; ride begins with long, moderately difficult climb

**Technical difficulty:** Moderately difficult; roads and trails in fair to good condition

**Scenery:** Forested ride passes through several high meadows; good views of Mt. Hood on climb

**Special comments:** Loop can be connected with other area trails and roads to form longer trips

The price of admission to this fun loop is a moderately difficult five-mile climb to High Prairie, cheap when you consider the guaranteed return on your investment. The drop from High Prairie to Bottle Prairie begins with a short descent on a rutted dirt road. Then you pick up Lookout Mountain Trail. Fun, dished-out corners help to make the top of the trail very memorable. This well-used trail receives a good deal of attention from forest maintenance crews. Sections of conveyer belt have been set into the ground to act as waterbars. When ridden across, the waterbars fold over, then they pop back up, standing ready to divert water off of the trail. These diversions help keep ditch-like conditions from developing. You can help, too—by not skidding. Expert mountain

# RIDE 89 · High Prairie Loop

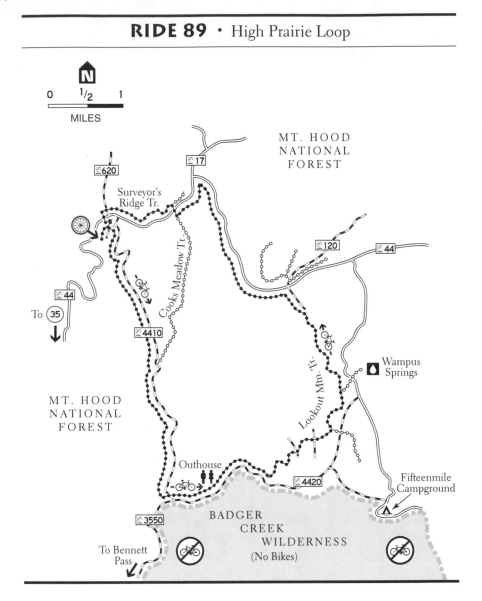

bikers slow down as they approach corners like these, then they roll through them. Try approaching turns at a pace that seems slower than necessary. Looking ahead is important, both for mastering this technique, and when you consider that hikers, equestrians, and cyclists enjoy climbing on Lookout Mountain Trail.

High Prairie Loop is 15 miles long. The initial ascent is on a gravel road in good condition. During dry periods, dust from passing motorists can be a problem. (The road is popular with people accessing trailheads for the adjacent Badger Creek Wilderness Area.) The trails on this outing include obstacles like roots, footbridges, and soft, sandy sections of tread. The trip includes 2.5 miles of pavement.

Clearings in the trees offer nice views of Mt. Hood from the road climb, and some distant peaks are visible to the north from the high point of the ride (near the hiking trailhead for High Prairie Trail). We had a crystal-clear day. Some locals informed us that the peak we were gazing at was Mt. Rainier, almost a hundred miles distant! Wildflower displays can be outstanding in the several high meadows that are passed on this loop. The ride's relatively high elevation can keep the trails and roads under a blanket of snow into the late spring, some years, even into the early summer.

**General location:** The trip begins about 30 miles south of Hood River.

**Elevation change:** The low point of the ride (4,200') occurs near the trailhead. The high point of the loop is 6,050'; attained on Forest Service Road 4420. Ups and downs add about 400' of climbing to the outing. Total elevation gain: 2,250'.

**Season:** Snow and wet conditions may linger into the late spring or early summer at the higher elevations of this ride. Dusty conditions on the roads and soft trail conditions can occur during periods of high traffic and dry weather. Call ahead to check on conditions and possible seasonal closures.

**Services:** There is no potable water on this ride. Water can be obtained seasonally at the Sherwood and Robinhood campgrounds on OR 35. There is an outhouse at the trailhead for High Prairie Trail 493 (at the high point of the ride, off of FS 4420). Limited groceries can be purchased in Mt. Hood. All services are available in Hood River.

**Hazards:** Watch for traffic at road crossings, and ride predictably and defensively on the roads followed on this loop. Descend with care on rutted FS 4420. Watch for obstacles and soft conditions while descending on Lookout Mountain Trail. The route briefly follows Surveyor's Ridge Trail (near the close of this loop); watch for cyclists approaching from the opposite direction. Carry a jacket in anticipation of cooler temperatures and winds at the higher reaches of this ride.

**Rescue index:** Help can be obtained at the Hood River Ranger Station during regular business hours. (Take FS 44 to OR 35; turn right and drive north for 11.7 miles to the ranger station on the left.) There is a pay phone at the Mt. Hood Country Store (just north of the ranger station on OR 35). Emergency services are located in Hood River.

**Land status:** Mt. Hood National Forest.

**Maps:** The district map of the Barlow Ranger District is a helpful directional aid for this ride. However, the district map does not show the connection of Lookout Mountain Trail 450 with FS 4420. The "Green Trails" maps 462, Mt. Hood, OR, and 463, Flag Point, OR, are good maps for this ride. USGS 7.5 minute quads: Badger Lake and Dog River.

**Finding the trail:** From locations to the north, drive south from Hood River on

OR 35 for 25 miles. Turn left (1.4 miles south of Sherwood Campground) onto FS 44/Dufur Mill Road. From locations to the south, drive north on OR 35. FS 44/Dufur Mill Road will be on your right, 6.8 miles north of Bennett Pass (2.6 miles north of Robinhood Campground). Follow FS 44 for 3.7 miles to FS 4410 (signed for High Prairie and just past the trailhead for Surveyor's Ridge Trail). Turn right onto FS 4410 and drive 0.1 mile to an unsigned gravel road on the right. Turn onto the gravel road. Parking is limited, but there is room to park 1 or 2 cars on the side of the road. The last choice for parking is at a dispersed campsite, 0.3 mile down the road, on the left. Other parking options include pullouts on FS 4410, or parking at the trailhead for Surveyor's Ridge Trail (often busy).

**Sources of additional information:**

Barlow Ranger District
P.O. Box 67
Dufur, OR 97021
(541) 467-2291

Hood River Ranger District
6780 Highway 35
Mt. Hood-Parkdale, OR 97041
(541) 352-6002

**Notes on the trail:** Head back to FS 4410 and turn right (south). In 4.6 miles, turn left at a **T** intersection onto FS 4420. (The road to the right is FS 3550; it goes to Bennett Pass). The high point of the ride is obtained in 0.6 mile, then the road descends for 0.9 mile to Lookout Mountain Trail 450. Turn left onto the trail and descend for 1.4 miles (crossing two gravel roads) to arrive at a **T** intersection. Turn left to remain on Trail 450. (Here, Trail 456 goes right toward Fifteenmile Campground.) In 0.8 mile, continue straight to stay on Trail 450 where Wampus Springs Trail 450A goes right toward FS 4420. Lookout Mountain Trail 450 becomes a double-track in another 1.6 miles. Follow the double-track out to paved FS 44. Use some care as you approach FS 44; don't roll out into traffic. (Note that FS 120 and the trailhead for Bottle Prairie Trail 445 is directly across from you at this point. Links with Knebal Springs Loop [Ride 90] and Eightmile Loop Trail [Ride 91] are possible here.) Turn left onto FS 44. In 2.3 miles, follow FS 44 hard to the left (where FS 17 goes right). In another 0.3 mile, at a low point in the road, turn right onto a trail signed "Cooks Meadow Trail." Enter the woods and immediately turn left to head west onto unsigned Trail 688. You will emerge from the woods in 1.5 miles at the trailhead for Surveyor's Ridge Trail 688. Turn left onto gravel FS 620, then turn left onto paved FS 44. Turn right in 0.1 mile onto FS 4410. In 0.1 mile, turn right onto an unsigned gravel road and ride back to your vehicle.

Several other rides can be created using all or part of the High Prairie Loop. A shorter ride can be enjoyed by riding up FS 4410 for about 2 miles to Cooks Meadow Trail 639 (on the left). Drop down Trail 639 to cross FS 44 and pick

Mt. Hood From
Forest Service Road 4410.

up Surveyor's Ridge Trail 688. Complete the loop by heading west on Trail 688, following the directions at the end of the above "Notes on the trail."

For longer options, consider tie-ins to Knebal Springs Loop (Ride 90) or Eightmile Loop Trail (Ride 91). Fit and adventurous cyclists may wish to consider riding south on FS 4410 and FS 3550 to the intersection with FS 4891, picking up Gunsight Trail 685 to return north to Gumjuwac Saddle. From the saddle, you can backtrack on the roads to descend on Cooks Meadow Trail 439. Pondering over the recommended maps is sure to produce other possibilities.

# RIDE 90 · Knebal Springs Loop

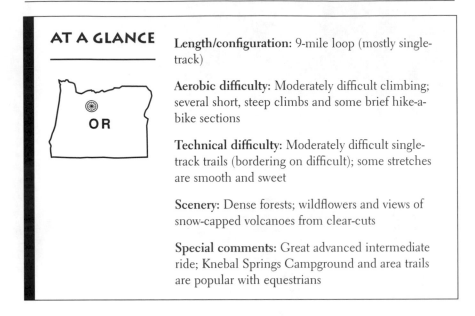

**AT A GLANCE**

**Length/configuration:** 9-mile loop (mostly single-track)

**Aerobic difficulty:** Moderately difficult climbing; several short, steep climbs and some brief hike-a-bike sections

**Technical difficulty:** Moderately difficult single-track trails (bordering on difficult); some stretches are smooth and sweet

**Scenery:** Dense forests; wildflowers and views of snow-capped volcanoes from clear-cuts

**Special comments:** Great advanced intermediate ride; Knebal Springs Campground and area trails are popular with equestrians

Buffed out single-track and awesome views of Mt. Hood, Mt. Adams, Mt. St. Helens, and Mt. Rainier highlight this fun, nine-mile loop. The ride includes short stretches on gravel roads and double-tracks, but most of the trip is on single-track (there are 1.3 miles of pavement near the start of the loop). Some of the trail miles are in less than perfect shape, and obstacles in the tread can create situations that require developed bike-handling skills. Energetic intermediate cyclists might enjoy this circuit, but they should be prepared to get off and walk their bikes from time to time. The trip includes some fun descending. Tight turns, a narrow tread, and soft conditions can complicate these drops.

The trailhead is in Knebal Springs Campground. This site is popular with equestrians, who enjoy trotting the area's many trails and forest roads. Local mountain bikers enjoy linking Knebal Springs Loop with Eightmile Loop Trail to create an outstanding longer ride.

**General location:** This outing is approximately 35 miles south of Hood River.

**Elevation change:** The trailhead in Knebal Springs Campground is at 3,800'. The high point of the loop, 5,040', occurs on Knebal Springs Trail 474 (about 3 miles into the ride). Ups and downs add approximately 700' of climbing to the trip. Total elevation gain: 1,940'.

**Season:** The trails and roads on this ride may remain blanketed with snow into the late spring. The summer and fall are good times for visiting the area. Call ahead to inquire about trail conditions and seasonal closures.

**Services:** Recent tests of the water at Knebal Springs Campground indicate that

Knebal Springs Trail.

it is not potable. (Further testing may demonstrate that the water is fit to drink; direct inquiries to the Barlow Ranger District.) You can get drinking water at the Sherwood and Robinhood Campgrounds (on OR 35). The Mt. Hood General Store (13 miles south of Hood River on OR 35) stocks a limited supply of groceries. All services are available in Hood River.

**Hazards:** Watch for vehicles on the roads. Watch for equestrians, mountain bikers, and pedestrians while traveling on the trails and roads of this loop. When approaching horses, stop and dismount to yield the trail. (When approaching from behind, stop well in back of equestrians, and announce your presence; do your best to avoid spooking the animals.) Talk to the riders in a normal tone of voice; ask if their horses are easily spooked and for instructions on how the equestrians would prefer you to facilitate passing. Your voice will help the horses recognize you as a human. The trails and roads on this trip include obstacles like roots, rocks, waterbars, narrow sections of tread, and soft conditions. Remain in control on the descents; the downhills near the end of the ride can be particularly hairy.

**Rescue index:** Help can be summoned during regular business hours at the

# RIDE 90 · Knebal Springs Loop

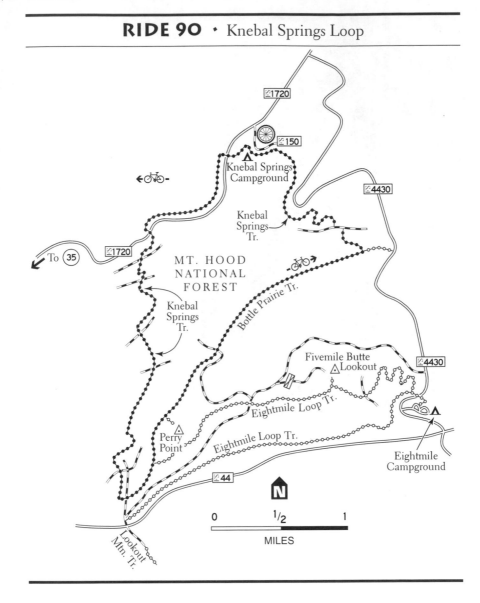

Hood River Ranger Station in Mt. Hood. (Take Forest Service Road 44 to OR 35; turn right and drive north for 11.7 miles to the ranger station on the left.) There is a pay phone at the Mt. Hood Country Store (just north of the ranger station on OR 35). Emergency services are located in Hood River.

**Land status:** Mt. Hood National Forest.

**Maps:** "Green Trails" maps 462, Mt. Hood, OR, and 463, Flag Point, OR, are good guides to this ride. The district map of the Barlow Ranger District is helpful as a guide to the trails and roads in the area, but it is incomplete in some regards (still worth carrying). USGS 7.5 minute quads: Fivemile Butte and Dog River.

**Finding the trail:** From locations to the north, drive south from Hood River on OR 35 for 25 miles. Turn left (1.4 miles south of Sherwood Campground) onto FS 44/Dufur Mill Road. From locations from the south, drive north on OR 35. FS 44/Dufur Mill Road will be on your right, 6.8 miles north of Bennett Pass (2.6 miles north of Robinhood Campground). Follow FS 44 for 5.3 to FS 17 (signed for Knebal Springs Campground). Continue straight onto FS 17 (where FS 44 curves right). In 0.5 mile, continue straight onto FS 1720 (signed for Knebal Springs) where FS 17 goes left. Stay on FS 1720 for 2.7 miles to FS 150. Turn right onto FS 150 and drive 0.2 mile to enter Knebal Springs Campground. Bear left through the campground to park on the left in an open grassy area.

## Sources of additional information:

Barlow Ranger District
P.O. Box 67
Dufur, OR 97021
(541) 467-2291

Hood River Ranger District
6780 Highway 35
Mt. Hood-Parkdale, OR 97041
(541) 352-6002

**Notes on the trail:** The ride begins across the road from the campground outhouse. Look for a faint trail that is marked by a "closed to motor vehicles" sign. (The trail goes between 2 campsites and heads into the woods.) Ride up this trail, turning left in 0.3 mile onto paved FS 1720. After 1.3 miles of pavement, turn left and climb up signed Knebal Springs Trail 474. Shortly, you will arrive at a gravel road. Turn right onto the road, then immediately turn left to regain the trail and ride into a clear-cut. In 0.3 mile, turn left onto a gravel road, then immediately turn right to regain signed Trail 474. You will arrive at a dirt double-track in 0.4 mile, bear right and ride through a clearing with incredible views of volcanic snow-cones. Soon, the roadbed becomes gravel and Trail 474 branches off to the left. Pick up the trail and pedal 0.3 mile to cross an overgrown double-track. In another 0.9 mile, cross a gravel road and follow the trail as it becomes a double-track. (The double-track is marked with a sign that directs you toward Trail 455 and Trail 450.) Travel down the double-track for 0.2 mile to signed Bottle Prairie Trail 455. Turn left and climb up this trail for 0.5 mile to an intersection with Eightmile Loop Trail 459. Here, continue straight (take the left fork) to remain on Bottle Prairie Trail 455 toward Knebal Springs Campground. You will pass a side trail in 0.4 mile; it goes right to Perry Point. (Follow this short trail if you would like another view of Mt. Adams.) After passing the side trail to Perry Point, continue in a northeasterly direction on Trail 455. The trail descends nicely to a double-track. Cross the double-track and ride 0.9 mile to an intersection where Knebal Springs Trail 474 goes left. Bear left to follow the trail toward Knebal Springs Campground. Some climbing leads to an unsigned gravel road. Turn left onto the road and ride 200 feet to regain the trail on the right. Descend and cross 3 creeks. (The first 2 creek crossings are followed by 2 brief, steep uphills, the third creek crossing is followed by a long, steep climb.) The ride ends with a descent into Knebal Springs Campground.

This loop can easily be linked with Eightmile Loop Trail (Ride 91). Follow the above ride description to the intersection of Bottle Prairie Trail 455 and Eightmile Loop Trail 459 (4.5 miles into the ride). Instead of continuing on Trail 455, turn right and follow Trail 459. Utilize the "Notes on the trail" for Eightmile Loop Trail (Ride 91) to return to the intersection of Trail 455 and Trail 459. Complete the ride by following the directions for the Knebal Springs Loop; ending at Knebal Springs Campground.

## RIDE 91 · Eightmile Loop Trail

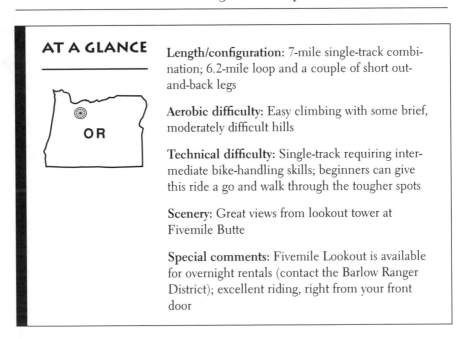

**AT A GLANCE**

**Length/configuration:** 7-mile single-track combination; 6.2-mile loop and a couple of short out-and-back legs

**Aerobic difficulty:** Easy climbing with some brief, moderately difficult hills

**Technical difficulty:** Single-track requiring intermediate bike-handling skills; beginners can give this ride a go and walk through the tougher spots

**Scenery:** Great views from lookout tower at Fivemile Butte

**Special comments:** Fivemile Lookout is available for overnight rentals (contact the Barlow Ranger District); excellent riding, right from your front door

You may enjoy Eightmile Loop Trail so much that you will be keen on doing it again. Better yet, consider renting the lookout tower at Fivemile Butte. The tower is adjacent to the trail. A stay here has you positioned to explore miles of top-notch single-track. Notable links include tie-ins to Knebal Springs Trail, Lookout Mountain Trail, Cooks Meadow Trail, and Surveyor's Ridge Trail. These riding opportunities are attractive, what's more, the lookout is very cool.

# RIDE 91 · Eightmile Loop Trail

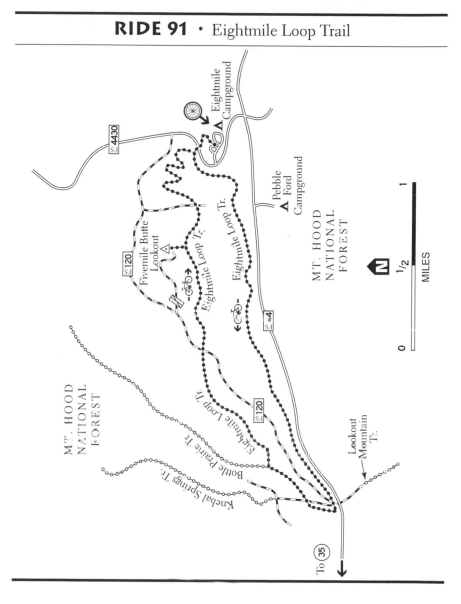

The circuit on Eightmile Loop Trail involves seven miles of good single-track with a smattering of minor obstacles. The climbs are mostly easy, with some short, moderately difficult grades. Energetic beginners may find this a challenging yet gratifying trip. Some of the hills and obstacles they come across may cause problems. Be prepared to walk your bike if you find the ride too difficult in spots.

**General location:** This loop is about 35 miles south of Hood River.

Michael Halls and David
Landolt enjoying
Eightmile Loop Trail.

**Elevation change:** The trailhead is at 3,840'. The high point of the loop (4,700') is reached about halfway through the ride. Undulations over the course of the trip add about 300' of climbing to the ride. Total elevation gain: 1,160'.

**Season:** The trail is usually free of snow from late June through October.

**Services:** There is no potable water on this outing. Water can be obtained seasonally at Sherwood and Robinhood campgrounds. (These campgrounds are on OR 35; you will pass one or the other on your way to the described trailhead.) All services are available in Hood River.

**Hazards:** Hazards on this ride include roots, rocks, waterbars, creek crossings, and sandy corners. The route includes switchbacks and other dangerous exposures. Control your speed while descending and watch for other trail users.

**Rescue index:** Help can be obtained at the Hood River Ranger Station (during regular business hours). To reach the ranger station, follow Forest Service Road 44 to OR 35. Head north on OR 35 for 11.7 miles to the ranger station on the left. There is a pay phone at the Mt. Hood Country Store (just north of the ranger station on OR 35). Emergency services are located in Hood River.

**Land status:** Mt. Hood National Forest.

**Maps:** The described trail is not delineated on the district map of the Barlow Ranger District. You will find a good map of the trail in *The Singletrack Anthology, Hood River*. This regional mountain bike guidebook by T. Barnes and K. Reynolds (published by Pinnacle Publishing) is widely available at local bike shops. USGS 7.5 minute quad: Fivemile Butte.

**Finding the trail:** From locations to the north, drive south from Hood River on OR 35 for 25 miles. Turn left (1.4 miles south of Sherwood Campground) onto FS 44/Dufur Mill Road. From locations to the south, drive north on OR 35. FS 44/Dufur Mill Road will be on your right, 6.8 miles north of Bennett Pass (2.6 miles north of Robinhood Campground). Follow FS 44 for 10.9 miles to FS 4430 on the left (0.6 mile beyond Pebble Ford Campground). Turn onto FS 4430 and drive 0.3 mile to FS 150 and Eightmile Campground. Turn right onto FS 150 and follow the signs to park at the campground picnic area.

**Sources of additional information:**

Barlow Ranger District
P.O. Box 67
Dufur, OR 97021
(541) 467-2291

Hood River Ranger District
6780 Highway 35
Mt. Hood-Parkdale, OR 97041
(541) 352-6002

**Notes on the trail:** Follow signed Eightmile Loop Trail 459. You will immediately cross a footbridge over Eightmile Creek. Follow the trail to cross the campground loop road and a double-track spur. The trail switchbacks to the right and then crosses paved FS 4430. Continue straight at the signed intersection to follow Eightmile Loop Trail 459. Cross a creek in 1 mile. From the creek crossing it is 1.4 miles to FS 120 (near its intersection with paved FS 44). Turn right onto the road and climb past a log loading ramp (follow the sign for Eightmile Loop Trail 459). Shortly, turn right at an intersection signed for Bottle Prairie Trail 455 and Eightmile Loop Trail 459. You will arrive at another intersection in 0.3 mile. (This intersection is reached after pedaling a total of 3.2 miles. Here, Bottle Prairie Trail 455 goes straight/left toward Knebal Springs Campground, and Eightmile Loop Trail goes right.) Turn right to remain on Eightmile Loop Trail. The trail rolls up and down, then descends nicely (stay alert; watch for some large waterbars on this descent). The trail crosses a road, then climbs through a clear-cut to reenter the woods and arrive at a **Y** intersection. Turn left to visit nearby Fivemile Lookout. Give a shout to see if the lookout is occupied; ask if you can come up for the view (Mt. Hood, Mt. Rainier, and Mt. Adams). Return to the last intersection and turn left to continue with the loop. A couple of gravel road crossing and some fun switchbacks bring you to the close of the loop. Turn left at the **T** intersection to return to the campground and your car.

This loop can be combined with Knebal Springs Trail to create a longer, more demanding ride. Follow the above directions for 3.2 miles to the intersection of Trail 459 and Trail 455. Continue straight (left) toward Knebal Springs Campground. Utilize the "Notes on the trail" from Knebal Springs Loop (Ride 90) to form a loop that closes back at this intersection. Complete the longer option by riding on Eightmile Trail to Eightmile Campground.

## RIDE 92 · Fifteenmile Creek Trail/Cedar Creek Trail

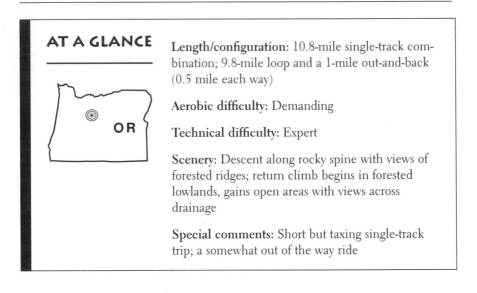

**AT A GLANCE**

**Length/configuration:** 10.8-mile single-track combination; 9.8-mile loop and a 1-mile out-and-back (0.5 mile each way)

**Aerobic difficulty:** Demanding

**Technical difficulty:** Expert

**Scenery:** Descent along rocky spine with views of forested ridges; return climb begins in forested lowlands, gains open areas with views across drainage

**Special comments:** Short but taxing single-track trip; a somewhat out of the way ride

Personally, we find that our favorite rides are often ones that begin with challenging climbs and end with rewarding descents. This single-track circuit fits a contrasting mold; it begins with a technical ridgeline descent and ends with a tough pull. After finishing the ride we found ourselves discussing our recent struggles with the climb and forgetting the fun parts of the ride. Some rest and some food helped us achieve a more balanced perspective on the trip. It is a fun ride, with many exciting aspects. It is well suited to strong cyclists who enjoy challenges. The trip is 10.8 miles long; a 9.8-mile loop and a 1-mile out-and-back (0.5 mile each way).

The riding down Cedar Creek Trail is a mixture of conditions and environments. It includes tricky switchbacks around huge boulders, cruises across open hillsides dotted with ponderosa pine, traverses across scree slopes, and precipitous drops. Things changed from moment to moment. One minute found us in dense woods, riding mellow terrain; the next brought us face to face with an

The top of Cedar Creek Trail.

exposed spine of rock and a steep, narrow section of trail. Where we felt vulnerable, or where we thought riding would further harm an already skid-damaged trail, we walked or carried our bikes (we walked a lot).

Fifteenmile Creek Trail is also a challenge; it regains the elevation you lose on Cedar Creek Trail. The climb begins gently, offering a warm-up through a damp environment of moss, mushrooms, and roots. Here, ditch like conditions were common, making the riding more difficult. We noted that sections of the trail had been marked with surveyor's tape, and wondered if some of the lower reaches of the trail were scheduled to receive some maintenance or rerouting. The trail becomes steep as it climbs out of the drainage. Some stretches mellow out and let you catch your breath, but these are often followed by additional periods of panting and grunting.

While not extremely remote, these trails are somewhat off the beaten track. Carry food, plenty of water, and be prepared for emergencies or difficulties that could develop. Budget plenty of time for the ride. While it is possible to link these trails with others in the area, we would recommend that you first ride this as a trip in itself, then judge whether you wish to include it into a longer circuit.

**General location:** The trailhead in Fifteenmile Campground is about 40 miles south of Hood River.

**Elevation change:** Fifteenmile Campground is the high point of the trip at 4,680'. The low point of the ride (2,720') occurs at the far intersection of Cedar

## RIDE 92 · Fifteenmile Creek Trail/Cedar Creek Trail

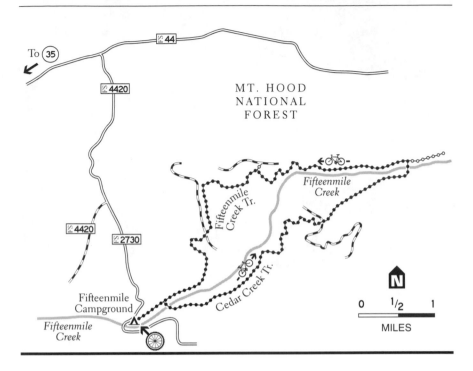

Creek Trail and Fifteenmile Creek Trail. Ups and downs over the course of the loop add about 300' of climbing to the outing. Overall elevation gain: 2,260'.

**Season:** Give the trails in the area time to dry out following the spring thaw. The trails here can typically support traffic from the late spring through the late fall. Call ahead for trail conditions and seasonal closures.

**Services:** There is no potable water on this ride. Water can be obtained seasonally at Sherwood and Robinhood campgrounds (on OR 35). You can purchase limited groceries at the Mt. Hood Country Store (13 miles south of Hood River on OR 35). All services are available in Hood River.

**Hazards:** The trails followed on this ride are strewn with obstacles and difficulties. Included in the mix are steep, loose descents and exposures where a wrong move could result in a bad fall. Watch for other recreationists on the trails. Please don't skid around switchbacks or lock your brakes in an attempt to negotiate steep descents.

**Rescue index:** Help can be found at the Hood River Ranger Station during regular business hours. (The ranger station is on OR 35, 11.7 miles south of the intersection of Forest Service Road 44 and OR 35.) There is a pay phone at the Mt. Hood Country Store (0.2 mile north of the ranger station on OR 35). Emergency services are located in Hood River.

**Land status:** Mt. Hood National Forest.

**Maps:** The "Green Trails" Map 463, Flag Point, OR, is useful as a guide to this ride. The district map of the Barlow Ranger District delineates Cedar Creek Trail 457 and a good portion of Fifteenmile Creek Trail 456. USGS 7.5 minute quads: Flag Point and Fivemile Butte.

**Finding the trail:** From locations to the north, drive south from Hood River on OR 35 for 25 miles. Turn left (1.4 miles south of Sherwood Campground) onto FS 44/Dufur Mill Road. From locations to the south, drive north on OR 35. FS 44/Dufur Mill Road will be on your right, 6.8 miles north of Bennett Pass (2.6 miles north of Robinhood Campground). Follow FS 44 for 8.4 miles to FS 4420 (just past milepost 8 on FS 44). Turn right and follow FS 4420. In 2.1 miles, continue straight, remaining on pavement and following FS 2730 (FS 4420 goes right and becomes gravel). Drive 1.9 miles to Fifteenmile Campground on the left. The campground is tiny, and parking is limited. The layout of the campground can cause problems for vehicles with long wheelbases or low clearance. If you plan on camping, take a site. If you are not going to camp, consider parking outside of the campground. There is room to park one vehicle just north of the campground (roadside; on the campground side of FS 2730). If that is taken, continue south to cross Fifteenmile Creek and look to the right as you round the bend in FS 2730; there is a wide spot in the road where you should be able to park one or two vehicles.

**Sources of additional information:**

Barlow Ranger District
P.O. Box 67
Dufur, OR 97021
(541) 467-2291

Hood River Ranger District
6780 Highway 35
Mt. Hood-Parkdale, OR 97041
(541) 352-6002

**Notes on the trail:** The trailhead for Fifteenmile Creek Trail 456 is just uphill from the outhouse. Follow the trail; you will immediately arrive at a **Y** intersection. Go straight (right) to follow Trail 456. Descend for 0.5 mile to signed Cedar Creek Trail 457. Turn hard to the right onto Trail 457 and cross a footbridge over Cedar Creek. (Don't miss this turn; you want to ride the loop in a counterclockwise direction.) The trail will cross a gravel road in 3.2 miles, then cross a footbridge over Fifteenmile Creek in another 1.5 miles. You will arrive at a **T** intersection after crossing the creek. Here, turn left onto Fifteenmile Creek Trail 456. In 2.8 miles, turn left at a **T** intersection to continue climbing on Trail 456 (the trail to the right goes out to a gravel road). Pedal 0.5 mile and turn left onto an overgrown road at signs for "Fifteenmile Trail #456." Follow this road/trail for 0.8 mile to a weathered sign that directs you to turn right to remain on Trail 456. Turn right onto the faint trail and push your bike up through rock outcroppings. The trail rolls up and down through rock outcroppings and reaches an open overlook at a rocky cliff. Soon, the trail reenters the woods, then descends briefly through ditch-like conditions before crossing signed Foster Creek. In 0.4 mile, cross a small footbridge over another creek, then continue straight to pass Cedar Creek Trail 457 on the left. Ride up to Fifteenmile Campground.

## RIDE 93 · Gunsight Trail

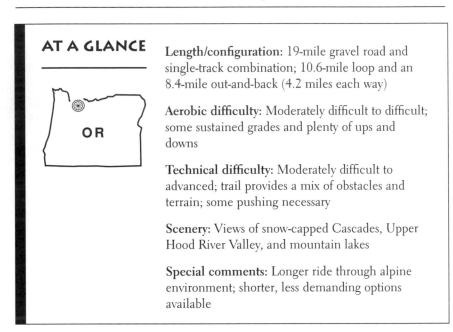

**AT A GLANCE**

**OR**

**Length/configuration:** 19-mile gravel road and single-track combination; 10.6-mile loop and an 8.4-mile out-and-back (4.2 miles each way)

**Aerobic difficulty:** Moderately difficult to difficult; some sustained grades and plenty of ups and downs

**Technical difficulty:** Moderately difficult to advanced; trail provides a mix of obstacles and terrain; some pushing necessary

**Scenery:** Views of snow-capped Cascades, Upper Hood River Valley, and mountain lakes

**Special comments:** Longer ride through alpine environment; shorter, less demanding options available

Gunsight Trail is a fun and challenging single-track that takes you to some spectacular sights. There is a great view of Mt. Hood near the halfway point. Another overlook is reached farther down the path. This vista includes the Upper Hood River Valley and Mt. Adams. The return on Forest Service Road 3550 sports some outstanding scenery as well. The ridge you are riding along suddenly drops away to the east. Far below are Jean and Badger Lakes, and in the distance is Mt. Jefferson.

This demanding 19-mile circuit is well suited to strong intermediate cyclists and advanced riders. It is a combination of a 10.6-mile loop and an 8.4-mile out-and-back (4.2 miles each way). The route follows gravel FS 3550 for 14 miles and Gunsight Trail for 5 miles. There are some sustained grades and plenty of short ups and downs. Most of the climbing is easy to moderately difficult. You will encounter a lot of rough surfaces, so wear your most heavily padded bike shorts.

# RIDE 93 · Gunsight Trail

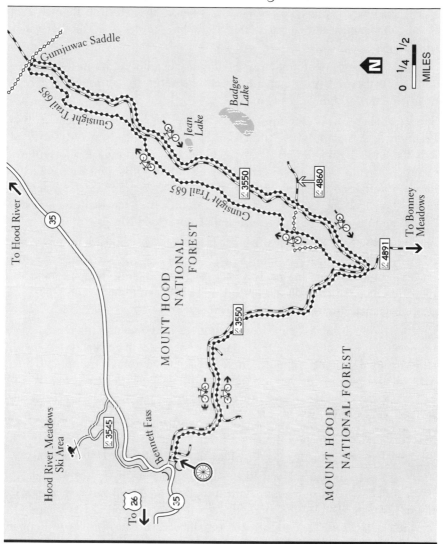

Gunsight Trail packs in a real mixture of riding surfaces and terrain. This fine path goes from stretches of smooth compacted dirt to areas littered with obstacles. Negotiating the trail requires good bike-handling skills. There are several places where you will need to push your bike.

**General location:** This ride begins at Bennett Pass on OR 35, approximately 32 miles south of Hood River.

**Elevation change:** The trailhead elevation at Bennett Pass is 4,674'. The route climbs to 5,340' at the intersection of FS 3550 and Gunsight Trail. A high point of 5,900' occurs on Gunsight Trail. Then you pedal to Gumjuwac Saddle, at 5,260'. Back on FS 3550, you reach 5,820' before the return to Bennett Pass. Rolling topography adds about 1,000' of climbing to the tour. Total elevation gain: 2,786'.

**Season:** The best opportunities for finding dry conditions are in the summer and fall. If the trails in the area are wet, check out the surrounding forest's nearly limitless supply of gravel roads.

**Services:** There is no water on the ride. Water can be obtained seasonally at Robinhood Campground; 4.3 miles north of the trailhead on OR 35. Food, lodging, limited groceries, gas, and pay phones can be found in Government Camp. (To get to Government Camp, drive south from Bennett Pass on OR 35 for about 6 miles, then head west on US 26. Drive west on US 26 for about 3 miles, then look for signs that direct you north off of the highway and into Government Camp.) All services are available in Hood River.

**Hazards:** Much of FS 3550 is degraded, with ruts, washboarding, rocks, and coarse gravel. Use extra caution when descending on this road. You may encounter motorists on the roads. Gunsight Trail presents obstacles including rocks, scree, sand, windfalls, narrow openings between boulders, drop-offs, and steep, switchbacking descents.

**Rescue index:** You will find a pay phone in Government Camp. (See "Services" for directions to this community.) There are ranger stations in Zigzag and Mt. Hood. (Zigzag is about 12 miles west of Government Camp on US 26. Mt. Hood is approximately 19 miles north of Bennett Pass on OR 35.) Emergency services are located in Hood River.

**Land status:** Mt. Hood National Forest.

**Maps:** The district map of the Hood River Ranger District is a good guide to this ride. USGS 7.5 minute quads: Badger Lake and Mount Hood South.

**Finding the trail:** From Hood River, drive south on OR 35 for 32 miles to Bennett Pass (about 1 mile south of the turnoff for the Hood River Meadows Ski Area). From locations to the south, drive to the intersection of US 26 and OR 35, then follow OR 35 northeast (toward Hood River) for 6 miles to Bennett Pass. Park in the paved pullout on the east side of the highway or turn east onto FS 3550/Bennett Pass Road and park in the gravel parking area on the right.

**Source of additional information:**

Hood River Ranger District
6780 Highway 35
Mt. Hood-Parkdale, OR 97041
(541) 352-6002

**Notes on the trail:** Head southeast and ride up FS 3550. Stay on the main road as several side roads branch off. After 4.2 miles, you will reach an intersection where FS 3550, FS 4891, and Gunsight Trail 685 meet. Turn hard to the left

Mt. Hood from Gunsight Trail.

onto Gunsight Trail. After 0.6 mile on Gunsight Trail stay right and uphill where an unsigned single-track goes left and descends. In another 0.5 mile, continue straight where a trail branches off to the right toward Windy Camp. From this intersection it is 1.3 miles to a large rock outcropping on the left. Climb up onto the outcropping for a view of Mt. Hood. Back on Gunsight Trail, you will descend rapidly and come to another observation point on the left (look to the left for a clearing in the trees near a pile of large, angular boulders). It is 0.7 mile from this second overlook to FS 3550. Turn left onto FS 3550 and follow it for 0.2 mile to rejoin Gunsight Trail on the left. This stretch of Gunsight Trail lasts for 1.8 miles and deposits you at Gumjuwac Saddle and FS 3550. Turn right onto FS 3550 and follow it back to your car.

You can shorten this loop without missing the nicest views. To do this, ride to the intersection of Gunsight Trail and FS 3550 (0.7 mile beyond the second overlook). Instead of turning left onto FS 3550, turn right and shorten the circuit by 4 miles. You will miss some exciting downhill single-track, but you will also avoid some bumpy climbing on FS 3550.

For an easy out-and-back trip, start at the described trailhead and follow FS 3550 for 1.8 miles. This stretch of FS 3550 is in fine condition and takes you to a good view of Mt. Hood.

# RIDE 94 · Frog Lake Buttes

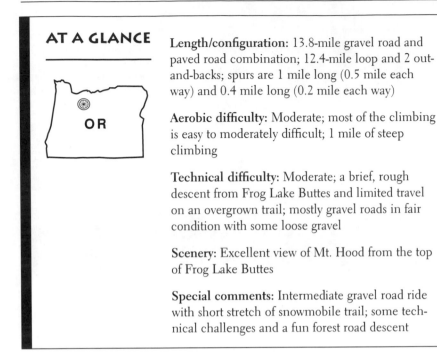

**AT A GLANCE**

**Length/configuration:** 13.8-mile gravel road and paved road combination; 12.4-mile loop and 2 out-and-backs; spurs are 1 mile long (0.5 mile each way) and 0.4 mile long (0.2 mile each way)

**Aerobic difficulty:** Moderate; most of the climbing is easy to moderately difficult; 1 mile of steep climbing

**Technical difficulty:** Moderate; a brief, rough descent from Frog Lake Buttes and limited travel on an overgrown trail; mostly gravel roads in fair condition with some loose gravel

**Scenery:** Excellent view of Mt. Hood from the top of Frog Lake Buttes

**Special comments:** Intermediate gravel road ride with short stretch of snowmobile trail; some technical challenges and a fun forest road descent

This ride is 13.8 miles long. It consists of a 12.2-mile loop and two out-and-back spurs. The out-and-backs are 1 mile long (0.5 mile each way) and 0.4 mile long (0.2 mile each way). One mile of the ride is paved cycling, and another 0.3 mile is a snowmobile trail; the remainder of the circuit is on gravel roads. The first 3.5 miles of the loop are the most demanding. A short warm-up is followed by two miles of moderately difficult climbing and then by a steep mile over a rough road. This ascent brings you to the top of Frog Lake Buttes and a big view of Mt. Hood. You make a technical descent from this high point, then do some route finding to locate an overgrown trail. Then you enjoy a fun three-mile descent. The remainder of the ride is an easy cruise over mostly level and downhill terrain.

**General location:** This ride starts at Frog Lake Sno-Park, about 8 miles south of Government Camp (approximately 60 miles southeast of Portland).

**Elevation change:** The ride begins at 3,920' and reaches 5,294' atop Frog Lake Buttes. Undulating topography adds about 600' of climbing to the loop. Total elevation gain: 1,974'.

**Season:** The roads followed on this ride are generally clear of snow from June through September. A great time for a visit is the period after Labor Day and before the beginning of hunting season.

Vista from Frog Lake Buttes.

**Services:** Water is available seasonally at Frog Lake Campground (0.4 mile south of the trailhead on Forest Service Road 2610). The community of Government Camp has lodging, gas, pay phones, and limited groceries. All services are available in Hood River.

**Hazards:** There are loose rocks and ruts on the descent from Frog Lake Buttes. Walk your bike down the steep, degraded snowmobile trail that connects FS 221 and FS 250. Watch your speed while descending on FS 250. This road contains some washboarding, and there is loose gravel in its corners. You may encounter some vehicular traffic on this ride.

**Rescue index:** The nearest pay phone is at a gas station 2 miles north of the trailhead on US 26. There is a ranger station in Zigzag. (Zigzag is about 20 miles northwest of the trailhead on US 26.) Emergency services are located in Hood River and Portland.

**Land status:** Mt. Hood National Forest.

**Maps:** The district map of the Bear Springs Ranger District is a good guide to this route. USGS 7.5 minute quads: Post Point and Wapinitia Pass.

**Finding the trail:** The intersection of US 26 and OR 35 is about 50 miles east of Portland and approximately 40 miles south of Hood River. From this interchange, follow US 26 south for 4.7 miles to the Frog Lake Sno-Park (on the left). From locations to the south, follow US 26 north from Madras for about 60 miles to the Frog Lake Sno-Park on the right (1.5 miles north of Blue Box Pass). Park in the large paved lot.

# RIDE 94 · Frog Lake Buttes

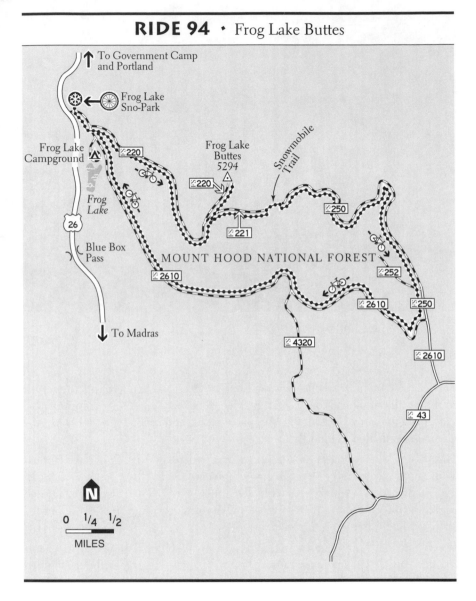

**Source of additional information:**

Bear Springs Ranger District
73558 Highway 216
Maupin, OR 97037
(541) 328-6211

**Notes on the trail:** From the parking lot, head south on FS 2610 toward Frog Lake. In 0.2 mile, turn left onto FS 220. Climb on FS 220 for 2 miles, then turn left to continue on FS 220 where FS 221 goes right. FS 220 ends at a clearing.

Backtrack to the intersection of FS 220 and FS 221. Turn left onto FS 221. Follow FS 221 to its terminus at a clear-cut. Walk your bike straight across the clear-cut; do not lose or gain elevation. After about 150', you will come to the edge of the woods. Look for a faint snowmobile trail that enters the forest. Follow this rough track downhill. After a few hundred yards, the trail becomes more obvious, and you will notice some orange and yellow diamond-shaped markers on the trees that border the path. The trail deposits you into another clear-cut at the bottom of the slope. Walk your bike out of the woods and bear to the right. Shortly you will come to a gravel road—the beginning of FS 250. Follow FS 250 downhill. Stay on this main road as it continues to descend. The road surface eventually changes to pavement. Coast down the pavement for just 0.4 mile to FS 2610 on the right (easy to miss). Turn right onto gravel FS 2610. Stay on this road to complete the ride.

# GLOSSARY

This short list of terms does not contain all the words used by mountain bike enthusiasts when discussing their sport. But it should serve as an introduction to the lingo you'll hear on the trails.

| | |
|---|---|
| *ATB* | all-terrain bike; this, like "fat-tire bike," is another name for a mountain bike |
| *ATV* | all-terrain vehicle; this usually refers to the loud, fume-spewing three- or four-wheeled motorized vehicles you will not enjoy meeting on the trail—except, of course, if you crash and have to hitch a ride out on one |
| *blaze* | a mark on a tree made by chipping away a piece of the bark, usually done to designate a trail; such trails are sometimes described as "blazed" |
| *blind corner* | a curve in the road or trail that conceals bikers, hikers, equestrians, and other traffic |
| *blowdown* | see "windfall" |
| *BLM* | Bureau of Land Management, an agency of the federal government |
| *bollard* | a post (or series of posts) set vertically into the ground which allow pedestrians or cyclists to pass but keep vehicles from entering (wooden bollards are also commonly used to sign intersections) |
| *braided* | a braided trail condition results when people attempt to travel around a wet area; networks of interlaced trails can result and are a maintenance headache for trail crews |
| *buffed* | used to describe a very smooth trail |
| *Carsonite sign* | a small, thin, and flexible fiberglass signpost used extensively by the Forest Service and BLM to mark roads and |

trails (often dark brown in color)

*catching air*     taking a jump in such a way that both wheels of the bike are off the ground at the same time

*cattle guard*     a grate of parallel steel bars or pipes set at ground level and suspended over a ditch; cows can't cross them (their little feet slip through the openings between the pipes), but pedestrians and vehicles can pass over cattle guards with little difficulty

*clean*     while this may describe what you and your bike won't be after following many trails, the term is most often used as a verb to denote the action of pedaling a tough section of trail successfully

*combination*     this type of route may combine two or more configurations; for example, a point-to-point route may integrate a scenic loop or an out-and-back spur midway through the ride; likewise, an out-and-back may have a loop at its farthest point (this configuration looks like a cherry with a stem attached; the stem is the out-and-back, the fruit is the terminus loop); or a loop route may have multiple out-and-back spurs and/or loops to the side; mileage for a combination route is for the total distance to complete the ride

*cupped*     a concave trail; higher on the sides than in the middle

*dab*     touching the ground with a foot or hand

*deadfall*     a tangled mass of fallen trees or branches

*decomposed granite*     an excellent, fine- to medium-grain, trail and road surface; typically used in native surface road and trail applications (not trucked in); results from the weathering of granite

*diversion ditch*     a usually narrow, shallow ditch dug across or around a trail; funneling the water in this manner keeps it from destroying the trail

*double-track*     the dual tracks made by a jeep or other vehicle, with grass or weeds or rocks between; mountain bikers can ride in either of the tracks, but you will of course find that whichever one you choose, and no matter how many times you change back and forth, the other track will appear to offer smoother travel

*dugway*     a steep, unpaved, switchbacked descent

*endo*     flipping end over end

| | |
|---|---|
| *feathering* | using a light touch on the brake lever, hitting it lightly many times rather than very hard or locking the brake |
| *four-wheel-drive* | this refers to any vehicle with drive-wheel capability on all four wheels (a jeep, for instance, has four-wheel drive as compared with a two-wheel-drive passenger car), or to a rough road or trail that requires four-wheel-drive capability (or a one-wheel-drive mountain bike!) to negotiate it |
| *game trail* | the usually narrow trail made by deer, elk, or other game |
| *gated* | everyone knows what a gate is, and how many variations exist upon this theme; well, if a trail is described as "gated" it simply has a gate across it; don't forget that the rule is if you find a gate closed, close it behind you; if you find one open, leave it that way |
| *Giardia* | shorthand for *Giardia lamblia*, and known as the "backpacker's bane" until we mountain bikers expropriated it; this is a waterborne parasite that begins its life cycle when swallowed, and one to four weeks later has its host (you) bloated, vomiting, shivering with chills, and living in the bathroom; the disease can be avoided by "treating" (purifying) the water you acquire along the trail (see "Hitting the Trail" in the Introduction) |
| *gnarly* | a term thankfully used less and less these days, it refers to tough trails |
| *graded* | refers to a dirt road that has been smoothed out by the wide blade on earth-moving equipment; "blading" gets rid of the teeth-chattering, much-cursed washboards found on so many dirt roads after heavy vehicle use |
| *hammer* | to ride very hard |
| *hardpack* | a trail in which the dirt surface is packed down hard; such trails make for good and fast riding, and very painful landings; bikers most often use "hardpack" as both a noun and adjective, and "hard-packed" as an adjective only (the grammar lesson will help you when diagramming sentences in camp) |
| *hike-a-bike* | what you do when the road or trail becomes too steep or rough to remain in the saddle |
| *jeep road, jeep trail* | a rough road or trail passable only with four-wheel-drive capability (or a horse or mountain bike) |
| *kamikaze* | while this once referred primarily to those Japanese fliers |

| | |
|---|---|
| *kamikazi* (continued) | who quaffed a glass of sake, then flew off as human bombs in suicide missions against U.S. naval vessels, it has more recently been applied to the idiot mountain bikers who, far less honorably, scream down hiking trails, endangering the physical and mental safety of the walking, biking, and equestrian traffic they meet; deck guns were necessary to stop the Japanese kamikaze pilots, but a bike pump or walking staff in the spokes is sufficient for the current-day kamikazes who threaten to get us all kicked off the trails |
| *loop* | this route configuration is characterized by riding from the designated trailhead to a distant point, then returning to the trailhead via a different route (or simply continuing on the same in a circle route) without doubling back; you always move forward across new terrain but return to the starting point when finished; mileage is for the entire loop from the trailhead back to trailhead |
| *multi-purpose* | a BLM designation of land which is open to many uses; mountain biking is allowed |
| *off-camber* | a trail that slopes in the opposite direction than one would prefer for safety's sake |
| ORV/OHV | a motorized off-road vehicle (off-highway vehicle) |
| *out and-back* | a ride where you follow a trail, then turn around and follow the same trail back; while this might sound far more boring than a loop route, many trails look very different when pedaled in the opposite direction |
| *pack stock* | horses, mules, llamas, etc., carrying provisions along trails |
| *point-to-point* | a vehicle shuttle (or similar assistance) is required for this type of route, which is ridden from the designated trailhead to a distant location, or endpoint, where the route ends; total mileage is for the one-way trip from the trailhead to endpoint |
| *portage* | to carry your bike on your person |
| *pummy* | soil with high pumice content produced by volcanic activity in the Pacific Northwest and elsewhere; light in consistency and easily pedaled; trails with such soil often become thick with dust |
| *quads* | bikers use this term to refer both to the extensor muscle in the front of the thigh (which is separated into four parts) and to USGS maps; the expression "Nice quads!" refers always to the former, however, except in those instances when the speaker is an engineer |

| | |
|---|---|
| *recreation opportunity guides (R.O.G.)* | handouts which identify and describe resources available to the public on national forest lands (camping facilities, trails, wildlife viewing opportunities, etc.); often available for the asking at Forest Service ranger stations throughout the Pacific Northwest |
| *runoff* | rainwater or snowmelt |
| *scree* | an accumulation of loose stones or rocky debris lying on a slope or at the base of a hill or cliff |
| *side-cut trail* | a trail cut on the side of a hill |
| *signed* | a "signed" trail has signs in place of blazes |
| *single-track* | a single, narrow path through grass or brush or over rocky terrain, often created by deer, elk, or backpackers; single-track riding is some of the best fun around |
| *skid road* | the path created when loggers drag trees through the forest with heavy equipment |
| *slickrock* | the rock-hard, compacted sandstone that is great to ride and even prettier to look at; you'll appreciate it even more if you think of it as a petrified sand dune or seabed (which it is), and if the rider before you hasn't left tire marks (from unnecessary skidding) or granola bar wrappers behind |
| *snowmelt* | runoff produced by the melting of snow |
| *snowpack* | unmelted snow accumulated over weeks or months of winter—or over years in high-mountain terrain |
| *spur* | a road or trail that intersects the main trail you're following |
| *squid* | one who skids |
| *stair-step climb* | climb punctuated by a series of level or near-level sections |
| *switchback* | a zigzagging road or trail designed to assist in traversing steep terrain; mountain bikers should not skid through switchbacks |
| *talus* | the rocky debris at the base of a cliff, or a slope formed by an accumulation of this rocky debris |
| *tank trap* | a steep-sided ditch (or series of ditches) used to block access to a road or trail; often used in conjunction with high mounds of excavated material |
| *technical* | terrain that is difficult to ride due not to its grade (steepness) but to its obstacles—rocks, roots, logs, ledges, loose soil . . . |

| | |
|---|---|
| *topo* | short for topographical map, the kind that shows both linear distance and elevation gain and loss; "topo" is pronounced with both vowels long |
| *trashed* | a trail that has been destroyed (same term used no matter what has destroyed it . . . cattle, horses, or even mountain bikers riding when the ground was too wet) |
| *two-track* | see "double-track" |
| *two-wheel-drive* | this refers to any vehicle with drive-wheel capability on only two wheels (a passenger car, for instance, has two-wheel-drive); a two-wheel-drive road is a road or trail easily traveled by an ordinary car |
| *waterbar* | an earth, rock, or wooden structure that funnels water off trails to reduce erosion |
| *washboarded* | a road that is surfaced with many ridges spaced closely together, like the ripples on a washboard; these make for very rough riding, and even worse driving in a car or jeep |
| *whoop-de-doo* | closely spaced dips or undulations in a trail; these are often encountered in areas traveled heavily by ORVs |
| *wilderness area* | land that is officially set aside by the federal government to remain natural—pure, pristine, and untrammeled by any vehicle, including mountain bikes; though mountain bikes had not been born in 1964 (when the United States Congress passed the Wilderness Act, establishing the National Wilderness Preservation system), they are considered a "form of mechanical transport" and are thereby excluded; in short, stay out |
| *windchill* | a reference to the wind's cooling effect upon exposed flesh; for example, if the temperature is 10 degrees Fahrenheit and the wind is blowing at 20 miles per hour, the windchill (that is, the actual temperature to which your skin reacts) is minus 32 degrees; if you are riding in wet conditions things are even worse, for the windchill would then be minus 74 degrees! |
| *windfall* | anything (trees, limbs, brush, fellow bikers . . .) blown down by the wind |

# INDEX

**CHRIS** and **LAURIE LEMAN** make their home in Ketchum, Idaho. Laurie was born in Vancouver, British Columbia and holds a degree from Simon Fraser

 University. She is employed as a waitress and freelance writer and helps coach the Sun Valley Nordic Ski Team. Chris is from Detroit, graduated from Michigan State University, and earns a living as a carpenter. They met while working as bicycle tour leaders in the Canadian Rockies.